The Measure of Things

The Measure of Things

of Things

Humanism, Humility, and Mystery

DAVID E. COOPER

CLARENDON PRESS · OXFORD

OXFORD

UNIVERSITY PRESS

Great Clarendon Street, Oxford OX2 6DP

Oxford University Press is a department of the University of Oxford
It furthers the University's objective of excellence in research, scholarship,
and education by publishing worldwide in

Oxford New York

Auckland Bangkok Buenos Aires Cape Town Chennai
Dar es Salaam Delhi Hong Kong Istanbul Karachi Kolkata
Kuala Lumpur Madrid Melbourne Mexico City Mumbai Nairobi
São Paulo Shanghai Singapore Taipei Tokyo Toronto

with an associated company in Berlin

Oxford is a registered trade mark of Oxford University Press
in the UK and in certain other countries

Published in the United States
by Oxford University Press Inc., New York

British Library Cataloguing in Publication Data

Data available

Library of Congress Cataloging in Publication Data

Cooper, David Edward.
   The measure of things: humanism, humility, and mystery / by David E. Cooper.
      p. cm.
   Includes index.
   1. Humanism. I. Title.
   B105.H8 .C68 2002   144—dc21   2002019897

ISBN 0-19-823827-4

10 9 8 7 6 5 4 3 2 1

Typeset by Invisible Ink
Printed in Great Britain
on acid-free paper by
Biddles Ltd.,
Guildford & King's Lynn

Acknowledgements

I would like to express my thanks to: the Leverhulme Trust and the AHRB for research grants that enabled research for and the writing up of parts of this book; the University of Durham for extending the periods of research leave made possible by those grants; the Department of Philosophy at East Carolina University, where initial work on the book was done, for the hospitality and stimulation afforded me as the Thomas W. Rivers Distinguished Professor in International Studies; the Thomas W. Rivers Professorship Foundation for its generosity; the many colleagues and PhD students who have commented on draft chapters of the book; the publisher's readers of the first draft for their helpful comments (one of which resulted in the title that the book now bears); Peter Momtchiloff at Oxford University Press for his encouragement and patience; and Angela Blackburn for her eagle-eyed copyediting.

Contents

Whoever goes beyond the measure is guilty of 'hubris', and 'hubris' is the worst thing that can befall a man.

George Seferis, *On the Greek Style*

—

CHAPTER I

Introduction

A Human World?

There is an ancient tension, still with us, over the relationship between human beings and a world which, to borrow from Kant, they can 'discursively' encounter—a world, that is, which they can bring under concepts, articulate, and describe. The tension emerges in answers to questions like the following, which go from the crude but curt to the cumbersome but more considered:

> Is there a way the world anyway is, irrespective of how we take it to be?

> Is an articulable world anything but the 'product' or 'construct' of human thought and attitude?

> Can sense be made of the idea of a world, accessible in principle to conceptual articulation, which is independent of human perspectives?

> Do concepts and descriptions truly apply to the world irrespective of the actual availability to, and exercise by, human beings of the appropriate conceptual and descriptive resources?

The ancient tension is between those who respectively answer such questions in the affirmative and the negative. For the latter, one might put it, any 'discursable' world is necessarily a 'human world': it is dependent on human attitude, perspective, or the like. Some such tension probably pre-dates systematic philosophizing, for it is discernible, arguably, among very early religions. Certainly it is there in the early thinking of the great philosophical traditions, east and west, as the following three examples indicate.

(a) According to the Indian Nyāya ('logic') school, we directly perceive the world as it is, except when subject to illusion. Moreover, we possess other 'means of knowledge' (pramāṇas) which enable us to conceptualize and articulate the world. In no way do perception and the other pramāṇas 'create' or 'shape' that world.[1] The Nyāya view was criticized by philosophers of the Madhyamaka school of Mahāyāna Buddhism. According to the philosopher Nāgārjuna, objects of knowledge cannot exist apart from the means of knowledge, and the things alleged to belong to the world are without 'own being' since they owe what existence they have to human language and discrimination.[2]

(b) Most of the classical Chinese schools of thought, including Confucianism, held that our concepts and terms, if 'properly rectified', 'correctly represent reality', since they correspond to divisions in the fabric of the world that exist independently of our discriminative activity.[3] Some Taoists, notably Chuang Tzu, retorted that our terms no more delineate an independent world than do the 'peeps of baby birds'. The world which Confucians take us to be 'representing' is a function of our conceptual and linguistic discriminations, which is why 'those who discriminate' necessarily fail to describe or 'see' a reality that exists independently of them.[4]

(c) Plato and Aristotle had different views of reality, but they agreed that human beings, if sufficiently rational, could come to know and conceptualize reality, one that did not depend on their coming to do so. In holding this, Plato and Aristotle saw themselves as criticizing some Sophist thinkers. Protagoras had stated that 'of all things man is the measure, of things that are that [or how] they are and of things that are not that [or how] they are not'.[5] This might plausibly be understood to mean that no account of how the world is could register more than a human perspective on it. A similar

---

[1] See the selections from *The Nyāya-Sūtras with Vātsyāyana's Commentary* in David E. Cooper (ed.), *Epistemology: The Classic Readings* (Oxford: Blackwell, 1998).

[2] See the selections from Nāgārjuna ibid. Nāgārjuna's views will be discussed in Chapter 12.

[3] Deborah H. Soles and David E. Soles, 'Fish Traps and Rabbit Snares: Zhuangzi on Judgement, Truth and Knowledge', *Asian Philosophy*, 8. 3 (1998), 154.

[4] Quoted ibid. 155 and 158.

[5] 'On Truth', quoted in G. B. Kerferd, 'The Sophists', in C. C. W. Taylor (ed.), *From the Beginning to Plato* (London: Routledge, 1997), 249. What Protagoras 'really meant' has, of course, been much disputed.

construal could be put on some of Gorgias's remarks. 'We communicate not about things which exist, but only speech' might be taken to mean that words do not refer to things which exist independently of our talk of them.[6]

Until the later stages of this book, when aspects of certain eastern traditions are discussed, I shall not dwell on forms the tension took in ancient times. The historical focus, in the early chapters, will be on its emergence in modern forms—on what has led up, for example, to Sartre's assertion that human beings are those 'by whom it happens that *there is* a world',[7] and on resistance to such assertions.

One illustration of the modern debate might be helpful at this stage. (I return to it in some detail in Chapter 8.) According to a familiar twentieth-century view, the theoretical terms of physics—an 'ideal' one of the future, if not today's—not only refer to actual entities and processes, but provide the vocabulary for an 'absolute account' that describes the world as it anyway is, free from any human perspective.[8] Many philosophers disagree: they may regard physics as an 'as if' story, useful only for organizing and predicting experience, or they may hold that physics is no less 'perspectival' than other, perhaps incompatible, accounts of the world.

Philosophers do not, unfortunately, neatly divide into those who respectively answer the questions with which I began affirmatively and negatively. For one thing, there are those who, while they may follow the letter of the affirmative view, hardly do so in spirit. They hold that, while there is a way things are irrespective of what we human beings think, any structured reality is nevertheless a function of intelligence, God's perhaps or a transcendental Mind's. That things are a certain way does not depend on the exercise by *us* of certain concepts, but it does depend on their exercise by, . . . well, Something. This view will crop up spasmodically in the book, usually by way of contrast with the thesis of 'the human world'. For another thing, some philosophers do not answer either affirmatively or negatively, because they don't like the questions. Even a notional contrast between the way

---

[6] 'On Nature', quoted in J. B. Wilbur and H. J. Allen, *The Worlds of the Early Greek Philosophers* (Buffalo, N.Y.: Prometheus, 1979), 255. Gorgias's meaning has also been much disputed.

[7] Jean-Paul Sartre, *Being and Nothingness: An Essay on Phenomenological Ontology*, trans. H. Barnes (London: Methuen, 1957), 552.

[8] See Bernard Williams, *Descartes: The Project of Pure Enquiry* (Harmondsworth: Penguin, 1978). Williams's position will be discussed in Chapter 8.

things are and how we take them to be, capable of giving rise to questions about the direction of dependence between the two, is one which these philosophers reject. Their position is discussed in several places, especially in Chapter 5.

The prospect of a *neat* division is spoiled in another way—as my illustrations might have suggested—by the variety of views found in both the affirmative and negative camps. In the former, opinions as to which world is the way it is irrespective of us can vary from, inter alia, the world as we ordinarily experience it, to the world as described by an 'ideal' physics, to a world of abstract essences or Forms. Nor is there uniformity of argument in support of the affirmative answer. That there is a way the world anyway is has been defended as self-evident, as deducible from theological premises, as presupposed by scientific enquiry or by ordinary linguistic practice[9]—and so on. Nor is there uniformity of argument among those in the negative camp. Self-evidence, deduction, the impossibility of a conceptual scheme which does not reflect human interests—these and much else have been appealed to in support of the thesis of 'the human world'.

There is one particular difference to be found among members of the negative camp that will assume considerable importance in the last four chapters. The more considered of the questions I posed asked whether any conceptualizable, 'discursable' world could exist and be the way it is irrespective of human perspectives and conceptual repertoires. Some philosophers have answered 'No' to those questions, but insisted that this does not exclude—and may even require—the existence of an unconceptualizable, ineffable realm, one that is necessarily 'mysterious'. That may have been Chuang Tzu's view: there is no articulable world without human 'discrimination', but there is the Tao, the Way, which does not permit 'discrimination' or description. In the Advaita Vedānta philosophy of Śaṃkara, the world of which there can be 'discursive' knowledge is the everyday one of *saṃsāra*, but this is *māyā* ('appearance' or 'illusion'). However, there is also *brahman*, the 'Absolute': but while *brahman* may be accessible to con-

---

[9] For a recent version of an argument of the last kind, see Robert B. Brandom, *Making It Explicit: Reasoning, Representing, and Discursive Commitment* (Cambridge, Mass.: Harvard University Press, 1994), who holds that our linguistic practices, such as reporting beliefs in the *de re* mode, presuppose a commitment to the possibility of 'objective correctness'—to, that is, the view that 'objects . . . are what they are regardless of what anyone takes them to be' (594–5).

templative vision, it is not conceptualizable. We can speak of it only as 'not this, not that'.[10]

As a modern advocate of this outlook, some people might propose Kant, with his distinction between the phenomenal world of 'appearances' and unknowable things in themselves. But this is a risky proposal. Kant will be an important figure in this book, but the meaning of his famous distinction and the status of his things in themselves are too much in contention for him to be cited, at this stage, to illustrate a particular position. A safer bet might be Henri Bergson. 'There is', he wrote, 'a reality that is external and yet given immediately to the mind',[11] but this reality defies conceptual articulation, which necessarily distorts its seamless character. Knowledge of an articulable kind is necessarily 'practical knowledge' that registers our interests and concerns, so that the world thus known is relative to human perspective.

Other philosophers in the negative camp do not entertain a realm beyond, behind, or otherwise related to 'the human world': that world is the only one there is. Nietzsche, who speaks of there being *only* perspectives, explicitly denies that there is a 'true world' beyond these, and takes to task those who decry the perspectival, human world as an 'appearance'.[12] That epithet would be in order only if there were another realm to contrast with the perspectival world—and there isn't.

This division within the negative camp needs to be borne in mind and, as mentioned, becomes important in the final chapters. One thing, certainly, that this division does is to complicate the anyway irksome job of finding appropriate labels for the affirmative and negative positions. That is a job I need to do straightaway.

The reason the division just mentioned causes terminological trouble is that any label apt to capture the idea of 'the human world' is liable to be unsuited for the further idea—Śaṃkara's, say—of a non-discursable realm distinguished from that world. Since this is true of all candidate labels, perhaps one should not complain, on this ground, about any one in particular. Still, some jar more than others. 'Anti-realist', for example, a term often applied to people who deny there is a way the world anyway is, sounds inept

---

[10] See the selections from Śaṃkara's *Brahmasūtrabhāṣya* in David E. Cooper (ed.), *Metaphysics: The Classic Readings* (Oxford: Blackwell, 1999).

[11] Henri Bergson, *An Introduction to Metaphysics*, trans. T. E. Hulme (New York: Liberal Arts, 1949), 49.

[12] These and further claims of Nietzsche will be discussed in Chapter 4.

when applied to Bergson, say, who insists that 'there is a reality external' to thought, albeit an unthinkable one. 'Relativist', too, is an unhappy term for someone, like Śaṃkara, who, while proclaiming the dependence of a describable world on human beings, also holds that there is an absolute reality, indescribable *brahman*. Both these terms, moreover, have the disadvantage of being embedded in various philosophical literatures, thereby acquiring connotations that may not be to the point. 'Anti-realism', for example, is often associated with a semantic theory which, though it might be drawn upon by those in the negative camp, is distinct from the 'human world' thesis.

A worse label still would be 'idealism', not least because some of the many idealisms which have been advanced do not belong in the negative camp at all. Berkeley was an idealist and held, in a sense, that the world depended upon mind. But, for him, this world—minds and the ideas occurring in them, including God's—is the way it is independently of what we take it to be. Moreover, even when someone in the negative camp is an idealist, that need not be the reason he belongs there. Śaṃkara is usually counted an idealist because he held that *brahman* is 'pure consciousness', *not* because he regarded the familiar world as dependent on human thought and talk. There are, to be sure, species of idealism which sound closer to the position of the negative camp. Dilthey characterized transcendental idealism as a philosophy which 'reaches behind what is given in consciousness to the creative capacity which . . . produces the whole form of the world'.[13] Transcendental idealism is an important episode in the development of the 'human world' position, but I am reluctant so to label the developed position. For one thing, it is too closely associated with theses of Kant's, not all of which survive in the final version of the story. For another thing, transcendental idealists typically maintain that 'the whole form of the world' is 'produced', not by *human* thought and activity, but by those of Mind, a Transcendental Ego, God, or whatever.

A label free from some of the drawbacks of previous candidates is 'anthropocentrism'. It doesn't, for example, carry much philosophical baggage, never having entrenched itself in the professional literature of philosophy. Moreover, it is suitably indicative of the idea of a 'human world'. But

---

[13] Wilhelm Dilthey, 'The Development of Hermeneutics', in *Dilthey: Selected Writings*, trans. and ed. H. P. Rickman (Cambridge: Cambridge University Press, 1979), 256.

it does carry its own burden: that of being too markedly pejorative. Anthropocentrism is something to avoid, and so we do best to avoid the term as one for a position which is not being prejudged. Still, we are getting warm. But, first, a brief digression.

The embryonic decision to write this book was formed when reflecting on some remarks by Thomas Nagel in *The View from Nowhere*. At one point, he is criticizing an 'idealist' position, which he associates (contentiously) with the later Wittgenstein, according to which 'the world is dependent on our view of it'. Against this, he defends an 'objectivist stance', on which 'the direction of dependence is the reverse' and the world is probably, in some respects, beyond our powers of conception, hence 'not *our* world even potentially'. A remark which especially caught my attention was Nagel's description of his position as 'a strong form of *anti-humanism*'.[14] I had not previously encountered 'humanism' as the name of an epistemological or metaphysical tendency, except in Heidegger, who applies it, for the most part, to a position akin to the view Nagel criticizes—one which 'explains . . . whatever is, in its entirety, . . . in relation to man'.[15] Further reading revealed that several twentieth-century philosophers have intended something like this position by the term, notably the pragmatists F. C. S. Schiller and William James, both of whom, unlike Nagel and Heidegger, *embrace* the position. James characterizes humanism as the 'doctrine that to an unascertainable extent our truths are man-made products', and recommends 'the humanistic principle' that 'you can't weed out the human contribution'.[16]

Others who have used 'humanism' in this way will be mentioned in due course, but enough has been said to indicate why this term suggested itself as a label for the 'human world' thesis. Once suggested, further advantages became apparent. First, like 'anthropocentrism'—but without being indelibly pejorative—it suitably indicates that 'the world is our world' and not one which is either independent of us or dependent on the thought of Something non-human. Second, unlike 'idealism' and 'anti-realism', it

---

[14] Thomas Nagel, *The View From Nowhere* (New York: Oxford University Press, 1986), 108–9 (my italics).

[15] Martin Heidegger, *The Question Concerning Technology and Other Essays*, trans. W. Lovitt (New York: Harper & Row, 1977), 133. Heidegger, one should note for future reference, also speaks of a 'true humanism' which he contrasts with humanism in his critical sense.

[16] William James, 'Pragmatism and Humanism', in *The Writings of William James* (Chicago: University of Chicago Press, 1977), 451 and 455.

doesn't have much of a pedigree in the philosophical lexicon, so there is less danger of confusing the intended sense with others. Certainly 'humanism' does have other senses, but most are so obviously different that confusion is unlikely: humanism as humanitarianism, for instance, or as the study of the *literae humaniores*.

For my purposes, the term has further advantages still. First, it rather naturally plugs us into a tradition of western thought. That will be a drawback if one thinks that, say, Renaissance humanism has nothing at all to do with humanism as characterized by James, Heidegger, Nagel, et al. But I shall argue, in Chapter 2, that it is a merit if the label encourages us to see humanism in my sense as a culmination of a tradition to which Renaissance humanism belongs. Second, the word has a moral, evaluative aura about it. Humanism, in different shapes, is something people defend or denounce as proper or perverse. Again, this would be a drawback if the humanisms thus defended or denounced were remote from the sense which concerns us. But I shall argue that there are deep connections between the 'human world' thesis and tendencies apt to attract evaluative judgement. Or better, it may be artificial to separate evaluative from epistemological-cum-metaphysical dimensions of the debate about that thesis. Since this intertwining of dimensions informs some of my discussion, I shall say more about it, by way of scene-setting, in the next section.

I end this section with four remarks on my use of 'humanism'. Boethius could not answer the question posed by the figure of Philosophy, 'Can you tell me what man is?'[17] Nor can I. I don't know, for example, whether some creature of the future, part metal, part flesh, will count as a human being. The point to make is that the 'human' in 'humanism' is not to be taken *too* seriously. It is not a thesis about the world's dependence on a particular biological species, but about its dependence on beings with, as Heidegger put it when characterizing *Dasein*, our 'manner of being'.[18] What the relevant manner is, and how different, biologically, a creature could be and still possess it, are not trivial questions. The present point, simply, is that the humanist, in my sense, need not insist that only members of *homo sapiens* have our, the human *kind* of existence.

---

[17] *The Consolation of Philosophy*, trans. V. Watts (Harmondsworth: Penguin, 1969), 51.
[18] *Being and Time*, trans. J. Macquarrie and E. Robinson (Oxford: Blackwell, 1962), § 4.

Second, we should distinguish 'global' humanism from various 'local' ones. It is possible, indeed common, to hold that things are only beautiful or ugly according to human perspectives, without taking a parallel view of spatial and other physical properties of things. So one can take a humanist view of aesthetics—or mathematics, ethics, or whatever—without subscribing to 'global' humanism, the thesis that nothing 'discursable' exists independent of human perspective, that the world *tout court* is a human one.[19] The main focus will be on this dramatic, 'global' claim, but sometimes more 'local' ones will be in view. Indeed, it will be interesting to observe how philosophers have disagreed over the support, or lack of it, the 'global' claim gets from the apparent success of some 'local' ones.

Third, we should distinguish 'generic' humanism from 'specific' ones. I introduced the term in a way which makes it applicable to any view which answers my four initial questions in the negative, irrespective of the specific form the view takes and the arguments deployed in support. But I also introduced it in connection with remarks by recent philosophers, such as Nagel, James, and Heidegger, and my focus will be on a humanism which is the culmination, in modern times, of a certain intellectual development. Typically, it will be humanism in this modern form which is intended by the term. When it becomes important explicitly to distinguish it from a more generic view, I introduce the required qualifiers. In particular, humanism in its characteristically modern form will, in later chapters, often be referred to as 'raw' humanism and distinguished from positions that 'compensate' for the bare thesis of 'the human world' by invoking an ineffable realm or 'mystery' that is 'beyond the human'.

Finally, who are the humanists' opponents? 'Realists', 'absolutists', 'cosmocentrists' share the drawbacks of 'anti-realists', 'relativists', and 'anthropocentrists'. Where economy, if not stylistic elegance, indicates a need, I shall speak of 'non-humanists' or 'anti-humanists'. Elsewhere, I speak simply of humanism's 'critics', 'opponents', and the like. From Chapter 7 on, however, and once the term has been properly circumscribed, I shall generally pit the humanist against the 'absolutist', less than ideal as that label might be.

---

[19] Compare Crispin Wright's advice, in his *Truth and Objectivity* (Cambridge, Mass.: Harvard University Press, 1992), to relativize anti-realism to particular, 'local', vocabularies. One can be anti-realist towards, say, talk about humour without being so towards, say, talk about space and time.

'Humility' and 'Vital' Matters

I suggested that it was a merit of the label that 'humanism' has an evaulative flavour to it, so that by employing it we are encouraged to connect discussion of the 'human world' thesis with matters of broadly moral or 'practical' concern. Since these matters will occupy much of our attention, I should expand on what I have in mind. The first thing to say, however, is that 'moral', in its contemporary philosophical usage, is not really the word I want. The 'matters of concern' are not, in the main, those of rights, obligations, justice, welfare, and other topics which currently preoccupy moral philosophy. The term 'ethical' would similarly be too narrow. So I shall speak of the 'vital' themes and matters with which my discussion of humanism will connect. These themes concern the proper stance human beings should adopt towards the world, and towards their beliefs and commitments—a stance that informs both their conception and conduct of their lives.

One connection between humanism and vital, including moral, matters is direct and predictable. Earlier I distinguished 'global' humanism from various 'local' ones, including humanistic treatments of moral belief. The idea that moral properties are human 'projections', not features of the world as it anyway is, is a familiar one. For some thinkers, it has provided something of a model for a more general, 'global' humanism, while for others, it has paved the way—by relocating 'values' in the 'subjective' domain—for a hard-headed account of a world uncontaminated by human perspective. That dispute will receive some attention later. The present point is simply to note that consideration of 'global' humanism encompasses discussion of 'local' humanisms about moral and other evaluative discourses.

But this is not the connection with the 'vital' that I have primarily in mind, though in order to introduce the sort I do, I need to make a further remark about 'local', moral humanism. Critics of that idea of morality are not always willing to treat it as the morally neutral, 'purely philosophical' analysis of moral discourse which its proponents generally present it as being. These critics subject moral humanism itself to a broadly moral, certainly 'vital', critique. It represents, not simply a mistaken account of moral discourse, but a perverse stance towards moral life. Writing of 'moral philosophy of an existentialist type'—which, for her, is not relevantly different from the 'non-cognitive' approaches familiar in English-language philosophy—Iris Murdoch complains that it is an 'egocentric' style of thought in which 'our picture of ourselves has become too grand . . . We have lost the vision of a reality separate from ourselves'.[20] Some of Murdoch's intended targets here, one should note, would not respond by pleading moral neutrality. Sartre, for one, regards his 'existentialist humanism', with its thesis that 'there is no legislator' of values but man himself, as something which a person should accept if he is to 'realize himself as truly human'.[21]

In the present context, what interests me about Murdoch's remarks on humanistic treatments of evaluative discourse is how they may modulate into a more general point about the 'vital' credentials of humanism *tout court*. Earlier, I cited a remark of Nagel's which had caught my attention. Here is another. Having recommended his 'strong form of anti-humanism', according to which 'the world is not our world even potentially', Nagel continues that 'to deny [this] shows a lack of *humility* . . . an attempt to cut the universe down to size'.[22] This charge of hubris generalizes Murdoch's complaint at our becoming 'too grand' and losing a 'vision of a reality separate from ourselves'. In levelling the charge, Nagel is, as we shall see in Chapter 7, following in the wake of many other critics of humanist epistemology, including Russell, Heidegger, and Max Scheler.

It is essential to observe, moreover, that, like some of Iris Murdoch's targets, there are humanists or their allies willing to reply to this charge on its own 'vital' terms and to return it against their critics. For Fichte, recognition of the human contribution to the nature of reality is not hubris, but a proper sense of 'self-sufficiency' in contrast to the 'spiritual servitude' exhibited by 'dogmatists' who imagine an independent world to be 'the explanatory ground of experience'.[23] More recently, it has been suggested that the truly 'immodest' or 'presumptuous' thought is not the humanist's, but the 'realist' one that although 'the world is determined independently of human

---

[20] Iris Murdoch, *Existentialists and Mystics: Writings on Philosophy and Literature*, ed. P. Conradi (Harmondsworth: Penguin, 1997), 338.

[21] *Existentialism and Humanism*, trans. P. Mairet (London: Methuen, 1966), 55–6. See also David Wiggins, 'Truth, Invention, and the Meaning of Life', in his *Needs, Values, Truth*, 3rd ed. (Oxford: Blackwell, 1998)—not only for criticism, akin to Murdoch's, of the 'vital' dimensions of non-cognitive moral theories, but for quotations from Aldous Huxley and André Maurois which, like mine from Sartre, affirm the 'vital' merits of moral humanism.

[22] *The View From Nowhere*, 109.

[23] J. G. Fichte, *Introductions to the* Wissenschaftslehre *and Other Writings*, trans. D. Breazeale (Indianapolis: Hackett, 1994), 17 ff.

cognitive activity, we are nevertheless . . . capable . . ., often, of knowing the truth about it'.[24]

The vocabulary of humility versus hubris, presumptuousness versus modesty, freedom versus servitude, and even decadence versus responsibility is, we shall see, liberally invoked in discussions of the 'human world' thesis, and by both warring parties.[25] Someone may worry, however, that, despite this, it is misleading to speak of 'vital' issues being involved. Surely the vocabulary invoked either is being used in an extended way, without the 'vital' or moral connotations the terms usually bear, or is bringing in considerations extraneous to the philosophical questions at stake. The humanist's 'hubristic' refusal to regard our beliefs as 'answerable' to an independent order of things should not be compared to the reprehensible hubris of the man who scornfully disregards the need to put his moral prejudices to the test. If the humanist is wrong, it is because he is mistaken about a purely philosophical, indeed technical, set of questions concerning the relation of words to things, the criteria of truth, and the like. It may be a good rhetorical ploy to accuse him of lack of humility, but such accusations should be taken no more literally than, say, one's criticism of an argument as 'perverse'.

This objection is too quick. It is, at the very least, harder than the objector imagines to prise 'vital' issues away from 'pure' or 'technical' ones. First, the objection begs questions. It begs one, for example, against someone like Fichte, who held that the resources of speculative reason are exhausted when it comes to the question of the direction of dependence between thought and the world, so that any rational considerations available can only be drawn from the sphere of practical reason.[26] More pertinently, perhaps, the objection skews matters in favour of the humanist's critics. A humanist, in my 'generic' sense, need not be a pragmatist, but he may be. And he may, like William James, be a generous one who places few constraints on the allowable criteria for what it is 'good to believe'. He will then find it quite illegitimate to make an exception for *philosophical* beliefs, including his own and his opponents'. If 'vital' considerations, including moral and even rel-

[24] Wright, *Truth and Objectivity*, 1–2.

[25] In connection with final pair of terms, Richard Rorty interprets Nagel as accusing pragmatists like himself of 'decadence', a refusal to be 'constrained . . . [by] something . . . men and women . . . must try to be "adequate" [to]'. *Consequences of Pragmatism: Essays 1972–80* (Brighton: Harvester, 1982), p. xxxix.

[26] Fichte, *Introductions to the* Wissenschaftslehre, 17 ff.

igious ones, are allowed to inform our beliefs at large, is it not arbitrary to outlaw them when it is philosophical positions that are up for appraisal? It is surely not *absurd* for James to argue that it counts as an objection to a philosophical doctrine that it endorses a servile, fatalistic temperament.

Second, one need not even be a humanist or pragmatist to suppose that it is proper criticism of a philosophical, or any other, position that it cannot be *lived*—that it is one which, though mouthable by some theorist, is necessarily suspended, and implicitly rejected, when the theorist is engaged in the business of living. Consider the charge often levelled against ethical 'non-cognitivists' that their view of moral judgement is one they cannot cling to when themselves engaged in making such judgements. Theirs, it is sometimes said, is a purely 'outsider' view of moral judgement, one impossible for the 'participant' to take. The phenomenology of moral experience excludes retention of the 'non-cognitivist' view during the course of such experience.[27] Now an analogous charge might be levelled against humanism at large. When in the thick of things—passively taking in the world around us, compelled to describe what we encounter thus-and-so—talk of a 'human world' which we 'shape', 'create', or 'carve up' seems idle. The thesis of the 'human world' lasts for as long as one is in one's study, and is necessarily abandoned once, re-engaged in life, the world, in all its brute independence, imposes itself. The thesis is a disingenuous one which no one can really believe unless reprehensibly blind to the obvious or adept at 'cognitive dissonance'. If this is so, is it not hubristic to go on trumpeting 'the human contribution'?

That is a fair question—as is one that the humanist, in a *tu quoque* manoeuvre, will set his opponents. It is, he argues, their thesis of an independent world which belongs in the study, manifesting a detached, 'spectatorial' view of the world which is belied once one is out and about in it. There, everything *is* encountered in relation to human concerns and 'projects', and is it not hubristic to pretend to a capacity to transcend such a relation and provide an account of how things independently and anyway are? This exchange of charges of hubris is chronicled in Chapter 7 and assessed in following chapters.

---

[27] See Wiggins, 'Truth, Invention, and the Meaning of Life', for this line of criticism of 'non-cognitivism'.

A third consideration is prompted by the suspicion that the 'ancient tension' is not only ancient but interminable and that arguments designed, without success, to clinch the case have been exhausted. In keeping with that suspicion, it is legitimate to wonder if the debate is best represented as a straightforward confrontation between philosophical arguments: to wonder, perhaps, whether it is not a confrontation between *visions* or *moods*, which 'orthodox' argument is insufficient to dispel. It is then legitimate to wonder if the recalcitrance of the dispute is not due to its engagement with 'vital' matters, exposure of which may be just what is needed to dispel one or both of the rival visions or moods. There is an analogy, here, in the history of religious controversy. Exposures of religious belief as, say, the refuge of the weak and oppressed have had more success in eroding faith than 'disproofs' of God's existence.

Some remarks of John McDowell, inspired by Wittgenstein, will help clarify the point. One of his critical targets is a 'philosophical realism' that seeks to view the relation between thought and the world 'so to speak, from sideways on—from a standpoint independent of all . . . human activities and reactions . . . [and] practices'. McDowell diagnoses this aspiration as a craving for 'consolation' and 'security' in 'recoil' from a sense of 'terror' and 'vertigo' induced by the thought that our beliefs and concepts 'rest on nothing more' stable than our contingent 'forms of life', on what Cavell called 'the whirl of organism'.[28] The 'felt distance' between thought and the world which the 'philosophical realist' experiences and tries to close from his 'sideways on' position is, says McDowell, something that should be 'exorcized', as should the vertigo it induces and the consequent yearnings for security and consolation.[29] (The language here unmistakably evokes familiar 'exposures' of religious conviction.)

All of this may sound like music to the 'anti-realist' humanist, but, for McDowell, humanism in its more muscular versions, such as 'social prag-

---

[28] McDowell, 'Non-Cognitivism and Rule-Following', in his *Mind, Value, and Reality* (Cambridge, Mass.: Harvard University Press, 1998), 212 and 207. The reference to Stanley Cavell is to his *Must We Mean What We Say?*, 2nd ed. (Cambridge: Cambridge University Press, 1976), 52.

[29] *Mind and World* (Cambridge, Mass.: Harvard University Press, 1994), 147. Here, McDowell's inspiration could as well have been Hegel as Wittgenstein. Hegel, too, diagnoses metaphysical disputes as often resting on 'useless ideas' about the opposition between cognition and absolute reality. See G. W. F. Hegel, *Phenomenology of Spirit*, trans. A. V. Miller (Oxford: Oxford University Press, 1977), §§ 73 ff.

matism', is subject to a related diagnosis. If the 'realist' is in recoil from the spectre of foundationless 'forms of life', the virulent humanist is in recoil from recognizing that the 'consolation' of 'realism' is illusory. Instead of exorcizing terror and vertigo, however, he has, like some thrill-seeking hang-glider, simply changed their valences into exhilaration and frisson— boasting of a dizzying freedom to create and shape the world. Were he not, deep down, subject to the same yearnings as the 'realist', he would have no need to over-compensate by trumpeting this 'arrogant anthropocentrism'.[30] (Perhaps only someone who regrets the death of God can conclude that, now, everything is permitted.)

McDowell's remarks nicely illustrate an intertwining of the ancient tension with 'vital' issues sparked by perception of the embeddedness of cognitive practices in 'forms of life'. Is the appropriate response one of peaceful accommodation, foundationalist bridling, or exhilaration? They indicate, too, how 'vital' considerations may serve to alter visions. The 'philosophical realist' cannot accept McDowell's diagnosis and then carry on business as usual. 'Intuitions' which he once saw it as his job to honour will now strike him as prejudices born of false yearnings. Arguments once deployed in a 'foundationalist' spirit will now be seen to be drawn 'from the midst' of the practices for which he once aspired to provide foundations. No more than the religious believer who is brought to see his faith as a refuge for the oppressed can the 'realist' pass off the exposure of his position as extraneous to its integrity. Suitably amended, these points apply, as well, to the 'vision' of the virulent humanist, the 'arrogant anthropocentrist'. (McDowell's own 'serene' or 'quietist' dissolution of the ancient tension will be criticized later on, especially in Chapter 9. But the criticism is not intended to detract from the value of the 'vital' terms in which he construes that tension.)

Finally, labels like 'arrogant anthropocentrism' are familiar in the literature of environmental ethics, and no book with 'humanism' in the title should ignore the pejorative use to which that label, too, is put by many environmentalists—as in titles like *The Arrogance of Humanism* and in demands for the replacement of 'humanist values systems by suprahumanistic values'.[31] As one pair of authors observe, 'anti-humanism' has become a slogan

---

[30] Ibid. 40.
[31] Quoted from a Greenpeace publication by Luc Ferry, *The New Ecological Order*, trans. C. Volk (Chicago: University of Chicago Press, 1995), 70. The author of *The Arrogance of Humanism* (Oxford: Oxford University Press, 1981) is David Ehrenfeld.

for that 'rejection of modernity' associated with 'deep' environmentalist thought.[32] So here is an area of 'vital' concern, involving the proper stance of human beings towards the natural world, which prima facie connects with our subject. Someone will object, however, that the connection is only superficial, that environmentalists who declaim against humanism do not intend it in my sense. They may have little more in mind than a 'chauvinistic' insistence that only human well-being is of moral moment, or the Stoic view, inherited by Christianity, that the natural world was created for the benefit of man. They may even intend something incompatible with humanism in my sense: for example, the view that '"man" is . . . "outside" the reality . . . given to him in consciousness', which 'endorses an instrumental conception of the relation between humanity and the . . . "natural" world' that men proceed to 'harness' 'by means of an objective knowledge of its workings'.[33]

It is clear, however, that many environmental philosophers do have in mind humanism in my, or a closely related, sense. For them, the 'human world' thesis is deeply implicated with a comportment towards the natural world which they decry. Part of what Stephen Clark means by 'humanism' is an 'anti-realist' picture of a natural world that we 'carve' into species and kinds, and which thereby encourages that insouciance towards creaturely differences displayed by, for example, transgenic procedures in modern biotechnology.[34] For other authors, a main culprit is a humanist treatment of values that excludes regarding them as discoverable ingredients of the objective natural order to which appeal could be made in criticism of our exploitation of nature.[35]

It is to Heidegger's later writings that one naturally turns for a prolonged attempt to implicate humanism in the 'devastation of the earth'. In effect, he collapses into the notion of humanism both the thesis of 'the human world' and a 'technological' way of 'revealing' the world responsible for that devastation. Humanism not only explains 'whatever is' in relation to man, but evaluates it 'from the standpoint of man'. Heidegger's characterizations of

---

[32] Luc Ferry and Alain Renaut, *Heidegger and Modernity*, trans. F. Philip (Chicago: University of Chicago Press, 1990), 1.

[33] Kate Soper, *Humanism and Anti-Humanism* (London: Hutchinson, 1986), 24.

[34] S. R. L. Clark, *Animals and Their Moral Standing* (London: Routledge, 1997), 7 ff.

[35] See, for example, Holmes Rolston III, *Conserving Natural Value* (New York: Columbia University Press, 1994).

humanism lend themselves, by design, to both an epistemological and an 'environmental' reading. For the humanist, man 'decide[s] whether and how beings appear',[36] both as a conceptual legislator and as the techno-logical 'master of the earth'.

While the suspicion may occur that Heidegger is illegitimately yoking together disparate humanisms, epistemological and technological, it would be too quick to dismiss his strategy in advance. Indeed, the presumption is that the connection is not accidental between an epistemology which treats the existence and structure of an articulable world as dependent on human practices and a view of the natural world as one at the legitimate disposal of human beings. After all, in its characteristically modern form, humanism understands the very identity of things to depend on their place within activities embedded in human 'forms of life'. It is difficult not to feel that this understanding threatens a sense of things' integrity and, perhaps, mystery which, for some philosophers, is prerequisite for an appropriately respectful or 'humble' stance towards nature.[37] (That stance is discussed in Chapter 13.)

Preview

The intertwining of some pretty 'abstract', even technical philosophical questions with 'vital' matters helps to make the structure and argument of this book relatively complex. Certainly it covers a lot of ground. Given this complexity and range, a brief chapter-by-chapter preview may prove help-ful.

Chapters 2–4 are an exercise in the history of ideas, undertaken less, how-ever, to cater to antiquarian tastes than in the belief that the temptations of humanism are best appreciated through understanding why people were in fact progressively drawn towards the 'human world' thesis. Chapter 2 charts the quickening pace, during the late medieval and Renaissance periods, of a confidence—one largely lost since classical times—that Hans Blumenberg

---

[36] 'Letter on Humanism', in *Basic Writings: Martin Heidegger*, ed. D. F. Krell (London: Routledge, 1993), 234.

[37] This is Iris Murdoch's position, as we'll see in Chapters 7 and 13. See also the interesting foot-notes 13 and 19 in Wiggins, 'Truth, Invention, and the Meaning of Life'.

has called human 'self-assertion'. Chapter 3 starts by noting a reaction against this process, but then identifies the emergence, towards the end of the eighteenth century, of certain innovations crucial to the later formulation of a full-blown humanism—in particular, Kant's 'Copernican revolution' and a 'Romantic' privileging of agency over reason. In Chapter 4, certain versions of just such a full-blown humanism, which I dub 'Promethean', are located in the writings of Nietzsche, Marx, and sundry thinkers around the turn of the twentieth century, including Bergson and some of the pragmatists.

Chapter 5 is a central one, for it articulates what I judge to be the most sophisticated and compelling version of the 'human world' thesis, one free from some of the difficulties confronting its 'Promethean' predecessors. I label this final version 'existential humanism'. While that label is intended to suggest close connections with the so-called existential phenomenology of Merleau-Ponty, Sartre, and the Heidegger of *Being and Time*, existential humanism is not to be identified with the position of any given philosopher or 'school'. It is a 'reconstruction' that draws on many authors, including Wittgenstein and even some philosophers, like Hilary Putnam and McDowell, whose self-description as robust realists belies, in my judgement, their proximity to humanism.

Chapter 6, by contrast, is one that could be skipped by readers not especially concerned for the fate of the term 'humanism', for it is something of an interlude in which I defend my way of understanding humanism—in terms of the 'human world' thesis—against certain rival ways, including Foucault's.

Chapter 7 begins by identifying an aspect of existential humanism ignored in Chapter 5: its advocacy of a certain stance or attitude towards our concepts, beliefs, and commitments that 'goes with' acceptance of the 'human world' thesis. I call this stance the 'dis-incumbenced' one. Roughly, the 'dis-incumbenced' person is one who, without abandoning beliefs and commitments, accepts that there can be no 'foundations' or independent 'grounding' for these. The chapter then proceeds to chronicle the charges of hubris or lack of humility that humanists and their opponents ('absolutists') level against one another. Two 'modes' of hubris are distinguished, those of belief and 'posture' respectively. The humanist accuses his opponents of the former, and is accused by them of the latter.

Chapters 8–10 proceed to assess these charges. In Chapter 8, I endorse the humanist's claim that absolutism—in the shape, for example, of 'scientific realism'—embodies an exaggerated, hubristic conception of human beings' capacity to attain, whether in practice or principle, to an 'absolute account' of the world 'uncontaminated' by 'the human contribution'. (The notion of such an account that is, in principle, beyond our attainment is, I suggest, incoherent.) Chapters 9–10 consider and finally endorse the charge that the 'dis-incumbenced' posture required by existential humanism—in its 'raw', 'uncompensated' form—is a hubristic one. Various attempts to celebrate or to render unproblematic this posture are, in Chapter 9, found to be unconvincing. Having appealed to the testimonies of people who have genuinely tried to embrace, rather than merely mouth, the thesis of 'the human world', I argue in Chapter 10 that human beings are incapable of that posture. It is an unlivable one. The main reason for this conclusion, given later in the chapter, is that reflective creatures cannot dispense with the conviction that their lives are 'answerable to', and find 'measure' in, something 'beyond the human'.

Chapter 11 is pivotal, for here there is a turn from attention to humanism to the topic named by the last word in my subtitle, 'mystery'. The chapter begins by bringing out the impasse that is seemingly reached with the demise, over the preceding three chapters, of both absolutism and 'raw' humanism. It proceeds to argue that the only escape from this impasse is a doctrine that, while recognizing the truth in the thesis of 'the human world', compensates for that thesis in its raw form by invoking an undiscursable, mysterious reality. Various pre-emptive dismissals of the very idea of mystery are rejected.

In Chapter 12, I draw upon the Mahāyāna Buddhist notion of 'emptiness' and Heidegger's meditations, in his later writings, on 'Being' and 'Enowning' (Ereignis) to elaborate a doctrine of mystery—one that, I hope, does not self-defeatingly try to 'eff' the ineffable. Chapter 13, the final one, explores—albeit in a fairly promissory way—the question of how a doctrine of mystery might provide 'measure' for our lives. If it cannot do this, that would be disappointing, since the prospect of such a provision was a main motive for entertaining the notion of mystery. I argue, however, that we may discern how various conceptions, beliefs, and comportments are or are not 'consonant' with an experience of, or 'attunement' to, mystery. For example, comportments that manifest the traditional virtue of humility turn out to be 'consonant'.

While on the topic of humility, let me say what I have and have not set out to achieve in this book. In some respects, the book is very ambitious. It attempts to identify, chart the development of, and subject to criticism what are, surely, the two main, rival trajectories of philosophical reflection on the relation between human beings—their thinking, perspectives, interests, and practices—and the world. It attempts, as well, to relate those trajectories to 'vital' issues, indeed to the question of the meaning of our lives. The later chapters, furthermore, attempt to rehabilitate, and 'apply' to 'vital' issues, a 'mystical' tradition that, it is argued, furnishes the only viable alternative to the rejected trajectories of humanism and absolutism. What the book does not set out to do is to demonstrate either the wrong-headedness of 'raw' humanism and its absolutist and other rivals or the truth of the doctrine of mystery urged towards the end. The most I may have achieved is to render my criticisms and proposals plausible. The latter, in particular, will, I suspect, only be found compelling by people already 'attuned' to experiencing the world in a certain way. But that, I also suspect—and for reasons briefly indicated earlier in this Introduction—is the lot of any philosophical proposals that, in effect, are urging something like a vision.

CHAPTER 2

'Self-Assertion': From 'Ockhamism' to Renaissance Humanism

History and Humanism

This and the following two chapters tell a historical story whose denouement, in Chapter 5, is that 'full-blown' humanism of our times which I call existential humanism. The present chapter takes us from a pregnant development in late medieval philosophy to the humanist thinking of the Renaissance and its immediate aftermath. Chapters 3–4 continue the story up from the Enlightenment period to the pragmatist thinking of some early twentieth-century philosophers.

Why do I tell this story instead of plunging, straightaway, into 'where we are at'? Partly because the story is, I hope, a good one, worth the telling for its own sake. Partly because we are unlikely to appreciate the temptations of humanism unless we understand those whom it in fact tempted. It is hard to sympathize with those philosophers who make a merit of treating venerable positions as if they might have come out of the blue, broadcast for the first time in this month's number of some journal. For we are unlikely, from our armchairs, to discern the 'mindset', the series of intellectual crises, and the constellation of rival views which formed the background against which a given position seemed compelling or repugnant. To suppose that, thus uninformed, one could appraise the position is no less cavalier than to pass confident judgement on an artwork from a culture about which one is pig-ignorant. Even if an ahistorical presentation of a philosophical position succeeds in exposing the more technical points germane to its appraisal, it will miss those 'vital' issues with which, I suggested, a thesis like that of 'the human world' is entwined. Those vital issues are not to be identified without attention to the moral and other significance with which the thesis and its precursors have actually been invested.

These reasons for telling the story which culminates in existential humanism would obtain even if one rejects that label. But another reason for the story is precisely to defend the label. There are two parts to that defence. First, I want to show that existential humanism is indeed heir to intellectual tendencies which belong to a broad tradition of humanism. We speak comfortably of Renaissance humanism, the humanism of Enlightenment, Marxist humanism, and pragmatist humanism. Properly construed, these historical humanisms move towards existential humanism, which therefore deserves the 'humanist' label more than other contemporary doctrines. Not everyone agrees, and so the second part of my defence takes the form of criticizing some rival characterizations of modern-day humanism. I won't do that until Chapter 6, but it will be useful briefly to list these characterizations which the story implies we should reject. One is the idea, urged by Althusser for example, that the defining feature of humanism is subscription to a concept of human *essence*, timeless and unconditioned. A second, popular among thinkers associated with Humanist Associations, equates humanism with a *naturalistic* view of human beings that eschews 'supernatural' agency as enthusiastically as it embraces a 'scientific image' of humankind. Finally, there is the currently fashionable characterization, associated with Foucault, that identifies humanism with doctrines of rational and autonomous *subjectivity*. Although I do not assemble my misgivings about these characterizations until Chapter 6, I shall sometimes indicate where episodes in my story count against them.

It might be useful, as well, to indicate what my story does *not* purport to be. It is not the tale of an inevitable and necessary direction of thought. How could it be, given that many philosophers of the first rank, though subject to the same intellectual pressures as the rest, never took it? Thus the 'crisis' in late medieval thought which invited a humanist response in the Renaissance also prompted rival ones. Kant's 'Copernican revolution', which decisively prepared a way towards pragmatism and existential humanism, was exploited by other thinkers in a different manner. So my claim is the lesser one that there is a coherent direction of thought to be identified, a story of an intelligible development to be told. It is, one might add, a story likely to be missed or only dimly perceived if we stick with the usual canon of 'great philo-sophers'. Certainly it becomes more vivid when attention is paid to thinkers such as Gassendi, Vico, Herder, Marx, and Dilthey, writers who rarely figure on the usual undergraduate menu of 'core' subjects like epistemology and metaphysics.

Stories need a beginning. A natural place, it might seem, for mine to begin would be the period whose scholars inspired the word 'humanism'. The term was coined, early in the nineteenth century, by J. F. Niethammer, to refer to ideas, especially in the sphere of education, associated with the Renaissance *umanisti*.[1] To start the story in the Renaissance would already be to begin earlier than adjacent ones told by some other historians of ideas. While these writers have not had a vested interest in the humanist creden-tials of the views whose origins they trace, those views are sometimes very close to the thesis of 'the human world'. I am thinking, especially, of Edward Craig's *The Mind of God and the Works of Man*.[2] This book, to which my two following chapters are especially indebted, is concerned with the displace-ment of an 'Image of God' doctrine, according to which man is 'first and foremost a spectator . . . who could, and should, acquire insight into the order of reality as God has disposed it', by 'the Agency theory' or 'the Practice ideal'. That theory exhorts us to 'turn to the concept of practice for a solution to metaphysical and epistemological problems', and in its fully developed form holds that man is not a 'spectator, but a being that actively creates, or shapes, its own world', with the effect that 'the realities which we meet with are the works of man'.[3] Those words should recall the character-izations of humanism by Nagel, James, and Heidegger cited in Chapter 1. Indeed, several of Craig's paradigmatic advocates of 'the Agency theory' are among my champions of contemporary humanism—James and Sartre, for example.

Where I depart from Craig is over dates. 'The Practice ideal', he writes, has been 'effective', with certain 'provisos', only from 1780, the eve of the

---

[1] On the origins of the term 'humanism', see Paul Oskar Kristeller, *Renaissance Thought and the Arts* (Princeton: Princeton University Press, 1990), 24 ff, and Hendrik Birus, 'The Archaeology of Humanism', *Surfaces*, 4 (1997), 4 ff, http://elias.ens.fr/Surfaces/vol4/birus.html.

[2] Oxford: Clarendon Press, 1987.

[3] Ibid. 224, 228 ff.

publication of Kant's first *Critique*.[4] Kant's 'revolution' is indeed a crucial episode in my story, but in this chapter I want to identify earlier episodes in the displacement of the 'Image of God' by embryonic versions of the 'Agency theory'. The displacement is certainly visible among some thinkers of the Renaissance, but it would be unsatisfactory to begin there, since these thinkers were themselves either developing earlier tendencies or, at any rate, responding to what had already been appreciated as a 'crisis' in the 'Image of God' doctrine.

Since there is nothing brand new under the philosophical sun—since any story can, with ingenuity, be taken back to the year dot—judgement is needed for beginning at a certain date. Fourteenth-century 'Ockhamism' was, to a degree, a replay of views, equally disturbing for the 'Image of God' doctrine, advanced by Muslim thinkers and indeed by some figures during the first centuries of Christianity. But my judgement is that no essential stage in the long journey towards contemporary humanism is missed by electing to start in the Fourteenth century, whereas something is lost by starting later.

'Ockhamism'

'[S]omething happened with Ockham', something which 'set the character of theories of knowledge', and of much else, during the following centuries.[5] In this section, I try to identify both what that 'something' was and the seeds of a style of response to it that deserves to be called humanistic. Notice that I speak of 'Ockhamism', not of Ockhamism or William of Ockham. The great Franciscan was a difficult thinker and I want to avoid exegetical issues concerning his exact position. Equally, I avoid the contested question of the fidelity to that position of the Ockhamist school which flourished, especially in Paris, during the fourteenth century. My concern is

---

[4] Ibid. 231. Compare the claim by Robert B. Pippin, who is also concerned to trace the increasing emphasis on 'activity in any account of experience', that 'the intellectual event which made possible' such an emphasis was Kant's first *Critique*. See his *Idealism as Modernism: Hegelian Variations* (Cambridge: Cambridge University Press, 1998), 9.

[5] John F. Boler, 'Intuitive and Abstractive Cognition', in N. Kretzmann, A. Kenny, and J. Pinborg (eds.), *The Cambridge History of Later Medieval Philosophy* (Cambridge: Cambridge University Press, 1982), 478.

to identify a position commonly perceived to have been proposed by Ockham and radicalized by his eponymous followers. It was that perception, not its scholarly accuracy, which mattered for subsequent developments.

I am not the first to suggest that what 'happened with Ockham' inspired developments which culminate in distinctively modern enthusiasms, including existential humanism. That suggestion was persuasively made by Hans Blumenberg in *The Legitimacy of the Modern Age*. For him, 'the modern age is the second overcoming of gnosticism', a 'new' gnosticism inaugurated by 'Ockhamism'.[6] Modernity, for Blumenberg, incorporates much more than humanism, and indeed that term occurs rarely in his book. Still, it is clear that, even when not so labelled, humanism is for Blumenberg, as it will be for me, a main trend in the 'overcoming' of 'Ockhamist' gnosticism.

Blumenberg is not without his critics, according to whom, for example, he ignores factors outside philosophy, ones of a social and political type, which helped to erode the medieval world view.[7] Nevertheless, his account of that view, of its erosion, and of the emergence of responses to that erosion, remains inspirational.

Why does Blumenberg describe 'Ockhamism' as a 'new' or 'second' gnosticism? The 'first' gnostics were a loosely connected group of religious thinkers who flourished in the early part of the first millennium CE. Their shared platform was that 'the true God is beyond the created universe and quite alien to it'.[8] The creator was not 'the true God', but a 'demiurge'—a being of evil, according to some gnostics, and, for the Manicheans among them, one engaged in a struggle against God. Gnostic theology was explicitly pitted against the emerging synthesis of monotheism, both Jewish and Christian, and neo-Platonism—a synthesis already elaborated by writers such as Philo of Alexandria, though yet to receive its most famous

---

[6] *The Legitimacy of the Modern Age*, trans. Robert M. Wallace (Cambridge, Mass.: MIT Press, 1983), 126. I am not the first, either, to relate Blumenberg's account to humanist and rival epistemologies which have flourished in both European and Anglo-American philosophy during the twentieth century. See, especially, Frank B. Farrell, *Subjectivity, Realism and Postmodernism: The Recovery of the World* (Cambridge: Cambridge University Press, 1996). In this lively book, 'Ockhamism' is the catalyst for the development of views which culminate in contemporary anti-realisms and the investment of 'subjectivity' with features of which the objective world has gradually been stripped.

[7] Several criticisms of Blumenberg are levelled in a generally sympathetic account by Pippin, *Idealism as Modernism*, 272 ff.

[8] Stuart Holroyd, *The Elements of Gnosticism* (Shaftesbury: Element Books, 1994), 4.

expression. If the world is created by a demiurge whose intentions are at best dubious, it is not a place that 'emanates' from the divine 'One', imbued with a *logos* which renders it a harmonious, benign, rational, and knowable whole. It is a place, rather, deserving of contempt. As for 'the true God', he is, since 'alien to' the world, a being knowable, if at all, only through an occult insight remote from ordinary reason.

I referred just now to the most famous expression of the synthesis of monotheism and Greek philosophy, and intended, of course, the writings of a man who, ironically, had been strongly attracted to gnostic ideas in his youth—St Augustine. When Blumenberg describes 'Ockhamism' as a 'second' gnosticism, he is drawing parallels between the gnostic onslaught on the early Christian–Greek synthesis and Ockham's rejection of the 'persistent Augustinian heritage in medieval thought',[9] one which, in relevant essentials, remained unaffected by later Aristotelian currents and was still dominant and intact during most of the thirteenth century. Blumenberg identifies 1277, the date of the Bishop of Paris's famous 'Condemnation' of 'Avicennism', as the 'exact point' when confidence in the 'rationality and human intelligibility of creation cedes priority' to a 'fascination' with God's absolute and unconstrained power[10]—a process which 'Ockhamism' was to intensify. Just as the 'first' gnostics' postulation of an 'alien' God 'beyond' creation was intended to dispel the image of the universe as an 'emanation' of divine *logos*, so the 'Ockhamist' conception of a '"hidden God" [with] His inconceivable absolute sovereignty' conspired towards 'destruction of trust in an ordered structure of the world oriented to man', towards a 'disappearance of order'.[11]

As a Franciscan monk, Ockham could not, of course, concur in a gnostic theology which opposed a demiurgic creator of the world to the 'true God'. What he does, rather, is to combine into one being, one God, crucial features of both the 'true God' and the demiurge of gnostic thought. Like the former, he is inscrutable, his mind and nature one to which the world provides no clue. Like the demiurge, he is a being of arbitrary and sovereign will and, while not evil, he is, in a sense, 'beyond good and evil', the sole source

[9] Joseph Owens, 'Faith, Ideas, Illumination and Experience', in Kretzmann, Kenny, and Pinborg (eds.), *Cambridge History of Later Medieval Philosophy*, 460.

[10] Blumenberg, *The Legitimacy of the Modern Age*, 160.

[11] Ibid. 136, 139, 137.

of moral commandments to which he himself is not subject. Given his inscrutability and unconstrained will, moreover, there can be no reason to suppose, as had Peter Lombard for one, that 'the world is made for the sake of man, that it may serve him'.[12] Ascription of any such abiding purpose to creation is an affront to God's sovereignty.

This is already to challenge elements of the 'Augustinian heritage', together with its Aristotelian accretions, which structured medieval thought. It is, for example, to reject the notion of a 'natural law' governing human behaviour which, though owing its status as *law* to divine command, is rationally discoverable through reflection on the purposes of man in a teleologically ordered universe. If, 'by the very fact that God wills something, it is right', and if he might suddenly will us to fornicate or even to hate him,[13] rational determination of morality is plainly impossible.

Equally challenging to 'the Augustinian heritage' were the 'Ockhamist' strictures on the very intelligibility of the world, at least to us humans. For Augustine, the world is the result of God's shaping a formless 'vehicle' by the forms that are co-eternal with him, divine ideas in effect.[14] As the order of forms in the divine mind is necessary and rational so, therefore, is the world order which reflects it. Nor is this world order opaque to us, since through 'divine illumination' our intellects enjoy a vision of how things truly are. On the Christian–Greek synthesis, 'this world is discoverable through the use of human reason because we are at some deep level in touch or tune with its maker and design'.[15]

No such confidence in a necessary order of the world or in a human capacity to know it is allowed by the 'Ockhamists'. The crucial premise, once more, is that of God's unbridled freedom, a premise from which Ockham or his followers quickly drew conclusions opposed to the prevailing tradition. To begin with, this premise was a main motive for Ockham's *nominalism*, his insistence that there exists 'no thing really distinct from

---

[12] Quoted by John Passmore, *Man's Responsibility for Nature*, 2nd ed. (London: Duckworth, 1980), 209. Passmore makes the point, to which I return, that such 'anthropocentrism' did not, at the time, serve to encourage 'domination' of nature but, rather, 'quietistic' confidence in nature's ways.

[13] William of Ockham, quoted by Frederick Copleston, *A History of Philosophy* (New York: Image, 1985), iii. 104.

[14] Augustine, *Confessions*, trans. R. S. Pine-Coffin (Harmondsworth: Penguin, 1981), bk. 12, chs. 6–7.

[15] S. R. L. Clark, *God's World and the Great Awakening* (Oxford: Clarendon Press, 1991), 108.

singular things' or particulars.[16] To suppose that there exist, in addition, universals or forms is to place limits upon God's freedom: he would be compelled to shape the 'vehicle' in accordance with a repertoire of forms, like a cook whose concoctions are restricted by the recipes available to him.

Ockham's nominalism was not the extreme thesis of later thinkers to the effect that something's being an X is simply a matter of its being *called* 'X'. For Ockham, words express concepts or 'natural signs' and it is these which, in the first instance, are general or universal through subsuming particulars on the basis of recognized similarities among them. Still, his position was radical enough: for it was not only the 'exaggerated realist', Platonic, thesis that universals may exist independently of particulars which was his target. Aquinas, too, had rejected that thesis, but continued to hold that our concepts, when felicitously formed and exercised, corresponded to the 'divine ideas' or 'eternal exemplars' in keeping with which God had created things.[17] For Ockham, however, *habit* alone accounts for the way we apply concepts, and God's creation is not in keeping with anything. No sense, therefore, attaches to the Augustinian thought that our picture of the world mirrors, because illuminated by, the divine understanding.

A second implication drawn by 'Ockhamists' from the premise of God's unconstrained freedom was the complete *contingency* of the natural world. Not even God can defy principles of logic, all of them perhaps reducible to the 'first principle' of non-contradiction: but that is the only necessity under which he labours. Since, as Nicholas of Autrecourt—'the medieval Hume'—put it, 'from the fact that some thing is known to exist, it cannot be evidently inferred . . . by the first principle, that some other thing exists',[18] relations between matters of fact, including causal ones, are therefore contingent. To suggest that one event could necessitate another entails, absurdly, that God is incapable of preventing that second event ensuing. Hence, as Nicholas's fellow 'Ockhamist', John de Mirecourt, argued, that *we* may be obliged to think and act on the basis of causal laws is no reason to infer that these laws register ways in which the universe is obliged to behave.[19]

---

[16] *Commentary on the Sentences*, I. ii. 4, in A. Hyman and J. J. Walsh (eds.), *Philosophy in the Middle Ages*, 2nd ed. (Indianapolis: Hackett, 1973), 691.

[17] Thomas Aquinas, *Summa Theologiae*, 1. 84. 5, in *Aquinas: Philosophical Texts*, trans. T. Gilby (Oxford: Oxford University Press, 1956).

[18] 'Letters to Bernard of Arezzo', in Hyman and Walsh (eds.), *Philosophy in the Middle Ages*, 710.

[19] Quoted in Copleston, *History of Philosophy*, iii. 132.

Both the above implications serve to disrupt the harmony, postulated in the Augustinian tradition, between thought and the order of reality. Nominalism severs the connection between our classification of things and an inherent order among them guaranteed by the 'divine ideas'. The doctrine of contingency proscribes projection onto reality of the necessity which attaches to our expectations of events. That harmony is further spoiled by a cluster of 'Ockhamist' views which conspired to 'weaken . . . the link between . . . cognition and its object',[20] between thoughts and things. As Ockham himself put it in a proposition which, significantly, was censored, 'intuitive knowledge in itself and necessarily is not more concerned with an existent thing than with a non-existent thing'.[21]

One such view is a legacy of nominalism. The universal judgements we make look to be about species or kinds, but this must be an illusion since nothing exists except particulars. Hence we must construe such judgements as being about terms or propositions, about 'dog' or 'white' rather than dog-hood or whiteness. But if the immediate objects of judgement or know-ledge are sometimes terms rather than things, why not always? In general, that is, 'the object of knowledge is mental, spoken or written propositions, and not any substance'.[22] If substances or things are known at all, this is only 'mediately', via the assumption that our terms 'supposit' for, and stand in some causal relation to, them. A second view follows more directly from the 'voluntarist' conception of God. It must be in God's power to dispense with 'secondary causes': that is, *directly* to produce in us experiences or intuitions of things *in the absence of* those things. We are never entitled, therefore, to assume that the explanation of our believing that something is such-and-such is an actual acquaintance with that thing and its properties.

Some 'Ockhamists' soon perceived the disturbing implications of this 'weakening of the link' between cognition and the world. They recognized, for a start, that it resurrected the whole problem of our epistemic access to the world that the doctrine of 'divine illumination' was supposed to have resolved. In particular, there could be no reason, any longer, to assert, with Aristotle's scholastic admirers, the identity of the objects of cognition with

---

[20] Boler, 'Intuitive and Abstractive Cognition', 470.
[21] Quoted in Copleston, *History of Philosophy*, iii. 64.
[22] Marilyn McCord Adams, 'Universals in the Fourteenth Century', in Kretzmann, Kenny, and Pinborg (eds.), *Cambridge History of Later Medieval Philosophy*, 435.

real objects, of thought with being. They recognized, too, how 'weakening the link' prepares for a thoroughly 'internalist' conception of the mind: for, that is, the attempt to explain and indeed identify cognitive states without reference to 'external' reality. And, most importantly, they appreciated the sceptical thrust of both internalism and the access problem. Autrecourt's strictures on logical inference from one thing's existence to that of another thing applied as much to the inference from a cognitive state to its external cause or correlate as to any other. Since, for him, there is no true 'certitude except the certitude of the first principle'—the law of non-contradiction and propositions reducible to it—it follows that while I may be 'evidently certain' of the immediate, internal objects of the senses, I cannot be similarly certain about the real objects which may, or may not, be responsible for those sensory experiences.[23] And while we can be certain of some universal judgements, this is only if they are, in later jargon, 'analytic' truths guaranteed by the meanings of our terms. No inference from such truths to the order of reality is permissible.

The something that 'happened' with Ockham—or, better, with 'Ockhamism'—might now be summarized as follows: a powerful challenge was laid down to the 'Augustinian heritage' according to which the world was created by a God whose purposes and demands are at least partially transparent to right reason, a world created to serve human beings and accessible to a human understanding illuminated by God—a world, moreover, which, for all its apparent vicissitudes, possesses an abiding and necessary order, natural and moral, that is for the good of man. In place of that heritage, 'Ockhamism' offers the bleaker vision of a God whose unconstrained freedom renders his will and purpose opaque to reason, and whose creation—the world—is a realm of contingency and sovereign diktat, a world of particulars which no longer mirrors an array of 'divine ideas' and which, for all we can know, possesses little or none of the structure we imagine. Nor, of course, is it a world that we can assume was created for our good: indeed, good itself is made the function, simply, of the divine will.

Any account of the 'crisis' occasioned by 'Ockhamism' should emphasize that it was as much a 'vital' one (in the sense indicated in Chapter 1) as an intellectual one. That it was at least the latter is obvious enough.

---

[23] 'Letter to Bernard of Arezzo', 709 and 708.

'Ockhamism' shook an established framework of philosophical theology within which broad solutions to ancient epistemological, moral, and metaphysical issues were available. But this framework was not the preserve of monks and scholars: it provided the world view by which medieval Christians lived. If a single expression can summarize what was under threat from 'Ockhamism', it is Blumenberg's—the 'anthropocentric illusion'. By this he means the conviction that the world is a divinely ordered, rationally accessible whole in which human beings have a secure and central place—a conviction which shaped the aspirations, values, and understanding of ordinary men and women. It was, for example, the conviction that informed the conduct of politics by conscientious rulers. As two Byzantine emperors respectively expressed it, 'we put . . . our trust . . . in the providence of the Supreme Trinity, from whence proceeded the elements of the whole universe and their disposition throughout the world', and the empire 'reflect[s] the motion of the Universe as it was made by the Creator'.[24]

The 'vital' implications of the 'Ockhamist' challenge might be sharpened by calling on Hegel's notion of the 'unhappy consciousness'. This was his term for an episode in the long history of human alienation that he more or less equates with medieval Christianity. Unlike the Stoic, the man of 'unhappy consciousness' is not indifferent to the natural world: rather he despises it, yearning instead for entry into a spiritual realm free from bodily shackles. Such a man is doubly alienated: from a world in which he cannot feel 'at home', and from himself, for he is 'split in two', a spiritual being akin to God, yet—protest as he might—a carnal creature as well. He sees himself, therefore, as a 'dual-natured, merely contradictory being'.[25]

One might think that any challenge to this world view would be welcome. The 'Ockhamist' one, however, did nothing to alleviate the dark view of the natural world, while at the same time it removed the props with which the 'unhappy consciousness' could, to a degree, console itself. 'Ockhamism' did not, for a start, dispel the impression of the world as a theatre of hardship and pain: rather, it emphasized the contingency and

---

[24] Justinian and Constantine Porphyrogenitus, quoted in, respectively, John Julius Norwich, *Byzantium: The Early Centuries* (Harmondsworth: Penguin, 1990), 181, and Steven Runciman, *Byzantine Style and Civilization* (Harmondsworth: Penguin, 1975), 121.

[25] G. W. F. Hegel, *Phenomenology of Spirit*, trans. A. V. Miller (Oxford: Oxford University Press, 1977), 126.

unpredictability of the world, denying the existence of an underlying rational order which, could we but discern it, would be revealed as necessary for our ultimate good. (It is no accident, perhaps, that 'Ockhamism' took root during the most disastrous event of the Middle Ages, the Black Death—proof, for many, that the 'anthropocentric illusion' was indeed an illusion.) Second, 'Ockhamism' rendered problematic the great consolation which Hegel saw the 'unhappy consciousness' as providing, 'a sense of . . . unity with the Unchangeable' through 'renouncing' bodily concerns.[26] The 'Ockhamist' God, after all, is not the rational Mind that we might seek more closely to mirror, not the source of forms or divine ideas that we might come to know through contemplation. Rather, he is a being of an unbridled will in comparison with which our own is almost nothing. For the 'Ockhamist', it seems, the bodily and the physical remain what they were for the 'unhappy consciousness'—'the enemy': but it is no longer clear what, for the 'Ockhamist', could count as 'the friend'. 'Ockhamism' seems to inaugurate a sense of alienation more profound, and with fewer potential consolations, than the medieval tradition identified by Hegel.

Because the 'crisis' was as much vital as intellectual, a crisis in a world view that shaped practice and purpose as much as doctrine and enquiry, it follows that an adequate response to it must itself address both dimensions. Or better, the response would itself have to take a form sufficiently encompassing to restore location and direction to human lives while confronting anew philosophical issues that, for several centuries, had been deemed resolved.

'Self-Assertion'

What were the available responses to the 'crisis' occasioned by 'Ockhamism'? Ones that were not available included a quick return to the *ataraxia* urged by the Greek sceptics and a quick advance to a cheerful 'postmodernist' celebration of uncertainties, the limits of reason, and 'incredulity towards metanarratives' purporting to 'legitimate' our 'discourses'.[27]

---

[26] Ibid. 134.

[27] Jean-François Lyotard, *The Postmodern Condition: A Report on Knowledge*, trans. G. Bennington (Manchester: Manchester University Press, 1986), pp. xxiii–xxiv.

Too much had happened on the journey from Hellenistic to medieval times, and too much needed to happen on the journey to contemporary times, for these to have been options. What had happened, and what needed to be dislodged, was, of course, the entrenchment of a religious metaphysics. Neither *ataraxia* nor 'postmodern play' is possible in a climate of thought where the body and the natural world are 'despised' or, at any rate, invidiously contrasted with a higher, spiritual realm. (In the fourteenth century, even thinkers from whom some indifference to scholastic controversy might be expected bear witness to that climate. Petrarch, famously, was sorely tempted, during his ascent of Mt Ventoux, to 'admire the high mountains, the vast floods of the sea', and the rest of nature: but a few lines of St Augustine were enough to make him 'angry with [himself] that [he] still admired earthly things' and remind him that 'nothing is admirable besides the mind'.)[28] Nor are such ancient or contemporary attitudes feasible unless the pursuit of pleasure, doing what one wants, is not merely tolerated, but regarded as so eminently sensible as to inspire indifference towards what is anyway held to be a fruitless concern with metaphysical certainty. This is hardly how pleasure and doing what one wants, even when the 'sackcloth and ashes' image is duly tempered, were viewed in the age of the 'unhappy consciousness'. How that view was to change will occupy us later: the present point is that this change could not take place 'just like that'.

What responses to the 'crisis' were available, then? One, to be sure, was 'business as usual'. During William of Ockham's last years, and for many to come, he and his followers experienced censorship and persecution. The scholastic philosophy which was achieving a dominance symbolized by Aquinas's canonization in 1323 was precisely the aristotelianized theology that 'Ockhamist' tenets challenged. Even at the high noon of Renaissance hostility to scholasticism, this was the philosophy predominantly taught in the universities of Europe, its critics being, for the most part, outside the precincts of academia. For these and earlier critics, this continuation of business as usual was an ostrich-like refusal, with rare exceptions, to engage in the rethinking of the 'Augustinian heritage' that 'Ockhamism' had surely made imperative. It was not, in fact, to be until the seventeenth century that

---

[28] Francesco Petrarca, 'The Ascent of Mt Ventoux', in E. Cassirer, P. Kristeller, and J. Randall (eds.), *The Renaissance Philosophy of Man* (Chicago: University of Chicago Press, 1948), 44.

a fresh attempt would be made, by Descartes, to revalidate assumptions called into question by 'Ockhamism'—a doctrine of innate ideas recalling that of the divine illumination of the mind, and a conviction that the understanding, unless distorted by the will, must reflect the real order of things. Seen from this angle, and despite his rejection of the 'anthropocentric illusion' of the world's being there for our sake, Descartes was less 'the father of modern philosophy' than the breather of fresh life into a wounded tradition.

A very different response from business as usual—one that was itself to invite censorship and persecution—was a current of thought more deserving of the 'new gnosticism' label than 'Ockhamism' itself. I refer to a Christian mysticism which flourished in the fourteenth century and beyond. The aim of figures such as Meister Eckhart and Jan Van Ruysbroek was not to reverse the 'Ockhamist' criticisms of orthodox theology, nor to deny that these had occasioned a 'crisis'. Instead, it was to press those criticisms to the end, but to find in the resulting 'crisis' something to celebrate, rather than bemoan. If, as the 'Ockhamists' had shown, God is a less scrutable being than imagined, why not frankly concede that he is a totally ineffable one? This will be true, at any rate, of the 'Godhead', the mysterious 'wellspring' of whom 'there is nothing to be said', which Eckhart, in gnostic fashion, distinguishes from the 'active' God incarnated in Christ.[29] Far from uselessly trying to fathom the Godhead's nature by reason, we should cultivate a 'learned ignorance' and dwell in a 'cloud of unknowing', to cite the titles of two famous mystical works. And if human capacities are as limited as 'Ockhamists' had argued, why not go further and concede that, in relation to the divine, 'all creatures are a pure nothing', at any rate no more than 'beans'?[30]

It might be the task of psychology as much as of philosophy to explain how such 'dying to self', such 'humility' before an ineffable Godhead, could bring the 'consolation' that men like Eckhart envisaged. The central thought, perhaps, was this: confessing our 'nothingness' as human beings is to recognize that reason and creaturely activities are obstacles to an experiential union with the Godhead for which we should free ourselves. Only in a 'God-seeing' experience, writes Ruysbroek, can anyone 'meet God with-

---

[29] Ursula Fleming (ed.), *Meister Eckhart* (London: Collins, 1988), 134.

[30] *Meister Eckhart: Selected Treatises and Sermons*, trans. J. Clark and J. Skinner (London: Harper-Collins, 1958), 124.

out intermediary'.[31] Thought and practical endeavour, philosophy and science and morality, are, so perceived, simply 'intermediaries' that intervene, usually unhelpfully, in the soul's 'marriage' with the divine.[32]

This offer of consolation would have meant little to those people who, whatever their opinion of the mystics' case in the abstract, lacked any confidence in their own capacity to enjoy 'God-seeing' experiences. Even for those with rather more confidence, the penalty for accepting that case—total disregard or scorn for a natural world that, in an earlier writer's words, becomes a 'Land of Unlikeness' to the soul[33]—was too high. So for those unable to follow the mystic path, as well as for those insufficiently phlegmatic to conduct business as usual, a quite different response to the 'crisis' would have to be found. That response is the one Blumenberg calls 'self-assertion' and it is the one which will eventually blossom into humanism in my sense. My account of this response does not follow Blumenberg at all closely, but nor does it contradict his characterization of self-assertion as 'an existential program, according to which man posits his existence in a historical situation', so as to 'deal with the reality surrounding him' and 'make use of the possibilities . . . open to him' in a 'world no longer reliably arranged in advance for [his] benefit' and the 'truth' about which is not 'any longer at his [immediate] disposal'.[34]

Instead of at once locating the beginnings of that response in various writings, let us first ask what kind of response *might* have been available to thinkers unimpressed by the alternatives. That will place us in a better position to identify those who actually *did* avail themselves of it. Given that the 'Ockhamist crisis' was a 'vital' one, the response would need to address 'vital' concerns. The 'crisis' was a 'vital' one because 'Ockhamism' had

---

[31] In F. C. Happold (ed.), *Mysticism: A Study and an Anthology* (Harmondsworth: Penguin, 1970), 290.

[32] Such pronouncements remind one of the Sūfis: which in turn should remind one that 'Ockhamism', its targets, and its aftermath have close parallels with developments, three hundred years earlier, in the Islamic world. The target of Al-Ghazāli was the Islamic–Greek synthesis in philosophical theology, effected by Ibn Sina and others, and one of the results of his onslaught on the 'incoherence' of that synthesis was to be the resurgence of a Sūfi mysticism to which Ghazāli himself became increasingly sympathetic. See my *World Philosophies: An Historical Introduction* (Oxford: Blackwell, 1996), 161–72, 186–93, for a brief account of these developments and references to relevant texts. Sūfi views, especially those of Rūmi, will be touched on in my final chapters.

[33] St Bernard of Clairvaux, in Étienne Gilson, *The Mystical Theology of Saint Bernard*, trans. A. Downes (London: Sheed & Ward, 1940), 133.

[34] *The Legitimacy of the Modern Age*, 138 and 205.

challenged a theological world view on which the standing and dignity of human beings owed to their special relation to God and the divine cosmos. By exposing the 'anthropocentric illusion' and, thereby, questioning the intimacy of that relation, it threatened to reduce human beings to mere 'beans' in the universe, virtual 'nothings' in a 'Land of Unlikeness'. What was required—by those unable to entertain a different, mystical union with God—was to identify respects in which humanity might nevertheless be *interesting*: sufficiently interesting to be set apart from and elevated above the run of creation, only this time for reasons other than a special relation to God and his purpose.

What might these respects be? Clearly they could not be features of human beings shared with other creatures. Even without the 'anthropocentric' tenet that the beasts are made to serve us, the animal kingdom enjoyed too low an esteem in the Stoic and Christian tradition for parallels between animals and man to be inspirational. If by 'naturalism' one intends the broad thought that all creatures, including men and women, are cut from the same cloth and subject to the same natural processes, then the response would need to be an anti-naturalist one. Almost as clearly, the respect in which humanity is 'interesting' could not be its possession of reason—not, at any rate, without recasting the traditional conception of reason as an instrument for discerning the truth of things. 'Ockhamism', after all, had cast doubt both on there being a rational order to discern and on our inferences to how things really are from the meagre deliverances of our senses.

It was, however, an 'Ockhamist' thesis—indeed, its central one of the unconstrained will and creativity of God—which shaped the 'self-assertive' response to the 'crisis' occasioned by that thesis. The purposeful activity and creativity of human beings are not, of course, unconstrained: but might they not, nevertheless, be precisely the respects in which humanity is 'interesting'? When proper attention is paid to the doings of artists, craftsmen, inventors, explorers, statesmen—even lawyers, merchants, and botanists—do we not discover what is truly distinctive of human beings? More generally, the recognition that human beings have a *history*—that, within God's world, they have made their own worlds—serves to set them apart from the beasts. So it is through emulating God's creativity, not through contemplative participation in a realm of 'divine ideas', that humanity is 'interesting'.

With this estimation of creative activity, there would come a new valorization of the prime instruments of such activity, the body and language. If, for example, the work of the artist manifests a distinctive, admirable, and specifically human mode of existence, then the body can no longer be simply the 'prison' or 'mire' that St Bernard, for one, described it as. Putrid and obscene it may often be, but it is also the instrument of creative work. Better, perhaps, a distinction should be made between the body as flesh, subject to all the usual temptations and decay, and the body as the indispensable vehicle of purpose and intelligence. Again, language cannot be viewed as simply a pale shadow of a divine *logos*, a set of labels for naming different bits of God's universe, when its role in creative activity is properly appreciated. Indeed, it is only when language itself is employed creatively that various human accomplishments—those of the poet, of course, but also of the lawyer and statesman—are possible.

With fresh valences attached to embodiment and linguistic accomplishment, further dimensions of human life might then be accorded an enthusiasm or indulgence rare in medieval Christianity. Three related ones would be active intervention in nature; enquiry into the gritty contingencies of the natural world, accompanied by the construction of classificatory schemes for ordering the furniture of that world—'science', one might say; and a concern to secure 'the commodities of life'. None of these could enjoy much respectability under the sway of a world view that regarded the body and nature itself as temporary 'prisons'. Under the 'anthropocentric illusion', moreover, the usual stance towards the natural world, *pace* recent environmentalist orthodoxy, was not an 'interventionist' one, but a quietistic confidence that, left alone, nature would work for the good of those creatures for whom, after all, it had been designed. As for 'science', this was something which, by the terms of the doctrine of 'divine ideas', was at best redundant, at worst offensive. Redundant, because the big truths which mattered were to be arrived at by contemplation, revelation, and reason, not by experiment and observation. Offensive, because classificatory schemes *constructed* by men in order to systematize data, unlike those deemed passively to mirror God's ideas, could only distort the real layout of the cosmos. Such attitudes to intervention in nature, empirical enquiry, and classificatory innovation could not, it seems, long survive the 'Ockhamist' exposures of the 'anthropocentric illusion' and the doctrine of 'divine ideas'. Fresh attitudes towards creative activities that manifested physical or linguistic agency might anyway be expected in the wake of the new valences attaching to body and speech.

In short, one can imagine how the 'crisis' might have suggested a 'vital' revaluation of human life, a strategy for rendering humanity 'interesting' quite apart from any special relationship with God. The strategy is centred on an esteem for creative agency that distinguishes humanity from other creatures. But the 'crisis' was a philosophical one, too: the product of a challenge to epistemological and metaphysical assumptions which had been integral to the medieval world view. Not only did that challenge call for a response in its own right, but without such a response the 'vital' strategy just described could not succeed.

The reasons for this were hinted at in the immediately preceding paragraphs. Central to the epistemological-cum-metaphysical dispensation of medieval thought was the following conviction: the only worthwhile form of enquiry—the only kind which can yield anything deserving the name 'knowledge'—is into the objective layout of things, one independent of human perspective. With that conviction in place, it is impossible to see how some, at least, of the 'self-assertive' activities described above could have received new and positive valences, how they could render humanity 'interesting' rather than presumptuous. For example, a 'constructive' classification of things accompanied by enquiry into the items so classified—what I gingerly referred to as 'science'—could only appear as a presumptuous and distorting rival to the passive mirroring of God's ideas. Again, creative and imaginative employment of language in the service of human ends could only seem an impious abdication from the proper endeavour to bring words into harmony with the *logos*. Quite generally, the strategy of esteem for creative agency must combine badly with a 'theological realism' that confines permissible intellectual activity to the adjustment of human thought to what is entirely independent of it.

But how might the 'realist' conviction be dislodged? A dramatic move would be to reject the very idea of an objective order there to discover and to which to adjust our thought. That move, however, was not to be made, on any 'global' scale (see p. 9 above), for many centuries to come. Still, the idea might surely be available in some 'local' areas of enquiry that one cannot be dealing with matters untainted by human purpose and perspective. In the case of morality, for example, 'Ockhamism' might suggest to some that moral truth, given God's inscrutability, is something *forged* rather than discovered by the light of reason. A less dramatic move might instead be made: this would leave intact the idea of an objective order, but question the value of enquiry into it in comparison with enquiry into what is frankly admitted to be relative to humanity. This second move would involve a sense that, though there may be a way things anyway are, it is legitimate and worthwhile to enquire into how things stand relative to human beings, and an accompanying sense that, here too, something deserving the title of knowledge is attainable.

What might have made this move seem attractive, imperative even? In part, no doubt, the move would be prompted by the discovery or heightened sense that humanity is 'interesting'. If people are 'interesting', so presumably are those matters which stand as they do only in relation to people. There would, however, be a more crucial consideration. People must live, and to live, their lives require guidance: beliefs, norms, and purposes which save them from being like Buridan's ass, incapable of taking one direction rather than another. Now an effect of 'Ockhamism' was, so to speak, to have 'flattened out' the world, to have stripped it of structures and purposes the rational discernment of which had, in the medieval scheme, provided human beings with a place in that world and guidance through it. (Autrecourt, consistent with his view that God's aims are unconstrained, adopted an atomist view which had no room for the idea of purpose or meaning *in* nature.) If the objective order of things can provide no guidance for lives, yet guidance is nevertheless indispensable, it must be sought elsewhere: in beliefs, norms, and purposes that make no pretence to mirror a scheme independent of human perspective and concerns.

The question would arise, naturally, of the warrant possessed by such guides, given that this could no longer be read off from 'the Book of God'. An attractively simple answer would be that honourable service in the provision of guidance is itself the warrant. Whether or not such a boldly pragmatist solution was available, one might certainly have predicted a turn to sources of beliefs and norms that had enjoyed little prestige in medieval thought: custom, tradition, common sense, history. Provided that the requisite guidance for life can be derived from such sources, one might then expect a certain impatience, or sceptical insouciance, towards the question of whether these sources can be validated by first principles discoverable by reason or contemplation. That insouciance might then extend to the question of whether, in the absence of such validation, these sources are really repositories of *knowledge*. Maybe the notion of knowledge would itself become 'humanized'.

I have been imagining a response to the 'Ockhamist crisis' which, if available, might have proved attractive to those sensible of the 'crisis'—a response offering a coherent and fresh direction in which both the 'vital' and more purely philosophical dimensions of that 'crisis' might be addressed. Involving as it does a revaluation of certain intellectual, linguistic, and bodily pursuits in the light of a new estimation of a distinctively human capacity for creative agency, it is not unreasonable to describe the response as one of 'self-assertion', of humanity's 'positing' itself as 'interesting'.

Renaissance Humanism

If it were available in the wake of 'Ockhamism', then, the response of 'self-assertion' might have proved attractive. But was it available and did some thinkers find it attractive? The answer is 'Yes', and in this section I add some proper names to the story and trace, albeit selectively, how 'self-assertion' was actually embraced and developed.

Among the 'Ockhamists' themselves, that response is only occasionally audible, and then in a muted form. True, one finds in Autrecourt an impatience with moral thinking that concerns itself with the niceties of Aristotle's *Ethics* rather than with the practical achievement of the 'common good', but there is not yet the idea that the conception of that good is itself a human achievement. In Autrecourt, too, as well as among the 'Balliol–Merton calculators', there was 'scientific' speculation about the mechanics of the natural world, but this was rarely accompanied by detailed empirical investigation. In the epistemological domain, the radical conclusions arguably implicit in 'Ockhamist' writings were not drawn. It has been suggested that Ockham's 'weakening of the link' between cognition and the world must imply a coherence theory of truth and knowledge, but this was not a theory Ockham or his followers articulated, let alone embraced.[35] It has been argued, too, that certain 'Ockhamist' principles might naturally indicate a significant degree of '"dictation" to nature and *a priori* construction' in any account of the world.[36] One thinks especially of Ockham's own injunction—his famous 'razor'—not to multiply entities

---

[35] Boler, 'Intuitive and Abstractive Cognition', 470.
[36] Copleston, *History of Philosophy*, iii. 164.

unnecessarily, and of Autrecourt's principle that a theory is to be preferred if it better coheres with our conception of a universe organized 'for the best'. But the 'Ockhamists' themselves did not construe such principles as purely pragmatic constraints on 'theory choice' in the manner of much later thinkers.

More generally, there is absent from 'Ockhamist' texts that celebration of human creative agency with which the further elements in 'self-assertion' are intimately connected. Maybe their authors, as good monks, were simply too close to the general spirit of the 'Augustinian heritage' whose letter they had rejected. Or maybe some outside help was needed for the 'self-assertive' response properly to begin, help denied to these monks but increasingly available over the next few centuries.

That 'outside help' was to come from an earlier age, from ancient Greece and Rome, especially the Graeco-Roman civilization of the Hellenistic era. It took the form of the rediscovery of texts lost, forgotten, or otherwise unavailable to western scholars for a millennium. We know the reception and appropriation of this help as the Renaissance, and the most prominent figures who studied and utilized these ancient sources as the humanists. Despite a recent tendency to define the *umanisti* as, simply, students and advocates of the *literae humaniores*, most of them were never only that. Theirs was also a 'worship' of and, hence, an attempt to appropriate antiquity.[37] A clue to a salient, and in the present context highly relevant, aspect of that 'worship' is the particular admiration extended to the first-century BCE statesman, lawyer, orator, and philosopher, Cicero. That he was all of these—man of action as well as thinker—was itself significant, indicative of an emerging ideal of 'the whole man'. More important, though, were some of Cicero's characteristic themes. These did not include his 'anthropocentric' conviction, bequeathed to a medieval era now passing, that the universe is divinely 'devised and ordered for the use of man'.[38] But they did include his concept of *humanitas*: not a human 'essence' distinguishing men from beasts, but an attained nobility which distinguishes civilized men from 'barbarians'. They included, as well, something that Petrarch

---

[37] James Hankins, 'Humanism and the Origins of Modern Political Thought', in Jill Kraye (ed.), *The Cambridge Companion to Renaissance Humanism* (Cambridge: Cambridge University Press, 1996), 125.

[38] Cicero, *The Nature of the Gods*, trans. H. McGregor (Harmondsworth: Penguin, 1972), 185.

had also emphasized: history as a record of human achievements and a repository of practical knowledge. Equally important was Cicero's concept of a 'second nature' that we create with our 'human hands . . . in the natural world' through irrigation, navigation, architecture, and so on, and which involves such a transformation from the merely creaturely that human beings even sense or perceive things quite differently from animals.[39]

What the Renaissance humanists' admiration for Cicero, man and author, indicates is a celebration of precisely the human potential for creative agency which is at the centre of 'self-assertion'. It is worth recalling that many humanists were not mere scholars, but 'civic humanists'—lawyers, civil servants, orators, merchants, navigators participating in the public life of the emerging Italian city-states. The ideals typically associated with humanism reflected the growing prestige of men who aspired to 'live honourably as well as actively and prosperously'.[40] The writings of the historian and republican Leonardo Bruni, for example, attest to a reversal of the medieval elevation of contemplation over engaged activity. In the terms employed in the previous section, it is in virtue of the creative agency manifested, inter alia, in the activities of such people, in contributions to forging a 'second nature', that human beings are 'interesting' in their own right, apart from any relation to God. For Juan Luis Vives, what makes man the most 'praiseworthy' creature is the capacity to 'bring forth extraordinary things'.[41]

Indeed, the famous humanist theme of the special 'dignity of man' is inseparable from that of creative agency. In his 'Oration' on that theme, Pico della Mirandola wrote, in the guise of God speaking to Adam, perhaps the most quoted lines by any Renaissance figure:

The nature of other creatures is defined and restricted . . .; you, by contrast, . . . may, by your own free will, . . . trace for yourself the lineaments of your own nature . . . We have made you a creature neither of heaven nor of earth . . . in order that you may, as the free and proud shaper of your own being, fashion yourself in the form you may prefer.[42]

---

[39] Ibid.

[40] John Hale, *The Civilization of Europe in the Renaissance* (London: Fontana, 1994), 206.

[41] Vives, 'A Fable about Man', in Cassirer, Kristeller, and Randall (eds.), *The Renaissance Philosophy of Man*, 392.

[42] Giovanni Pico della Mirandola, *Oration on the Dignity of Man*, trans. A. R. Caponigri (Chicago: Gateway, 1956), 7. Pico's view was not idiosyncratic. Paul Kristeller tells us that it was becoming a

Far from having an 'essence', divine or natural, human beings are distinguished and in possession of a special dignity precisely because they enjoy no given, fixed place in the hierarchy of beings. They are agents, shapers, and the most 'extraordinary things' they are able to create are themselves.

In keeping with my account of 'self-assertion', we should expect to find, among Renaissance humanists, new valences being attached to those primary instruments of creative agency, language and the body. For Vives himself, the most 'extraordinary things' man has 'brought forth' are 'the designations and names of all things', achievements which set him apart from animals and are 'the precondition of religion and memory' and much else.[43] There is no mention, significantly, of language being a gift from God, a replica of the divine *logos*: rather, it is something 'brought forth' by human beings for their use, like towns and houses. That is a point endorsed by the greatest of the humanist students of language, exposer of the fraudulent Donation of Constantine, Lorenzo Valla. For Valla, language, like everything belonging to 'second nature', is a 'cultural artifact . . . [with a] historical development' that has taken it a very long way from the original gift to Adam.[44] Certainly, language was at the heart of humanist concerns. I do not have in mind, for present purposes, the enthusiasms for philology and for purging Latin of its medieval accretions, but the appreciation of language as an instrument both of self-expression and the practical ordering of things. Nor, of course, should one overlook the central place that rhetoric—language employed for the shaping and changing of opinions—occupied in the humanist curriculum.

Renaissance art alone would be sufficient testimony to a new, or rather revived, attitude towards the human body. We are, after all, speaking of the age in which Leonardo and Vesalius produced their admiring studies of anatomy. For humanists, both the person and the works of Michelangelo stood as exemples of a proper attitude to the body. Whereas the medieval artist had been an anonymous cipher of God's creativity, Michelangelo was, for Vasari, a creative genius whom we should 'admire and follow . . . [a]

familiar view in the fifteenth century that man has no pivotal place in a hierarchy, and so can 'move upward or downward according to his free will'. Human beings are 'set apart from the order of objective reality'. *Renaissance Thought and the Arts*, 109–10.

[43] 'A Fable about Man', 392.

[44] Charles G. Nauert, *Humanism and the Culture of Renaissance Europe* (Cambridge: Cambridge University Press, 1995), 37.

perfect exemplar in life, work, and behaviour',[45] at once depicting the human form as something to esteem and embodying what is estimable in his own muscular activity with chisel or brush. Some of Michelangelo's portraits, moreover, are testimony to further respects in which the body was being rehabilitated. Doubtless medieval men and women had preened themselves and been admired for physical courage: but preening had been officially disapproved of, while courage was esteemed when exercised in the service of God. In Michelangelo's portraits, however, the viewer is stared back at by men proud of their physique and appearance, exuding a courage and determination which belonged to a man's *virtù*. *Virtù* belongs to the well-formed constitution of 'the whole man', something he should aspire to because he is a human being and not because of a special relationship he stands in to God.

With new valences attached to language and the body, one should expect revised attitudes towards concerns largely ignored or even condemned during medieval times. One of these was 'science': enquiry into, and the classificatory ordering of, the furniture of nature. Certainly, by the sixteenth century, 'the rise of science' in a recognizably modern shape was plainly visible. But was this associated with the 'self-assertive' tendency of the humanists? It is commonly assumed that the focus of the *umanisti* on human affairs virtually excluded interest in the natural world. Had not Francis Bacon, sharing that assumption, counted the 'delicate' learning of the humanists among his 'vanities of learning'?[46] It would be difficult, however, to explain the emerging interest in the natural world except as riding on the back of a revived interest in human beings as embodied agents who move and act in that world. Moreover, the image of humanist indifference to nature is untenable. Some humanists, like Marsilio Ficino and, later, Giordano Bruno, were dedicated to developing 'philosophies of nature', even if, as Bacon complained, these owed precious little to observation and disciplined inference. Many others, though, were engaged in the pursuit of, by present lights, 'orthodox' science, even if, in most cases, this was confined to taxonomy.[47]

---

[45] Giorgio Vasari, *Artists of the Renaissance*, trans. G. Bull (Harmondsworth: Penguin, 1982), 233.

[46] Francis Bacon, *The Advancement of Learning* (Oxford: Clarendon Press, 1974), bk. 1.

[47] See Anthony Grafton, 'The New Science and Tradition of Humanism', in Kraye (ed.), *Cambridge Companion to Renaissance Humanism*, for a critical discussion of the assumption.

We miss important connections between 'self-assertion' and 'science', however, if we confine the latter to 'orthodox' enquiry. Bacon did not know whether to 'laugh or weep' over Renaissance magic. While he criticized the magi both for their congenital secrecy and for failing to deliver the goods they promised, Bacon was, however, entirely sympathetic to the overall aim of magic. For magic aspired to precisely that increase in 'human utility and power' which, for him, was the proper end of science. 'Knowledge itself is power', Bacon wrote in 'Of Heresies': Paracelsus could have written the same. The dominant form taken by 'science' in the period, then—the attempt to harness and exploit hidden natural powers—was one whose ambitions were just what we should expect in a climate of burgeoning 'self-assertion'.

These ambitions belonged, predictably, with a reconception of the human stance towards nature, with what Blumenberg calls the investment of nature as a 'counterworld of manipulability'.[48] It is with this reconception and not, as often supposed, with the emergence of Christianity, that 'hubristic' exploitation, and dedicated mastery, of nature could begin. As noted earlier, a commitment to altering the world for human benefit presupposed the atrophy of an 'anthropocentric illusion' according to which the world is already arranged for our good. Bacon's is only one, late, statement of this new stance: but despite his calls to put nature 'to the question' and 'command nature in action' for the 'relief of man's estate',[49] the technological 'ordering' of nature was yet to gather pace. More vivid testimony than technology to this stance is to be found in art of the period.

It is no accident that, for Bacon, the 'purest of human pleasures' was gardening,[50] the artful transformation of nature. An activity long confined within the precincts of monastery or palace was soon to be extended to large areas of land in a spirit of improving and controlling what nature had provided. This same spirit was evident in the plastic arts, where wild scenes which had once formed merely the backdrop to representations of people and cities now became contrived landscapes populated by men, women, and their artefacts. Changing attitudes were nicely symbolized by Tribolo's

---

[48] *The Legitimacy of the Modern Age*, 173.

[49] Francis Bacon, *The New Organon and Related Writings* (Indianapolis: Bobbs-Merrill, 1960), 19.

[50] 'Of Gardens', in Bacon's *Essays* (London: Grant Richards, 1902), 127. For an interesting account of the significance of gardens for changing attitudes towards nature, see Simon Schama, *Landscape and Memory* (New York: Knopf, 1995).

sculpture of 'Nature', depicted as a voluptuous woman, with sprouting vegetables and a score of heavy breasts being milked by both children and adults—a 'homage', as one writer puts it, to 'the capacity of nature to be seduced into the service of man'.[51] The transformation of the land for purposes of delight and utility, and as an emblem of the human stamp upon nature, was not only the development attested to by artists. If, for Bacon, the scientist must 'put nature to the question' so, for Albrecht Dürer, the painter must 'wrest from' nature and 'possess' it if he is to produce art.[52] Representation of the world is not the outcome of its passive contemplation, but requires aggressive imposition of form by the creative artist.

The pleasures to be got from gardening and the use of the environment were, of course, only some among those now condoned or encouraged in an age which, if not hedonistic, was distinctly more favourable than the medieval one towards enjoyment. To be 'the whole man', a person could hardly refuse to satisfy the more physical aspects of his being. It is now such relatively lusty men as Michelangelo who are held up as 'perfect exemplars' of humanity. Erasmus himself may have wanted nothing more than to live in a library, but he was willing, as a good humanist, to encourage others to 'clap [their] hands, live well, and drink'.[53] And while the Epicureanism which, by the sixteenth century, was gaining followers was hardly a sybaritic gospel, the very fact that pleasure could at all be regarded a proper end of human life demonstrated the success of 'self-assertion' in rehabilitating sides of life more darkly regarded in medieval Christendom.

The 'vital' strands of the 'self-assertive' response to the 'Ockhamist crisis', then, were there in the thinking of Renaissance humanists. Can the same be said of the epistemological-cum-metaphysical elements without which, I suggested, the 'vital' response would lack legitimacy? Today, the blunt question 'Did humanist *philosophy* take the direction of "self-assertion"?' would generally receive a negative answer—not on the grounds that it took a different direction, but because there was no such philosophy. In the wake of Kristeller's warning, against Burckhardt's sweeping generalizations, that there was no 'body of uniform philosophical opinion . . . com-

[51] Hale, *The Civilization of Europe in the Renaissance*, 513.

[52] Quoted in Mark Roskill, *The Languages of Landscape* (University Park, Pa.: Penn State University Press, 1996), 64.

[53] Desiderius Erasmus, *In Praise of Folly*, in E. Rummel (ed.), *The Erasmus Reader* (Toronto: Toronto University Press, 1990), 168.

mon to all humanists', it is now common to encounter such pronouncements as 'Renaissance humanism was neither a philosophy nor an ideology', but simply a movement loosely bound by a regard for classical
culture.[54]

I make three comments on such pronouncements. First, one can happily
concede, as Burckhardt himself did, that the humanists were a 'miscel-
laneous' crowd,[55] and that the philosophers among them took no uniform
line. It is enough, for my purposes, that many of them did make 'self-
assertive' responses and that these include writers—Pico, Machiavelli, Vives,
Montaigne, for example—more likely to be recalled by the word 'humanism' than the scholars who laboured to produce textually impeccable interpretations of Plato and Aristotle. Second, it won't do to characterize
Renaissance humanism simply in terms of a regard for antiquity, for this
rather obviously ignores the basis for the admiration of, say, Epicurus or
Cicero. Part of that basis was the detection in such authors of themes fit for
modulation into a 'self-assertive' philosophical outlook to complement the
'vital' programme of humanism. Third, and most important, pronouncements à la Kristeller surely betray a strangely narrow conception of philosophy—philosophy, roughly, as systematic metaphysics. This produces a
bias against discerning a distinctive philosophical attitude among thinkers
whose primary concerns were, typically, in moral and political theory. More
crucially, it prevents the recognition that the explanation for an animus
against system-building might itself lie, not in indifference or ignorance, but
in a *philosophical* turn of thought.

There was such a philosophical turn of thought among leading humanists and those they influenced, best characterized, perhaps, by Jacques
Maritain's phrase 'metaphysical modesty'[56]—to be more exact, a relatively
cheerful modesty about the human capacity to discover ultimate truths, one
no longer accompanied by a sense that there is therefore nothing worthwhile to enquire into or know. Just such a turn, I argued, was needed if such
'assertive' activities as constructive classification and the transformation of
nature were not to seem, as they would have to many medievals, hubristic

[54] John Monfasini, 'Humanism, Renaissance', in Edward Craig (ed.), *Routledge Encyclopedia of Philosophy* (London: Routledge, 1998), ii. 533.

[55] Jacob Burckhardt, *The Civilization of the Renaissance in Italy*, trans. S. Middlemore (Harmonds-worth: Penguin, 1990), 136.

[56] *True Humanism*, trans. M. Adamson (London: Centenary, 1938), 3.

challenges to the divine order which it is our business to mirror and acqui-
esce in.

Characteristic of Renaissance humanists, argues one historian of ideas,
was a relegation of concern for 'absolute truth', a sense that the human
mind is 'unsuited' to the 'elabor[ation of] a comprehensive picture of reality'. It is suited, rather, to addressing 'specific problems' of a practical kind
and with the modest ambition of attaining truths which are 'particular, conditional, and subject to many limitations'.[57] Even Pico, with larger metaphysical ambitions, thought that a 'comprehensive picture' could only
emerge from an eclectic survey of past philosophies and religions, a picture
which no one rational mind could ever have generated. This blend of 'metaphysical modesty' and confidence in the importance of enquiries into the
more tractable domain of 'things in reference to man', as Bacon put it,[58] is
just what we expected to find in the 'self-assertive' response. Its natural
corollary is a pragmatic attitude towards knowledge and truth of a kind
found not only in Bacon, but in a writer like Pierre Gassendi. Though we
cannot know 'the inner nature of things', it is nevertheless 'advantageous' to
hypothesize hidden causes and the like. Moreover we can enquire into 'what
things appear to be and . . . what is revealed by the senses'.[59] This will not
yield knowledge of the objective order, but what it yields is surely worthy of
the name of knowledge, given the indispensable role it plays in guiding our
lives and enabling us to achieve what we want. (Gassendi was an Epicurean,
something he managed to combine with being a Catholic priest.) The idea
that 'things in reference to man' constitute a legitimate field of enquiry and
knowledge surfaces in several forms during the sixteenth and seventeeth
centuries: for example, in the thoughts that while the 'real essences' of
things may not be knowable, their 'nominal essences' are, and that for most
purposes this latter knowledge is quite good enough.

The pragmatic attitude just sketched falls short of a pragmatism or 'constructivism' which denies the existence of, rather than simply the availability of, 'absolute truth'. That more radical standpoint, while not developed
into a general philosophical thesis, is, however, discernible in humanist writings on the moral and political. Whether or not it is accurate to regard

---

[57] Nauert, *Humanism and the Culture of Renaissance Europe*, 21, 196, 20.
[58] *The New Organon*, 142.
[59] *The Selected Works of Pierre Gassendi*, ed. C. G. Bush (New York: Johnson, 1972), 294.

Petrarch, Poggio Bracciolini, and others as endorsing 'an incipient form of cultural relativism',[60] the humanists' heightened perception of history had convinced many of them that the moral, political, and, indeed, religious systems of men were the products of artifice, constructions to be judged, not by their accord with 'natural law', but by their efficiency in doing the job they were designed for. A central figure here was Machiavelli. His notorious advice to the Prince to break faith with moral constraints where need be, to become a 'great pretender and dissembler',[61] presupposed his view that morality itself is simply a device for satisfying, in an efficient and harmonious way, people's selfish desires. Where a community's morality is failing in this aim, the Prince should not be squeamish about departing from it or exploiting it. Machiavellian *virtú*, unlike Thomistic virtue, is not the disposition of a rational soul to actions laudable at all times and in all circumstances, but the possession of a man in 'harmony with his time and the type of its affairs'.[62] Nor can *virtú* go unrecognized: for it belongs to the successful man, and there is no success where there is no esteem from his fellow humans.

There were, to be sure, humanists for whom the unavailability of 'absolute truth' was no reason to inflate the importance of knowledge of 'things in reference to man', let alone to forge some radical 'constructivist' notion of truth. Rather it was cause to recall the wisdom of Pyrrhonian scepticism: not only its rejection of certainty about reality, but its treatment of this rejection as bringing in its wake, instead of despair over our epistemic frailty, a contented *ataraxia*, a freedom of the soul from disturbance. Following the line taken by Cornelius Agrippa and François Sanchez, Michel de Montaigne was sufficiently impressed by the contradictions among men's opinions, the unreliability of the senses, and the circularity of justifications for reason to assent to Philip Melancthon's pronouncement that there is 'a plague on Man: the opinion that he knows something'.[63] But, really, this is nothing to grieve over, not even that God is a *deus absconditus*, rational understanding of whom is impossible. Thus while our classifications of

---

[60] Hankins, 'Humanism and the Origins of Modern Political Thought', 128.

[61] Niccolò Machiavelli, *The Prince*, trans. W. Marriott (London: Dent, 1960), 98.

[62] Quoted in A. J. Parel, 'The Question of Machiavelli's Modernity', in Tom Sorell (ed.), *The Rise of Modern Philosophy* (Oxford: Clarendon Press, 1993), 269.

[63] Michel de Montaigne, *The Complete Essays*, trans. M. Screech (Harmondsworth: Penguin, 1991), p. xxxii.

things into species may not correspond to any objective order—'all things',
after all, 'are connected by *some* similarity'—we are guided by actual 'practice' or 'habituation' which enables us to 'feel our way'. When we reach the
narrow 'limits and . . . boundaries of knowledge', we may nevertheless pros-
per and achieve peace of mind, even in our religious beliefs, by 'keep[ing] to
the beaten track' of established tradition and common sense.[64] Given what
they share in the way of a cheerful metaphysical modesty, the difference
between those, like Montaigne, who subscribe to sweeping sceptical pronouncements, and those, like Gassendi, who are willing to speak of knowledge of 'things in reference to man', is not perhaps a great one.

One thing they shared, along with humanists of the period at large, was a
greater appreciation of sources of belief and value—tradition, common
sense, history, taste—which had enjoyed little prestige in the medieval mind.
Esteem for sources that do not even pretend to yield knowledge that is independent of human concerns is, I suggested, an important component in
'self-assertion'. And it is surely an important ingredient of any adequate
characterization of the humanist tradition during this period. Gadamer
wisely remarks that Kant, by 'limit[ing] the concept of knowledge to the
theoretical and practical use of reason' and so downgrading the status of
consensus and good taste, historical precedent, and human sentiment,
marked 'the end of [that] tradition'.[65]

I conclude, then, that not only were both the 'vital' and more purely
philosophical components of 'self-assertion' present in humanist thinking
of the Renaissance, but that precisely this presence is central to our recognition of this thinking as *humanist*. In Chapter 3, we shall examine how
humanist 'self-assertion', after some delays and necessary detours, was to
gather momentum.

---

[64] Ibid. 1222, 1229, 629.
[65] Hans-Georg Gadamer, *Truth and Method*, trans. W. Glen-Doepel (London: Sheed & Ward,
1981), 38.

Reason and Agency: Enlightenment, Kant, and Romanticism

'Self-Assertion' in Abeyance

In the previous chapter, I described a response to the vital and intellectual crises occasioned by the 'Ockhamist' challenge to the 'Augustinian heritage' which had provided the framework for medieval life and thought. I borrowed Blumenberg's term 'self-assertion' as a label for this response, which I traced as far as some characteristic views of Renaissance humanists. In the present chapter, I continue the story up to the emergence, in the eighteenth and nineteenth centuries, of positions that prepared for those 'full blown' doctrines of 'the human world' to be discussed in Chapter 4.

The story is not without interruption. The momentum of the 'self-assertive' response was lost during the seventeenth and eighteenth centuries, especially during the heyday of European Enlightenment. It picked up again, now unstoppably, only when Enlightenment thinking was seen to generate 'crises' not dissimilar from those occasioned by 'Ockhamism'. The primary testimony to this perception of crisis was the 'Copernican revolution' inaugurated by Kant, an event essential to a renewed and more virulent mood of 'self-assertion'. That more virulent mood was already palpable among a number of thinkers—close contemporaries of Kant, such as Herder—whose writings provided the main philosophical impetus to the romantic movement. It was this mood which enabled the completion of a turn, by Marx, Nietzsche, and those they inspired, from the humanism of the Renaissance to a 'full-blown' humanism.

The differences between these earlier and later phases of humanism are sufficiently marked to invite a special label for the latter. One which suggests itself is 'Promethean'. It will not be until Chapter 7 that one motive for this label properly emerges. There I discuss the charge that humanism is an outlook 'lacking in humility'. The figure of the Titan who, in Aeschylus's *Prometheus Bound*, rejects 'servile humility' to Zeus and refuses to 'speak humbly and fear Nemesis',[1] is an apt symbol for a philosophy which seemingly denies the answerability of human thought and purpose to any independent measure which might prove to be their nemesis. But Prometheus has also become a symbol with more immediate relevance to my discussion. Grandson of Sky and Earth, creator of men from clay and water, Prometheus is, for a start, a being in and of nature, and like the race he has formed, he is 'natural' in the further sense of being a creature of passion, one who, in Goethe's poem, suffers, weeps, enjoys, and rejoices.[2] Second, as the bearer of fire to human beings and, in Aeschylus's words, the giver of 'all human skills and science', Prometheus is a symbol of the practical and technological dimensions of human enterprise. Since the versions of humanism with which the following chapter in particular closes are, in some sense, 'naturalistic' and also emphasize the role of practical interests and endeavour in shaping our conception of the world, invocation of Prometheus is apposite.[3]

This chapter and Chapter 4 aim, then, to continue my story up to the entrenchment of Promethean humanism. As before, I shall first recount what might have been a fictional, hypothetical story before showing how it was enacted in the history of ideas. The advantage of this is that the hypothetical story serves as a guide to where to look in actual history.

'Self-assertion' was one response to the perception that 'Ockhamism' had successfully challenged the 'Augustinian' pretension of human access to the

---

[1] Aeschylus, *Prometheus Bound and Other Plays*, trans. P. Vellacott (Harmondsworth: Penguin, 1961), 48–9.

[2] J. W. von Goethe, 'Prometheus', in L. Forster (ed.), *Penguin Book of German Verse* (Harmondsworth: Penguin, 1959), 203. His words are: 'Hier sitz ich, forme Menschen / Nach meiner Bilde, / Ein Geschlecht, das mir gleich sei, / Zu leiden, zu weinen / Zu geniessen und zu freuen sich.'

[3] It's interesting to note that the title originally proposed by Isaiah Berlin for *The Roots of Romanticism: The A. W. Mellon Lectures in the Fine Arts, 1965* (London: Chatto & Windus, 1999), which partly covers the same developments as my discussion, was *Prometheus: A Study in the Rise of Romanticism in the Eighteenth Century*.

objective, divine order of things and had thereby spoiled the image of human uniqueness which had compensated for the 'unhappy consciousness' engendered by the medieval world view. The response took the form of locating what is 'interesting' about human beings in their capacity for creative agency, with the result that new and positive valences attached to activities—bodily, linguistic, artistic—which emphatically manifested that capacity. Necessary to the success of this strategy was a revised, and again positive, estimation of beliefs, values, and their sources that did not even pretend to reflect an objective order now become opaque. Schemes of classification and scientific hypotheses, for example, might be admired—even dignified as 'knowledge'—partly because they enabled successful 'coping' with the familiar world, partly as paradigmatic expressions of creative agency.

Why might the momentum of this response be lost, except for occasional bursts? For a start, this response to 'Ockhamism' was never the sole one: it had to compete against a 'mystical' tendency to concede but, as it were, revel in 'Ockhamist' strictures on our cognitive capacities, and—more relevantly—against thinkers who strove to continue philosophical business as usual by reaffirming the prospects for objective knowledge. It would not be surprising if some of those thinkers, while sensitive to 'Ockhamist' criticisms of the 'Augustinian heritage', managed to reassure people that reality has a knowable structure to which, with the use of right reason, we can gain access. One might expect, too, that some of the systems developed would restore a more traditional conception of what is 'interesting' and 'dignified' about human beings, even one that once again treated the human mind as the image of God's.

There is, however, a more interesting reason why self-assertive humanism should have gone into relative abeyance. It fell victim to its own success—one which came to be explained in terms of categories quite different from those of 'self-assertion' itself. It is not that the activities of scientific enquiry, technological endeavour, classification and taxonomy, and artistic production ground to a halt. On the contrary: it is rather that the achievements in these domains inspired the thought that those responsible for them were *getting things right*— divining the order of the universe, discovering the laws of nature, discerning the laws of beauty, or whatever. Established scientific hypotheses, say, could not simply be successful instruments for controlling nature and securing 'the commodities of life', welcome as these 'spin-offs' might be: rather, their success must owe to right reason, to faithful depiction of the natural order.

With this view of science and other activities inspired by the mood of 'self-assertion', a more traditional conception of what is 'interesting' and unique about human beings is reinstated. Creative agency and its expressions are not ignored or despised, but are seen as testimony to something more fundamental that distinguishes human beings —their capacity for reason. With this perception would come revisions to the new valences urged by self-assertive humanism. If bodily activity is to be admired, this is less as an expression of creative agency than as the workings of an ingenious mechanism belonging to a universe that itself operates according to rationally discernible principles. Language is to be esteemed less as an instrument of creative expression than as the mirror of an order of ideas which in turn mirrors an order of things. The achievements of great artists are to be put down to their insight into the right rules of proportion, balance, and so on.

'Self-assertion' was not simply a 'vital' programme for rendering human beings 'interesting' independently of any relation to God: it also incorporated characteristic views about knowledge and its limits. But with the momentum of the 'vital' programme lost, victim of its own success, atrophy of these accompanying epistemological views was ensured. For with the reaffirmation of the power of rational enquiry to delineate the objective order, there would be no temptation either to entertain pragmatic and constructivist conceptions of knowledge, or to retreat into an irenic scepticism. Of course, that reaffirmation by itself entails no particular conception of knowledge, but it would be surprising if the conceptions which emerged did not reflect the methods of precisely those enquiries—mathematics, the natural sciences—whose prestige inspired it. These would be conceptions which, in contrast to the self-assertive stance, allowed scant scope for such alleged sources of knowledge as tradition, authority, and a *sensus communis*—'sources' which the new scientists prided themselves on ignoring. On other issues, such as the relative weights to be given to disciplined observation and a priori reasoning within rational enquiry, one would expect opinions to differ.

Differences are what one might expect, as well, among the metaphysical schemes proposed by the reaffirmers of reason. With the theological constraints of the 'Augustinian' framework no longer in place, various schemes meeting the criteria of rational coherence could be proposed. Still, one might predict that those schemes would come to prevail which were reckoned best able to accommodate and validate the rational, scientific enquiries whose achievements were primarily responsible for renewed confidence in metaphysical system-building. It would be no surprise, therefore, if broadly materialistic systems came to prevail. These metaphysical schemes, including the materialistic ones, need not exclude God, though exclusion was now an option that had been unavailable at the time of the 'Ockhamist crisis'. The God who remained would not, however, be the pre-'Ockhamist' one, repository of a stock of 'divine ideas', creator of a world designed for the sake of human beings, and whose purposes for man are the primary objects of enquiry—though there might remain echoes of such a conception. More likely, he would be a God required by reason only to explain the origin and maintenance of the ingenious mechanism examined by natural scientists.

He might be required, too, to explain the troublesome conviction that there are *moral* truths, ones seemingly resistant to legitimation by the methods of rational enquiry. But here, too, one might encounter other options. There would be some, surely, who would deny that moral truth is thus resistant: arguing, say, that reason or experience demonstrate that all creatures must act out of self-interest and that moral truths are summations of how people best serve their own interests. There would likely be others who would deny that there are moral *truths* at all, arguing that moral convictions simply register 'sentiment' or feeling, and thereby dissolving the problem of accommodating moral truth within the picture of reality inspired by the natural sciences.

Such is a sketch of how, in the wake of an over-successful episode of 'self-assertion', developments in philosophy and in 'vital' conceptions of human beings and their special place in the world might have gone. 'Self-assertion' would be in abeyance, the reaffirmation of reason in ascent. Let me continue with an account of why this situation may have been unlikely to persist and, indeed, have occasioned a new 'crisis'.

To begin with, the plethora of systems that one would predict now that the theological constraints of old were eased must itself, sooner or later, become an embarrassment to the reaffirmers of reason. If neither a priori reasoning nor empirical enquiry could resolve the differences between the systems, one would predict the re-emergence of scepticism towards the claims of reason—a scepticism, moreover, which, in an age where faith and authority were spurned, could not be the irenic, ataraxic one of earlier times.

I also suggested that, with the increasing prestige of natural science, one would expect the gradual dominance of metaphysical systems of a broadly materialistic kind, deemed especially consonant with scientific enquiry. But this dominance would itself create unease. Unlike the self-assertive emphasis upon creative agency, an emphasis upon rationality might anyway strike many people as a failure to appreciate 'the whole man'. Coupled with a materialistic conception of human beings, it could seem quite incapable of rendering those beings 'interesting'. The exercise of reason would not mark any ontological distinction, of the kind affirmed by Pico, between humans and other creatures. Reasoning would, rather, be the particularly ingenious operation of mechanisms visible in cruder forms throughout organic nature, indeed throughout the material universe at large. Surely, people might feel, it would demean linguistic and technological accomplishment to regard them not as creative expression, but only as devices—sophisticated extensions of ones employed by animals—for representing the world and pursuing interests.

Those same people might also feel that the world, on the increasingly dominant conceptions of it, was a flat or thin one—insufficiently rich, at least, for knowledge of it to provide guidance to life. Richer metaphysical conceptions, it might appear, could be arrived at only through speculations that exceeded the strictures of the mathematized sciences, while conceptions that did not exceed them portrayed a world stripped of those ingredients—purpose and beauty, for example—which could serve to guide our activities. It could even strike people that such conceptions made no room for *moral* activity, not only because they encouraged the reduction of moral belief to prudential calculation or subjective sentiment, but by rendering human freedom problematic. Instead of a *sui generis* capacity for creative agency, what was on offer, apparently, was a freedom no more elevated than that enjoyed by dogs—action in the absence of obstacles, perhaps, or in accordance with character.

With these responses to the reaffirmation of reason, a 'crisis' would be on hand with parallels to the one induced by 'Ockhamism', but in important respects more acute. For one thing, neither the 'Ockhamists' nor their self-assertive descendants queried the assumption that, opaque as it must be to our intelligence, there is a divinely ordered reality some of whose broad features we can be confident about. The plethora of systems accompanying the reaffirmation of reason, however, suggested that any confidence at all might be misplaced, and that robust scepticism was the only responsible response. Second, it had once been the conviction that rational discovery of the order of things would reveal truths capable of providing guidance. But the world revealed by the increasingly favoured forms of enquiry seemed to do nothing of the sort. They were, moreover, enquiries which boasted of dispensing with older, alternative sources of guidance, those of tradition and taste, for example. Worse still, perhaps: not only was the world revealed by these enquiries duller than people had once imagined, but their everyday world had largely become, if not quite an illusion, then at any rate a highly distorted mask of the real—colourless, smell-less, let alone beautyless and purposeless—thing. If dignity and self-esteem were a function of rational understanding, as the reaffirmers of reason urged, then such desiderata, it seemed, were the prerogative of the very few who pursued the favoured methods of enquiry.

If a 'crisis' was looming—'vital' and philosophical—what responses might have emerged? Ones similar, but not identical, to those which greeted the 'Ockhamist crisis'. First, one would expect there to be those who, disillusioned with the claims of reason, yet unwilling to forsake the prospect of access to the real order of things, would take a 'mystical' turn—though this time, perhaps, one of a secular character, with, say, the inspired artist replacing the contemplative monk as the figure to achieve insight into the ineffable. Second, one would expect there to be the continuers of business as usual: if reason and scientific enquiry have not yet settled on the proper account of reality, that's because it's still too soon or because of insufficient diligence. There would no longer be the optimism, probably, that the account eventually settled on would be one with which everyone could happily live—but in a tough-minded age, with superstition consigned to the past, that would be no reason to soften the account.

Finally, one would predict a renewal of 'self-assertion', now modulated in keeping with the acuteness of the new 'crisis'. There could be various dimensions to this renewal: not only rehabilitation of sources of guidance dismissed by the reaffirmers of reason, but a search for new ones—the instinctual wisdom of a people, say, or nature as encountered by the poet. More momentously, one might expect the emergence of the thought—a radicalization of earlier self-assertive proposals—that the whole trouble with the reaffirmation of reason is the assumption of an objective order, independent of human contribution, accessible to rational enquiry. Such a thought could take the form of alleging that language is not essentially an instrument for representing the world, nor even, primarily, a vehicle for creative expression, but an important shaper of the world that we then strive to represent or express ourselves in. Or maybe our technological endeavours should be seen not only as means to achieve our ends but as serving to organize the world in which it is possible to pursue them. At its most dramatic, the thought would culminate in the proposal that any world we can experience or grasp is, in some sense, projected or constituted by human minds—a world which would not be there without us.

In the context of the 'crisis' described, the charms of such thoughts should be apparent. What, to begin with, could do more to make us 'interesting' and unique than the idea that we are responsible for the world, that in Coleridge's words 'we receive but what we give, / And in our life alone does Nature live'[4]—the idea, in more recent idiom, that 'the realities we meet with are the works of man'?[5] How better to brighten the depressing picture that science offers of the world than to insist that it is precisely that, a picture *we* have drawn, useful for certain purposes, but with no claim to represent the real order of things and necessarily incapable, in particular, of accounting for the 'we' who have constructed the world of science? Finally, don't such thoughts as these reawaken the possibility of genuine freedom, and hence of morality? For if the world we meet is the work of man, then he is no mere mechanical component of that world.

Enlightenment

My story was not well told if it did not strike readers as a regimented, selective narrative of developments from Descartes's reaffirmation of reason to Kant's critique of 'dogmatism', his 'Copernican revolution', and their aftermath.

In setting out to 'seek no knowledge other than . . . in myself or . . . the

---

[4] 'Dejection: An Ode', in *The Portable Coleridge* (Harmondsworth: Penguin, 1977), 170.
[5] E. J. Craig, *The Mind of God and the Works of Man* (Oxford: Clarendon Press, 1987), 232.

great book of the world', and 'upon a foundation which is all my own',[6] Descartes declared his rejection of the humanism, cultivated by Sanchez and Montaigne, that set the intellectual tone of his youth. By seeking knowledge in the world itself, he denied that the only 'knowledge' to which we can aspire is belief which serves us well. By insisting that the foundation must be 'all my own', he denied that the best we can do is to follow the 'beaten track'. What is 'all my own', of course, is reason. Descartes's manifesto registers the older conviction of an objective, independent order that, with the right use of reason, we can know. For him, as Blumenberg puts it, there is an 'assertoric quality [to] reality':[7] the world demands to be taken as what it appears to be once we have disciplined our wilful tendency to go beyond that which is clearly and distinctly presented to us. With the will in check, massive error could only owe to the machinations of an evil demon, a possibility itself excluded by reason.

Descartes, we all learn, was a 'modern' philosopher: and certainly he was neither exhorting wholesale revival of the 'Augustinian heritage' nor immune to some attractions of 'self-assertion'. Thus he scoffed at the 'anthropocentric illusion' of a universe created for the sole benefit of man, and the Galilean physics he endorsed rejected the notion of purposes in nature. While scornful of fledgling pragmatism about the truths of science, he agreed, in Baconian vein, that one important reason for the pursuit of science is that, thereby, we shall become 'the lords and masters of nature'.[8]

Still, in the convictions that rational enquiry can gain access to the objective order and that, because this is a divinely ordained order, 'the greatest joy of which we are capable in this life'[9] resides in gaining such access, Descartes is unmistakably retrieving conceptions of knowledge and human excellence from an older heritage. (In his doctrine of innate ideas, like that of perfection, he even recalls the doctrine of 'divine illumination'.) These convictions Descartes bequeathed to the philosophers of his century. Few of them doubted that, with the proper exercise of reason, we 'could, and should,

---

[6] René Descartes, *Selected Philosophical Writings*, trans. J. Cottingham, R. Stoothoff, and D. Murdoch (Cambridge: Cambridge University Press, 1988), 24, 27.

[7] Hans Blumenberg, *The Legitimacy of the Modern Age*, trans. Robert M. Wallace (Cambridge, Mass.: MIT Press, 1983), 187.

[8] Quoted by Blumenberg, 182.

[9] *Selected Philosophical Writings*, 98.

acquire insight into the order of reality as God had disposed it'.[10] Writers like Spinoza and Leibniz, moreover, repeat the Cartesian conviction that the capacity for such knowledge is the distinguishing human excellence. For the former, metaphysical knowledge is at once our 'greatest joy', the bringer of calm, the dispeller of 'despair', and what sets us apart from the brutes.[11] For the latter, such knowledge 'make[s] us more perfect' and 'alone is good in itself'.[12]

Mention of these three 'rationalists' should not be taken to imply that such convictions were peculiar to them. Provided that 'reason' is not confined to a priori knowledge of necessary truths, but is applied as well to disciplined scientific enquiry, the same convictions that reason can deliver truths about the objective order of reality, and that its exercise is the distinctively human virtue, were shared by an 'empiricist' like John Locke. All these thinkers were impressed by the achievements of mathematized natural science, and competing emphases on the roles of a priori understanding and empirical enquiry pale in significance when compared to those shared convictions.

One thing they could agree upon was to demote the status and 'dignity' attached, by self-assertive humanists, to creative agency. If insight into reality required the taking up of a 'passive' stance from an 'Olympian position' then, as Edward Craig puts it, 'man's powers of action were not something which this epoch prized very highly'.[13] Indeed, one finds among these writers attempts to redefine action, in so far as it is something to admire, in terms congenial to their convictions. For Spinoza and Leibniz, we should be 'active', not in the sense of being 'men of action', but through minimizing our susceptibility to influences external to reason. A result of such demotion or redefinition was, predictably, a reversal of the valences ascribed by self-assertive humanists to manifestations of creative agency. One thinks, for

---

[10] Craig, The Mind of God and the Works of Man, 224. Craig is right to regard the seventeenth century as dominated by the 'image of God' picture. My reservation (pp. 23–4 above) was with his suggestion that this picture held uninterrupted sway before Kant: a suggestion which the 'self-assertive' tendencies I described in Chapter 2 contradict. But, then, Craig himself is not concerned with developments prior to the seventeenth century. Let me acknowledge again my debt, especially in the present chapter, to his account.

[11] Benedict de Spinoza, Ethics, V prop. 27, IV app. 32, in his Collected Works, trans. E. Curley (Princeton: Princeton University Press, 1985).

[12] G. W. Leibniz, Basic Writings, trans. G. Montgomery (Chicago: Open Court, 1962), 170.

[13] The Mind of God and the Works of Man, 225.

example, of Locke's castigation, in opposition to Renaissance rhetoricians, of figurative language as 'a powerful instrument of error and deceit'.[14]

I have mentioned several names from the seventeenth century. When one adds others—those, say, of the Cambridge Platonists—the variety amply confirms the prediction that, with the reaffirmation of reason and of the possibility of metaphysics, there would be a plethora of competing systems developed in an age where older theological constraints had been relaxed. Certainly there were striking differences between the systems on offer, especially concerning the nature of *substance*, of what truly and fundamentally *is*, and the means of cognitive access to this nature. Certainly, too, some of the views advanced on such issues would have been too heretical to win favour in an earlier climate. Indeed, for 'orthodox' theologians, Spinoza's seemingly pantheistic references to 'God *or* Nature', or Hobbes's materialistic conception of spirit, *were* heretical. Such voices, however, were no longer in a position to police the philosophical scene.

I also predicted that, despite this plethora, time would favour those systems deemed especially consonant with the outlook of natural science. And these were favoured by the main spokesmen for Enlightenment in its mature period, when it was not Descartes and Leibniz, but Hobbes and Locke, who were regarded by many as the wisest heads of the preceding century: the first an unrepentant materialist, the second a prophet of science's capacity to reveal the 'real essences' of things. Most Enlightenment thinkers, for all their talk of 'reason', were not 'rationalists' in the textbook sense, but enthusiasts for empirical scientific method. For men like La Mettrie and Baron d'Holbach, nothing beyond the physical mechanisms exposed by the sciences was required for full description and explanation of reality. 'Reality', here, included human beings. In a radical execution of Hume's ambition to do for man what Newton had done for nature, men were to be regarded only as especially complicated 'plants' or 'machines', to borrow from the titles of La Mettrie's books. For Holbach, thought and will are but 'a modification of the brain' as a result of physical 'impulse'.[15]

Not all Enlightenment thinkers concurred in the atheistic conclusions which Holbach, who credited theology with 'all those errors by which man

---

[14] *Essay Concerning Human Understanding* (London: Dent, 1961), bk. 3, ch. 10.
[15] Paul-Henri d'Holbach, *Système de la nature* (Hildesheim: Olms, 1966), 228.

is blinded',[16] drew from such claims: but few of them found a place for God except as designer of the universal mechanism. God as a constant intervener, or as a presence of which the world is an epiphany, was a 'superstition' of the kind Diderot dismissed when he extolled the scientist or philosopher who 'trampling underfoot prejudice, tradition, . . . authority . . . dares to think for himself . . . to admit nothing save on the testimony of his own reason and experience'.[17]

One may wonder why, if reason does not produce understanding which is an image of God's and is nothing but 'modifications of the brain', the life of reason should have invited such dithyrambs. The answer is only in part the confidence, expressed by Condorcet, that, 'emancipated from its shackles', a rational human race will surely advance towards 'virtue and happiness'. Equally important was his insistence on the '*pride*' that men, no longer 'abased . . . before the transports of supernatural religion', ought to take in reason's attainment of truth.[18] Human beings are indeed unique, 'interesting', and 'dignified' independently of any relation to God: not for the reasons urged by self-assertive humanism, but for one with an older pedigree—their capacity to know the order of things.

Self-assertive enthusiasms were no more in favour than they had been in the previous century. Paradigmatic manifestations of creative agency were, if admired at all, interpreted in accordance with Enlightenment predilections, as testimony to people's rational capacities. Technological accomplishment, for example, was not treated, as before and after, in terms of self-expression or the imposition of will upon nature, but as a requirement of prudence. As Isaiah Berlin remarks, nature was regarded as 'on the whole [a] benevolent . . . well-composed system', something to stay in gear with, not (as yet) an 'enemy or neutral stuff' to be mastered.[19] This was nature as depicted in paintings by Gainsborough and Francis Wheatley of prosperous merchants contentedly admiring their estates: amenable nature which may

[16] In J. B. Schneewind (ed.), *Moral Philosophy from Montaigne to Kant: An Anthology* (Cambridge: Cambridge University Press, 1990), ii. 444.

[17] Denis Diderot, quoted in Charles Taylor, *Sources of the Self* (Cambridge: Cambridge University Press, 1989), 323.

[18] Antoine-Nicolas de Condorcet, *Sketch for a Historical Picture of the Progress of the Human Mind*, trans. J. Barraclough (London: Weidenfeld & Nicolson, 1955), 201 and 136.

[19] *The Roots of Romanticism*, 76–7.

invite amendment into 'culturally tractable form'[20]—into 'prospects', into 'landscapes'—but not nature as putty for human moulding. As for another great vehicle of creative agency, language, here the predominant Enlightenment perception, Condillac's for example, was inherited from Locke. Language is essentially a system of signs for our ideas, its rhetorical employment permissible, at best, on recreational occasions. Even on those, the speaker or poet more likely to be admired was one who followed classical canons, not one who stretched the rules of language in pursuit of self-expression.

We saw in Chapter 2 that it was in the moral arena that 'self-assertion' came closest to 'constructivist' accounts of truth of a kind familiar in much later times. Later, certainly, than the eighteenth century, for this was not the Enlightenment strategy, despite the perception that moral truth posed a problem, since on the surface neither pure reason nor scientific enquiry can deliver moral principles. One predictable strategy was to remove morality from the sphere of truth altogether, to treat evaluative judgements as recording our 'sentiments', thereby ensuring that truth was the monopoly of the rational disciplines. This would not sever all connection between morality and rationality, for it was argued that the universal sentiments in question, rather like the desire to procreate, contributed to the overall, harmonious economy of life—testimony, perhaps, to an ingenious designer of the universe. Such a strategy came under strain, however, when the anthropological data collected by Montesquieu and others suggested that human sentiments were not universal and could indeed conflict. Hence, in the later decades of Enlightenment, the preferred strategy was to put moral truth on a sound, rational basis. 'Morality', wrote Helvétius, 'ought to be treated like all the other sciences, and founded on experiment'.[21] The favoured approach, evident in Bentham and Holbach, was to claim that rational reflection demonstrates a single universal 'passion'—self-interest. Evaluative judgements, in that case, can only register what people think serves their interests, and the role of 'experiment' is to determine what really does serve those interests. If 'stealing is wrong' can, in Hobbesian fashion,

---

[20] Mark Roskill, *The Languages of Landscape* (University Park, Pa.: Penn State University Press, 1996), 112.

[21] Claude-Adrien Helvétius, *On the Mind*, in Schneewind (ed.), *Moral Philosophy from Montaigne to Kant*, 416.

only mean something like 'stealing adversely affects our interests', then it is a judgement as 'scientific' as any other truth.

Humanism Revived?

My selective account of the reaffirmation of reason during the seventeenth and eighteenth centuries has demonstrated, I hope, that humanist 'self-assertion' indeed went into abeyance. Earlier, my hypothetical story predicted that this reaffirmation would generate a sense of 'crisis'. In the present section, I look at one very famous expression of this sense.

First, however, I raise a question related to my wider strategy, though only to postpone it until Chapter 6. By describing Enlightenment as a period when humanistic 'self-assertion' was in abeyance, I imply that today's references to 'Enlightenment humanism' are unwarranted—or, more circumspectly, that they are not references to humanism in a philosophically interesting sense of the sort indicated in Chapter 1. If our understanding of humanism is shaped by themes distinctive of the Renaissance thinkers discussed earlier, and by the radical development of those themes to be discussed later, then talk of 'Enlightenment humanism' is infelicitous.

Why, then, the recent references to such a phenomenon? One reason is the 'popular' meaning of 'humanism' as, roughly, humanitarianism. When a member of the British Humanist Association writes that 'to commit oneself to Humanist values is to . . . adopt [human] goods as the ultimate criterion of right and wrong', and hence to oppose 'any religious ethic [which] has to put God's will first',[22] the commitment is recognizable as one already made by Helvétius, Holbach, and Bentham. So we can concede that there was Enlightenment humanism in this sense—and pass on. A second reason is the influence of Foucault. He proposes several grounds for regarding Enlightenment as the forge of humanism, all of which, in my judgement, are uncompelling. It would be question-begging to assert this simply because Foucault's 'Enlightenment humanism' cannot be humanism in *my* sense. But I hope to do better than that, suggesting, for example, that some

---

[22] Antony Flew, in P. Kurtz (ed.), *The Humanist Alternative: Some Definitions of Humanism* (London: Pemberton, 1973), 112.

views he ascribes to Enlightenment thinkers are more distinctive of *critics* of Enlightenment. (I am thinking especially of Foucault's association of humanism with the emergence of man as a 'problem', a being at once in nature and able to stand back from it, at once a known object and a knowing subject.[23] That awareness indeed becomes acute with Kant and his successors, but was not something which perturbed the likes of Holbach and Condorcet.)

I return to this in Chapter 6 when trying to 'locate' humanism in my sense in relation to rival accounts. Let me now turn to the business of lending historical substance to my hypothetical account of a perceived 'crisis' for the reaffirmation of reason. I begin with the first and last of the products of that reaffirmation which, I predicted, must eventually cause unease—the plethora of metaphysical systems and the treatment of morality. These may seem unrelated, but for one philosopher they combined to motivate a revolution, a 'Copernican' one, in the understanding of our relation to the world.

Kant acknowledges these motives in the Prefaces to his first *Critique*. At the outset, he laments the dishonour into which metaphysics, once 'queen of all the sciences', has fallen. The reason for this, he explains, is that differences among 'dogmatists'—philosophers who have failed to attend to the limits of reason—have resulted in 'endless conflicts . . . civil wars . . . complete *anarchy*'. Admittedly, for a time, there was a near consensus in favour of an empirically minded metaphysics descended from Locke, but that time is past. Unsurprisingly, 'anarchy' has resulted in a mood of scepticism, leading to sheer 'indifference', towards metaphysical enquiry (A viii–x).[24] Kant soon accuses 'dogmatism' of another crime: it is the 'source of all the lack of faith which conflicts with morality'. Here he has in mind those mechanistic accounts of reality that multiplied during the Enlightenment period—ones which, Kant argues, can make no room for the presupposition of morality, *freedom* (B xxix–xxx). In rejecting 'dogmatism', therefore, Kant fulfils his two main ambitions to save the honour of metaphysics by ending the 'civil wars' caused by unbridled confidence in 'reason', and to remove an 'obstacle that . . . threatens to annihilate' moral reason (B xxv).

---

[23] Michel Foucault, *The Order of Things: An Archaeology of the Human Sciences*, (London: Tavistock, 1970), 318.

[24] References to Kant prefixed by A and B are to the original pagination of the first and second editions respectively of *Critique of Pure Reason*, trans. W. S. Pluhar (Indianapolis: Hackett, 1996).

The antidote to 'dogmatism' is the 'Copernican' turn from the assumption that 'our presentation of things . . . conform[s] to them as things in
themselves' to the view that 'these objects are, rather, appearances that conform to our way of presenting' (B xx). Of things in themselves we can have
no knowledge at all, in which case the 'endless conflicts' among metaphysicians as to their nature have been pointless. This is not, however, to agree
with sceptics and empiricists that there is no role for metaphysics, that
knowledge, if possible at all, can only be derived from experience. For the
proper role of metaphysics is to articulate the conditions under which experience of objects, their 'appearing' to us, is possible. Knowledge of these
conditions is neither trivial, 'analytic' knowledge, nor is it acquired through
experience: it is 'synthetic a priori' knowledge. Such knowledge does not, of
course, register how reality in itself is, but only how it must be experienced
in order to 'conform' to our forms of perception and understanding. That
means, for Kant, that 'all we cognize a priori about things is what we ourselves put into them . . . what the thinking subject takes from itself' (B xviii,
xxiii). For example, space does not characterize reality in itself, but is only
'the subjective condition of sensibility under which alone outer intuition
[perception, roughly] is possible for us' (B 42).

This doctrine—transcendental idealism—also removes the 'obstacle' to
morality. If the mechanistic account of nature suggested by the sciences
were true of reality in itself, there could be no genuine freedom: everything
in nature, including people, would be subject to causal law. However, the
possibility is now open to conceive of moral agents as belonging, not to
nature, but to the 'noumenal' realm of things in themselves. Freedom, and
so morality, is possible provided that I think of myself in a 'twofold way': as
'belonging to the world of sense', but also as a noumenal being or intelligence, subject only to the laws of reason (FP 86).[25] Since we cannot understand ourselves qua things in themselves, we 'do not comprehend the
practical unconditioned necessity of the moral imperative': however, we at
least 'comprehend its incomprehensibility' (FP 97)—a happier situation than
accepting an account of reality which contradicts our ineradicable conviction of freedom. Moreover, even if some notion of freedom could survive

[25] References prefixed by FP are to Kant's Fundamental Principles of the Metaphysic of Morals, trans.
T. K. Abbott (Buffalo, N.Y.: Prometheus, 1987).

the scientific account, it would surely not be one which allowed us, any longer, to recognize the special *dignity* which attaches to us as moral agents: for this is the dignity of 'a rational being, obeying no law but that which he himself . . . gives'(FP 63). A moral philosophy able to secure our dignity must be 'perfectly cleared of everything which is only empirical, and which belongs to anthropology'. The attempt to ground morality in 'human nature'—to treat moral principles as maxims of enlightened self-interest, say, or as expressions of sentiment—merely 'substitutes for morality a bastard'(FP 11, 55).

By locating dignity in a capacity which sets us apart from merely natural creatures, Kant recalls Pico's 'self-assertion'. Indeed, it seems that Kant does not simply retrieve, but thoroughly radicalizes humanist 'self-assertion': for, in holding that space, time, causal relations, and so on are what 'we ourselves put into' the world, is he not embracing a full-blown version of 'the human world' thesis? No sense, surely, can attach to the existence of the world independently of us if, when 'we annul ourselves as subject . . . space and time themselves . . . would vanish' (B59).

It is no objection to attributing this thesis to Kant that he postulates, besides the empirical world, a realm of unknowable and independent things in themselves. As explained in Chapter 1, the humanist, in my sense, holds that no discursable—describable, conceptualizable—world can exist independently of human beings. This is compatible with postulating the independent existence of an undiscursable reality. (Later, I shall refer to a humanism unaccompanied by any such postulate as 'raw' humanism.) It could, perhaps, be argued that there is this much connection between humanism and the doctrine of things in themselves: without that latter doctrine, there would be no motive for humanist talk of the empirical world as existing only 'for us', since there would be no 'absolute' realm with which invidiously to contrast that world.[26] But the implicit assumption here, that Kant's grounds for making the empirical world dependent on 'us' presuppose that contrast, is questionable. For example, his claim that only if space is a form of our sensibility can we account for the necessity of geometrical truths does not, as it stands, require that there are things in themselves.

---

[26] John McDowell argues like this when he writes that, without his insistence on there being a 'supersensible' world, Kant could have retained 'a commonsense respect for the independence of the ordinary world'. *Mind and World* (Cambridge, Mass.: Harvard University Press, 1994), 44.

However, as recent discussions of 'Kant's humanism' have shown, there are good reasons to deny that Kant embraces the 'human world' thesis. The question, as Quassim Cassam poses it, is whether 'the knowing subjects', the 'we' to whose cognitive faculties the world must conform, are 'human subjects or . . . knowing subjects in general, human or otherwise'.[27] The first reason for concluding that 'we' is not restricted to the human species—nor to humans *plus* 'honorary' humans (creatures pretty much like us in relevant respects, but made of metal, say: see p. 8 above)—is that Kant's more considered remarks support this. Even in the Transcendental Aesthetic, where humanist rhetoric is pronounced, Kant ends by saying that 'there is . . . no need for us to limit . . . intuition in space and time . . . to the sensibility of man' (B 72). We just don't *know* whether the sensibility of 'all beings' is like the human one. If it is, then space and time do not vanish simply because we humans are 'annulled'. So, in this part of the *Critique*, the thesis is at most what Cassam calls the 'weak humanist' one that an empirical world *may*, for all we know, be a specifically human one.[28] In the Transcendental Analytic, Kant's position is explicitly 'universalist': the categories of understanding are ones to which objects of intuition or experience must conform 'whether this intuition is similar to ours or not, as long as it is sensible rather than intellectual' (B 148). That is, all beings whose mode of access to objects is perceptual—and we can't imagine what an alternative mode would be like, though God may enjoy it—must operate with those categories. Hence a world understood in terms of such 'pure concepts' as plurality, substance, and causality is not a merely 'human world', but the world as it necessarily figures for any discursive intelligence.

The second reason for doubting that Kant embraces the doctrine of 'the human world' is that none of his arguments for the dependence of the world on 'us' exploits factors which are distinctively human. They do not, for example, appeal to human interests or motives, nor to the roles played by human language or conventions, nor to creative agency. So, even if it should

---

[27] Quassim Cassam, 'Realism, Idealism and Transcendental Arguments', unpublished paper read to University of Durham Research Seminar, 1997, 4.

[28] Ibid. 7. Cassam attributes the terminology to Paul Guyer. Notice that 'weak humanism' in this epistemological sense should be distinguished from what might also be called by that name: the claim—*my* humanist's claim, in fact—that the world is not relative to humans alone, but to them and those 'honorary' humans who are relevantly like them in much more substantial respects than simply being creatures whose access to objects is experiential. (More on that in Chapter 5.)

turn out that no other beings represent the empirical world as humans do, this would, as it were, be a brute, inexplicable fact, not grounded in considerations about the human form of life. Kant, then, is not a proponent of 'the human world': for the humanist, the world's dependence on the human is *due to* something distinctive about humans—their interests, practices, or whatever—and not a fact that just happens, for no fathomable reason, to obtain.

To doubt that Kant's Copernican turn was a humanist one is not, however, to doubt the importance of that turn for the development of full-blown humanism. (Nor, incidentally, is it to deny that other Kantian theses—concerning 'regulative principles' and 'the primacy of practical reason'—are distinctly humanist in tone.) Earlier philosophers, notably Hume, may have emphasized the responsibility of mind, of the imagination especially, for shaping our beliefs about the world: but none had arrived at the concept of that 'subtle compound of belief and impression . . . the world-as-we-experience-it'[29]—a world notionally or actually contrasted with reality as it is in itself, and a world which is 'an expression of mind',[30] but not one which is therefore reduced, in the manner of Berkeley, to the contents of mind. That concept, or its relatives, will play a central part in the subsequent story of humanism. If Kant is not a humanist, it is because his 'we' are not human agents, but something more 'abstract'.

Someone may challenge my suggestion that creative agency is missing from Kant's approach. To begin with, does he not emphasize the role of the *will*? Certainly, for Kant, human dignity resides in a capacity to will, possibly against all inclination, submission to the moral law. In that sense, Berlin is right to say that, for Kant, 'the will is the thing which distinguishes human beings from other objects in nature'. But Berlin's further claims that, according to Kant, 'values were entities which human beings generated themselves', 'a value is made a value . . . by human choice', and 'the only thing worth possessing is the unfettered will',[31] grotesquely distort Kant's position. The moral will is thoroughly 'fettered', in the sense of being subject to laws of reason, and it is reason—not the act of will or commitment—which

---

[29] Craig, *The Mind of God and the Works of Man*, 236.
[30] Jonathan Lear, 'The Disappearing "We"', *Proceedings of the Aristotelian Society, Supp. Vol.* 58 (1984), 219–42, at 232.
[31] *The Roots of Romanticism*, 70, 71, 72, 78.

guarantees the 'value' of, say, truth-telling and repaying debts. There is no suggestion in Kant that moral truth, or any other kind of truth, is a product of will and commitment.

But, second, isn't the vocabulary in which Kant talks of the 'I's' relation to objects a distinctly 'voluntarist' one? Isn't a leading thought in the Transcendental Deduction that the 'I' actively 'unites' or 'synthesizes' the manifold data of intuition (B 137–8), that it is 'spontaneous' as well as 'receptive'? It can be argued, even, that there is a 'short' argument from such talk to Kant's transcendental idealism: for if an empirical object is nothing but a unity of intuitions which have been synthesized by an active intellect, then it would be absurd to regard it as a thing in itself, independent of cognition.[32]

Certainly Kant's 'voluntarist' vocabulary was to exert great influence, notably on his German idealist successors. It was the spur, for example, to Fichte's view that 'the intellect, for idealism, is an act, and absolutely nothing more'.[33] But it would be mistaken to regard this vocabulary as expressive of 'the agency theory'. First, it would be wrong to model the Kantian 'I's' synthesis of a manifold of intuitions into an object on, say, a collage artist's assembling disparate materials into a single picture, or a scientist's subsuming diverse hypotheses under a unifying theory. In the Kantian synthesis, there is nothing intentional and purposeful, nor anything—as in paradigmatic cases of action—presupposing bodily agency. Second, there is nothing distinctively human in the 'I's' unifying activity: rather, it is an operation which any being capable of objective experience must engage in—'a primordial action', as Fichte puts it, of '*the* intellect', rather than of individual, finite human agents. Indeed, references to such an operation as 'active' and 'spontaneous' seem to have a purely negative point: the 'I's' synthesizing is *not* caused or determined by something 'external'. (How could it be, the argument goes, if the external or objective is the product of the synthesis?) Now, it may be part of the notion of creative agency that it not be causally explicable: but the notion is much richer than that. For the thinkers discussed in the previous chapter and in the section to follow, it is embodied, interested, purposeful, human agency.

---

[32] See Robert B. Pippin, *Hegel's Idealism: The Satisfactions of Self-Consciousness* (Cambridge: Cambridge University Press, 1989), 33 ff.

[33] J. G. Fichte, *Science of Knowledge: With First and Second Introductions*, trans. P. Heath and J. Lachs (New York: Appleton-Century-Crofts, 1970), 21.

Put succinctly, a main reason Kant is not a humanist is precisely the absence of any central role given in his scheme to agency in this richer, fuller-blooded sense. It is, in fact, to other critics of the reaffirmation of reason, earlier than or contemporary with Kant, that one should turn for the revival of 'self-assertion' and for intimations of the Promethean character this revival would assume in the following century and beyond. Kant's Copernican turn would play a decisive role, but only when yoked to an appreciation, found in these thinkers, of agency in the fuller-blooded sense.

Agency Restored

These other critics were ones who decried the reaffirmation of reason, and on grounds more several than Kant's; who intensified an earlier humanist sense that creative agency is the locus of human uniqueness and dignity; and who, in varying degrees, anticipated the Promethean doctrine of a world shaped by distinctively human engagements. As critics of the reaffirmation of reason, they were men who prepared for and, in some cases, applauded the emergence of romanticism. They included Goethe, Schiller, J. G. Hamann, and, perhaps most importantly, J. G. Herder. (Anachronistically, I include in their ranks an earlier figure—Giambattista Vico.)

Kant's objection to Enlightenment rationalism was a focused one, aimed at the 'dogmatic' assumption that rational enquiry can delineate reality in itself. In other respects he was, of course, a child of Enlightenment. As much as Diderot, he welcomed the emancipation of thought from traditional authority, inherited 'prejudice', and 'the wisdom of the ages'. Moreover, provided that rational enquiry confined its ambition to exploring the phenomenal world, it could expect success. It was, after all, one of Kant's stated aims to underwrite Newtonian physics as an account of empirical reality. As for moral truths, these, for Kant, could be ascertained by logic, by reflection on which principles might, with consistency, be willed as universal laws.

The figures to whom we now turn shared little of this enthusiasm for the reaffirmation of reason. As when discussing earlier episodes of self-assertive humanism, it will be convenient, if artificial, to treat the 'vital' and 'intellectual' dimensions of their hostility separately.

It was, I argued, characteristic of reaffirmers of reason, not to impugn creative agency, but to regard it as testimony to the truly distinctive human capacity for reason. So when the dramatist Jakob Lenz, late in the eighteenth century, declares that 'activity is the soul of the world', not pleasure or reason, and that 'only by action does one become the image of God',[34] we are returned with a vengeance to the thought that human dignity rests in agency. A more famous poet and dramatist corroborates that thought. 'In the beginning was the deed', wrote Goethe, and added that 'everything is hateful to me which merely instructs, without . . . enlivening my activity'. The school to which Wilhelm Meister sends his son strives, admirably, to cultivate 'the highest kind of reverence, reverence of oneself' in order that a person may *do* to the utmost 'what he is capable of'.[35]

As we might expect from an earlier episode of 'self-assertion', fresh and positive valences are once again ascribed to those human accomplishments that paradigmatically manifest creative agency—to linguistic, artistic, and technical mastery. In the writings of Kant's fellow Königsbergers, Hamann and Herder, we find a rejection of the standard Enlightenment view of language as, in essence, an ingenious device for recording and communicating ideas. Language is not a product or spin-off of reason: rather, as Hamann and Herder respectively put it, 'reason *is* language' and is 'inconceivable without the use of language'.[36] Indeed, almost nothing distinctively human is conceivable without language. Even emotions—all but the most primitive—presuppose linguistic discrimination: only a linguistic being could be resentful, say, as distinct from jealous or indignant. Again, it is through language that there can be that 'perpetuation of thoughts and feelings' which is 'the essence of [the] tradition' of a people[37]—a tradition to which, for Herder, a person must belong in order to be a person, possessed of a human identity, at all. In sum, linguistic activity is 'a thing without which [man] was not man'.[38]

[34] Quoted in Berlin, *The Roots of Romanticism*, 55.

[35] Quoted and discussed in my *Authenticity and Learning: Nietzsche's Educational Philosophy* (London: Routledge & Kegan Paul, 1983), 52 and 129 ff.

[36] Terence J. German, *Hamann on Language and Religion* (Oxford: Oxford University Press, 1981), 7; J. G. Herder, *On Social and Political Culture*, trans. and ed. F. M. Barnard (Cambridge: Cambridge University Press, 1969), 137.

[37] Herder, *On Social and Political Culture*, 164.

[38] Ibid. 139. Charles Taylor rightly identifies Herder as a 'hinge figure', the first, perhaps, to demonstrate that human beings exist as such only in 'the linguistic dimension': 'The Importance of Herder', in his *Philosophical Arguments* (Cambridge, Mass.: Harvard University Press, 1995), 79 and 84. See also my 'Johann Gottfried Herder', in R. Arrington (ed.), *The Blackwell Companion to the Philosophers* (Oxford: Blackwell, 1998).

Language, of course, is also a main medium for forms of creative expression we call art. Among romantic critics of Enlightenment, elevation of the artist was to become de rigueur, though often this reflected a 'mystical' penchant for attributing to the artist insights into reality denied the plodding scientist or concept-bound philosopher. But in the writings of Friedrich Schiller, the dignity conferred on art was of a piece with that of creative agency as such. What is paramount in the 'play' of the artist is not the enjoyment it gives or knowledge it displays, but its epitomizing what is most truly human—genuinely free creativity. Someone 'is only fully a person when he plays'.[39] It is in the 'play' of art that two drives are combined, either of which, left rampant and isolated, destroys the integrity of the person—the one, a 'material' drive to submit to experience, the other, a 'formal' drive wilfully to impose form on what is given in experience. For Schiller, genuine freedom, hence full personhood, excludes both complete submission and wilful caprice. Only in the 'play-drive' of the artist is there a proper balance between respect for the material which experience provides and creative lending of form to that material.

For some figures of the times, these were also the appropriate terms in which to applaud the achievements of science and technological mastery over nature. Whether those achievements testified to a true understanding of reality as such, and whether they yielded material benefits—these, for some writers, were not the crucial considerations. What invited esteem, rather, was—to recall Ovid's description of Prometheus—the technologist as *plasticator*, the shaper and moulder of the natural world. Vivid testimony to this was a book significantly sub-titled 'The Modern Prometheus'—Mary Shelley's *Frankenstein*. What drives Frankenstein is not a desire for knowledge for its own sake, nor for benefiting humanity, but an urge to create. Shelley was well acquainted, through her husband and his circle, with contemporary scientific advances and with the Promethean climate in which they took place. More than one character in her book mouths sentiments that echo those expressed by Humphry Davy:

Science has . . . bestowed upon [man] powers which may be called almost creative; which have enabled him to change and modify the beings surrounding him,

[39] Friedrich Schiller, *Über die ästhetische Erziehung des Menschen* (Stuttgart: Reclam, 1979), 63.

and . . . to interrogate nature with power, not simply as a scholar . . . seeking only to understand . . . but rather as a master.[40]

If the 'vital' status of language, art, and technology were reappraised in a humanist vein, so was that of something else which had received a bad press in mainstream Enlightenment thought. I mean such sources of guidance in life—ones plainly of human devising—as myths and historical traditions. It was such 'authorities' that had been a main target of Voltaire, Diderot, Kant, and others who taught that man reaches maturity only when his own reason becomes his sole source of authority. It soon became a familiar perception, however, that the rational enquiries favoured by Enlightenment spokesmen, though they might furnish truths about the world, were incapable of providing guidance to the sense and conduct of our lives. Goethe recalls his perception of Holbach's mechanistic system as something 'grey . . . corpse-like . . . a spectre', while Herder complained that while 'Light' may nourish the head, it 'does not nourish men', not their 'heart, . . . humanity [and] life'.[41] If rational enquiry reveals a grey, neutral universe, and if the wisdom of the ages, revealed religion, and tradition are abandoned as 'prejudices', then men and women are bereft of guidance.

A striking response to this situation was the rehabilitation of myth. Among many romantics, enthusiasm for mythopoesis had a 'mystical' tinge. For the young Schelling, rational enquiry was incapable of articulating an anyway ineffable Absolute, and for intimations of that Absolute a promising place to turn was the 'collective intuition' embedded in myths.[42] But it was not on grounds like these that Herder and, before him, Vico urged respect for people's myths. For Vico, these exhibit a 'poetic logic', 'sublime' in its way, that enables a people to make sense of, and hence cope with, the world about them.[43] For Herder, myths are important vehicles of the accumulated wisdom of a *Volk*. It is no objection to their authority, in his view, that by some criterion they may not be true. For one thing, we should rid ourselves,

[40] Quoted in Maurice Hindle's introduction to Mary Shelley, *Frankenstein: Or The Modern Prometheus* (Harmondsworth: Penguin, 1992), p. xxvi.

[41] Johann Wolfgang von Goethe, quoted in Frederick Copleston, *A History of Philosophy* (New York: Image, 1985), vi. 50; Herder, *On Social and Political Culture*, 193.

[42] F. W. J. Schelling, *Ideas for a Philosophy of Nature*, trans. E. Harris and P. Heath (Cambridge: Cambridge University Press, 1988), 55.

[43] Giambattista Vico, *Selected Writings*, trans. and ed. L. Pompa (Cambridge: Cambridge University Press, 1982), 214.

at least in the moral realm, of the 'illusion that everything is true or false' once and for all. One needs to know the 'individual and unique' ethos of a people, its peculiar aspirations, to judge which beliefs and priorities are suited to it. For another thing, a person should submit to, and be guided by, what is a requirement for his being a person at all. Since 'a man's humanity is connected by spiritual genesis . . . with his countrymen and forefathers', and since myths are prime channels of that spiritual heritage, a person's very humanity is threatened by insouciance towards these and other repositories of a community's tradition.[44]

In these remarks on myth, 'vital' criticism of the reaffirmation of reason slides into a challenge to its epistemological assumptions. Herder is not simply lamenting the failure of rational enquiry to provide guidance, but denying that there are general truths about human nature and conduct for such enquiry to uncover. When Vico censures his contemporaries' arrogance towards primitive thought, he is also challenging their conception of knowledge. With some justice, Vico has been described as 'reject[ing] Cartesianism in favour of a purely constructivist theory of knowledge'.[45] It is one to which he lent literal expression in his so-called 'verum-factum' doctrine: 'the true is what is made'. In 'Ockhamist' vein, he holds that God's universe is one which God alone, as its maker, can properly know. Human knowledge, correspondingly, is restricted to truths entirely 'fashioned' by men—for example, the axioms of mathematics. Human beings have also 'fashioned' the world they experience, by 'dissecting'—and thereby distorting—the 'unitary' world of God. Thus, in an area like physics, we lack proper knowledge, and our beliefs are true only to the degree that there is some resemblance between God's world and what our concepts have fashioned.[46]

Hamann and Herder endorse Vico's explanation of the certainty of mathematics, but in their case, the constructivist tendency is furthered by their perception of the 'linguistic dimension'—for here, too, 'vital' criticism of an Enlightenment failure properly to esteem a human accomplishment merges with epistemological criticism. When they insist that without language there can be no thought, they are not making a purely conceptual

[44] Herder, *On Social and Political Culture*, 203 and 312.

[45] Leon Pompa, 'Vico', in T. Honderich (ed.), *The Oxford Companion to Philosophy* (Oxford: Oxford University Press, 1995), 518.

[46] Vico, *Selected Writings*, 51–5.

point about what it is to think. Their more radical point is that languages inevitably shape the conceptions of their speakers and that, since thought cannot rise above language, there is no way of privileging any one of these conceptions. 'Our mother tongue embodies the first universe we saw', writes Herder, and while we may learn other tongues, we shall never be able to 'see' the universe except as refracted through some tongue or another.[47]

Accompanying these constructivist reflections is a pronounced pragmatist inclination. The truths we 'fashion', the concepts we deploy to 'dissect' the world, are not dreamt up from the armchair. They answer to our purposes and needs, at the most general level the need to produce 'unity' and 'order' out of multiplicity and disorder if we are to embark on intelligent activities at all.[48] In other figures of the period, too, this pragmatist note is sounded. Fichte, for example, insists that 'we know [only] because we are called on to act', and he heralds the point, elaborated by later pragmatists, that the very identity of things which we take ourselves to encounter depends upon their relation to our actions—their identity, for example, as items of food.[49]

Have we, then, arrived at Prometheanism and so, at last, at a full-blown version of humanism? The pieces seem to be in place: a robust reassertion of the 'dignity' of creative agency, a critique of the pretension of reason to penetrate to objective reality, and constructivist rhetoric about a world 'fashioned' by humanly devised concepts and languages. Nevertheless, one hesitates to state that the thinkers discussed in this section themselves assembled the pieces into a Promethean structure. By that structure, I mean the combination of the Kantian thought that any discursable world is constituted by 'us' with the un-Kantian insistence that the 'us' in question are we human agents.

One reason to hesitate, in the case of several of the thinkers, is that their own remarks in the more philosophically speculative reaches of their discussions are sketchy. Neither Vico, Schiller, and Goethe, nor the two Königsbergers, saw themselves primarily as metaphysicians or epistemo-

---

[47] Herder, *On Social and Political Culture*, 164.

[48] Herder, *Reflections on the History of Mankind*, trans. T. Churchill (Chicago: University of Chicago Press, 1968), 99. In this work, Herder proclaims, apparently contradicting his earlier position, that there is only 'one human reason'. But since reason is defined precisely in terms of the activity of seeking order and unity, it is not clear that his position violates the earlier 'relativism'.

[49] Quoted in Berlin, *The Roots of Romanticism*, 89.

logists. In none of their writings is there an unambiguous endorsement of the 'Copernican turn', and where various of their remarks suggest this, others go in a different direction. For example, the constructivist tone of Vico's comments on physics jars with his claim that experiment can determine a 'resemblance' between reality and the world as depicted by physics—for that claim suggests that reality does after all, and 'in itself', exhibit a determinate structure, albeit one which we cannot fully know, not having 'made' it ourselves. One hesitates, for a different reason, to label Fichte a Promethean, despite his anticipations of pragmatism, his insistence on the primacy of action, and his talk of the world as a 'posit' of the 'I'. The reason was indicated earlier (p. 68): the Fichtean 'I', like the Kantian 'we', is nothing essentially human. What 'constitutes' the world is not human agency, but a 'pure act' which, as Fichte himself remarks, might just as well be referred to as God or the Absolute.[50]

The story needs to be continued, then, before we can confidently claim to encounter an unequivocal champion of the thesis of 'the human world'.

[50] I am not very confident, anyway, about my remarks on Fichte, in the light of the revisionary scholarship on this philosopher in recent years by, among others, Philonenko, Pippin, and Breazeale. I am grateful to my Ph.D. student, James A. Clarke, for drawing my attention to this work.

CHAPTER 4

Prometheanism: Marx, Nietzsche, Pragmatism, and 'Reactionary Modernism'

Production and Power

In continuing the story told towards the end of the previous chapter, I advance, without much more ado, to two robust humanists of a Promethean stamp, Marx and Nietzsche. Before that, however, I briefly comment on my leap-frogging over a figure whose omission from even a highly selective narrative might seem odd. Hegel is usually understood to hold that, in some sense, the existence of the world is inseparable from that of thought, and hence sounds to belong in the vicinity, at least, of humanism. Well, my problem is suggested by the words 'in some sense'. Because of the opacity of Hegel's metaphysics, I do not know whether he counts as a humanist. What is certain is that on two leading interpretations of his position, it would be mistaken to foist on him the thesis of 'the human world'. 'Hegel's idealism', writes one commentator, 'is ambiguous: [the] claim that . . . the [world]-process as a whole is, or is analogous to, a mind . . . might be interpreted as a thoroughgoing spiritualist doctrine or as a relatively modest doctrine concerning the conceptual structure of the world.'[1] On the former interpretation, Hegel is not a humanist for the sort of reason that Kant and Fichte weren't, for the 'Spirit [which] is the cause of the world' is nothing peculiarly human.[2] On the second, Hegel is not proposing that the

---

[1] Michael Inwood, *A Hegel Dictionary* (Oxford: Blackwell, 1992), 23.
[2] G. W. F. Hegel, *The Encyclopedia Logic*, trans. T. Geraets, W. Suchting, and H. Harris (Indianapolis: Hackett, 1991), § 8.

world is dependent on our thought, only that it is structured so as to be accessible to thought. Far from the articulation of the world being 'imposed', Promethean-style, its intrinsic articulation is precisely what we register in our thought. So interpreted, Hegel is nowadays presented as offering a *rival* to humanist conceptions.

It is with two critical comments on Hegel by Marx and Nietzsche that it is convenient to introduce these two Percheans. Marx complains that, for Hegel, things are the 'products of abstract mind', of merely 'mental labour', and hence only 'conceptual beings' (163).[3] Nietzsche complains that Hegel 'delayed the triumph of atheism' by persuading people of 'the divinity of existence' (GS 357).[4] What both men are criticizing is not Hegel's view, as they took it, that the world is a product of intelligence, but his identification of intelligence with the 'spiritual', the merely 'mental' and 'abstract'. In effect, they are heralding their own Promethean substitutes for Hegel's idealism.

Marx and Nietzsche are not always paired in the history of ideas, but in the present context the affinities between their positions are striking. To begin with, both proclaim the thesis of 'the human world': there can be no discursable reality independent of human beings. Second, both are Percheans: what constitutes or shapes 'the human world' is creative human agency. Third, for both men there is an intimate connection between Percheanism and 'vital' matters of human existence. Finally, in the writings of both, there is a tension between their humanism and their 'naturalism'—one bequeathed to later Percheans and which was to become a prime objective of existential humanism to resolve.

The 'young' Marx, who concerns us here, writes that 'Nature . . . taken . . . in its separation from man is nothing for man' (173). Anodyne readings of that remark are possible: maybe it is the virtual tautology that we can find no significance in something when it is considered in isolation from all our concerns. But other remarks show that Marx intends something far from trivial. A thing, he tells us, is 'an objective human relationship . . . to man' (152), and

---

[3] References to Marx in the text are to page numbers of his *Economic and Philosophical Manuscripts*, in *Karl Marx: Early Texts*, trans. and ed. D. McLellan (Oxford: Blackwell, 1979).

[4] References to Nietzsche in the text are to section numbers of *The Gay Science* (GS) (New York: Random House, 1974); *The Will to Power* (WP) (New York: Random House, 1968); *Beyond Good and Evil* (BGE), *Genealogy of Morals* (GM), and *The Wanderer and his Shadow* (WS), in *Basic Writings of Nietzsche* (New York: Random House, 1968); and to *The Antichrist* (A) in *The Portable Nietzsche* (New York: Viking, 1954)—all translated by W. Kaufmann.

an object of sense-perception is 'a social, human object produced by man' (152), who also 'creates and posits objects' (167). If idealism, by equating man with something 'spiritual', is wrong, so is materialism, which ignores the constitutive role of man altogether.

Leszek Kolakowski plausibly attributes this 'anthropocentric monism' to Marx's 'nominalist' attitude towards universals or properties. A thing is only 'definite'—and hence identifiable and discursable—in virtue of its properties, of the general terms or concepts that apply to it. But, for Marx, these terms or concepts do not correspond to any 'alleged natural classification' or 'cleavages of the world into species': rather, they are 'the product of the practical mind', devices for organizing 'chaos' into convenient collections of objects. Nor is there anything sacrosanct in the familiar battery of concepts we employ for this purpose. 'In abstract . . . we could build a world where there would be no such objects as "horse", "leaf", "star".'[5]

This was certainly Nietzsche's position, too. In his early writings, Nietzsche held that general concepts and terms were 'metaphors', applied to particulars not because these fall into natural divisions but in consequence of our determination to force together items among which there are, objectively, no more similarities than dissimilarities.[6] Later he writes that concepts are 'possible only where there are words—the collecting together of many images' under convenient labels (WP 506). It would be wrong to suppose that the application of a word to some item is dictated by the latter's alleged place in an objective order. 'As if all words were not pockets into which now this and now that has been put, and now many things at once!' (WS 33). Nietzsche's 'nominalism' feeds directly into his own proclamations of 'the human world'. Addressing 'you realists', who take it that 'the world really is the way it appears', he challenges them, impossibly, to 'subtract . . . every human *contribution*' to the world of mountains and clouds—and of horses, leaves, and stars—and be left with anything over (GS 57). No sense can be made of a world which is not structured by our constructed concepts. 'We can comprehend only a world that we ourselves have made' (WP 495). This is why, for Nietzsche, there are no truths, in the sense of propositions that picture how matters independently stand, only inter-

---

[5] L. Kolakowski, *Towards a Marxist Humanism*, trans. J. Peel (New York: Grove, 1968), 45–8.

[6] See *Philosophy and Truth: Selections from Nietzsche's Notebooks of the Early 1870s*, trans. D. Breazeale (Atlantic Highlands, N.J.: Humanities, 1979).

pretations or 'perspectives'. So-called 'truth', he writes, is 'the kind of error without which a certain species of life could not live' (WP 493).

That last remark indicates the Promethean character of Nietzsche's 'human world' doctrine. It is, he immediately adds, 'the value for *life* which is ultimately decisive' for the concepts we employ, the 'perspectives' we adopt. The 'human world' doctrine, by itself, implies nothing about the role of practical agency. It is compatible with supposing that our concepts are spun from our minds, or with holding, in Kantian style, that the seemingly indispensable ones are a priori conditions for conscious experience. But these are not possibilities taken seriously by Marx and Nietzsche. When Marx writes that nature is 'the tool of [man's] vital activity' or that the 'production' of the 'objective world' is through man's 'active species-life' (139-40), and when Nietzsche claims that 'synthetic *a priori*' judgements 'must be *believed* to be true, for the sake of the preservation of creatures like ourselves' (BGE 11), they pronounce that it is human activity, in response to needs and aims, which is the constitutive source of 'the human world'.

Neither man sees this as a bit of educated guesswork, supported perhaps by anthropological observation. Both have a deep reason for denying that the source could be the armchair mind or the a priori structures of consciousness—for denying, indeed, that references to mind and consciousness are felicitous in this context. The reason is that, despite hallowed tradition, mind and consciousness are not the primary or defining aspects of intelligent life. To 'have a mind', to be conscious in the human way—to make judgements, have thoughts, and so on—presupposes a prior immersion in social, linguistic activity. This, perhaps, is Marx's point when he says that 'the essence of man' is not 'inherent in each separate individual', but is 'the ensemble of social relations'[7]—and also in his diatribe against Hegel's treatment of 'abstract . . . mental labour' as primary (164). It is certainly Nietzsche's point when he argues that 'consciousness has developed only under the pressure of the need for communication', which is needed, in its turn, for reasons of 'social or herd utility' (GS 354). Kant, it is implied, stopped short in attributing responsibility for the shape of the empirical world to conditions of thought: for we need, as well, to explain the latter on the basis of what Nietzsche called 'the conditions of life'.

---

[7] Marx, 'Theses on Feuerbach', in *The Portable Karl Marx*, ed. E. Kamenka (Harmondsworth: Penguin, 1983), 198.

It is important to emphasize how far-reaching this Prometheanism is. It is not intended as an interesting, but limited, claim about the conditions under which human beings as they happen to be are able to experience and describe the world. To be sure, one can imagine other human beings—or 'honorary' ones—whose worlds would be signficantly different from ours. But that is because we can imagine 'creatures like ourselves' who nevertheless have very different interests, needs, and purposes. What we cannot conceive are 'pure spectators', creatures who experience and articulate a world, but who are not agents.

Nietzsche, at least, explicitly offers two related reasons for this. The first is that *evaluation*—something that only interested, purposive creatures could practise—is presupposed in experience. Even 'sense perceptions are permeated with value judgements (useful, harmful . . .)' (WP 505). For anything to be an item of experience or judgement for a creature, it must 'stand out', and this it can only do if it *concerns* the creature, fits into its economy of 'fors and againsts'. When Nietzsche writes that 'something that is of no concern to anyone *is* not at all' (WP 555), he is emphasizing that point, but also making a further one. This is to the effect that our very sense of a world existing at all depends on our being concerned, engaged creatures. 'We have only drawn the concept "real, truly existing" from the "concerning us"; the more we are affected in our interest, the more we believe in the "reality" of a thing.'[8] A disengaged being, whom nothing could touch, would therefore not 'have a world' at all.

Are they points to which Marx also subscribes? One might reasonably construe his remark that nature is only 'given to me as a social product' (150) as implying the general claim that only to social—therefore purposive, therefore evaluating—creatures can anything 'stand out' for experience and judgement. Something like Nietzsche's second point, moreover, is suggested by Marx's mixed response to a view expressed by Fichte, but which Marx attributes to Hegel. This is the view that the 'external' world is 'a creature of thought' posited to serve precisely as 'the opposite of thought'. Marx, naturally, rejects the idea that it is 'abstract mental labour' which does the positing, but he is sympathetic to the thought that our sense of the world is of something that 'opposes'. As 'the tool of his vital activity' (139), nature does

---

[8] Quoted in Peter Poellner, *Nietzsche and Metaphysics* (Oxford: Clarendon Press, 1995), 89. Poellner provides an excellent account, and defence, of this neglected point of Nietzsche's.

not 'oppose' a creature's projects in the form of sheer recalcitrance. But it is in virtue of a degree of resistance it puts up—as well as of the opportunities it offers—that we acquire any notion of nature as 'real' and 'external'. If so, then—as for Nietzsche—experience of the 'real, truly existing' is impossible for creatures who are not agents.

The third affinity between our two Prometheans is their insistence that a life appropriate to human beings is only available to those with a 'lived' appreciation of Prometheanism itself. In previous chapters, we recorded the need felt by champions of 'vital self-assertion' to address epistemological and metaphysical issues. Without an appropriate understanding of knowledge, truth, and the place of human beings in the world, celebration of creative agency could seem an affront to God or, at best, an arbitrary privileging of one human capacity over others—the capacity for reason, say. Hence, for example, Herder's attempt to connect his enthusiasm for language as a vehicle of self-expression to the idea of language 'fashioning' the world we experience.

In the writings of Nietzsche and the young Marx, we find direct attempts to ground 'vital' proposals in their Prometheanism. Crudely put, we ought to be self-assertive, creative agents because that is what Prometheanism shows us to be. Two rather different claims should be distinguished here. The first is that what makes human beings 'interesting' and distinguishes them from everything else in nature is a capacity for creative agency. For Marx, it is the special character of his productive, 'conscious vital activity' that 'differentiates man immediately' from animals and enables a distinctive and uniquely human way of perceiving the world (139, 152). Nietzsche, though he likes to stress man's affinity to animals, nevertheless accepts that he is 'of course the most *interesting*' creature (A 14), and that in virtue of his 'creative powers'. Still, a capacity or power may remain more or less unexercised, and this leads to the second point.

A central theme of both philosophers is that most human beings fail properly to exercise their capacity for creative agency. They are 'botched', 'weak', and 'herd-like', or 'alienated' from their very humanity. They are the victims of religious mystification, the machinations of 'ascetic priests', or of the drudgery that production becomes under the division of labour. The details of Marx's and Nietzsche's very different explanations of why human beings generally fail to enjoy the 'dignity' for which they have the potential do not concern us here. But the differences should not mask the shared insistence that the properly human life requires appreciation of what humans are *au fond*. To be a creative agent is, in important part, to recognize that one is. Nietzsche's heroes—the 'free spirits', 'genuine philosophers', 'higher specimens', 'overmen'—have abandoned 'the ascetic ideal' of discovering the truth about an independent reality, and act accordingly. The 'genuine philosophers' are 'commanders and legislators . . . their "knowing" is *creating*' (BGE 211). The free-spirited artist, unlike the scientist, recognizes that he is not representing an objective order, but self-consciously exercising a 'will to power', 'organiz[ing] a small portion' of the world (WP 585). For Marx, men are returned to their 'species-life' and become truly human when they cease to regard the world as 'exterior existence . . . independent and alien' and instead recognize it as *their* 'work and . . . reality', *their* product and 'inorganic body' (135, 140, 139).

These remarks confirm Marx and Nietzsche's enthusiasm for just those vehicles of creative agency prized by earlier humanists—art, technical mastery, linguistic and conceptual innovation. The emphases are different, of course. Nietzsche's is on the 'true philosophers' who 'make and create' concepts (WP 409), on 'free spirits' who inscribe their own 'table of values', and on artists, especially those 'artists of life' who mould themselves into, as it were, works of literature.[9] Marx's is on the producer, the worker for whom nature has become 'the tool of his vital activity'. But for Nietzsche, too, mastery over oneself involves 'mastery over nature' (GM II 2), while the Marxian producer has more than a little of the artist in him, 'fashion[ing] things according to the laws of beauty' (140), not under the law of necessity.

It is in the Prometheanism of these writers, and not in something called 'the Enlightenment project', that environmentalist critics of humanism and anthropocentrism should seek their target. Marx, for whom nature should be 'fashioned by industry [into] true anthropological nature' (154), really does come out with the sort of remarks wishfully credited by these critics to Enlightenment thinkers. It was, he writes, a 'great civilizing influence' to have dispensed with the 'deification of nature', so that 'nature becomes for the first time simply an object for mankind'. One Soviet historian nicely captures the flavour of Marx's notion of *Homo plasticator* when he looks forward

---

[9] The allusion is to Alexander Nehamas, *Nietzsche: Life as Literature* (Cambridge, Mass.: Harvard University Press, 1985), in which the theme indicated by the sub-title is skilfully explored.

to the time when 'nature will become perfect wax in [man's] hands'.[10] Nietzsche may be less enamoured of technological ambitions, but it is not unreasonable of Heidegger to suggest that, in the doctrine of 'will to power', we observe a 'transition' from an earlier 'phase of the modern age' to its 'consummation' in the form of a technological world view [11]—a consummation, we'll soon see, realized only a few decades later by such self-declared 'Nietzscheans' as Oswald Spengler.

In the case of Marx, there is another reason why he should figure on the list of humanists denounced by some environmentalists: his use of that very term in a sense closely related to theirs (and mine). With the abolition of private property and, so, of alienation, writes Marx, there is a 'reappropriation of the human essence by and for man'. Thereby is achieved a 'completed humanism' (148).[12] The connection between this 'completed humanism' and humanism in my sense is this: the former is realized when men and women come to recognize the natural world for what it is—a human product—and act accordingly. 'Completed humanism' therefore presupposes appreciation that the world is 'the human world'—appreciation, in other words, of the truth of humanism in my sense.[13]

The final affinity between Marx and Nietzsche is of a different stripe. Here it is not a matter of a shared platform, but of a common tension which neither man attempts explicitly to relieve. The tension is between their

---

[10] Marx, The Grundrisse, and M. N. Pokrovskiy, both quoted in John Passmore, Man's Responsibility for Nature, 2nd ed. (London: Duckworth, 1980), 24–5. Marx, to be fair, was not advocating the exploitation of nature for profit: on the contrary, he complains of the 'debasement of nature' under 'the domination of private property and money', and of the way 'all creatures have been turned into property'. 'On the Jewish Question', in The Portable Karl Marx, quoted in Richard D. Smith, 'Karl Marx', in J. Palmer (ed.), 50 Key Environmental Thinkers (London: Routledge, 2000); Smith provides a succinct, balanced account of Marx's attitudes towards the environment.

[11] Martin Heidegger, Nietzsche, ed. D. F. Krell (San Francisco, Calif.: Harper & Row, 1987), iii. 6.

[12] Elsewhere, Marx uses 'humanism' in a pejorative sense when referring to 'airy' doctrines of an 'inaccessible, peculiar' human essence. The German Ideology, trans. R. Pascal (New York: International, 1960), 92 ff.

[13] Nietzsche did not use 'humanism' in a similar way. If he had, this might have discouraged references to him as an 'anti-humanist'—ones that indicate either a different understanding of the term from mine or a misunderstanding of Nietzsche. Both are indicated in David West's claim that Nietzsche rejects humanism because it postulates 'our access to . . . ideals [truth, goodness, etc.] which confirms the almost godlike status of humanity, our transcendence of merely animal existence': An Introduction to Continental Philosophy (Oxford: Polity, 1996), 128. On the understanding of humanism I am urging, humanists—like Nietzsche himself—don't base our 'dignity' on our having access to truth and the good, but on our active role in generating truths and values. As for 'our transcendence of merely animal existence', this is not something Nietzsche denies. He refers to man as a 'super-beast', a creature on a rope between the ape and the Übermensch.

humanism and their 'naturalism'. Alongside the Promethean passages I
have cited, we find Marx asserting that 'man is a directly natural being... like
animals and plants' (168), and Nietzsche boasting of 'placing man back
among the animals' (A 14) or of 'translating man back into nature' (BGE
230). I speak of a tension here, since it is surely problematic to understand
how the world or nature can be a 'product' of human beings, something
'constituted' through human agency, if men and women are simply 'parts of
nature'. It is surprising how many philosophers miss this problem.
Schopenhauer, for example, cheerfully advanced the incoherent view that it
is the brain, an object *in* the experienced world, which is responsible *for* there
being such a world.[14] Interestingly, Nietzsche did note the incoherence of
the view that 'the external world is the work of our organs', on the grounds
that this would entail, absurdly, that 'our organs themselves would be—the
work of our organs!' (BGE 15). Yet he does not address the tension between
his own proposals that 'Life' is the source of all 'perspectives' and yet, at the
same time, something only 'biological' or 'physiological'.

Something, it seems, has to give. Either the Promethean rhetoric masks a
less radical position—perhaps the empirical claim that our activities play an
important role in influencing how we perceive and conceive things—or the
naturalistic remarks are not to be taken at face value. The first option is
adopted by commentators who represent Marx and Nietzsche as purely naturalistic thinkers with a penchant for hyperbolic, metaphysical expression of
their views—a penchant which Marx, at least, managed to overcome in
works later than the 1844 manuscripts. On that option, the two men's positions would be compatible with holding that there is, after all, a way the
world objectively is—a way expounded by biologists and other natural
scientists. So understood, neither thinker is a humanist at all. On the second
option, it is the naturalistic rhetoric which needs to be deflated. Maybe it has
the primarily negative purpose of ridiculing the thought that human beings
are 'souls', 'abstract minds', vehicles of 'Spirit', or whatever. Or maybe
Nietzsche intends 'biology' and 'physiology' metaphorically: certainly he
says things about our 'biological' drives and instincts that make it difficult to
regard them as objects of natural scientific study—for example, that they
'interpret' and 'have perspectives' (WP 481). Or maybe he talks at two levels,

---

[14] Arthur Schopenhauer, *The World as Will and Representation*, trans. E. Payne (New York: Dover,
1969), ii. 18.

an empirical and transcendental: at the former it is legitimate to explain our-selves biologically, but at the latter biology is itself 'just a perspective' we have devised for 'organizing' experience. As for Marx, maybe the material nature he says we belong in is not what those words suggest to the modern ear—the subject matter of physics—but only something like the realm which 'opposes' our purposes (see p. 82 above).

Perhaps, through such manœuvres, it is possible to defuse either the Promethean or the naturalistic remarks cited. It has to be repeated, howev-er, that neither Marx nor Nietzsche explains how the tension is to be released, or indeed clearly recognizes a need for this. It is worth remarking, moreover, that this tension is present even in their detailed discussions of various matters, not simply at the level of general rhetoric. Consider, for example, what they say about sense-perception. Nietzsche, we saw, advanced the seemingly exciting claim that perception cannot be of what is just 'given', since it is 'permeated with value judgements'. But a moment later, he adds that this is true even of an insect's reaction to colours. The point, presumably, is that an ant's reactions are constrained by what is useful to it. If this, however, is all that the involvement of 'value judgements' amounts to, then not only is Nietzsche's terminology misleading, but noth-ing of any moment would be implied about the possibility of 'objective' per-ception. Not dissimilarly, Marx's interesting reference to our senses as 'theoreticians' looks like an attack on the view that we have direct, uncon-ceptualized access to the 'given'. That attack, though, looks to be spoiled by remarks which suggest that, under certain conditions, we are, like animals, 'passive' in the face of 'sensuous, alien objects'. These remarks seem to imply that, however matters may now stand with human perception, there can be 'bare' sensory experience of the directly 'given'.

In the next section, we will see that the tension in question is one that Marx and Nietzsche bequeathed to later Prometheans. This is hardly sur-prising for, resolvable or not, it is surely a tension which is endemic to the Promethean tendency. That tendency, I suggested, was made possible only by the 'Copernican' image of the world as 'our' product. It is distinguished from Kant's own 'Copernicanism', however, by an insistence that the 'we' in question are human—or 'honorary' human—beings, that the constitutive source of the world is human agency. The insistence that 'we' are nothing mysterious, but simply ordinary human beings and their kin, may sound attractive: but the more familiar, the more 'worldly', 'we' become, the harder it is to understand how, in any philosophically exciting sense, 'we' could be responsible for the world, how the world can be 'the human world'. Or put it like this: Kant could avoid the problem of how 'we' could at once belong in nature yet be constitutive of it by viewing 'us' in a 'twofold way'— as phenomenal creatures and as denizens of the noumenal realm. Any such dual vision, however, is one of the targets of a Prometheanism which 'translates' 'us' back into ordinary, active, flesh-and-blood creatures. And now the problem seems to be—to ape Nietzsche—that 'flesh-and-blood themselves would be—the work of flesh-and-blood!'.

Life, Power, and Meaning

The writings from the early decades of the twentieth century to which I now turn are not mere footnotes to Nietzsche, but they support the remark that 'there is scarcely anything in [subsequent] arguments against the possibility of absolute representations'—representations of a world independent of human perspective—'that cannot be found somewhere, in some form, in Nietzsche'.[15] Since it would be tedious to reiterate points familiar from Nietzsche, I focus on the emergence of themes, less clearly identifiable in Nietzsche's writings, which feed into the existential humanism articulated in the following chapter. I shall also support my claim that later Prometheans inherited a tension between the thesis of 'the human world' and 'naturalism'.

The thinkers who concern us are a mixed bag: several of the pragmatists, some neo-Kantians, various 'philosophers of life', and two of the figures felicitously labelled 'reactionary modernists' by the historian, Jeffrey Herf. As good Prometheans, these writers—at times, at least—subscribe to the thesis of 'the human world', the grounding of that thesis in the ineliminable role of action and purpose, and the conviction that both the thesis and its ground are essential to the 'vital' matter of human self-estimation.

To take that last point first: these thinkers militate against what they perceive as the predominant '-isms' of their times—'intellectualism', 'rationalism', 'positivism', 'scientism'. They do so, not solely on the grounds that

---

[15] A. W. Moore, *Points of View* (Oxford: Clarendon Press, 1997), 103

these doctrines are mistaken, but because they are enervating, degrading even. In partial replays of early romantic reactions against Enlightenment, scientism is rejected not only because of its pretence that the natural sciences offer a complete account of the world, but because any such account would be a grey, flat one providing nothing by way of guidance to life. Intellectualism—the idea that there can be a detached, objective account of the world—is not only a pipe-dream, but diminishes human beings by refusing them any creative role in the constitution of the world. Rationalism exaggerates the powers of reason, and devalues those deep human experiences that indicate our participation in a 'great river of life' which flows through everything.

Those words are Henri Bergson's, the most eloquent critic of the offending *fin de siècle* '-isms', from his *Creative Evolution*, a title suggestive of the central role which agency plays in his philosophy.[16] In fact, creative agency plays two roles. First, human agency is a precondition for what is ordinarily regarded as thought—the application of concepts to things. The 'work of the intellect', Bergson insists, is not 'disinterested': in employing concepts, we 'take sides, . . . draw profit . . . satisfy an interest', so that all 'knowledge' is 'from a certain point of view'.[17] Even the aim of the sciences cannot be 'to show us the essences of things': rather, they show us 'the best means of acting' on things.[18] Bergson is fond of the familiar image of the intellect 'carving up' what is, in reality, seamless. For Bergson, as Russell wittily puts it, the intellect is like a butcher who 'imagin[es] that the chicken always was the separate pieces into which the carving-knife divides it'.[19]

Clearly enough, Bergson's view of this role of purpose and agency is close to pragmatism but, more idiosyncratically, he ascribes them a different, grander role. As remarked in Chapter 1, Bergson does think there is an 'external reality', an 'Absolute', 'given immediately to the mind'. His conception of this Absolute—the 'great river of life'—is itself thoroughly modelled on purposive agency. Life, the *élan vital*, is 'unceasing . . . action, freedom', an 'internal push' which 'expresses' itself in nature and human activity.[20] Since the words, symbols, and concepts we employ necessarily

---

[16] Henri Bergson, *Creative Evolution*, trans. A. Mitchell (London: Macmillan, 1911), 284.

[17] Henri Bergson, *An Introduction to Metaphysics*, trans. T. E. Hulme (New York: Liberal Arts, 1949), 38. [18] *Creative Evolution*, 98.

[19] Bertrand Russell, *History of Western Philosophy* (London: Routledge, 1961), 759.

[20] *Creative Evolution*, 262, 107, 101.

register 'points of view', this Absolute, though 'given' to the mind, is 'consequently inexpressible'. There can be no 'discursive' knowledge of reality, only an 'intuition' of, or 'intellectual sympathy' with, it. 'Description' always 'leave[s] me . . . in the relative'.[21]

Bergson, then, is a Promethean humanist: for although he postulates an 'independent' reality, this is not a discursable one. Any world we can conceptually articulate we have 'carved' out in response to our interests. Bergson, however, is not typically Promethean in the 'vital' lessons he draws: for while he castigates the conceits of 'rationalism', he does not proceed to a celebration of human 'self-assertion', of our capacity to shape our world, in the style of Nietzsche or the young Marx. Bergson's 'heroes' are the mystics who, relighting the 'lamp' of intuition which has been all but extinguished by 'practical knowledge', will 'pierce the darkness of the night in which the intellect leaves us'.[22]

For a more characteristically Promethean response to a view no less intoxicated with 'Life', one might turn to Oswald Spengler and Ernst Jünger, the two exemplary figures among those 'reactionary modernists' who, as Herf puts it, 'reconciled the antimodernist, romantic and irrationalist ideas present in German nationalism' with that 'most obvious manifestation of means–ends rationality . . . modern technology'.[23] If, as suggested earlier, environmentalists will find more of a target in Marx than in Enlightenment rationalism, they will discover a whole shooting-gallery in the writings of these two figures. Spengler's heroes are 'Faustian' men, such as engineers, who mark 'the victory of technical thought' in a 'pitiless no-quarter battle of the will to power' to 'enslave and harness' nature.[24] Jünger's are the 'steely', 'chiselled' Workers (*Arbeiter*)—'cybernetic storm-troopers'—who are at once 'bees and titans', caught up in, yet proudly advancing, the 'total mobilization of matter' through industrial and military technology.[25] Neither the

---

[21] *An Introduction to Metaphysics*, 22–4.

[22] *Creative Evolution*, 282.

[23] Jeffrey Herf, *Reactionary Modernism: Technology, Culture and Politics in Weimar and the Third Reich* (Cambridge: Cambridge University Press, 1984), 1. I give fairly detailed accounts of 'reactionary modernism' in 'Modern Mythology: The Case of "Reactionary Modernism"', *History of the Human Sciences*, 9. 2 (1996), and 'Reactionary Modernism', in A. O'Hear (ed.), *German Philosophy Since Kant* (Cambridge: Cambridge University Press, 1999).

[24] Oswald Spengler, *Man and Technics: A Contribution to the Philosophy of Life*, trans. C. Atkinson (London: Allen & Unwin, 1932), 77, 16, 84.

[25] Thomas Nevin, *Ernst Jünger and Germany: Into the Abyss 1914–1945* (London: Constable, 1997), 135, 140; Ernst Jünger, *Der Arbeiter*, in *Essays II* (Stuttgart: Klett, 1964), 164.

Faustians nor the Workers take part in this battle or mobilization as a means to such unheroic Enlightenment ends as material progress and the general happiness. Spengler's hero despises 'progress-philistines', his 'passion . . . has nothing whatever to do with its consequences', but is instead the 'self-assertive' one to 'build a world oneself, to be oneself God'.[26] For Jünger, indeed, technology is not instrumental activity as much as the 'stamp' or Gestalt of the Worker—a whole way of interpreting the world as so much material for 'mobilization'. When Heidegger called technology a metaphysical 'way of revealing' that drives out all others, he has in mind precisely what Jünger had celebrated.[27]

As that remark suggests, this celebration did not float free from a wider conception of the relation of human beings to the world. The legal theorist Carl Schmitt, himself one of Herf's 'reactionary modernists', relates it to an 'activist metaphysics', while Heidegger applauds writers like Spengler and Jünger for vividly 'communicat[ing] an experience of being . . . as the will to power'.[28] Certainly the rhetoric of will to power and 'Life' is pervasive, but the debt is as much to neo-Kantian thinkers such as Wilhelm Dilthey as to Nietzsche or Bergson. Dilthey was among those neo-Kantians whose strategy was to agree with the Master's insight that experience presupposes what 'we ourselves put into' the world, but then to 'historicize' that insight. The preconditions of experience are not timeless a priori principles and categories structuring all possible thought, but historical conditions—'life-forms' that, Dilthey explains, constitute the 'cultural wholes' that are the 'basis . . . for our experience, understanding, expressions'.[29]

Spengler and Jünger, in effect, mix a heady cocktail concocted from Nietzschean and neo-Kantian ingredients. History is a 'destiny', driven by the will to power, of successive 'forms' that 'express' that will. These 'expression-forms', as Spengler calls them, are whole 'organic' cultures which put their 'stamp', to use one of Jünger's favourite terms, on every dimension of culture—science, art, and so on—and on the human beings

---

[26] Man and Technics, 85 f.

[27] See Martin Heidegger, The Question Concerning Technology and Other Essays, trans. W. Lovitt (New York: Harper & Row, 1977).

[28] Carl Schmitt, quoted in Herf, Reactionary Modernism, 120; Martin Heidegger, The Question of Being (New Haven, Conn.: College & University Press, 1956), 43.

[29] Wilhelm Dilthey, Dilthey: Selected Writings, trans. H. Rickman (Cambridge: Cambridge University Press, 1968), 232.

who belong to them.[30] The Faustian epoch of the Worker is only the latest 'expression-form', though a peculiarly authentic one, of the will to power manifested in each epoch's attempt to shape and order its world.

Both men draw predictable conclusions for the status of truth and knowledge. Since all human activity bears the stamp of a 'form', beliefs are merely 'expression[s] of the will to power', and 'there can be no eternal truths', only 'life-symbols'.[31] No belief can be said to correspond to how reality independently is, for nobody can avoid the 'stamp' of an 'expression-form' so as impartially to adjudicate among the belief-systems of different cultures. Indeed, since everything that can be experienced and articulated is a 'symbol', a 'shape' with which a 'mythopoetic power' has invested the world, the very intelligibility of a belief's corresponding to an objective state of affairs is excluded. Consistently enough, Spengler and Jünger see themselves as advancing 'myths', which are none the worse for that, since even the pronouncements of natural science and mathematics are 'deep myths'.[32] If their own myths are superior, this is because they dare to speak their name in a way that those of religion and science do not.

There are four themes in the writings I have been discussing which, with later developments in view, I want to highlight. The first is the continuing presence of humanism-versus-naturalism tensions. These take the form of simultaneously holding that human beings are responsible for there being a discursable world and placing them as items within that world. That combination implies—to amend Nietzsche's remark (p. 86 above)—that 'human beings themselves would be—the work of human beings'. It would, for example, be incoherent of Bergson to identify the 'we' who 'carve up' reality into particular objects with individual flesh-and-blood people: for these would then be both carvers and carved. Perhaps he doesn't do this and the 'we' are what he calls 'selves', where a 'self' is 'a continuous flux' that may be 'intuited', but not 'analysed'.[33] As such, 'we' belong to or express that seamless 'movement' Bergson refers to as 'Life' or the Absolute. Since this is 'inexpressible', it is not, then, a discursable, carved-out world to which 'we'

---

[30] See, for example, Oswald Spengler, *The Decline of the West: Form and Actuality*, trans. C. Atkinson (New York: Knopf, 1939), 1–22, and Jünger, *Der Arbeiter*, 158 ff.

[31] Spengler, *The Decline of the West*, 41; Jünger, *Der Areiter*, 76.

[32] Spengler, *The Decline of the West*, 41 and 427.

[33] Bergson, *An Introduction to Metaphysics*, 24 ff.

belong. Unfortunately, Bergson says rather a lot about what is, allegedly, unsayable. For example, Life apparently evolves into different and increasingly higher species. More generally, Bergson's biological vocabulary makes it sound as if Life is a natural force or energy. In that case, he faces the same problem that Nietzsche, with his penchant for biological terminology, did. 'We' somehow constitute any conceptualizable world but, as belonging to Life, are processes falling under quasi-biological concepts—and hence are 'our' own 'work'. A similar tension pervades the writings of the two 'reactionary modernists'. The world, Spengler tells us, is an 'anthropomorphic' one and concepts like 'energy' and 'force' are 'mythological' ones which we impose upon it. Yet these very concepts are invoked to explain our anthropomorphizing activities, our 'stamping' order upon the world. We are, says Jünger, 'inscribed' in a 'raging process', as much 'stamped' by prevailing forces as 'stamping'.[34] Impossibly, surely, we both project and are inscribed in the same processes. Something has to give: either the full-blown thesis of 'the human world' or the inscription of 'us' in that world.

A second theme is related to the first. Whether or not these writers were alert to the tensions described, they at least hint at a resolution. They do so by gesturing towards a source of 'the human world' that, unlike a transcendental self, is human enough but which, unlike a flesh-and-blood person, is not an item in that world. Bergson was doing this when identifying 'us' with 'selves', even if his biological rhetoric finally prevented him from relieving the tension. Spengler and Jünger attempt something similar. It is not particular persons, individually or collectively, who 'stamp' and order the discursable world. Rather, it is 'morphological forms', cultural 'life-forms' and *Gestalten* which do the ordering. Individuals are at once the tools and products of this activity. The individual worker, for example, is a 'symbol' of the *Gestalt* of the Worker that 'stamps' identity on particular objects, including the workers themselves. Again, the thinking person is only 'the organ through which [a] language' helps to confer order on the world.[35] Such gestures get spoiled by subsequent 'naturalistic' talk of 'inscription' in 'raging processes', but at least they are made.

[34] Spengler, *The Decline of the West*, 381; Jünger, 'Total Mobilization', in R. Wolin (ed.), *The Heidegger Controversy: A Critical Reader* (Cambridge, Mass: MIT Press, 1993), 128.

[35] Jünger, *Der Arbeiter*, 170.

In the case of Dilthey, arguably, they do not get similarly spoiled. His candidates for the constituting source of 'the human world'—for 'the basis for . . . our experience, understanding' and 'valuation'—are also the 'forms' that Life assumes. These 'life-forms', however, are manifested only in human activity, not in 'animal' and natural processes. It is the central contention of Dilthey's account of *Verstehen* that these forms and their expressions cannot be explained in the terms of natural science. Indeed, Life as 'that behind which it is impossible to go' cannot be characterized in terms of anything more basic. In particular, it would be wrong to analyse a 'life-form' into the actions of individual human beings, for the latter are intelligible only as 'point[s] where webs of relationships intersect', as 'woven into th[e] common sphere' of a 'life-form'.[36] My present brief is not to defend Dilthey's particular gestures towards the constituting agent of 'the human world', only to applaud his recognition that if the tension between humanism and naturalism is to be eased, this agent is not to be identified with creatures who populate that world.

The third theme is that of holism—the idea that individual items in a domain cannot be understood except in relation to that whole domain. It is unsurprising that writers whose rhetoric is one of all-encompassing 'Life', of cultural wholes, *Gestalten*, and the like, should subscribe to this idea. Bergson rails against the 'analytic' tendency to understand a whole by identifying its components, as if the world and our experience of it were like a film composed of separate frames. 'Consciousness', he writes, 'cannot go through the same state twice', because any conscious state relies for its identity on the whole flow of experience.[37] Since our conscious life involves the understanding of concepts, this implies what is sometimes called conceptual or semantic holism—a thesis explicitly advanced by Dilthey. 'Meaning means nothing except belonging to a whole.'[38] Concepts have sense only in relation to a whole scheme or language, just as musical notes have significance only in relation to a whole piece.

The contribution of holism to the humanist cause may not be immediately apparent, and I defer elaboration until the next chapter. For the

---

[36] The citations from Dilthey and a fuller account of his position may be found in my 'Verstehen, Holism and Fascism', in A. O'Hear (ed.), Verstehen *and Humane Understanding* (Cambridge: Cambridge University Press, 1996).

[37] *Creative Evolution*, 6.

[38] Dilthey, *Selected Writings*, 233.

present, I mention the following consideration: the holistic character of conceptual understanding calls for explanation, and surely a plausible explanation would be the embeddedness of concepts in an integrated 'life-form' that, so to speak, puts an indelible stamp on those concepts. Someone might suggest a different explanation: maybe conceptual holism reflects the holistic character of the world. But this is not a suggestion from which our Prometheans demur: they would agree with Jünger that a world organized by a *Gestalt* is a 'whole [which] encompasses more than the sum of its parts'.[39] Indeed, if items of experience are themselves analogous to 'symbols' or 'expressions', the holism of things is of a piece with the holism of concepts. Anyway, the holism of things requires explanation, and isn't the most plausible explanation, once more, in terms of an integrated 'life-form' in relation to which things assume their identity?

A fourth theme is suggested by some further remarks of Bergson and Dilthey on meaning, although it is one usually associated with a school of thinkers mainly domiciled across the Atlantic. Reference to a 'school' of pragmatists is, perhaps, dangerous, since there were striking differences among these figures. All of them might agree on an anti-intellectualist stance—on John Dewey's insistence that 'the organ of thinking . . . [is] an organ of conduct',[40] not of detached contemplation—and that 'truths should have practical consequences': but such pronouncements allowed for conflicting interpretations. For example, F. C. S. Schiller, but not C. S. Peirce, interpreted the second pronouncement to mean that 'truths *consist* in their practical consequences'.[41] Certainly we should heed one commentator's placing of the pragmatists on a 'reformist'-'revolutionary' spectrum,[42] while duly noting that even a 'reformist', like Peirce, says things with seemingly radical implications and that even a 'revolutionary', like Schiller, sometimes backslides.

When Peirce writes that the truth is 'SO . . . whether . . . anybody thinks it is so or not',[43] he sounds far from the 'revolutionary' spirit of Promethean

---

[39] *Der Arbeiter*, 38.

[40] 'The Practical Character of Reality', in H. Thayer (ed.), *Pragmatism: The Classic Readings* (Indianapolis: Hackett, 1982), 280.

[41] F. C. S. Schiller, *Studies in Humanism* (London: Macmillan, 1912), 3.

[42] Susan Haack, 'Pragmatism', in N. Bunnin and E. Tsui-James (eds.), *The Blackwell Companion to Philosophy* (Oxford: Blackwell, 1996).

[43] Quoted in Susan Haack, *Evidence and Inquiry: Towards Reconstruction in Epistemology* (Oxford: Blackwell, 1995), 202.

humanism. Many utterances of William James, Schiller, and Dewey are, however, precisely in that spirit. Indeed, 'humanists' is just what they call themselves. James endorses 'the humanistic principle' that 'you can't weed out the human contribution' (p. 7 above). In doing so, he follows Schiller, for whom humanism is the 'spirit' of pragmatism and the 'great principle that man is . . . an ineradicable factor in any world he experiences', engaged in the very 'construction of a real external world'.[44] Like Bergson, both of them are partial to metaphors of carvery and the like. For James, 'we carve out everything . . . to suit our human purposes', as if from a undifferentiated 'block of marble'; for Schiller, reality is something 'plastic' that we mould in accord with our interests.[45] In rejecting a world with an intelligible structure independent of human construction, James—now in company with Dewey—shifts to printing metaphors. There can, he says, be no 'absolute edition of the world', only 'finite' ones which register practical perspectives; there is, writes Dewey, no 'subject-matter of awareness' passively 'mimeographed . . . upon . . . mental carbon-paper'.[46] For these 'revolutionary' pragmatists, as for Nietzsche, the very concept of reality has implicit reference to human purpose. To count things as real, according to Dewey, is to recognize them as being 'good for what they lay claim to in the way of consequences which we . . . are after'.[47]

Like other Prometheans, these pragmatists emphasize the 'vital' implications of their position for human self-esteem. Only pragmatism, says Schiller, is able properly to affirm 'the ultimate reality of human activity and freedom'; while, for James, the notion that 'man *engenders* truths upon' a malleable world is an 'inspiring' one that 'add[s] both to our dignity and responsibility'. A 'radical pragmatist' will be the 'happy-go-lucky anarchistic sort of creature' James admires.[48] That is not an especially Nietzschean turn of phrase, but allowing for the difference in idiom, James's pragmatist is not far from Nietzsche's 'free spirit' who, unburdened of 'the true world', 'dances' through life.

Like other Prometheans, too, these pragmatists are not entirely steady in

[44] *Studies in Humanism*, 13.

[45] William James, 'Pragmatism and Humanism', in *The Writings of William James* (Chicago: University of Chicago Press, 1977), 452 ff; Schiller, *Studies in Humanism*, 19.

[46] James, 'Pragmatism and Humanism', 459; Dewey, 'The Practical Character of Reality', 284.

[47] 'The Practical Character of Reality', 284.

[48] Schiller, *Studies in Humanism*, 19; James, 'Pragmatism and Humanism', 456–7.

their humanism. In Dewey, for example, insistence on the constructive role of 'the humanistic factor' rubs uncomfortably against a 'frankly realistic . . . acknowledging [of] brute existences . . . in no way constituted out of thought'—a friction Dewey tries, unpromisingly, to soothe by arguing that humanly accessible objects are not these 'brute existences' but things which 'in becoming known' thereby 'undergo . . . qualitative change'.[49] As in other Promethean writings, moreover, the humanism-versus-naturalism tension is often visible in those of the pragmatists. Only two pages before referring to our purposive construction of an external world, Schiller describes purposiveness as a 'biological function' of a mind which is an 'instrument for effecting adaptations'—thereby placing 'us' within the world 'we' are alleged to construct.[50]

The pragmatists advance few arguments for their Promethean humanism which, to recall an earlier citation, cannot be found somewhere, in some form, in Nietzsche. For example, like Nietzsche, they embrace the idea that any description of the world is invested with 'valuations' that only purposive agents could make. There is, however, a characteristic pragmatist thesis about meaning, at best implicit in Nietzsche, that promises to support that of 'the human world'. Here is what I had in mind by the fourth and final of the themes to be identified in this section—one already sounded by Bergson and Dilthey (and maybe by Fichte before them: p. 82 above). Bergson wrote that 'to label an object with a certain concept is to mark . . . the kind of action or attitude' the object invites, while Dilthey held that I only understand what anything is in relation to 'the goal of some striving or a restriction on my will'.[51]

What such remarks indicate is a thesis which goes beyond the already familiar one that our concepts register human purposes and interests. It is to the effect that in understanding the sense of a concept or general term, we understand the place in human activity of any object to which the concept or term applies. Reference to such activity, therefore, belongs to the very specification of a concept's sense, and not simply to an account of the

---

[49] John Dewey, *Essays in Experimental Logic* (Chicago: University of Chicago Press, 1916), 35 and 280. I am willing to take Richard Rorty's word for it that, at times, James, too—despite the robustly humanist remarks I have quoted—has 'no sympathy with the notion of nature as malleable to thought': Rorty, *Philosophy and the Mirror of Nature* (Oxford: Blackwell, 1980), 279.

[50] *Studies in Humanism*, 10.

[51] Bergson, *An Introduction to Metaphysics*, 38; Dilthey, *Selected Writings*, 178.

concept's aetiology and purpose. This thesis is suggested when Peirce writes that the meaning of a concept consists in the 'general modes of rational conduct' consequent upon applying it to things[52]—in which case Schiller may be right that Peirce did not appreciate the radical implications of some of his claims. For it looks as if this thesis about meaning immediately delivers the thesis of 'the human world'. Consider, say, Dewey's proposal that 'the use of language to convey and acquire ideas is an extension and refinement of the principle that things gain meaning by being used', so that to understand a word is to 'become mentally a partner' with those who use what the word refers to.[53] If something like that is right, then no discursable world independent of human agency is imaginable. The sense of any word or concept we could apply with understanding cannot be specified without reference to purpose and action.

Like the earlier themes I identified—the tension between humanism and naturalism, the search for an appropriate 'source' of 'the human world', and the holism of concepts and things—this last one of pragmatic meaning helps provide the context for the emergence of humanism in its developed, final form.

---

[52] C. S. Peirce, *Selected Writings* (New York: Dover, 1958), 204.
[53] John Dewey, *Democracy and Education* (New York: Free Press, 1966), 16.

CHAPTER 5

Existential Humanism

Prometheanism, Naturalism, and Humanism

The final form of humanism referred to at the end of the previous chapter is what I call existential humanism, exposition of which will occupy the present chapter, with further significant elaboration to come in Chapters 7–8. It is, for example, only in Chapter 7 that the 'vital' aspects of existential humanism become a focus of attention. For the time being, it is to the more 'pure' dimensions of this philosophy that we attend. My exposition will be sympathetic for, although by the end of Chapter 10, humanism in its 'raw' form will have been rejected, the thesis of 'the human world' is defended.

Who are the existential humanists? Nobody, possibly, since I do not want to identify the position to be described with that of any particular philosopher. Rather, it is one assembled from the writings of several thinkers, none of whom, perhaps, would buy the whole package.[1] That said, the label is intended to evoke the views of those often described as existential phenomenologists—Heidegger, Sartre, Merleau-Ponty, Ortega y Gasset, and others, during at least some phase of their careers. Existential humanism certainly comes close to the positions advanced by the first three of that quartet in *Being and Time*, *Being and Nothingness*, and *Phenomenology of Perception* respectively. But I draw, where appropriate, on the thoughts of other philosophers, including Dilthey and Wittgenstein, and even of ones whose pronouncements sound hostile to the thesis of 'the human world', such as Donald Davidson and John McDowell.

---

[1] In a previous book, *Existentialism: A Reconstruction* (Oxford: Blackwell, 1990, 2nd ed. 1999), I employed a similar strategy when inventing a figure, 'The Existentialist', not necessarily to be identified with any particular existentialist philosopher, but representing, so to speak, the best wisdom to be culled from several. My existential humanist in the present book is, of course, a close relative of the Existentialist in the earlier one.

Lest this eclectic list suggests that 'existential humanist' is a catch-all label for anyone subscribing to the thesis of 'the human world', let me stress that it does not apply to all such subscribers. In several cases, the elements intended by 'existential'—ones pertaining to human life, agency, and purpose—are missing. Consider, for example, Nelson Goodman's account of the 'world-making' we perform, 'not with the hands, but with . . . languages and other symbol systems'. This worldmaking, he continues, is to be taken literally, for 'surely we make versions, and right versions make worlds'.[2] No sense, there-fore, can be made of how the world is independently of conventional, sym-bolic systems ('versions'), for there are as many worlds as there are right versions. This is a form of the 'human world' thesis, and arguably 'a form of idealism as extreme as Hegel's or Fichte's', as Putnam maintains.[3] But it does not belong in the tradition of humanism I have traced since, although Goodman makes passing mention of our practical concerns, his arguments make no essential appeal to agency and purpose. Rather they appeal to 'logico-mathematical considerations'[4]—to, for example, the absurdity, as Goodman sees it, of supposing there is a 'fact of the matter' at issue between seemingly competing descriptions when these are relative to, say, different spatial coordinates or different conventions for counting. Whether con-siderations of that sort can be inflated into a general doctrine of 'world-making', they are at any rate of a different kind from those I discuss.

Considerations of the kind met with in previous chapters have been vari-ous, from authors themselves as various as Herder, Fichte, Marx, Nietzsche, Dilthey, James, and Dewey. Such considerations as the following emerged in support of the 'human world' thesis: the concepts we apply to the world necessarily reflect human values and interests; concepts cannot be extricat-ed from the traditions and ways of life in which they are embedded; the things concepts apply to are intelligible only in relation to our purposive practices; the holistic character of possible descriptions of the world is due, not to the world, but to the human life they register; no sense can be made of what it is for something to exist except as 'concerning us'.

The existential humanist does not add anything brand new to such con-

---

[2] Nelson Goodman, 'On Starmaking', in P. McCormick (ed.), *Starmaking: Realism, Anti-Realism, and Irrealism* (Cambridge, Mass.: MIT Press, 1996), 145.

[3] Hilary Putnam, 'Irrealism and Deconstruction', in McCormick (ed.), *Starmaking*, 180.

[4] Hubert L. Dreyfus and Charles Spinosa, 'Coping with Things-in-Themselves: A Practice-Based Phenomenological Argument for Realism', *Inquiry*, 42 (1999), 67.

siderations, but assembles, elaborates, and, where necessary, amends them, weaving them into a coherent whole. That general picture will emerge in the following sections: in the present one, I bring out two important respects in which existential humanism takes issue with the Promethean humanism which figured in the latter stages of my narrative. The first of these I have already flagged: abandonment of the flirtation with naturalism which many of those Promethean authors conducted. The second is abandonment—at any rate, a muting—of the Promethean rhetoric of the world as something we 'carve out', 'create', 'construct', or 'make'. The two manœuvres are not unrelated.

'What is the status', asked Husserl, 'of the paradox . . . of humanity as world-constituting subjectivity and yet as incorporated in the world itself?'[5] Whether or not that is quite the way to express the 'paradox', there is a real tension between holding that the world is dependent upon human beings and regarding them as, simply, natural parts of the world they are allegedly responsible for. At its most acute, it is Schopenhauer's paradoxical view that the human brain, a natural item in the empirical world, is somehow responsible for there being such a world. Attempts to combine the two terms of the paradox turn out to be bogus. Consider, here, Richard Rorty, who seems to endorse the 'human world' thesis in denying that we can ever 'encounter . . . reality except under a chosen description' and in rejecting all pretensions, including that of the 'positivist's God', science, 'to get back behind language to something . . . to which it might hope to be "adequate"'.[6] Elsewhere, however, Rorty professes to be a 'bald naturalist' who regards us simply as 'organisms . . . programmed to respond . . . to, among other things, the impact of environment'.[7] How can Rorty combine his humanism with a bald naturalism that, in the words of the coiner of that expression, McDowell, 'hold[s] that reality does have an intrinsic character, which is captured by . . . the natural sciences'?[8] The answer, predictably, is that this is not what Rorty means by 'bald naturalism'. Instead, he means by it, peculiarly, a

[5] Edmund Husserl, *The Crisis of European Sciences and Transcendental Phenomenology*, trans. D. Carr (Evanston, Ill.: Northwestern University Press, 1970), 182.

[6] Richard Rorty, *Consequences of Pragmatism: Essays 1972–80* (Brighton: Harvester, 1982), pp. xx and xli.

[7] 'McDowell, Davidson, and Spontaneity', *Philosophy and Phenomenological Research*, 58 (1998), 389.

[8] 'Reply to Commentators', *Philosophy and Phenomenological Research*, 58 (1998), 420. McDowell goes on to note that Rorty is not, of course, a bald naturalist in the sense defined.

denial that reality has an intrinsic character combined with a conviction that the natural sciences provide our currently most useful vocabulary. This pragmatic naturalism does not contradict the thesis of 'the human world', since it does not even purport to make a claim about what humans or the world are really like. Initial appearances to the contrary, then, Rorty is not even trying to combine the two terms of Husserl's paradox.

Husserl had his own way of resolving the paradox, but not one available to the humanist. It consists in denying that the 'world-constituting subjectivity' is 'humanity'. The human belongs only to the 'constituted' phenomenal world, while the 'constituter' is a transcendental 'I', or 'ego-pole', in which 'nothing human is to be found, neither soul nor psychic life nor real psychophysical human beings'.[9] As philosophers who, in the nineteenth century, reacted against a transcendental idealism for which subjectivity was 'nothing human', humanists can hardly follow Husserl's own transcendental route.

One way of expressing the tension between naturalism and the thesis of 'the human world' is that for the former, the only relations between the human and the world are contingent—spatial, temporal, causal ones—between independently identifiable items in the natural order. For the humanist, the fundamental relation must, one might put it, be more 'intimate'. Clearly the natural order as a whole does not 'depend' on the human in the contingent manner in which, say, the temperature in a stadium depends on the body-heat of the spectators. This more 'intimate' relation will emerge later. I mention it at this stage because it is relevant to the other main modification to Promethean humanism urged by the existential humanist: rejection of what might be dubbed the 'sculptural' rhetoric of Prometheanism—the talk of the world as carved or cut out, moulded or made by, human beings. For the existential humanist, this rhetoric encourages acceptance of an insufficiently 'intimate' relationship between the human and the worldly. In effect, he is advocating that humanism divests itself of one main theme in Prometheanism, retaining only the insistence that there could be no discursable world except through human purposive agency—a thought to be divorced from the sculptural image often associated with it. This is what Merleau-Ponty is urging when, while insisting that the world is 'inseparable from subjectivity and intersubjectivity', he never-

<hr />

[9] *The Crisis of European Sciences*, 183.

theless denies that it is something 'constructed or formed', 'the law of [whose] making' we have in our possession.[10]

Taken seriously, the sculptural rhetoric indeed conjures up quaint images. One encouraged by some of Nietzsche's passages is that of human beings stuck in a world that is so much featureless porridge until their conceptual sculpturing or carvery lends it contour and form. That is an incoherent picture, not least because it makes an arbitrary exception of human beings: *they* cannot be the shapeless, featureless stuff that everything around them is. Alert to the incoherence of that picture, other philosophers propose a second one, in which the conceptual sculptors, the source of objects in the world, themselves stand outside it. Hovering above it, they emit, as it were, rays which cut up the otherwise porridgy world into objects, animals, or whatever. That picture is suggested by Husserl's talk of an 'ego-pole' that he himself describes as the source of 'rays' which 'constitute' objects. This picture looks no more appealing than the first and, for the reason given two paragraphs earlier, it is anyway not a humanist picture. The transcendental 'ego-pole' is 'nothing human'.

For the existential humanist, sculptural rhetoric with its quaint imagery betrays a failure to appreciate the special 'intimacy' of the relation between the human and the world. This cannot be remotely like the relation of the sculptor's chiselling to the uncarved block before him, or to the eventual statue which is its product—not a relation, however magical, modelled on contingent relations between items within the world. In this respect, the sculptural rhetoric of Prometheanism combines with the thesis of 'the human world' no better than naturalism does.

Someone may retort that the sculptural vocabulary is, after all, *rhetoric*, mere metaphor, and not, therefore, to be taken poker-faced. Isn't it, moreover, a rhetoric indulged in by some existential humanists, notably Sartre? It is true, certainly, that this rhetoric dies hard.[11] It is true, as well, that as an

---

[10] Maurice Merleau-Ponty, *Phenomenology of Perception*, trans. C. Smith (London: Routledge & Kegan Paul, 1962), pp. xx, x–xi.

[11] The rhetoric is still very much around. 'We . . . grope our way through being by carving entities out of it and gradually constructing ourselves a World', writes Umberto Eco in *Kant and the Platypus: Essays on Language and Cognition*, trans. A. McEwen (London: Secker & Warburg, 1999), 20. Going back a few years, and from the sculptor's studio to the kitchen, we find Roland Barthes writing that language 'attacks, sizzles, hardens and browns', transforming raw material into objects 'as the raw slice of potato is transformed into a *pomme frite*': *The Rustle of Language*, trans. R. Howard (Berkeley: University of California Press, 1989), 355.

occasional device for dramatically affirming the thesis of 'the human world' it can be effective. But metaphor, when overindulged, can be misleading and, for reasons beyond those already mentioned, existential humanists do well to use sculptural rhetoric sparingly. For one thing, it encourages an assimilation of our usual experiential encounters with the world to ones which, of necessity, are unusual. There are occasions when the metaphors of carving out, cutting up, and the like are fitting—as when an intrepid botanist stumbles across weird, unfamiliar flora that he must, if only provisionally, sort and label. Or as when a legatee must lend some system to the chaotic papers left him by an eccentric author. Such occasions need only to be described for their contrast with our usual situation to be obvious. In the usual case, we smoothly, unreflectingly, and without need for 'decision' recognize things for what they are.

Second, the sculptural rhetoric can mislead, even in the unusual cases, by encouraging blindness to the unreflective exercise of conceptual skills presupposed by the botanist's or legatee's procedure. While he may 'carve up' the exotic specimens into types X, Y, and Z, or 'construct' categories A, B, and C for organizing the papers, no similar procedure was needed to recognize that he was faced with some plants or sheets of writing. It is illegitimate to extrapolate from such examples to the thought that we might be, or might once have been, confronted with material so raw—with a block so uncarved—that we must start from scratch, unable to apply any concepts except those constructed on the hoof. Construction of concepts, classificatory decisions, and the like presuppose, however novel and unregimented the data before us, that we come to situations 'always already', as Heidegger puts it, equipped with an understanding that is not itself in the process of being constructed or decided upon.

The existential humanist is urging, then, a distinction, within the broad Promethean tendency that he in part continues, between the sculptural rhetoric of that tendency and its central insight of the dependence of the discursable world on human agency. Not only is the former inessential to the latter, it is at odds with it: for the talk of our being in the perpetual business of carving up or constructing the world combines badly with the idea of a world opening up for us in relation to an understanding that is carried by our typically unreflective, smooth, and, in an important sense, passive encounter with the world in everyday activity. That human agency is responsible for there being a discursable world does not mean that the agency in question is that of deciding what the world is, choosing its structure, or imposing form upon it. None of those terms plausibly expresses how human beings relate to 'the human world'. The existential humanist is therefore doubly at odds with those writers, of whom there are many, who indulge in sculptural rhetoric but reject the thesis of 'the human world', usually on the grounds that we should not confuse 'construction' of concepts with 'construction' of reality.[12] For him, if the world is dependent on human agency, this is not because, in any serious sense, we are always devising or fashioning categories to which we then suit a world, as if it were a jig-saw cut up in accordance with its designer's plan.

The existential humanist is equally at odds, naturally, with those who think that the thesis of 'the human world' collapses once the sculptural rhetoric is abandoned. That it does not collapse he will need to argue: but in advance of that, he can reasonably warn against any quick move from the unsuitability of sculptural rhetoric in a given area of discourse to rejection of a humanist treatment of that discourse. For example, it would be bad phenomenology to speak of us carving up situations into the funny and unfunny, or of imposing funniness on certain remarks. Typically we are as passive in our recognition of situations or remarks as funny as in our perception of objects as trees or tables. Yet it is more than plausible to deny that funniness is a feature of situations or remarks that belongs to them independently of human responses and interests. A humanist treatment of humour is a 'local' humanism (p. 9) which is hard to fault.[13] It would be hardly less rash, arguably, to abandon a humanist treatment of moral judgement on the grounds, simply, of the unsuitability of sculptural rhetoric in ethics. *Pace* an army of ethical 'non-cognitivists'—subjectivists, emotivists, and so on—it is wrong to describe us as, at all typically, experiencing in a 'neutral' way a world to which we then 'give' or 'attach' values, 'choosing' or 'deciding' what to regard as good, noble, mean, or evil. This does not entail, however, that 'moral realists' are right to hold that moral qualities belong to the

---

[12] Eco (see preceding note) is a good example, at once fond of the sculptural rhetoric, as we've seen, yet insisting that there is a real 'grain' of the world in no way dependent on human agency.

[13] For a persuasively 'anti-realist' account of humour, see Crispin Wright, *Truth and Objectivity* (Cambridge, Mass.: Harvard University Press, 1992). Both Wright and the existential humanist will, therefore, resist the idea suggested, perhaps, by John McDowell's remark that the passivity of our experience is, by itself, sufficient indication of 'constraint [which] comes from outside thinking': *Mind and World* (Cambridge, Mass.: Harvard University Press, 1994), 28. They will, at any rate, if McDowell includes things like finding something funny under the heading of 'thinking'.

world as it anyway is, independent of human purpose and concern.[14] Again, then, the fate of a 'local'—this time, moral—humanism is not tied to the appropriateness of a certain rhetoric.

Ex-istence (1): The Language Analogy

Existential humanism embraces the thesis of 'the human world', but sheds both the naturalist tendency and the sculptural rhetoric of Prometheanism that proved seductive to earlier cohorts of humanists. Both those attractions betray a failure to appreciate the 'intimate' relation between human being and the world that a cogent thesis of 'the human world' requires. The relation cannot be a contingent one between items in the natural world, nor can it permit that 'distance' between human beings and their world suggested by the sculptural imagery. The degree of intimacy is suggested by Heidegger's remark that 'self and the world belong together . . . [They] are not two beings, like subject and object', but 'the unity of Being-in-the-world'.[15] Such is this 'unity' that, Heidegger continues, 'we' who are in-the-world, the world we are in, and our being in it, may only be 'provisionally' separated. In the final analysis, none of the terms is intelligible in abstraction from the others. We are not, therefore, related to things as substances to substances—not if a substance is understood in the traditional, Cartesian sense as something which 'needs no other entity in order to exist', as one which might, logically, have existed by itself.

---

[14] Like the existential humanist, Simon Blackburn's 'quasi-realist' denies that moral values are features of how the world anyway is, since they are 'spread' or 'projected' through our 'attitudes', while rejecting any 'reduction' of moral judgements to expressions of choice, preference, or acts of will. While the moral world is 'stained' through 'sentiment', it gains 'its own life', our responsiveness to which can be as receptive and will-less as non-moral sensory experience typically is. *Spreading the Word: Groundings in the Philosophy of Language* (Oxford: Clarendon Press, 1984), 219. Blackburn, however, is no humanist. At least, I assume he isn't on the basis of his insistence that, despite the 'staining' of the world through our sentiments, no sense can be attached to the claim that moral values are 'mind-dependent' which could make that claim generally true. *Spreading the Word*, 217 ff, and *Ruling Passions: A Theory of Practical Reasoning* (Oxford: Clarendon Press, 1998), 311–12. I return to that insistence—a peculiar one in my view—in the penultimate section of this chapter. See, for example, n. 49.

[15] Martin Heidegger, *The Basic Problems of Phenomenology*, trans. A. Hofstadter (Bloomington: Indiana University Press, 1982), 297. Generally, of course, Heidegger prefers, in such early works as this and *Being and Time*, to speak not of 'we' or of 'human beings', but of *Dasein*, 'the manner of Being which . . . man . . . possesses', though not necessarily only 'man': *Being and Time*, trans. J. Macquarrie and E. Robinson (Oxford: Blackwell, 1980), 32. His motive is to set aside what he sees as irrelevant connotations—biological, for example—of terms like 'human'.

The first task, then, is to provide an account of that 'intimate' relation, the upshot of which will be that human being should be understood in terms of a purposive engagement with a world that could not be encountered or experienced at all in the absence of that engagement. That is the task of the present and following section. In the last two sections, the move from that conclusion to the thesis of 'the human world', which is completed in Chapter 8, is begun.

In keeping with Heidegger and Sartre, let's call the relation in question 'ex-istence'. I write it that way, as Heidegger sometimes does, in order, first, to emphasize that this is a term of art and, second, to draw attention to an etymological feature that helps explain its being favoured by existential phenomenologists. Etymologically, to 'exist' is to 'stand out from'. The idea that a human being, in some sense, stands out from himself—is always directed beyond himself—will play an important part.

What, then, is human ex-istence? A useful strategy is to begin with a relation that is at once an important dimension of ex-istence and, in instructive respects, a model for it. This is the relation between speakers / hearers and their language, their repertoire of meaningful words and devices for combining those words into communicative utterances. To begin with, this relation is, surely, 'intimate'. It is not, in fact, a truism to hold that verbal communication presupposes a language, nor that a language presupposes communicative use. Maybe primitive acts of communication do not require a language, and maybe there are artificial languages that cannot be put to communicative use. But I shall take it that, once attention is focused on communication of any sophistication and upon natural languages, it is true to hold both that communication requires a language and that the existence of a language requires speakers / hearers who use it for communicative purposes. (This would need tightening up to cater for 'dead languages'.) For words to have meaning, people must mean something by them, and to mean something by them, they must be able to intend to communicate something by them. And if, at a sufficient level of sophistication, people communicate and mean by employing sounds, then these sounds have meaning and belong to a language.[16]

---

[16] To say this is not to agree, necessarily, with Paul Grice that the meaning of a word can be *analysed* in terms of speakers' meanings and intentions. My much weaker claim is simply that, whatever the exact connections between intentions and word-meaning, there wouldn't be meaningful words,

Next, the relation between speakers/hearers and their language is not a natural one to be explicated in terms of spatial, causal, and other natural connections between people and words. It is because I *understand* various English words, and *understand* how they may be combined, that I am able to employ them in communication and to be a successful recipient of other people's communications. In both the vernacular and the phenomenologists' more technical sense, a language user's relation to the words of his language is 'intentional'. The words mean what they do in virtue of communicative purposes, and speakers are 'directed towards' words—recognizing them as the words they are—in virtue of their understood meanings.[17]

Next, it would be implausible to depict the relation between speakers/hearers and their language by a sculptural, Promethean image according to which the former are constantly in the business of conferring meanings on noises, of performing 'mental acts' which weld meanings to noises. Doubtless there are occasions, as when we need to coin new words to understand old ones employed in an unexpected way, or to make sense of words in a foreign language we are learning, when such a vocabulary is suitable. Generally, however, it would be bad phenomenology to describe our experience of language as one of hearing mere noises accompanied or rapidly followed by a 'mental act' of interpretation or semantic 'processing'. Typically no such 'act' is required, for we passively hear the words as the meaningful items they are. If our relation to words is, in the more technical sense, 'intentional', the intentionality in question is that non-reflective type, implicit in our everyday dealings with language, that Merleau-Ponty calls 'operative intentionality'.[18]

The 'mental act' model is implausible for other reasons. First, it encourages an overly atomistic conception of one's understanding of language, as a sum of so many discrete acts of understanding the words in a repertoire. Understanding a language cannot, however, be the result of stitching together such discrete acts, since to understand individual words I must grasp how they relate to and combine with other words. Indeed, I must

---

and they wouldn't mean what they do, in the absence of communicative intentions. See Grice, 'Meaning', *Philosophical Review*, 66 (1957).

[17] In Husserl's technical sense, intentional states (experiences, recognitions, etc.) have the 'peculiar feature of being related to ... things through their ... posited meaning': *Ideas: General Introduction to Pure Phenomenology*, trans. W. Boyce-Gibson (London: Collier-Macmillan, 1962), 346.

[18] *Phenomenology of Perception*, p. xviii.

already have some grasp of the language to which they belong, for their intelligibility is a function of their place in that language. This is part of what Heidegger has in mind when he writes, apropos of 'the being of words', that familiarity with a whole realm of 'significance' is a condition for appreciating the 'significations' of particular items within that realm.[19] Second, the model implies that people could, in principle, be masters of their language without ever actually employing it, since understanding words is construed as a matter, simply, of welding items to them—mental images, senses, essences, semantic rules, or whatever. This implication must be rejected for a reason elaborated by Wittgenstein. Whatever item is welded to a word, it too must be understood or interpreted properly if it is to supply the actual meaning of the word. But what could be the criterion of appropriate interpretation other than appropriate use of the item? That criterion, however, could have been applied to the understanding of words themselves, thereby rendering redundant the appeal to items allegedly welded to words by 'mental acts'.

It is important to appreciate, moreover, that the employment of a language required if people are to be credited with understanding it cannot, in general, be some hived-off one—such as referring to things and describing them 'just for the sake of it'—disengaged from the more practical activities in which speaking is involved. To be sure, language can 'go on holiday': one can impart information 'for its own sake', in abstraction from the cooperative activities—building, preparing dinner, buying and selling, or whatever—for which the sharing of information is typically required. But just as summer vacations presuppose a way of life from which a break is being taken, so the possibility of 'off-duty' uses of languages rides on the back of the employment of language in situ. It is the engaged employment of language for cooperative purposes which shapes the criteria of relevance—of what count as appropriate ways of referring to and describing things—without which not even those on holiday from such purposes could successfully communicate. This is the element of truth in Dewey's remark (p. 98 above) that using words to convey ideas is an 'extension' of the principle that meaning is acquired through more practical employment. Our relation to language is one of 'operative intentionality', not only in the sense mentioned above—that of a pre-reflective understanding implicit in our intercourse

---

[19] *Being and Time*, 121.

with words—but in the further sense that, typically, we use words in the course of our operations, of getting on in various ways with the practical business of life. All of this, I take it, is what Wittgenstein had in mind when he wrote that 'speaking a language is part of an activity, or of a form of life'. To speak a language is to understand the contributions it can make to the practices that characterize our life—which is why 'to imagine a language means to imagine a form of life'.[20]

The connection between language and forms of life is something to which we shall return. The immediate topic is the existential humanist's deployment of the relation between speakers and their language as a model or analogy for the wider relation of human beings to their world. His claim is that, in crucial respects, human beings stand to their world as speakers stand to their language. Let's briefly remind ourselves of the aspects of this latter relation to which attention has been drawn. It is an 'intimate' one in the sense, first of all, that there cannot be speakers or communicators of any sophistication without a language in which to communicate. Nor, second, can there be a natural language—a repertoire of meaningful words and their combinations—without speakers who put it to communicative uses. The relation is 'intimate', too, in that linguistic understanding is typically smooth and unreflective, not a matter of confronting an array of noises to which meanings are then welded, from the outside, as it were, by 'mental acts'. We saw, as well, that this 'operative intentionality' is operative in the further sense that the primary use of language which is the vehicle of implicit understanding is in the service of the practical business of life.

Those last points might be put by saying that people who speak a language understandingly are 'out there' in the world, their understanding of it a function of engagement with their world, not some treasure stored in a mental museum to which, in principle, access would be possible in the absence of wordly involvement. The expression 'out there' recalls the name

---

[20] Ludwig Wittgenstein, *Philosophical Investigations*, trans. G. E. M. Anscombe (Oxford: Blackwell, 1963), §§ 23 and 19. More argument than I have had time for would be needed to establish the artificiality of separating the understanding of a language from the capacity successfully to communicate through it in the course of engaged activities. Indeed, various qualifications need to be made to the general idea of meaning and understanding as presupposing use. My remarks, incidentally, do not commit me to any precise interpretation of the slogan 'meaning is use'—to the view, for example, that a word has as many meanings as it has distinct uses. That, typically, a word must be used to have meaning does not entail that, once its meaning is in place, it cannot be put to uses which do not affect that meaning.

given by the existential humanist to the intimate relation he hopes to establish between human beings and the world—'ex-istence'. For the name intimates the idea of a human being as one who essentially, not contingently, 'stands outside' of himself, out there in the world which is the environment of his engagement. We are not, as Sartre says Husserl's 'bracketing' of the world implies, like so many 'flies bumping their noses on the window without being able to clear the glass', beyond which—for all the difference it could make to our mental life—there might be no world at all.[21]

Ex-istence (2): Meaning and Practice

The existential humanist will elaborate this notion of ex-istence by analogy with the relation of language users to their language: but, first, a disclaimer. His immediate point is not that human being is essentially linguistic. Given the range of characteristically human practices—legal and educational ones, say—that are inconceivable in the absence of language, this is not a claim with which he wants to take issue. But his present concern is to exploit an analogy, not to offer a definition of man as *Homo loquens*. Indeed, when that definition is offered—as it is by some philosophers convinced that reason presupposes language—as an extension of the characterization of man as *Homo rationalis*, it is one whose spirit the existential humanist will reject.

The first part of the intended analogy between ex-istence and speakers's relationship to their language is this: just as to be a speaker *is* to be engaged in certain ways with a language, so to be human *is* to be engaged in certain ways with the world. The negative import of this claim emerged a little earlier, with the denial that human beings are minds or selves which, like Sartre's flies, could even notionally be 'self-enclosed' entities that do not reach 'out there' among things. The positive point is that a description of a typically human life is one of a practical involvement in the world. To be sure, animals too are practically involved in the world, and humans can, within limits, 'slacken the intentional threads which attach us to the world',

---

[21] Jean-Paul Sartre, *Being and Nothingness: An Essay on Phenomenological Ontology*, trans. H. Barnes (London: Methuen, 1957), 100. I try to explain the objections of Sartre and other existential phenomenologists to Husserl at greater length in my *Existentialism: A Reconstruction*—as I do several other matters treated briefly in the present chapter.

take stock, and reflect.[22] Not only, however, are these limits severe, but as Merleau-Ponty's words suggest, detachment is parasitic on a more basic, operative intentionality that infuses our practical dealings with things. Those dealings, as he puts it, manifest an understanding 'in the hands', and the 'kind of concern' registered in these dealings has, to cite Heidegger, 'its own kind of "knowledge"'.[23] It is the character of this understanding or knowledge that distinguishes human being from that of other animals—a character which emerges in the course of making out the second part of the analogy.

The further point of analogy is this: just as language requires speakers, so the world requires human beings—and for the reason that things in the world, like the words of a language, are meaningful items that presuppose the existence of creatures in virtue of whose practices they are meaningful. This is the claim made by Merleau-Ponty when he writes that 'the world is inseparable from' our being-in-the-world, since it is a 'cradle of meanings', and by Heidegger when he states that 'the sign-structure . . . provides an ontological clue for "characterizing" any entity whatsoever'.[24]

To appreciate this claim, it is helpful to prescind, for the time being, from the strong contention that, like words, things *are* (nothing but) meaningful items, and to focus on the more modest one that, typically and 'primordially', human beings do and must experience things as meaningful. In the remainder of this section, then, it is ex-istence as a phenomenological relation between human beings and the world as they encounter it which is under examination. The move from phenomenology to ontology becomes an issue in the final section of the chapter.

Before seeing how existential phenomenologists secure the analogy between words and things as we encounter them, a brief remark about meaning is in order. Why do we speak of words being meaningful or significant at all? The broad answer is that it is because people use words to *refer* one another—to 'point' or 'direct' one another—to things, situations, and so on 'beyond' the words themselves. To understand words is to be suitably referred. This is true even of those words, like 'if' and 'but', that are not happily spoken of as referring to anything. For, in combination with other words, they are used to form sentences which do serve to refer people to

---

[22] Merleau-Ponty, *Phenomenology of Perception*, p. xiii.   [23] *Being and Time*, 95.
[24] Merleau-Ponty, *Phenomenology of Perception*, 430; Heidegger, *Being and Time*, § 17.

states of affairs, actual or notional. Words can be used for this very general purpose, it was argued, only in virtue of practices in which language is engaged. The existential phenomenologist's suggestion is that things are meaningful or significant for the same reason. They are encountered or experienced, within our practices, as items which refer, point or direct us towards further things, situations, people, or whatever.

The details of this suggestion emerge during the existential phenomenologist's defence of why some such suggestion must be true. It must be true, he argues, if 'the problem of access' is to be solved. To experience or encounter something is—or so we'll assume for the time being—to experience or encounter it *as* this or that, as a dog, say, or a stone. What gives us access to objects like dogs and stones? How is such objective experience, to speak in Kantian idiom, possible? That question, the existential phenomenologist holds, is indeed basic, in a way that the usual questions posed by epistemologists are not. Questions like 'How do we know that the objects of our perception correspond to real things?' presuppose that our experience is objective—which is precisely what calls for explanation. A proof that our perception of things is veridical would not explain our knowledge of the world in the absence of an account of how experience of things is possible in the first place.

The Kantian question is one that ought to have taken centre stage with the demise of the doctrine of 'divine illumination', according to which the concepts in virtue of which it is possible to experience things are ideas divinely planted in our minds. But it did not: attention quickly turned to less fundamental epistemological issues. While Kant rightly gave pride of place to the question of the 'subjective condition' under which objective experience is possible, his own answer was, at best, a limited one, for he confined attention to what we 'cognize a priori about things'. Appeal to the subjective forms of sensibility and the innate categories of the understanding might explain why, say, we experience things as spatially extended or as causally related. But it does not explain how that experience could be of dogs or stones. As Umberto Eco puts it, 'the first *Critique* fails to deal with the problem of how we understand that a dog is a dog', and remains at too 'high [a] level of abstraction' to explain how we can say 'This . . . is a stone'.[25]

---

[25] *Kant and the Platypus*, 70 and 73.

But why speak of a 'problem' here? Don't we just look and listen, take in the items about us, notice similarities among some of them, group these together under a concept X, and then perceive the next item belonging to the group *as* an X? It is the contention of existential humanism that this 'spectatorial' account of access to and experience of things is hopeless. Doubtless, I can now go into a room, look around, take things in, notice similarities—and so on. But that is because I am a creature for whom the world is *already* 'lit up' in various ways, for whom things have *already* 'shown up' as this or that. I bring a whole background of understanding and experience into the room with me. Heidegger writes that 'cognition in the . . . spectator sense . . . presupposes existence'.[26] Unless, that is, we are already related to the world in a more fundamental way—unless we ex-ist—spectating would yield nothing of the world to us. The spectatorial account assumes that, simply by spectating, we can individuate items, identify them as remaining the same items, and group them into classes according to criteria of resemblance. But how, asks the existential humanist, can mere spectating determine that anything is experienced as *an* item, rather than as part of a larger one or a collection of lesser ones? And how could it settle whether an item, despite the changes it will have undergone, remains the same one? And why should just these, and not innumerable other, points of resemblance among items serve as the bases for classification, for subsumption under concepts?

Wittgenstein asked why a broom counts as one object, and not as two (a stick and a brush)[27]—or as twenty, or as a twentieth of some greater whole. His implied answer is that it does so because of its distinctive role in an activity, sweeping. It is that role, too, which enables one to say that the broom remains the same one, despite various changes—including a new handle—which take place in its career. And it is similarity of purpose or role which is the basis for grouping various items together as brooms. The existential humanist wants to generalize these points. It is in virtue of the significance an item has—the way it figures for and matters to us—in relation to our purposeful practices that it is identifiable, and reidentifiable, as *an* item of experience. It is in virtue of this, too, that it falls, along with other similarly significant items, under a certain concept.

[26] *The Basic Problems of Phenomenology*, 276.
[27] *Philosophical Investigations*, § 60.

The existential humanist is prepared, of course, to respond to a critic's predictable observation that we have moved away from dogs and stones to brooms and other functional artefacts. It is hardly surprising, the critic will continue, that criteria of identity and resemblance for things made to perform functions are relative to practical purposes—but this is surely not the case when we turn to dogs, stones, winds, planets, and the panorama of natural items that largely make up the world we encounter. The response to this objection is that, while indeed natural items are not purpose-made functional items, it is true of them as well that, if they are to show up for us at all, they must 'matter' and hence have their place in our practices.

Elucidation of the kind of place they have requires focusing on an aspect of functional items so far left implicit—their meaningfulness, in the sense briefly discussed above. According to the existential humanist, a phenomenology of our 'operative' understanding of brooms, hammers, and other 'equipment' should articulate the complex manner in which such items refer us—the 'us' who understandingly employ them—to what is beyond the items themselves. In unreflectively, though not blindly and without intelligent purpose, taking hold of the broom, I am directed towards the floor-dust for whose removal brooms are designed, and thence to the state the house should be in if other domestic activities, like cooking, are to be properly conducted. Through such activities, I am referred to my family with whom I eat, and thence to the ways of my society which shape when, what, and how families eat together.

Eventually, I am directed towards a whole 'Life', to what Dilthey called the whole 'context of interactions' which 'forms the basis . . . for our experience [and] understanding' (p. 94 above). Encapsulated in the broom, as it were, is that whole form of life without which our 'operative' understanding would not be of a broom at all. Such understanding, as one writer on Wittgenstein puts it, 'reverbrates with the characteristic structures of our form of life'.[28] This is why, in possible forms of life, an activity which looks much like sweeping the floor with a broom might not be anything of the sort—but a battle fought with a weapon, say, or a solitary game played with something sold in the same shop as golf-clubs. A form of life is not simply, as

[28] Marie McGinn, *Wittgenstein and the* Philosophical Investigations (London: Routledge, 1997), 94.

Wittgenstein put it, the 'whole scene of our language-games',[29] to which therefore our words refer us, but the whole scene of our wider and connected practices, to which therefore the things with which we deal refer us. Put differently, in our 'operative' encounters with a broom we are referred to the world, in Heidegger's sense of a 'relational totality', a 'structural whole of meaningful connections'.[30]

The point could be made by saying that brooms and so on are 'sign-like', and the existential humanist urges that natural items are no less so. That they are not designed to play roles in our practices is not relevant: after all, a fallen branch might be used as a broom. Whether or not a natural item is dragooned into practical service, it can—indeed, must—'signify' if it is to be anything for us at all, to stand out as an item and to be classified together with other like items. As Heidegger puts it, 'our concern discovers nature as having a certain direction', so that, for example, winds are first 'discovered' in the context of activities like farming, where they serve to direct the farmer to the impending threat to his crops, the need to bring in his cattle, or whatever.[31] Without such direction, there is no recognition of a wind, only a confrontation with sensory stimuli whose elevation into significant, conceptualized objects of experience is left unexplained. If the wind itself does not encapsulate a form of life, then 'discovery' of it, understanding of it as the wind, is integrated in the form of life of creatures for whom such items as the wind can matter.

Let me summarize this long discussion. The existential humanist's ambition is to secure the thesis of 'the human world'. To that end, he embarked on elucidating the character of the relationship between human beings and the world. So far, he has not been doing quite that: for, prescinding from the ontological issue of whether any discursable world must be dependent on human being, he has limited himself to the phenomenological enterprise of illuminating the relation between human beings and the world as it is experienced in their basic, pre-reflective, 'operative' encounter with it. He has argued, partly by analogy with the relation between language users and their language, that this relation of ex-istence is an 'intimate' one. It is not a contingent one between different sets of substances which are indepen-

---

[29] *Philosophical Investigations*, § 179.

[30] Martin Heidegger, *History of the Concept of Time*, trans. T. Kiesel (Bloomington: Indiana University Press, 1985), 210.

[31] *Being and Time*, 100 and 112.

dently conceivable. Rather, just as speakers need a language to speak and a language needs speakers to speak it, so human beings must be engaged in the world, and the world as engaged in is intelligible only in relation to them. The reasons are that a distinctively human way of life is one 'out there', purposefully and intelligently dealing with things in the world, and that these things as 'operatively' experienced are, like words, meaningful or significant, and hence presuppose the presence of those for whom they have meaning.

Ex-istence is an 'intimate' relation in a further respect. Just as meanings do not accrue to words through conferment of the former on the latter by 'mental acts', but in virtue of the employment of words in the furtherance of our practical business, things do not get their significance through our imposition of meanings upon 'neutrally' experienced items, but through the place they occupy in the related practices that constitute a form of life. Things do not, so to speak, stand over against us awaiting an imprint of significance. As Sartre puts it, we immediately encounter things as belonging in 'a world of tasks'.[32] Here he expresses the characteristic animus of the existential humanist against any 'spectatorial' account of cognition, for this leaves it inexplicable how things become 'lit up' for us as individuatable items of experience and how they can be grouped, under concepts, into significant classes. In fine, the phenomenology of ex-istence presents us with a vision of ourselves as unthinkable in abstraction from a world in which we are practically engaged, and of a world which, as it shows up for us through this engagement, is unthinkable in abstraction from it.

I close this section with some remarks on the connections between existential humanism and the earlier humanistic tendencies whose development I narrated. I remarked (pp. 100–1) that existential humanism does not add anything brand new to those tendencies. Certainly it is not difficult to see how it picks up on earlier themes and weaves them into a coherent composition. Thus, the emphasis, in Nietzsche and others, on the role of interests and values in shaping thought is surely implicit in the existential humanist's conception of practice as the primary vehicle of understanding—for it is integral to the idea of purposeful practice that it answers to concerns, and hence to a sense of what is worth doing. Again, earlier references, by Dilthey and others, to the 'life-forms', *Gestalten*, and the like in

---

[32] *Being and Nothingness*, 15.

relation to which alone anything can be meaningful are recalled by the existential humanist's notion of a form of life to which meaningful items—be they words, things, actions, or whatever—ultimately refer us. Again, the hints dropped by Bergson and the pragmatists concerning the relation between meaning and practical use are taken up by the existential humanist and developed into his account of 'operative intentionality'.

Despite these points of continuity between earlier humanistic tendencies and existential humanism, there are also, as noted, differences. Thus, while the latter retains a perception of the centrality of 'creative agency'—of purposeful practice—this is now freed from the older 'sculptural', Promethean rhetoric. If one insists on speaking of human beings 'making' their world, this should not register the thought that they impose form on a cosmic porridge, but the insight that it is in and through typically unreflective 'coping' that a world of significant items can 'show up'.

There is also a difference from earlier tendencies in the tone, as it were, in which the centrality of agency is proclaimed—a difference related to existential humanism's divestment of the naturalistic leanings of previous versions. Possibly despite their intentions, earlier humanists often sound as if they are proposing what is, basically, a sociological thesis. The picture sometimes conjured is one of human beings swimming about in the world, unable quite to get at what its ingredients really are because of the distorting influence of desires, interests, perspectives, or values. That is not the picture intended by the existential humanist, who has a clearer perception of being engaged in philosophy, not sociology. Consider, for example, what Sartre has to say about the role of values. In encountering things and situations in our 'world of tasks', we are constantly experiencing them as 'lacks'—as calling for action on our part to repair them, adjust them, and so on because, relative to our purposes, they are not as they *should* be.[33] Evaluation, therefore, is integral to our very experience of things, not a dogged habit which we can't kick. The more general point is that the practices which register our interests and values do not prevent access to things visible, so to speak, to a disengaged spectator for whom those interests and values figure as obstacles that stand in our way. Rather it is precisely in and through our practices that access to things is possible, and the disengaged spectator for whom those practices merely distort is a myth. This is, admittedly, to jump ahead, for the

[33] Ibid. 85–95.

existential humanist has not yet shown that, once access to the world is secured, there cannot be an ascent to a disengaged cognition of it. His attempt to show this is not made until Chapter 8, when he takes on the real rivals to his position.

A 'Realist' Alternative?

How does the existential humanist proceed from his account of ex-istence, that 'intimate' relation between human beings and the world encountered as meaningful items 'lit up' through human practices, to the thesis of 'the human world'—to his 'anti-realist' denial that sense can be made of a deter-minate, discursable world independent of such practices? His strategy is one of counter-punch, of dealing with critics who stand in his path. If the world as it is ordinarily encountered is one from which 'the human contribution' cannot be removed, then there is a presumption in favour of the 'human world' thesis. It is up to critics to defeat that presumption.

With one kind of critic, whose resistance is only a verbal feint, he can be brief. This critic argues that the existential humanist's credentials as an anti-realist, indeed as a *humanist*, are spoiled by his insistence on the 'interdependence' of human practices and the world. An authentic anti-realist should be an 'idealist' or 'constructivist' for whom the only direction of dependence is from the world to us. By recognizing our 'intimate' dependence on the world in which we engage, the existential humanist shows that he is as much a realist as an anti-realist or humanist.[34] The short response to this is that an anti-realist or humanist does not need to be an idealist or constructivist. He is someone, simply, who rejects the realist thesis of an independent dis-cursable world. Whether he then proceeds, like certain idealists, to regard the world as a 'product' of mind or, like the existential humanist, to dismiss the notion of world-independent minds as well, is irrelevant.

With two other kinds of critic, existential humanists must contend at greater length. One kind is willing to concur in the existential humanist's account of our everyday, 'operative' encounters with the world, but insists

---

[34] This is how Jeff Malpas criticizes the view that 'the impossibility of separating everyday prac-tices and everyday objects' has anti-realist implications. 'The Fragility of Robust Realism: A Reply to Dreyfus and Spinosa', *Inquiry*, 42 (1999), 91–2.

that we are capable of ascending—or perhaps descending—to modes of experience and description that are not similarly shaped by, and reflective of, practical purposes and interests. The possibility, at least, exists of attaining to an 'absolute conception', disengaged from forms of life, of the world as it in itself is. Let's call critics of this sort 'absolutists', and speak of them as endorsing an 'independence' thesis in response to the 'human world' thesis. Absolutism, including the version that envisages the achievement by science of an 'absolute conception' of reality, is discussed in Chapters 7–8.

It is a different kind of critic who will now occupy us. This one agrees with the existential humanist that there can be no ascent to an absolute standpoint whose occupants have floated free from the concepts operative in everyday, engaged life. What this critic denies is that such concessions imply agreement with the thesis of 'the human world'. For him, the existential humanist's account of ex-istence is perfectly compatible with a robustly realist conception of the world, with an 'independence' thesis.

Critics of this second kind belong to a larger school of philosophers—'concept-bound realists', I'll label them—who, in recent years, have argued against relativists, constructivists, and their kin, whilst cheerfully accepting some of the premises on which such opponents often rely. Those premises are ones of an 'anti-foundationalist' type, directed especially against the view, espoused by some absolutists, that there is an unconceptualized 'given' against which the adequacy of the concepts and beliefs we form can be measured. These premises get picturesquely expressed by talk of the impossibility of 'getting outside our skins' so as to confront our concepts as a whole with the data of experience, or of obtaining a view 'from sideways on' of the correspondence between language and reality. The attitude of concept-bound realists to such premises is that they are virtual truisms, from which nothing dramatic could follow. Their suspicion is that, among relativists, epistemological nihilists, postmodernists, and others, 'the tautological is being transmuted into the tendentious'—as when the move is made from 'We can't describe anything except in language' to 'There is nothing outside language for our descriptions to represent accurately or inaccurately'.[35]

---

[35] Susan Haack, *Evidence and Inquiry: Towards Reconstruction in Epistemology* (Oxford: Blackwell, 1995), 184. Her particular target here is Rorty. Compare Michael Devitt and Kim Sterelny, *Language and Reality: An Introduction to the Philosophy of Language* (Oxford: Blackwell, 1987), 219, who take a

The more positive tenet of concept-bound realism is that the exercise of our concepts, and perhaps language, which experience presupposes is not a lamentable obstacle to encountering the world as it is, but a precondition of this. Except when we are 'misled', writes McDowell, our concept-bound experience 'takes in . . . how things anyway are', and is our mode of 'openness to the lay-out of reality'.[36] Donald Davidson agrees: there can be no experience, properly speaking, without language, one which, moreover, 'reflects our native interests and our historically accumulated needs and values'. Nevertheless, 'we perceive the world through language' and we should 'resist' the thought that truth is at all 'bent or distorted by language'.[37]

The target of concept-bound realists is wider than humanism, but sometimes it is Promethean and existential versions of the 'human world' thesis that are unmistakeably under attack. One finds it argued, for example, that practical interests indeed constrain what we experience and describe, just as the mesh of a fishing-net constrains which fish will be caught in it. But just as the latter constraint does not tell against the independence of fish from fishing, nor does the former preclude that it is an independent reality of which our conceptual 'nets' allow us admittedly partial views.[38] Again, it has been argued, by Maudemarie Clark, that Nietzsche's 'perspectivism'— which, we saw, emphasizes the ineliminability from experience and judgement of interest-related concepts—is perfectly compatible with 'commonsense realism'. This is because 'commonsense' or concept-bound realism requires only that the world has its own nature 'whether or not anyone actually knows what it is'. It does not require, in addition, that the truth of judgements should be unrelated to certain of our interests, such as one in the predictive success that theories must have if they are to serve us.[39] For

structuralist author to task for thinking it 'only a small step' to move from saying that language is our 'characteristic means of coping with the world' to saying that language 'constitutes the characteristic structure of human reality'.

[36] Mind and World, 25–6.

[37] Donald Davidson, 'Seeing through Language', in J. Preston (ed.), Thought and Language (Cambridge: Cambridge University Press, 1997), 17 and 27.

[38] See David Wiggins, 'On singling out an object determinately', in P. Pettit and J. McDowell (eds.), Subject, Thought and Context (Oxford: Oxford University Press, 1986). Wiggins defends a 'plural realism': just as different fishing-nets catch different but real enough fish, so conceptual 'nets' capture different but real enough ways the world is.

[39] Maudemarie Clark, Nietzsche on Truth and Philosophy (Cambridge: Cambridge University Press, 1990), 45. Clark claims not to be criticizing the mature Nietzsche who, she thinks, himself came to embrace 'commonsense realism' and to reject only an untenable 'metaphysical realism'. She sees herself, therefore, as criticizing only a younger Nietzsche and those Nietzscheans who have failed to

Clark, as for other concept-bound realists, proclamations of the 'human world' thesis are warranted, if at all, only as an antidote to an extreme realism that has strayed from common sense by severing all connection between reality and our 'cognitive interests'.

With much of the concept-bound realist's position, the existential humanist can sympathize. He agrees that it is illegitimate to move from truisms of the 'Any description of the world will be *our* description' variety to substantive conclusions. He agrees that concepts 'go all the way down' and that there can be no 'sideways-on' assessment of the adequacy of concepts to reality. He accepts that we should resist the thought that our language and concepts inevitably 'distort' how things are. Not only does he agree on these points, but he reminds his critics that it was philosophers of his persuasion, such as Heidegger, who were among the first to stress them—when rejecting the 'spectatorial' view of knowledge, for example, or when erasing the 'sculptural', Promethean image of conceptual imposition on a cosmic porridge.

It is with a certain tetchiness, then, that the existential humanist views weapons from his own arsenal being turned against him. He will complain, to begin with, that his position is being lumped together with ones that he, as much as his critics, impugns. In particular, he pleads innocent to the charge of moving straight to the 'human world' thesis from such anti-foundationalist slogans as 'We can't jump out of our conceptual skins' and 'Concepts reach all the way down'. It is not, for him, the mere fact that our experience and encounter with things are 'mediated' by concepts, but the way they are, which motivates that move. Indeed, he might agree that *if* certain rival notions of the place of concepts in experience were right, then talk of 'the human world' would be unwarranted. According to several concept-bound realists, for example, the primary employment of concepts is in 'active thinking': the only reason for speaking of conceptual capacities being 'drawn on in experience' is that judgements of experience are 'linked' to other judgements through inferential, 'rational relations'.[40] There is no

---

discern the Master's conversion to 'commonsense realism'. That Nietzsche underwent this conversion is hard to sustain unless, like Clark, one decides to ignore his remarks in *The Will to Power* and other late writings unpublished in his lifetime.

[40] McDowell, *Mind and World*, 11–12. For a similar view of the place of concepts, see Robert B. Brandom, *Making It Explicit: Reasoning, Representing, and Discursive Commitment* (Cambridge, Mass.: Harvard University Press, 1994).

indication in this account, as it stands, of a more primitive, pre-reflective conceptual capacity exercised in experience—the 'operative' capacity to encounter things as this or that which, if the existential humanist is right, is inseparable from the role of practices in allowing things to 'show up' as significant. The appreciation that experiences and exercises of concepts are those of people in the swim of a form of life, replete with the purposes and interests integral to that life, is at any rate more hospitable to talk of 'the human world' than a view according to which the primary exercise of concepts is performed by 'thinkers' occupied with 'rational relations' between judgements. That latter notion, conversely, encourages talk of our 'openness to the world' more than one which might instead inspire images of our being 'caught up in' and 'fallen into' particular ways of life.

With the distinctive character of his premises understood, the existential humanist will now express puzzlement as to how a critic can concede these, yet baulk at the 'human world' thesis. What, for example, does talk of experiencing the world as it really is amount to once it is conceded, as by Davidson, that experience requires the exercise of a language which 'reflects' our native and historical interests and needs? Recall, in this connection, Clark's attempt to combine a 'commonsense realism' with Nietzsche's interest-based 'perspectivism'. The puzzle here is to understand why, if the world has an independent nature or constitution, this is not something it has irrespective of *any* interests—in prediction and control, for example—that constrain the theories we could accept.[41] To concede that no sense can be made of how the world is apart from such interests surely rescinds the idea of its having an independent nature or constitution.

Recall, too, the suggestion that, while any conceptual scheme must reflect practical purposes and interests, this merely shows that it only partially captures the order of things—like a net which lets in only some of the fish. This attempt to combine a humanist premise with ('plural') realism collapses once the question is pressed whether we can have access to the order of things other than through our interest-related conceptual 'nets'.[42] If, as the fishing-net analogy suggests, we can, then the concession to humanism

---

[41] Peter Poellner, *Nietzsche and Metaphysics* (Oxford: Clarendon Press, 1995), 24, expresses the same puzzlement.

[42] Jane Heal, *Fact and Meaning: Quine and Wittgenstein on the Philosophy of Language* (Oxford: Blackwell, 1989), 168 ff, criticizes Wiggins along similar lines.

turns out to have been bogus: for it is being allowed that we may, after all, transcend our interests, just as we can tell what fish there are in the sea without having an interest in catching them. If we cannot, then this is either because one has conceded the 'human world' thesis (no sense can be made of an independent order of things) or because one thinks there is a conceptually inaccessible, undiscursable order of things. Accepting the first disjunct is to give up the realist objection to humanism; accepting the second is to renounce concept-bound realism in favour of some other variety—'noumenal' realism, or whatever.

The puzzle, then, concerns the status of the concept-bound critic's proclamations of realism, despite the concessions made to humanists and their relatives. In the existential humanist's opinion, none of the motives, explicit or implicit, for these proclamations is compelling. Some of them, indeed, are distinctly feeble. Sometimes, for example, the proclamations of realism are made, it seems, in a purely *pis-aller* spirit: concept-bound, 'modest', 'internal', or whatever realism is the best one can aspire to given that more traditional versions of realism ('metaphysical', 'noumenal', etc.) have been exposed as too silly to countenance.[43] In the existential humanist's view, this is like describing the sparkling plonk, which was the best we could afford, as a champagne—a 'modest' one, of course. Anyway, he does not agree that there are no traditional versions of realism that deserve to be taken seriously, for example the absolutist one to be examined in Chapter 8. Another peculiar strategy is to proclaim oneself a realist in virtue of subscribing to a position that is at any rate *more* 'realist' than some very 'minimal' ones that someone or other has nevertheless described as 'realist'. For example, the concept-bound realist may rightly insist that he is proposing something more robust than, merely, that a distinction may be made between P's being the case and someone's believing that P. But, of course, it is eccentric to hold that one is a realist—even a 'minimal' one—merely because one makes that distinction. In that case, however, no one proves their realist credentials merely by subscribing to something a bit stronger than that. One may as well claim to be a democrat on the grounds that one is at least *more* of a democrat than, say, a fan of the old German Democratic Republic.

---

[43] See, for example, Putnam's defence of the label 'internal realism' in the Preface to his *Realism and Reason: Philosophical Papers, Vol. 3* (Cambridge: Cambridge University Press, 1983).

A more interesting motive is suggested by some remarks of John McDowell's, alluded to in note 26 to Chapter 3 (p. 67). McDowell argues, in effect, that Kant would never have made noises of a humanist or idealist kind, describing the empirical world as lacking independent reality, were he not already committed to a noumenal order in comparison with which the phenomenal world has only a 'fraudulent' claim to reality. Once that dichotomy is abandoned, insistence that the world is 'only' a human one loses its point. (Nietzsche, we saw, made a similar observation: p. 5 above.) I have already questioned this diagnosis of Kant's idealistic idiom (p. 67), pointing out, for example, that his case for the ideality of space and time does not obviously presuppose the existence of things in themselves. Certainly the existential humanist will reject a similar diagnosis of his own embrace of the 'human world' thesis. That thesis requires no acceptance of an independent, undiscursable reality. The humanist's point is not that the discursable world is a 'veil' masking such a reality, but that it is one whose description is bound to register human interests and purposes. No such description, therefore, can pretend to be of the 'objective' kind that a puta- tively detached observer would provide, and to count, therefore, as a description of the kind whose feasibility the rhetoric of realism primes one to expect.

Yet another motive for proclamations of realism is suggested by Davidson's and McDowell's remarks, cited a few pages back (p. 121), to the effect that we are committed to realism by accepting that, except when we are 'misled', our thought and talk about things do not 'distort' how they are. The existential humanist, however, rejects the dichotomy implied here. Our thought and talk in general neither distort the way the world anyway is nor get it right, for there is no way the world anyway is. It is incumbent on the humanist, certainly, to preserve a distinction, at the level of more particular thoughts and statements, between truth and falsity—but this is something he claims to do without invoking the notion of the world as it anyway is (see Chapter 9). Moreover, the existential humanist will continue, it can anyway be misleading to pose the issue of realism as one about the adequacy of *thought* to the world. It indeed sounds wrong to suppose that our considered judgements might be inadequate, on any massive scale, to the world. One can agree with Robert Brandom that the 'conceptually articulated grasp' manifested in such judgements is a genuine grasp of 'a conceptually articu- lated world—the world consisting of everything that is the case, all the facts, and the objects they are about'.[44] What the existential humanist insists, however, is that this world is 'the human world', the one whose objects only 'show up' in, and are dependent upon, our practices. That world indeed has a conceptual articulation which reflective thought can 'grasp': but this is an articulation, as Heidegger emphasizes, 'grounded in' our being-in-the-world, an articulation inseparable from that 'primordial' mode of 'interpretation'—of encountering things 'as'— whose vehicle is not 'theoretical statements', but 'concerned', active engagement.[45] Certainly, thought and talk do not 'produce' the articulated world, but that does not mean—to risk a bit of 'sculptural' rhetoric—that it is not 'produced' at all.

A final factor that lurks behind some concept-bound critics' proclamations of realism is of a meta-philosophical kind. Like myself, Anthony Grayling is puzzled by the refusal of these critics frankly to declare an *anti-realist* affiliation. He speculates that, in their view, traditional 'philosophical problems prompted by reflection on the relation of thought (etc.) to the world just have no content' and our concepts are in order just as 'they seem to be when we are sufficiently unreflective about them'.[46] The view identified here—sometimes referred to as 'quietism'—is one advocated by several writers who have taken to heart Wittgenstein's remark that philosophy leaves everything as it is. As understood by Grayling, their point, in the present context, seems to be that, at the 'unreflective' level, we apply concepts to things without a sense, typically, that these things 'depend on us'—or indeed with a sense that they do *not*. 'From "inside" our ways of thinking . . .', Barry Stroud puts it, 'only realism seems correct.'[47] If, therefore, we remain at that level or on the 'inside', our idiom will be a thoroughly realist one: and if, to boot, we *ought* to remain at that level, eschewing the old 'philosophical problems', then the only proper idiom will be that of unreflective realism. There will then be no level at which, so to speak, what the anti-realist wants to say can be sensibly said.

---

[44] *Making It Explicit*, 623.

[45] *Being and Time*, 200.

[46] Anthony Grayling, *Introduction to Philosophical Logic*, 3rd ed. (Oxford: Blackwell, 1997), 293. Grayling includes Putnam, Davidson, and Wittgenstein among those whose 'non-anti-realistic anti-realism' he finds so slippery.

[47] Barry Stroud, 'The Allure of Idealism', *Proceedings of the Aristotelian Society, Supp. Vol.*, 58 (1984), 257.

The existential humanist makes two responses to this quietism—over and above an expression of the qualms that many people must share with him about the authority with which unreflective talk is being invested by quietists. First, in *ad hominem* style, he will point out that when quietists diagnose—as, at some point, they must—people's unreflective realist idiom, the diagnosis typically fails either to preserve anything that the unreflective users of that idiom would own to or to justify the quietist's proclamations of commonsense realism. Consider, for example, one quietist sympathizer's assertion that claims about how things independently and anyway are should not be construed as stating truths about reality—for that would be to attribute too reflective, too 'metaphysical', a stance to ordinary speakers. Rather, such claims should be construed as 'grammatical' ones 'registering what we *allow* to be said'.[48] Not only would this construal be resisted by most speakers but, treated as an account of what their idiom, despite that resistance, must 'really' be registering, it is surely an *anti*-realist diagnosis. Just as it is music to the atheist's ear to hear that 'God exists' can only register certain human emotions or needs, so it is welcome news to the anti-realist that 'This is the way reality anyway is' only registers 'our' determinations and permissions as to what can be said.

The existential humanist's second response, predictably, is that, despite reflectively engaging with the old 'philosophical problems', he *has* managed to say something sensible. He has provided an account of human ex-istence which, if well taken, lends sense to the idea that what our concepts apply to are meaningful, sign-like items which only 'show up' within practices integrated into a form of life—an idea which, unless genuine obstacles are put in the way, naturally leads to the notion of those items belonging only to a 'human world'. Something more than distaste for departures from the unreflective level is needed to impugn the intelligibility of that account.[49]

[48] Cora Diamond, *The Realistic Spirit: Wittgenstein, Philosophy and the Mind* (Cambridge, Mass.: MIT Press, 1995), 215.

[49] The existential humanist will also claim that his account of ex-istence and his counters to the concept-bound realist furnish a sufficiently clear sense of the 'dependence' of things on human life to answer Simon Blackburn's scepticism (see n. 14 above) concerning the intelligibility of any notion of dependence other than that of an empirical kind—the kind exemplified, say, by the dependence of hammers on their manufacturers. See his *Ruling Passions*, 311–12.

Concepts, World, and Life

With the rejection of various motives for refusal of the 'human world' thesis, the question arises whether there is any tenet of concept-bound critics that would both register a substantive disagreement with humanism and provide warrant for their realist idiom. Perhaps what is sometimes referred to as 'the contractual model of meaning' would perform both these roles. According to this model, once a concept or word-meaning is established, the concept or word acquires 'a definite pattern of application which . . . extends "of itself" to new cases quite without further assistance from us'.[50] 'Contractualists' might agree with Wittgenstein that the concepts we possess owe to our interests, education, and the like, and hence do not 'reside . . . in the nature of things',[51] but they will insist that, whatever the genesis of these concepts, their subsequent careers—how they get applied—owes simply to the world. The factors which the existential humanist emphasizes—practices, forms of life, values, and so on—shape only the genesis of concepts, not their careers. To the extent that the correctness of a concept's application to new items is independent of those factors—that it is determined solely by those items themselves—it would be appropriate to invoke a realist idiom. That 'things are . . . thus and so anyway' might be read as recording that 'the pattern of application that we grasp, when we come to understand [a] concept . . . extends, independently' of, inter alia, our judgements and interests.[52] To the extent that reference to 'the human world' suggests that application is 'up to us', it is thoroughly misleading.

The existential humanist rejects the contractual model. He can, to be sure, accept that a pattern of application of concepts 'extends independently' of judgements and interests if that means, simply, that we are typically 'passive' when we describe a dog, say, as a dog. We do not, normally, need to

---

[50] Bob Hale, 'Rule-Following, Objectivity and Meaning', in Bob Hale and Crispin Wright (eds.), *A Companion to the Philosophy of Language* (Oxford: Blackwell, 1997), 380. This article usefully surveys debates adjacent to the one which presently concerns us, notably the exchanges between Crispin Wright and John McDowell on the relation between 'objectivity' (or 'investigation-independence') and criteria of meaning. Hale's sympathies are with the modified 'anti-realism' of Wright—sympathies shared by the existential humanist, though he advances considerations rather different from Wright's.

[51] See, for example, *Philosophical Investigations*, 230, and *Zettel* (Oxford: Blackwell 1967), §§ 357–8, 387–8.

[52] John McDowell, 'Wittgenstein on Following a Rule', *Synthese*, 58 (1984), 325.

agonize about and 'decide' on the appropriate description. This much was cheerfully conceded by the existential humanist when distancing himself from Promethean humanism (p. 103 above). But he will reject the idea of independent extension if that amounts to something more substantial than the admission of a 'passivity' that, he is confident, his own position can accommodate. For him, as for Wittgenstein on Jane Heal's interpretation, 'to use any concept is to make a move in one sort of life rather than another', and thereby to testify to 'the interconnectedness of our concepts, practices and interests'. The supposition that the whole burden of determining the acceptable use of a concept 'falls entirely on the world' is a 'will o' the wisp', the fantasy of a 'mirroring realism' according to which the careers of concepts should proceed along 'the real joints at which the world is . . . sliced'.[53] The idea that our practical engagements should shape the array of concepts we possess, yet play no role in determining their subsequent extension, is unappealing. The point is not an empirical one, analogous to incredulity that the personal interests which drove someone to acquire possessions should then in no way influence what he or she does with them. The point, rather, is that the sharp distinction made by the 'contractualist' between coming to possess a concept and using it is artificial. To possess a concept is not to come by some booty, store it in a 'mental museum', and occasionally give it an airing. It is, to recall Heal's words, a capacity to make moves in a sort of life, and to respond to the similarities between new items and old by which we are impressed. What that capacity is—what the concept it registers extends to—cannot be determined independently of our interests and practices: not, at any rate, if the existential humanist's claims about the interconnectedness of practices and judgements of similarity are well taken.

It might seem incumbent on the humanist to cite some clear-cut examples where interests rather than the world determine how concepts have been applied. Such a demand, however, betrays a misunderstanding. As Heal rightly emphasizes, the thesis is one of 'the interdependence of concepts and interests', not of 'the *priority* of interests over concepts'.[54] The idea, that is, is not the 'sculptural', Promethean one that we generally

---

[53] Heal, *Fact and Meaning*, 226–7, 190, 210.
[54] Ibid. 176.

consult our practical purposes and then decide how items will be conceptualized. Clear-cut examples where *that* happens—as when lawmakers
decided, for reasons of legal simplicity, to call roller-skates 'vehicles'—do *not*
illustrate the general way in which interests and concepts are interdependent. On the contrary, such examples do not exemplify the same concept
being applied to new items, but a change of concept. ('Vehicle' has been
given a special meaning in the law.) The existential humanist in no way
denies that, where the same concept is being applied to new items, there is a
sense that the application is *compelled*—a sense missing in those cases where
interests and purposes are explicitly consulted before deciding to call an item
this or that. That we feel so compelled, he will add, is due, of course, to 'the
sort of life' we live.

While he rightly resists furnishing examples of the type envisaged in the
previous paragraph, the existential humanist is not reluctant to provide
examples which serve to sharpen awareness of the interdependence of concepts, interests, and life. That purpose would be served by cases where it
seems fairly obviously true that a concept which has had a certain career—
has gone on to be applied to certain items, but not to others—might easily
have had a different career which it would be invidious or 'whiggish' to
regard as a perverse or deviant one. Its actual, historical application might
have felt natural, even compulsory: yet we can easily imagine that, had life
gone a bit differently, other applications would have struck us as equally natural. An example often used in this connection is that of games. It is not hard
to imagine that people with a way of life not markedly different from our
own would have found it natural to apply the concept to what we, instead,
have classified as rituals, say, or have described as games but with a sense of
speaking metaphorically. Similarities between novel activities and paradigm
examples of games might have been salient for them in a way they were not
for us. It matters little whether we say that these people would have changed
the idea of a game or that they would, simply, have been applying it to activities that we too might have done, but in fact did not. The important thing is
that nothing in the earlier understanding of the concept determined a pattern of application independent of judgements and responses that are
moves in a way of life.

The example of games might appear too special to illustrate a general
phenomenon. Indeed, it may seem unsurprising that the application of a
concept to a certain kind of purposeful activity should itself be sensitive to

purposes and interests. It would be politic, therefore, for the existential humanist to show that a concept whose application might appear to be wholly independent of practical purpose fails, on reflection, to obey the 'contractual model'. Consider, then, colour concepts. While our having the particular colour concepts we do presumably reflects our way of life—remember the eskimos and their snow—the usual view is that the correct application of these concepts, once in place, is wholly dictated by the world's impingement upon us. This view, according to the existential humanist, is mistaken. That we call things red even when it is too dark to see them properly, or under conditions of lighting where, to the uneducated eye, they look to be some other colour—these and many other features of our use of 'red' are explicable only by reference to broad purposes that the vocabulary of colour serves. Crudely, but crucially, our use of that vocabulary registers an interest in prediction. Since the behaviour of an object is rarely affected by the lighting conditions under which we view it, and since there are often correlations between its behaviour and its colour—brown apples rot, grey clouds presage rain—various features of our uses of colour terms are just what we would expect if they are to serve our interest in predicting what things will do.[55] Had we been inveterate aesthetes, whose interest in colours was—like Walter Pater's, apparently—confined to the delicious or offensive sensations they provide, our colour talk might have been very different. We might, for instance, happily have spoken of the apple's ceasing to be brown as night falls.

It matters little whether one says that the aesthetes have different colour concepts from ours or that, simply, they apply them differently. The important thing is that the burden of determining the acceptable application of concepts is seen, once more, not to fall entirely on the world. Like the concept of a game, though less obviously so, the use of our colour concepts testifies to the interdependence of concepts and interests. As Merleau-Ponty puts it, our concepts and words are not a 'simple notation' mirroring the order of things: rather, they are ones 'into which the history of a whole language is compressed', a history inextricable from the wider history of those 'fundamental activit[ies] whereby man projects himself towards a

---

[55] Related points are made by Heal, ibid. 197 ff, Charles Travis, 'On Constraints of Generality', *Proceedings of the Aristotelian Society*, 94 (1994), and Alasdair MacIntyre, 'Colors, Cultures, and Practices', *Midwest Studies in Philosophy*, 17 (1992).

"world"'.[56] That ongoing history is inevitably at work in shaping the application of concepts and words, and we need only reflect on how different that application might have been had aspects of our 'fundamental activities' themselves been different. One is tempted to say that it is a lack of imaginative reflection which is responsible for a 'contractual model' on which the world alone, and not 'man's project', carries the burden of settling what is what.

The existential humanist must deal with more critics than those discussed in this section. But if his response to these concept-bound critics is right, then at least one type of obstacle to moving from his account of ex-istence to the thesis of 'the human world' has been removed. For he has tried to show that, once his account of ex-istence is conceded, as it is by many concept-bound critics, their persistence in a realist idiom opposed to the notion of 'the human world' is without warrant. The existential humanist's further struggles will be charted in later chapters, following a brief interlude during which an earlier promise is redeemed.

---

[56] *Phenomenology of Perception*, 188, 191.

CHAPTER 6

Interlude:
Rival Humanisms

The story told over the preceding chapters has stretched from a certain response to the 'Ockhamist' rejection of 'the Augustinian heritage', seven hundred years ago, to the emergence of a twentieth-century philosophy that continues to appeal to many contemporary thinkers. It has taken us from a fledgling to a mature humanism. That label was not chosen arbitrarily. I suggested in Chapter 1 that it is a more suitable one than several contenders for the tendency of thought I have charted, and my story has occasionally been punctuated by brief justifications for choosing it. Indeed, the story as a whole was intended, in part, to justify the label and thereby contribute to an understanding of humanism. However, I also pointed in Chapter 1 to the obvious fact that my way of understanding the term 'humanism' is not the only one on the market. Since the term is variously used, it would be cavalier simply to reject rival characterizations as 'mistaken': but I argue in this brief chapter that not only do these involve misconceptions, but that, by a number of reasonable criteria, my own characterization has the better claim to capture a currently central understanding of humanism within philosophy. (Readers who are not especially taxed by the issue of the best characterization of humanism may prefer to proceed straightaway to Chapter 7, where critical consideration of existential humanism gets underway.)

The words 'within philosophy' are significant, for there are characterizations of a 'popular' kind that are not rivals to my own since they do not even pretend to capture a concept whose main domicile is philosophy. One thinks, for example, of humanism in the sense of humanitarianism, or as the study of the *literae humaniores*, but also of humanism as the resolution to focus on human well-being, or as a 'triumphalist' celebration of the sort expressed by a Chekhov character who proclaims that 'man must regard himself as higher . . . than anything [else] in nature . . . otherwise he is not a man, but a mouse'.[1]

With such 'popular' characterizations set aside, mine is left with three rivals, regarded by their champions as identifying the broad thought at the core of western philosophical humanism. These rivals, briefly mentioned early in Chapter 2, understand by humanism a doctrine of, in turn, human essence, naturalism, and rational subjectivity. Before considering them, I recommend three criteria that, surely, it is desirable for a characterization to satisfy. First, it should capture a position whose spokesmen as well as its critics have actually referred to as humanism. Second, given the pervasive charge of humanism levelled by environmental thinkers, a characterization should make it readily understandable why the position characterized is a critical target in these circles. Finally, there should be historical justification: the position characterized must be intelligibly related to, preferably heir to, older views whose humanistic pedigree is not in question.

By those three criteria, my own understanding of humanism fares well. Marx, James, Schiller, Dewey, and Sartre were self-confessed humanists, using the term in ways closely akin to my own for a thesis of 'the human world'. It is now familiar, moreover, for scholars who think that Kant subscribed to that thesis to describe him as a humanist. 'Humanism' is also the label employed, we saw, by such critics of that thesis as Nagel and the later Heidegger. Second, it should be readily understandable why my humanists should be a critical target of environmentalism. 'Self-assertion' in the shape of technological control of nature has been a recurrent theme in the development of humanism, culminating in Marx's perception of nature as 'simply an object for mankind', a theatre for creative agency, and Jünger's view of technology as impressing the Worker's *Gestalt* upon a 'totally mobilized' natural world. In both cases, technological 'self-assertion' is explicitly linked with a Promethean notion of a natural world devoid of any structure beyond that imposed by schemes of human thought. It is easy to appreciate, therefore, why the later Heidegger, whose understanding of the technological *Gestalt* is borrowed from Jünger, should regard the critique of technology as being of a piece with criticism of humanist metaphysics. If we are to 'let things be', we must first recognize their intrinsic integrity. One can

[1] Anton Chekhov, *Lady With a Lapdog and Other Stories* (Harmondsworth: Penguin, 1964), 219.

appreciate, as well, why contemporary environmental thinkers, such as Stephen Clark, continue to regard humanism in my sense as a main villain of the piece—especially in the context of a recent 'green backlash' from sociologists, a main platform of which has been an insistence that nature is only a 'social construct'. In a book indicatively titled *Against Nature*, the implication of its author's remark that nature 'never appears as it "is" but rather always as already the nature of a particular social order' is that technological 'interference' in nature is only a continuation by other means of that more fundamental 'interference' whereby there is 'nature' in the first place.[2]

Finally, my whole story, if accurately told, is historical justification for understanding humanism as I do: for there is a relatively smooth path to be traced from the leading philosophical themes of Renaissance humanism to the Promethean tendencies of Marx's humanism and later humanisms, such as pragmatism and 'reactionary modernism'. To that story I add just one general comment: when intellectual historians speak, appropriately enough, of the humanist tenor of a period of thought—of 'Chinese humanism' in the classical period, for example—they usually have in mind the pivotal place which, in that period, reflection on human beings plays in a wider reflection on reality. One commentator on 'the classic age' of Islamic and Jewish philosophy, for instance, describes its leading figures as 'portend[ing] a humanism', though not, of course, one which is 'in opposition to theism': rather 'it is a humanism in that it speaks insistently from the role that it assigns to man'.[3] One does not have to be a humanist in my sense of embracing the thesis of 'the human world' in order to be a humanist in this wider sense. But my humanists are vivid instances of thinkers for whom there can be no understanding of the world at large independently of an understanding of human existence. As such, my characterization of humanism locates it within a tradition at odds with one that affords no special place to reflection on human beings in the endeavour to delineate the reality to which they belong. That, as we will now see, is more than can be said for the rival characterizations.

---

[2] Steven Vogel, *Against Nature: The Concept of Nature in Critical Theory* (New York: SUNY Press, 1996), 37. I am indebted to Gill Aitken, 'A New Approach to Conservation' (Ph.D. diss., Lancaster University, 1999), for referring me to this and other works mentioned in this section.

[3] Lenn E. Goodman, *Jewish and Islamic Philosophy: Crosspollinations in the Classic Age* (Edinburgh: Edinburgh University Press, 1999), 29–30.

With the first, 'essentialist', rival, I shall be brief, since either it cannot be taken seriously or it collapses into the other rival positions. Louis Althusser charges the young Marx, who concerned us in Chapter 4, with humanism and congratulates the older Marx on his anti-humanism. The difference, it seems, is that the former postulated a 'definite pre-existing essence' of human beings, while the latter rejected any such doctrine of an 'ideal essence'.[4] But what does reference to a human essence amount to? It might indicate—though this is not what Althusser intends—that human beings constitute a 'natural kind', a view I discuss shortly. Or it might mean that there are defining properties necessary and sufficient for counting as a human being. This seems to be the meaning of those who equate the doctrine of a human essence with there being a 'determinate answer to the question of what it is to be human'.[5] If this is the intended meaning, it is hard to see what 'essentialism' has to do with humanism. Certainly it fails my three criteria. For a start, I can think of no self-confessed humanist who counts himself as such simply on the grounds of holding that there is, in this sense, a human essence. Indeed, some of them seem explicitly to reject this essentialism—as when (young) Marx denies that there is an essence 'inherent in each separate individual' and locates the essentially human in 'the ensemble of social relations' (see p. 81 above), or when Sartre identifies the 'fundamental meaning' of humanism with *rejection* of a 'pre-existing [human] essence'.[6]

Second, it is impossible to see how essentialism of this sort could, by itself, be a sensible target of environmentalist critique. At most, it might be a prelude to an objectionable definition of 'man'. When Heidegger writes that every humanism 'has presupposed [a] universal "essence" of man', it is not this presupposition that he complains about, but the particular specifications of that essence which have prevailed.[7] Finally, essentialism so understood has no historical warrant for providing a characterization of humanism. Some Renaissance humanists may have been essentialists, but

---

[4] From L. Althusser, *For Marx*, trans. B. Brewster, in W. McNeill and K. Feldman (eds.), *Continental Philosophy: An Anthology* (Oxford: Blackwell, 1998), 273 and 275.

[5] See e.g. David Owen, *Maturity and Modernity: Nietzsche, Weber, Foucault and the Ambivalence of Reason* (London: Routledge, 1994), 221.

[6] Jean-Paul Sartre, *Existentialism and Humanism*, trans. P. Mairet (London: Methuen, 1966), 55 and 28.

[7] 'Letter on Humanism', in *Basic Writings: Martin Heidegger*, ed. D. F. Krell (London: Routledge, 1993), 226.

that is not why they were humanists: and some of them appear to reject essentialism. Recall Pico's remark that in contrast with other creatures, whose nature is 'defined and restricted', a human being is the 'shaper' of his own nature and being (p. 42 above).

It is not, then, the bare doctrine of essentialism which could constitute humanism, but only some versions of what the human essence consists in. Predictably, Althusser turns out to have a rather particular version in mind, not just the general idea of 'a definite pre-existing essence'. It is the doctrine of 'liberal-rationalist humanism', to the effect that 'the essence of man makes history, and this essence is freedom and reason', which is 'the philosophical myth of man' that Althusser wants 'reduced to ashes'.[8] This characterization of humanism is closely in line with Foucault's, to which I shortly turn.

One thing, I suggested, that might be intended by speaking of a human essence is that human beings are a natural kind, and in a more interesting sense than, merely, that they are members of a species. The idea would be that 'human being' is a natural kind term since it 'rigidly designates' creatures with underlying properties of a sort exposed by the natural sciences, ones deemed explanatory of the phenomenal or 'manifest' properties on the basis of which our everyday identifications of creatures as human typically proceed. Those underlying properties are essential to counting as human rather as, some hold, being H_2O is essential to counting as water.[9] This is a thesis about the type of meaning possessed by the term 'human', and one to which not all of those who characterize humanism as naturalism may subscribe. What they do subscribe to, however, is the thought that human life may, in principle, be exhaustively accounted for in natural scientific terms.

For reasons rarely made explicit, 'humanism' suggested itself to several writers—especially those associated with the American and British Humanist Associations—as a suitable term for this type of scientism. For Sydney Hook, 'scientific humanism'—the only serious sort—is equivalent

---

[8] *For Marx*, 272.
[9] I allude here to the understanding of natural kinds and essence made familiar by Saul Kripke, *Naming and Necessity* (Oxford: Blackwell, 1980). A natural kind term, like 'water' (allegedly), is said to 'rigidly designate' if it refers to the same stuff—H_2O, as it has turned out—in all possible worlds, irrespective of the stuff's phenomenal properties, such as being drinkable or tasteless.

to 'naturalism', while Roy Wood Sellars's humanism is a 'physical naturalism' perfectly capable of 'fit[ting] man into the picture' and explaining 'the
development of human culture'.[10] Two motives behind such characterizations might be these: in calling naturalism 'humanistic', one emphasizes, to
begin with, that men and women are, in the first—and indeed last—
instance, members of a species, and not, say, immortal souls; and one registers, second, that, with the 'supernatural' excluded, moral attention can
squarely focus on 'the welfare of human beings', not accordance with 'God's
will' (see p. 64).

So, the characterization of humanism as naturalism meets my first criterion: it is adopted by some self-confessed humanists. Two points should be
added, however. First, I have been at pains to show that the apparent naturalism of several of *my* self-confessed humanists, such as Dewey, was either
bogus or at odds with the basis for their humanism. Second, while naturalism or scientism has indeed been the target of much criticism, it is never
under the heading of 'humanism' that it is attacked. When, for example,
McDowell criticizes it, he does so under the heading of 'bald naturalism',
and for that reason has himself been described as a humanist.[11]

If critics of naturalism do not refer to it as humanism, nor do critics of
humanism have naturalism in mind. This is true, in particular, of humanism's environmental critics, from whose lips such naturalistic slogans as
'Man is just part of nature' are more than familiar. The reference by the
editor of *The Humanist* to science's demonstration that man is not a 'special
product', with its implication that 'anthropocentrism [is] laid to rest', is
music to most environmentalist ears.[12] The humanism they decry is guilty
of hubristically placing humankind above the rest of nature. Now, whatever
the faults of the naturalism embraced by Hook, Sellars, and others, that is
not one of them. Some environmental philosophers with humanism in
their sights do, it is true, attack the notion of human beings as a natural kind,
for they think there is something arbitrary in dividing nature's creatures into
distinct kinds. They do so, however, not out of any anti-naturalistic animus,
but because, in their view, a science of nature properly informed by ecology

[10] In P. Kurtz (ed.), *The Humanist Alternative: Some Definitions of Humanism* (London: Pemberton,
1973), 33 and 137.
[11] John Haldane, 'Rational and Other Animals', in A. O'Hear (ed.), Verstehen *and Humane
Understanding* (Cambridge: Cambridge University Press, 1996), 21.
[12] Paul Kurtz, in his introduction to *The Humanist Alternative*, 5.

would abandon the categories of individual and species or kind. Instead, it would recognize the primacy of 'process' and 'relation', with the individual insect or man 'reduced' to a mere 'node' or 'intersection' of such processes and relations.[13]

The characterization of humanism as naturalism does no better by my third criterion of historical warrant. Humanists in and around the Renaissance period, I argued, were animated, from Petrarch to Montaigne, by the conviction that not only was cultural history irreducibly necessary for explaining the ways of men, but that—through displaying the prejudices of each age—history must inspire scepticism towards global claims of the sort aspired to by the natural sciences. Moreover, as Gadamer remarks, the emphasis of these thinkers was on the human capacity to 'break with the immediate and the natural', to 'wrench free' from nature.[14] This is a tendency continued, we have seen, down to such modern self-confessed humanists as Marx (with some vacillation) and Sartre (with none). When earlier humanists spoke of the importance of nature in human history, this was 'second nature', the human environment of building, trade, art, and so on, whose creation by men and women sets them apart from all other creatures. Humanism and naturalism have a common source in their rejection of theological metaphysics, but my argument in earlier chapters was that they represent opposed reactions to that rejection. Naturalism—in the shape, for example, of eighteenth-century materialism—emerged from a 'reaffirmation of reason' and was 'business as usual' in the sense of aspiring to the delineation of an objective order of things. Humanism rejects that aspiration, whether in the form of a theological or scientific metaphysics.

The point just made recurs when appraising the third rival characterization of humanism, as a doctrine of rational subjectivity, to which I now turn. The essentialism attacked by Althusser was, it turned out, a 'liberal-rationalist humanism' according to which 'the essence of man is freedom and reason'. Whether or not they use the vocabulary of essence, what many contemporary opponents of humanism—notably, Foucault—attack is some such idea of human beings as autonomous rational subjects. Foucault,

---

[13] This is a main theme in Neill Evernden, *The Natural Alien: Humankind and Environment* (Toronto: University of Toronto Press, 1985).

[14] Hans-Georg Gadamer, *Truth and Method*, trans. W. Glen-Doepel (London: Sheed & Ward, 1981), 13.

in fact, discusses humanism in two different, though related, ways. In some places, he means by 'humanism' our 'modern thought about man, our concern for him' as a 'problematical' being, the subject-matter of the human sciences. 'As constituted in modern thought', Foucault argues, man appears as a 'strange empirico-transcendental doublet', a creature standing at once within the empirical order and outside of it as the source for all knowledge of that order.[15] This is perceptive: from the time of Kant, with whom the issue of the 'empirico-transcendental doublet' becomes acute, we saw several of my humanists, or their precursors, failing to reconcile a Promethean image of human beings 'constituting' their world with a naturalistic urge to place them within it.

Elsewhere, however, Foucault means by 'humanism' one of the sides taken on the issue posed by 'modern thought'—by humanism, in the first sense, that is. 'The theory of the subject', he writes, 'is at the heart of humanism'—the subject being, inter alia, what 'rul[es] the body' and is 'sovereign in the context of judgement'.[16] It is a theory that 'gives absolute priority to the observing subject', or 'knowing subject', and inexorably 'leads to a transcendental consciousness'.[17] In one commentator's words, humanism, for Foucault, is 'the grounding of reason, history and truth in the figure of the transcendentally free and creative subject'.[18] For the humanist, in this sense, a human being is an autonomous individual consciousness, at once the shaper of history and the ascertainer of truth and right, capable as he is of a detached, rational survey of the world, society, and language. Since, in Foucault's view, this conception of human beings is a myth, we can cheerfully anticipate the day when man will be 'erased, like a face drawn in the sand at the edge of the sea'.[19]

Perhaps one scores only a hollow victory against this characterization by noting that no modern philosopher has, to my knowledge, called himself a humanist in virtue of subscribing to what Foucault calls the 'theory of the knowing subject'. This is because few recent philosophers subscribe to that theory at all. The testimony of those who do, however, does nothing to

---

[15] Michel Foucault, *The Order of Things: An Archaeology of the Human Sciences* (London: Tavistock, 1970), 318 ff.

[16] *Language, Counter-Memory, Practice: Selected Essays and Interviews*, trans. D. Bouchard and S. Simon (Oxford: Blackwell, 1977), 221 f.

[17] *The Order of Things*, p. xiv.

[18] Owen, *Maturity and Modernity*, 221.   [19] *The Order of Things*, 387.

endorse Foucault. Husserl, who indeed postulates a 'transcendental con-sciousness', remarks that, in 'reducing' the empirical self to a transcenden-tal one, he 'puts out of play' the '*human* ego'—which hardly suggests that Husserl could have welcomed the name 'humanism' for his procedure.[20] As for perhaps the best-known contemporary philosopher with some sympa-thy for 'the theory of the knowing subject', Thomas Nagel, we have already encountered his declared adherence to 'a strong form of *anti-humanism*' (p. 7).

Turning to my second criterion, Foucauldian humanism has been a declared target of several environmental thinkers. Earlier I quoted one writ-er's suggestion that it is the view of man as '"outside" the reality . . . given to him in consciousness' which 'endorses an instrumental' attitude towards nature (p. 16). Another asserts that this instrumental ideology 'rests upon a dualistic image of the relationship between human beings' and nature, and is committed to 'Cartesian rationality'.[21] It is unclear, however, why these writers connect transcendental subjectivity with instrumentalism. Two thoughts, perhaps, encourage the connection, neither of them compelling. The first is that a transcendental consciousness, being 'outside' the world, is not 'integrated' with nature in a manner to encourage a sense of caring dependency. But why, one wonders, wouldn't the attitude of this detached 'knowing subject' be one of aesthetic contemplation—as Schopenhauer in fact held? Or one of contemplative wonder—of the type, ironically, that environmentalists often call for? It is Iris Murdoch's view, certainly, that it is precisely a 'selfless respect' for the 'independent existence', the 'otherness', of nature which is the proper antidote to instrumentalism.[22]

The second thought may be that, since the transcendental subject is alleged to be the sole source of value, the world that is an object for it is with-out intrinsic value, hence an object in the further sense of something to use as the subjects will. But there is confusion here. That nature is without intrinsic worth in the sense that its worth is necessarily *for* conscious subjects does not entail that it is without intrinsic value in the sense of having only instrumental value. That nothing could have value without being valued

---

[20] Edmund Husserl, *The Paris Lectures*, trans. P. Koestenbaum (The Hague: Nijhoff, 1975), 10.

[21] John A. Livingston, quoted in Aitken, 'A New Approach to Conservation', 93.

[22] Iris Murdoch, *Existentialists and Mystics: Writings on Philosophy and Literature*, ed. P. Conradi (Harmondsworth: Penguin, 1997), 378.

does not mean that everything is valued only as a means. Relatedly, that the 'knowing subject' is blessed, it seems, with 'Cartesian rationality' hardly entails that the sole exercise of its reason must take the form of calculative, means–ends reasoning. So, even if 'the theory of the knowing subject' has been a target of environmentalists, it is doubtful that it is, per se, a legitimate one.[23]

Finally, Foucault's (second) characterization of humanism is without historical warrant. Far from regarding men as capable of a detached, rational appraisal of our inherited beliefs and norms—of a transcendental stance—the characteristic attitude of Renaissance humanists was one of scepticism towards this possibility. What distinguished human beings was not a potential for objective knowledge, but creative agency, 'self-assertion'. Descartes's 'reaffirmation of reason' was in conscious opposition to such humanistic tendencies, and Kant—as Gadamer rightly observed—marked the end of a certain humanistic tradition in elevating reason over the traditions and the *sensus communis* that, for the *umanisti*, must provide our main guidance, theoretical and practical (p. 50).

'Humanism', I have earlier remarked, sounds a peculiarly inept title, moreover, for a tradition of thought which, in postulating a transcendental consciousness capable of a 'God's-eye' survey of reality, posits something from which, so to speak, the characteristically human has been stripped away—bodily activity, emotion, interest, motivation, and the rest. From Descartes's meditator, through the noumenal self of Kantian moral reflection, to Husserl's pure ego, the transcendental subject is what remains when everything characteristically human—and everything that distinguishes one human being from another—is, to speak with the last of those philosophers, 'bracketed' or 'put out of play'. It is perfectly understandable, indeed, why philosophers, such as Averroes and Husserl himself, worried whether one

---

[23] The writers I am criticizing might, I suppose, appeal to the authority of Heidegger, for does he not associate the 'devastation' of nature with a 'dualism' of rational subjects versus a world of objects? Well, yes, but only because he thinks that dualism was always bogus, since the objects were always determined according to a 'ground-plan' laid down by human beings. It is only when that is recognized by Nietzsche that the way is open for the exploitation of a nature now seen to be a 'product' of human will—when, in other words, dualism has transmuted into the thesis of 'the human world', into humanism in my sense. See Heidegger's 'The Age of the World-Picture' in his *The Question Concerning Technology and Other Essays*, trans. W. Lovitt (New York: Harper & Row, 1977). A plausible target of environmentalist criticism, I argue in Chapter 13, would be a privileging of *theory*, but this is not peculiar to doctrines of rational subjectivity.

could speak of rational selves or subjects in the plural at all: for have not the 'selves' which participate in universal reason, which share in a transcendental stance, lost whatever individuates them as persons? In that case, a humanism understood in terms of transcendental consciousness would be a humanism without any humans.

What matters in the end is not, of course, that the title 'humanism' jars with the tendency of thought it is being used to label. More important is the encouragement that Foucault's use of the label gives to assimilating that tendency to a tradition which represents a fundamentally opposed response to the break-up of 'the Augustinian heritage'. That is a main reason why Foucault's characterization, like the other rival ones already rejected, fails adequately to capture the notion it set out to elucidate.

CHAPTER 7

Humility

Authenticity and 'Dis-incumbence'

Whether or not existential humanism is the true heir to the humanist tradition in modern times, it is the version that will occupy us over the next four
chapters. In Chapter 5, I presented the existential humanist's account of
human ex-istence and argued that, in the absence of further obstacles, its
natural expression is the thesis of 'the human world', the denial that any discursable world is independent of 'the human contribution'. An obstacle
does remain, in the shape of the 'absolutist' conviction that it is possible to
ascend to a conception of a structured world which indeed transcends
human perspective. The attempt to dispose of that obstacle is made in
Chapter 8, in the context of a characteristic charge, briefly rehearsed in my
Introduction, that is levelled at—and returned by—humanists: the charge of
hubris or lack of humility. In the present chapter, I provide that context, but
only after repairing an omission from Chapter 5.

When describing earlier developments in humanism, I drew attention, as
indeed did the architects of these developments, to their 'vital' import—
their bearing on life and conduct—and not simply to their more narrowly
intellectual implications. In my account, so far, of existential humanism, its
'vital' aspects have remained in the background. When brought into promi-
nence, they will invite, from some quarters, a charge of hubris which soon
inflates into a charge against the whole approach of existential humanism.

Our initial question is this: if one concurs in the account of ex-istence and
the anticipated removal of absolutist obstacles to the 'human world' thesis,
what 'vital' implications might one draw? What stance towards the world
and other people, suggestive of how one should go about life, would be indicated? Even if no specific moral directives are indicated, is there nevertheless
a 'tone' one should strive to give to one's life, a 'mood' to be cultivated? I

pose the question in that way because one would search in vain among the various philosophers from whom I culled the position of existential humanism for a single, concrete, 'vital' programme—an agreed list, say, of moral prescriptions. But it is not similarly fruitless to try to identify a tone, mood, or stance whose cultivation, according to most of these writers, is encouraged by the 'human world' thesis. To identify it, we need to examine two related themes prominent among those writers, those of estrangement and authenticity.

These themes are scarcely new, even if they have not always gone by those names. 'The groundwork of all true philosophy', wrote Wordsworth, has been the conflict between an 'intuition . . . of ourselves, as one with the whole' and one that 'places nature in antithesis' to us.[1] Certainly, the whole history of philosophy, and of other human endeavours, reveals a preoccupation with the 'oppressive' and 'unhappy' sense, as Hegel calls it, which people have of being placed in a world which is 'out and out other' than themselves.[2] This sense of estrangement has its roots, no doubt, in an appreciation of human uniqueness—of, for example, the capacities for reason, free decisions, and moral deliberation that set men apart from everything else. It has been a characteristic philosophical endeavour to resist or mitigate the stark dualistic opposition between human existence and the world in which that appreciation seems to result. For example, idealist attempts to locate the world within the precincts of mind, like materialist ones to treat human life as only an especially complicated process of nature, are better viewed as responses to the wider issue of estrangement than as solutions to a narrower 'problem of knowledge' which dualistic oppositions engender.

The theme of estrangement has certainly been prominent in the humanist tradition I earlier traced. The issue of estrangement becomes acute, it seems, when people's accommodation to the world, their settled 'location' in relation to it, is challenged. It is in these terms that one could characterize the effect of the 'Ockhamist' challenge to an 'Augustinian heritage' that had long consoled the 'unhappy consciousness' with a vision of human beings' 'unity with the Unchangeable'. It was the loss of that consolation which, we

---

[1] Quoted in Charles Taylor, *Sources of the Self* (Cambridge: Cambridge University Press, 1989), 574.

[2] *Phenomenology of Spirit*, trans. A. V. Miller (Oxford: Oxford University Press, 1977), 2. The claim I make here is developed and documented at some length in my *World Philosophies: An Historical Introduction* (Oxford: Blackwell, 1996, 2nd rev. ed. 2002).

saw in Chapter 2, was a spur to the 'self-assertive' tendencies that developed into Renaissance humanism. The same terms are appropriate for the effect of the dominant tendency in Enlightenment rationalism. With its stark opposition of mind to a mechanical, 'disenchanted' natural world devoid of significance and worth, the Age of Enlightenment was, for Hegel, 'the Age of self-alienated spirit'.[3] As noted in Chapter 3, the language of estrangement or alienation was pervasive among such critics of Enlightenment as Hamann, Herder, and Goethe. Friedrich Hölderlin's Hyperion speaks for them all when he laments an Enlightenment science which has 'spoilt everything' by requiring him radically to 'distinguish myself from what surrounds me'.[4] It was precisely the refusal to have everything spoilt, to concede that the world exists 'in antithesis to us', that palpably informed the Promethean tendencies described in Chapter 4.

For Marx, as for Hegel, it is the express mission of philosophy to 'overcome' estrangement, which is why philosophy can only be 'realized' by the abolition of those socio-economic conditions that,[5] via the 'reifying' pretensions of metaphysics and religion, prevent people from recognizing that the 'objective world' is 'produced' through their 'active species-life' (see p. 84 above). For Nietzsche, too, it is the 'laughable . . . juxtaposition of "man *and* world"' which must go, for it breeds estranged, 'sickly' creatures incapable of stomaching life as it is and yearning, instead, for the comforts of an illusory 'true world'.[6] The same aspiration to 'overcome' estrangement is visible in other Promethean authors. 'God only knows how many of the sufferings of life', proclaimed Dewey, may be put down to the 'rupture', preached by 'analytic realism', between 'the world and the knower as something outside of it'.[7] James and Bergson would have applauded.

There's something else on which these authors agree: it is not enough, in order to 'overcome' the sense of estrangement, simply to give intellectual assent to a philosophical truth. Rejection of the 'out and out other', of the 'true world', of 'analytic realism', must be a 'vital' exercise, informing and colouring the lives we lead. It is here that the notion of authenticity, though

---

[3] Ibid. 294.

[4] *Gedichte: Hyperion* (Augsburg: Goldmann, 1981), 161.

[5] 'Contribution to the Critique of Hegel's *Philosophy of Right*', in *The Portable Karl Marx*, ed. E. Kamenka (Harmondsworth: Penguin, 1983), 124.

[6] *The Gay Science*, trans. W. Kaufmann (New York: Random House, 1974), § 346.

[7] *Essays in Experimental Logic* (Chicago: University of Chicago Press, 1916), 72–3.

the term is borrowed from the lexicon of a later existentialist literature, enters in. If estrangement owes to crediting, or handing over, to the world itself what is in fact a 'human contribution', then the authentic (*eigentlich*) life is one of retrieval, of human beings' regaining what is their 'own' (*eigen*), one conducted in 'lived' appreciation of the extent of the human contribution. This is why, for Marx, an end to alienation requires the 'fashioning' of nature, through creative labour, into a recognizably 'anthropological nature'; why, for Nietzsche, it requires the 'free spirit' self-consciously to fashion a 'gay science', his own 'table of values', and indeed himself; and why, for Dewey, education must cultivate a spirit of 'what the Yankee calls gumption', practical engagement with a 'reality-of-use-and-in-use', not an allegedly independent reality which 'may go hang' so far as we are concerned.[8]

The twin themes of estrangement and authenticity continue to play loudly amongst existential humanists, modulated, however, in keeping with their rejection of Prometheanism. The 'juxtaposition of "man *and* world"' continues to be both a source and product of a failure to appreciate the dependence of a structured world on human agency. When, writes Merleau-Ponty, we ignore our ordinary activities within a world which is a milieu of significance, and instead pay 'disinterested attention' to it, the world becomes 'hostile and alien, no longer an interlocutor'.[9] 'Overcoming' that sense of hostility, however, is impeded by Promethean flirtations with both the naturalism and the 'sculptural' imagery criticized by the existential humanist in Chapter 5. The gap between man and world is to be closed neither by a Nietzschean 'translat[ion of] man back into nature' nor by a vision of values and concepts carving up a cosmic porridge. The former, as Sartre notes, only makes matters worse: for now I become estranged from myself as a 'Me-Ego' that has been relegated to just one more natural item.[10] The latter, too, fails to close the gap for, as Heidegger remarks, the image of imposing values on an indifferent stuff that confronts us is one of those which has surely *helped* to 'achieve' a 'maximum of *uprootedness*'.[11] It is not,

---

[8] 'The Practical Character of Reality', in H. Thayer (ed.), *Pragmatism: The Classic Readings* (Indianapolis: Hackett, 1982), 277–8.

[9] *Phenomenology of Perception*, trans. C. Smith (London: Routledge & Kegan Paul, 1962), 322.

[10] *Cahiers pour une morale* (Paris: Gallimard, 1983), 429.

[11] *An Introduction to Metaphysics*, trans. R. Manheim (New Haven, Conn.: Yale University Press, 1959), 198.

then, in these directions that authentic 'retrieval' of a 'human world' is to be sought.

According to some critics, it should not be sought anywhere. Given the existential humanist's emphasis upon the 'absorption' in 'public norms' and practices—in a form of life—presupposed by any individual's understanding, it becomes 'incomprehensible', argues Hubert L. Dreyfus, that an individual's life can be an authentic one, retrieved from this immersion in 'average everyday' understanding. If so, Heidegger's talk in *Being and Time* of *Dasein* authentically 'choosing itself' and becoming 'something of its own' is an unfortunate Kierkegaardian excrescence on his insight into the essentially public character of ex-istence.[12] Even if this were fair comment on Heidegger's position, it is not obvious that the only conception of authenticity available to the existential humanist is that of the individual soaring free from absorption in public norms and understanding. In earlier chapters, we have met with thinkers in the humanist camp whose conception has a more 'collectivist', even 'tribal', character. Ernst Jünger's authentic 'Worker', for example, proudly recognizes himself as a 'cog' in the 'mobilization of matter' effected by the mass to which he belongs. Herder's celebration of those who fully identify themselves with a world-constituting *Volkgeist* helped spawn a modern ideology of 'roots' that encourages people to view themselves not as their own 'personal possession but a patrimonial construct'.[13] Neither of those precedents, perhaps, makes a 'collectivist' conception of authenticity sound inviting, but it can take a more moderate and benign form.

Putnam, for example, has argued that Wittgenstein's humanist 'rejection of metaphysics is a *moral* rejection'. The aspiration to provide an account of how the world is in itself is not only vain, but pernicious—for two reasons. First, it illegitimately pretends that an account of the world—that of science, say—could escape practical and evaluative constraints, and hence distracts from the primary question of 'whether the form of life', to which it owes, 'has practical or spiritual value'. Second, it implies that such an

---

[12] Hubert L. Dreyfus, *Being-in-the-World: A Commentary on Heidegger's* Being and Time, *Division I* (Cambridge, Mass: MIT Press, 1991), 333–4. I address Dreyfus's criticism in 'Inverting the Image', *Inquiry*, 35 (1993), 233–48.

[13] Régis Debray, quoted in Alain Finkielkraut, *The Undoing of Thought*, trans. D. O'Keeffe (London: Claridge, 1988), 94—a book that charts Herder's influence on both fascism and 'roots' ideology.

account could be used to sit in magisterial judgement on different world views, when in fact it is not even possible for those views, and the forms of life in which they are embedded, to be understood by 'those who are unable to share its evaluative interests'.[14] Here Putnam may be thinking of Wittgenstein's remarks on *The Golden Bough*, with their contempt for those who would measure the validity of alien concepts by a parochial yardstick.[15]

The conception of authenticity—of retrieving the 'human contribution' to the world—indicated here is not an 'individualist' one: it is the conception realized in the lives of people alert both to the values and interests which all views of the world manifest and to the dangers of ignoring these when passing judgement on views bound up with other, seemingly strange forms of life. People alert in these ways are no longer just going along with the crowd, for they display a degree of reflection that is not an 'average everyday' one. But the possibility of such alertness is compatible with an emphasis upon public norms and practices as conditions of intelligibility. That no one could, in the absence of these, conceptualize and evaluate at all, does not entail that, once equipped to do so, he or she cannot adopt a reflective stance towards these conditions, and indeed recognize them *as* conditions of intelligibility. Nor is that emphasis incompatible with a more 'individualist' conception of authenticity. Dreyfus's claim, following Heidegger, that a human being 'can never choose itself from the ground up', hardly implies, as he imagines, that no one can be 'an individual with an identity of its own'.[16] Only a peculiarly exacting criterion of what it is to be an individual could warrant that inference.

Admittedly, in the writings of some figures I associated with existential humanism, just such a criterion seems to be imposed: notably in those of the younger Sartre, with his penchant for speaking of a person making an 'original choice' of his life and 'creating' his own world. But that was not the position of other figures, and it was one from which the post-war Sartre, of *Truth and Existence* and other works, retreated. A more sober conception of individual freedom and authenticity is found in Merleau-Ponty. Although the world is not independent of—nor, therefore, 'hostile and alien' to— human 'projection', this does not mean that anyone can 'choose [himself]...

[14] Hilary Putnam, *Pragmatism: An Open Question* (Oxford: Blackwell, 1995), 50–1.
[15] *Remarks on Frazer's* Golden Bough, trans. A. Miles (Retford: Brynmill, 1979).
[16] Dreyfus, *Being-in-the-World*, 308.

from nothing at all', or 'transform' and 'annul' his beliefs or values 'just like that'. Choice, in any serious sense, presupposes 'a previous acquisition', including a sense of what matters, gained through immersion in shared practices. Equally, however, the impossibility of 'choosing oneself from the ground up' does not mean that the individual is without the capacity to 'modify' his 'acquisition', without powers of 'general refusal' and 'begin[ning] something again'. That a person is 'always already' in a world of significance not of his own making does not exclude his 'taking up a position', a distinctive one of his own, in and towards that world.[17]

Since it is of small relevance to subsequent discussion, I shall not pursue the question of how 'individualist' a conception of authenticity the existential humanist is entitled to entertain. Of greater moment for the 'vital' dimensions of his position is the existential humanist's proposal of the mood or attitude that, in Dilthey's words, should 'give colour to whatever presents itself to life'.[18] It is not difficult to predict some of the aspects of life and the world that it is proposed we 'celebrate'. It is unsurprising, first, to find Heidegger and Merleau-Ponty, like Dewey, celebrating the 'operative' wisdom or 'knowledge in the hands' of the carpenter and the forester: an understanding that, on their accounts, necessarily precedes that of the chemist, say, or the geographer, who only 'stops and stares'. We should expect, second, that 'celebration of the ordinary', of what figures for us in our everyday dealings and of those very dealings themselves, that several commentators find in Wittgenstein's later writings. They are thinking especially, perhaps, of passages where he impugns the pretence of the sciences to unique authority on what things are like—as when he laments the tendency to suppose that knowing what water is consists in knowing its chemical formula.[19] Relatedly, we should expect a 'celebration' of what Paul Feyerabend describes as 'the rich, colourful and abundant world that affects us in so many ways'. To diminish that world in the manner of metaphysicians seek-

[17] Merleau-Ponty, *Phenomenology of Perception*, 447, 452, 191 ff.

[18] *Dilthey: Selected Writings*, trans. H. Rickman (Cambridge: Cambridge University Press, 1968), 240.

[19] Ludwig Wittgenstein, *Culture and Value*, trans. P. Winch (Oxford: Blackwell, 1980). On Wittgenstein's 'celebration of the ordinary', see David Pears, *The False Prison*, 2 vols. (Oxford: Oxford University Press, 1987–8), which speaks eloquently of how, for the later Wittgenstein, 'wonder' is not, as in the *Tractatus*, directed at the mystery of the existence of the world, but something 'diffused over the whole range of human life . . . all the ordinary modes of human thought and activity': i. 17.

ing a 'real' order of things independent of how we are affected is not only illegitimate: it is alienating and 'devalues human existence', for it is to the 'abundant' world that belong 'all the properties and events that make our existence important'.[20] (These 'celebrations' are returned to, in a rather different context, in Chapter 13.)

These 'celebrations' of what 'presents itself to life' do not, however, indicate the special tone of the authentic life as conceived by the existential humanist, the characteristic mood which goes with a sense of retrieving the 'human contribution'. This is the tone or mood gestured at by some favourite terms from the lexicon of existentialism—'Angst', 'absurdity', 'guilt'—and by the word 'irony' in something close to Rorty's sense. None of them is quite suitable, but it is instructive to glance at what their users intend to convey. Angst, for Heidegger, has little to do with nail-biting nervousness: indeed, it can be a 'sober' and 'joyful', albeit 'uncanny', mood. It is the mood in which 'entities *within* the world . . . *sink away*',[21] lose their air of belonging to an independent order of things, and are experienced instead as owing their being and identity to the places they occupy in that vast theatre of significance which Heidegger calls 'the world'. In Angst, we are brought before 'the world as such', before that 'relational totality' which is at once unthinkable in isolation from human agency and the precondition for there being those entities which, when 'tranquillized', we take to belong to a realm set over against us.

One aspect of Angst will be an experience of the contingency of our picture or 'interpretation' of the world. The point is not that we might, for biological or historical reasons, have failed accurately to depict the order of things, but that this very order owes to a form of life that might have been different. If the argument in the last section of Chapter 5 is well taken, it is contingent, in this sense, that our concepts extend as they do: no 'contract' determines that just these objects fall under just those concepts. The point could be put by saying that there can be no 'final vocabulary' required by reality and in comparison with which the accuracy of our actual vocabularies could be measured. That expression is Rorty's, whose 'ironist' is

---

[20] Paul Feyerabend, *Conquest of Abundance: A Tale of Abstraction versus the Richness of Being* (Chicago: University of Chicago Press, 2000), 16.

[21] Martin Heidegger, *Being and Time*, trans. J. Macquarrie and E. Robinson (Oxford: Blackwell, 1980), 232.

precisely someone who rencounces the aspiration to a 'final vocabulary' and recognizes the 'redescriptions' we venture as being just that—redescriptions, without any pretence of getting closer to a vocabulary endorsed by reality.[22]

In *Angst* or the 'ironic' mood, one might say, our vocabularies and encounters with the world are experienced as being 'without foundations'. With this way of putting it, we arrive at Sartre's notion of 'absurdity'. To live in the mood of absurdity is not to regard one's life as silly or crazy, but to live with a certain 'feeling of unjustifiability', a recognition that the 'choices' a person makes, though these may be 'fundamental' in shaping his life, are themselves 'beyond all reasons', without foundations in an independent order.[23] What invites the label 'absurd' is not this absence of foundations per se, but the tension between appreciation of that absence and the seriousness, energy, and commitment with which the person continues to pursue his 'projects' and engage in life. A similar tension inspires Karl Jaspers to speak of the 'guilt' that imbues the authentic life: a tension between the recognition that 'we have to occupy a standpoint at every moment' and a reluctance to count any standpoint as 'objectively valid'.[24]

Talk of tension indeed helps to capture the conception of authentic life advanced by the existential humanist. On the one hand, it is a life lived 'in the midst of the world'. The pretension of the hermit or existentialist 'loner' to detach himself from it or soar above it is no more than that. For if he is to act, think, and speak at all, his instruments will be things, concepts, and words that owe their identity to a form of life from which his self-exile is, therefore, only superficial. Yet it is a life which, though in the midst of the world and informed by the perceptions of salience, of what matters, and of what is possible that a form of life furnishes, is also one whose tone is gestured at by the terms invoked above, 'irony', 'absurdity', and so on. For it is a life led in the midst of a 'human world' that is recognized as such: one which is not 'exterior' to a form of life whose practices and perceptions are, therefore, seen to be 'without foundations'.

---

[22] Richard Rorty, *Contingency, Irony and Solidarity* (Cambridge: Cambridge University Press, 1989), 80 ff.

[23] Jean-Paul Sartre, *Being and Nothingness: An Essay on Phenomenological Ontology*, trans. H. Barnes (London: Methuen, 1957), 479–80.

[24] Karl Jaspers, *Philosophy*, trans. E. B. Ashton (Chicago: Chicago University Press, 1970), ii. 109.

None of the terms invoked is especially apt for labelling this delicate and 'tense' mood or stance. 'Absurdity' and 'guilt' are overdramatic, while 'irony', with its connotation of amused detachment, fails to bring out that necessity of 'occupying a standpoint' in the midst of the world which, as Jaspers puts it, is a crucial ingredient in the 'antinomical structure' of authentic life. *Angst*, despite Heidegger's glosses on it, remains too redolent of nail-biting. So let's invent a label, one as ugly as such neologisms usually are. Let's say that the tone of the authentic life, the stance of an authentic person, is one of 'dis-incumbence'. Note the second 'i': the term is coined from the Latin word meaning 'to lean on', from which words like 'incumbent' derive, not from the French word meaning 'to block', from which 'encumber' comes. Hence my term pleasingly picks up on William James's characterization of humanism as the doctrine that 'experience as a whole . . . leans on nothing'. The dis-incumbenced mood, then, is that which imbues one's comportment in the midst of a 'human world' that is experienced as such, the tone of a life led in the 'tension' between occupation of a standpoint and the perception that no standpoints, at the final count, have solid ground beneath them.

In this section, I have tried only to characterize, not to question, the existential humanist's 'vital' response to the issue of estrangement, a response that advocates the cultivation of an authentic, dis-incumbenced stance.[25] With that characterization in place, we are in a position to examine the familiar charge of hubris levelled against humanism.

Hubris: Charge and Countercharge

In the present section, I chronicle not only that charge, but the countercharge of hubris levelled by humanists against their rivals. To the surprise,

---

[25] One may reasonably ask how distinctive of existential humanism is the cultivation of dis-incumbence. Certainly there are parallels between dis-incumbence and the sense of 'spontaneity' or 'freedom' that, according to Fichte, it is the 'vocation of man' to acquire when properly educated by the *Wissenschaftslehre* ('doctrine of knowledge') into the truth of idealism. For what the doctrine cultivates is a similar, 'tense' combination of release from the 'fetters of things in themselves' and appreciation of the 'necessity' our thought and experience are under as creatures who owe their identity to 'intersubjective' activity. See Fichte's letter to J. Baggeson cited in his *Introductions to the Wissenschaftslehre and Other Writings*, trans. D. Breazeale (Indianapolis: Hackett, 1994), p. vii. I am grateful to James A. Clarke for the comparison and reference.

perhaps, of some readers, it will emerge that the language of humility and hubris is pervasive in the debate between humanists and their critics. In the following section, I make a distinction between two modes of humility. With the help of that distinction, I proceed, in the final section, to identify, in fairly schematic ways, what I take to be the real force of the charge and countercharge of hubris. The three subsequent chapters elaborate on, and appraise the effectiveness of, these mutual charges.

The charge against existential humanism is best introduced in connection with the normative, 'vital' dimensions described in the previous section. It is one, as we briefly saw in Chapter 1, eloquently presented by Iris Murdoch. In 'moral philosophy of an existentialist' and 'humanist' type, with its central emphasis on authenticity, 'our picture of ourselves has become too grand . . . [and] we have lost the vision of a reality separate from ourselves'. We should be making the 'attempt to look right away from the self towards a distant transcendent perfection'. In doing so, we would be cultivating 'one of the most difficult and central of all virtues'—humility, not in the sense of 'self-effacement', but that of 'selfless respect for reality'.[26] As the several references to the self suggest, Murdoch's complaint is specifically against an 'individualist', Sartrean conception of authenticity or 'dis-incumbence'. But it is easily converted into a more general one: for the core of the complaint is that any injunction to authenticity is hubristic in its refusal to countenance a 'transcendent' source of demands, to 'respect' the normative requirements imposed by a 'reality separate from ourselves'.

Murdoch points out that a similar complaint can be made against much of twentieth-century English-language ethical theory—against 'emotivists', 'prescriptivists', 'projectivists', and others who also deny that moral principles have a source in a 'reality separate from ourselves'. Since philosophers of these persuasions, hostile to the 'moral realism' advocated by Murdoch herself, have held sway in modern analytical ethics, hers has been a relatively lone voice in its complaint of hubris. On the dis-incumbenced character of moral life, these philosophers could, in round terms, agree with the existential humanist.

There is, however, a fundamental difference between most proponents of those Anglo-American 'isms' and the existential humanist. I noted earlier

[26] See *Existentialists and Mystics: Writings on Philosophy and Literature*, ed. P. Conradi (Harmondsworth: Penguin, 1997), 338.

that a humanist treatment of ethics can be welcomed by thinkers of very different stripes (p. 10 above). For some, it has provided a prelude to, model for, or ingredient in a wider, 'global' thesis of 'the human world'. For others, it has conveniently removed the obstacle that moral judgements seem to pose for a naturalistic, scientific account of reality. Generally, the emotivists and their brethren have belonged to this second group. By denying that good, right, and so on are features of a world independent of human purpose or feeling, the problem of how such 'queer' properties could be fitted into a scientific picture of the world is removed. Put differently, these philosophers construe the humanist line on ethics as one that rightly honours a division of facts and values. Far from endorsing a 'global' humanism, then, these philosophers resist any move in that direction from the position of a more 'local', normative humanism.

For the existential humanist, on the other hand, just such a move is imperative once it is recognized that any account of the world necessarily owes to practices and a form of life that presuppose evaluation—a sense of what matters, what is worth achieving, and so on. Evaluation is not some bolt-on extra to life, a matter of imposing values onto a world of neutral facts, for in the absence of evaluation there would be no world encountered at all. We do not, as Heidegger put it, first encounter the 'naked thing', and only later 'throw "signification" over' it or 'stick a value on it'.[27] Or, as Sartre writes, 'there is no consciousness which is not haunted by . . . value', and we should appreciate that there are a 'thousand projects', unthinkable in the absence of evaluation, behind the possibility of confronting and reporting any so-called 'brute fact'.[28]

Emotivists, prescriptivists, and so on do not, then, join Murdoch in castigating existential humanism for its lack of humility in the normative sphere. But what they and many other philosophers have done is to convert her charge into one against the 'global' thesis of 'the human world'. While it may not be hubristic to deny a *moral* reality 'separate from ourselves', it surely is hubristic, they argue, to deny that reality *tout court*—the world of 'facts'—is thus separate. For a perfect specimen of this widened charge, let us recall the words of Thomas Nagel (p. 11 above). Humanism, in rendering the world 'dependent on our view of it', displays a 'lack of humility', indeed

---

[27] *Being and Time*, 190.
[28] *Being and Nothingness*, 463.

'blind self-importance'. In its 'attempt to cut the universe down to size', not least by excluding the possibility that much of that universe may be 'incomprehensible' to us, humanism rejects the 'objective stance' that is the proper 'form of humility'.

The levelling of this charge is hardly surprising given the tenor of the remarks made by many writers in, or in the vicinity of, the humanist tradition—remarks that seem to boast of the sins of which critics accuse them. Sometimes the tenor is explicitly theological, as when Friedrich Schiller refers to humanity as 'God-like' in its 'aesthetic' production of the world, or when his pragmatist namesake (F. C. S.) and William James speak of our 'divinely creative functions' in 'creating' objects from the malleable 'raw materials' of the senses.[29] Even when the theological rhetoric is not explicit, capacities once regarded as the preserve of the gods are proudly ascribed to humanity. For the Hegelian idealist, the 'I' is the 'crucible and fire' which produces the 'unity' of a world out of the 'plurality of sense', a world which it is man's 'endeavour' to 'appropriate and subdue', 'crush and pound', through 'idealizing' it.[30] The Fichtean idealist, meanwhile, derives a 'full feeling of . . . absolute self-sufficiency' from his realization that the world is but 'the reflection of our own inner activity'—a feeling which enables him to 'look down with . . . disrespect' on the 'spiritual servitude' of the 'dogmatist' who still requires the crutch of a world separate from that activity.[31] We soon find Nietzsche writing that 'one may certainly admire man', not as a discoverer of truth, but as a 'mighty genius of construction' who 'piles up' a vast edifice of 'thoroughly anthropomorphic truth' that is not 'valid apart from man'.[32] And so it continues into the following century. Sartre invites us to embrace an optimistic, existentialist humanism whose central aim is to 'remind man that there is no legislator but himself' (p. 11 above). Rorty extols a pragmatist humanism that denies any criterion of truth or rationality other than 'obedience to our own conventions', and which, in appreciating that men and women are in the business of 'making worlds rather than

[29] Quoted in E. J. Craig, *The Mind of God and the Works of Man* (Oxford: Clarendon Press, 1987), 227 and 263–4.

[30] G. W. F. Hegel, *The Encyclopedia Logic*, trans. T. Geraets, W. Suchting, and H. Harris (Indianapolis: Hackett, 1991), § 69.

[31] *Introductions to the* Wissenschaftslehre, 17, 145, 19–20.

[32] *Philosophy and Truth: Selections from Nietzsche's Notebooks of the Early 1870s*, trans. D. Breazeale (Atlantic Highlands, N.J.: Humanities, 1979), 85.

finding them', enables them proudly to stand 'alone', their 'links to something beyond'—to God or to 'the positivist's God of science'—now sev-
ered.[33]

Given the barrage of such remarks and the attraction which humanist
thinking has exerted over the past couple of centuries, it is understandable
that modernity should have been described as an age of 'a grossly hubristic
humanism'.[34] But the charge of hubris goes back a long way, to times when
extreme proclamations of the kind just cited had yet to be heard. Earlier figures in the humanist tradition may have prudently avoided boasts of
humanity's 'God-like' powers, but as we glimpsed in Chapters 2–3, this did
not prevent critics noting and excoriating the transfer of responsibilities
from God to 'self-assertive' man that was quietly being conducted. Such critics, observes Jacques Maritain, regretted the erosion of a 'metaphysical
modesty' which had 'kept the eyes of medieval man' averted from his own
cognitive and creative accomplishments, an erosion that threatened to
replace 'the cult of the God-man, of the word made flesh' by a 'self-assertive'
cult of 'Humanity, of man alone'.[35]

Still, it is not until the emergence of the Promethean forms of humanism
made possible by Kant's 'Copernican turn' that accusations of lack of humility become commonplace. The young Nietzsche, though not in an especially critical spirit, notes how Kant's philosophy, construed as showing that 'the
world has reality only in man', was 'immediately employed . . . for [man's]
self glorification'.[36] Pragmatist humanism was to prompt some particularly
tart accusations. Frank Lovejoy, for example, castigated those who turned
'realities' into 'mere obsequious shadows' of man,[37] and it was pragmatism
that Russell had in mind when he accused philosophers who deny that there
are 'facts largely outside human control' of inhumility, 'cosmic impiety',
and worse—'a certain kind of madness—the intoxication of power'.[38] Half
a century on, the charges continue: whether the target goes by the name
of humanism, anti-realism, constructivism, pragmatism, or idealism, the

---

[33] *Consequences of Pragmatism*, pp. xlii, xxxix, xliii.

[34] Robert B. Pippin, *Idealism as Modernism: Hegelian Variations* (Cambridge: Cambridge
University Press, 1998), 4.

[35] *True Humanism*, trans. M. Adamson (London: Centenary, 1938), 3, 8.

[36] *Philosophy and Truth*, 38.

[37] Quoted in S. R. L. Clark, *Animals and their Moral Standing* (London: Routledge, 1997), 121.

[38] Bertrand Russell, *History of Western Philosophy* (London: Routledge, 1961), 782.

constant refrain is that of a lack of humility, of an 'arrogant anthropocentrism', of a 'baseless confidence' in our powers.[39]

Although the refrain and the broad target are constant, it is worth recording for future reference that, on closer inspection, different critics direct their charge against rather different aspects of humanism. They differ, that is, on the precise locus of humanist hubris. For some, it is the refusal to hold our concepts, beliefs, and norms as a whole answerable to anything beyond themselves—the insistence that 'there is in the world nothing to lean on'.[40] For others, it is in humanist proclamations of unbounded human powers of creativity and construction that lack of humility is most visible. For yet others, the real immodesty resides in a pre-emptive denial that the world may, in large part, be unknown to us, even unknowable by us. I postpone until the final section the question of how the charge of hubris should be construed if it is to be maximally effective.

Before that, I now chronicle the countercharge of hubris that humanists level against their accusers. For the humanist, claims like Nagel's, to the effect that humility requires the 'objective stance' and openness to facts independent of the 'human contribution', are bogus. Such claims have, of course, a long pedigree. Science, wrote T. H. Huxley in stentorian tone, continues in the spirit of the Christian conception of humility when it enjoins one to 'sit down before the facts as a little child, . . . give up every preconceived notion, follow humbly . . . or you shall learn nothing'.[41] As remarks like Huxley's indicate, the claim is not simply that there are independent realities or facts, not just 'obsequious shadows' of human thinking, but that by 'humbly' submitting to them, we can hope to discover and articulate them. Correspondingly, the charge of lack of humility that such remarks have invited is directed, not against the bare realist or objectivist claim, but against the epistemological claim that we can achieve at least approximate knowledge of what the world 'separate from ourselves' is like.

One does not, of course, have to subscribe to the thesis of 'the human world' to level that charge. It is one commonly heard coming from those

[39] John McDowell, *Mind and World* (Cambridge, Mass.: Harvard University Press, 1994), 40.

[40] Isaiah Berlin, *The Roots of Romanticism: The A. W. Mellon Lectures in the Fine Arts, 1965* (London: Chatto & Windus, 1999), 143.

[41] Letter to Charles Kingsley, quoted in R. Hookyaas, *Religion and the Rise of Modern Science* (Edinburgh: Scottish Academic Press, 1972), 51.

sceptics—Montaigne, Pascal, and Alexander Pope, for example—for whom human powers of observation and reason are so frail and unreliable that only blind overconfidence could credit them with resulting in knowledge. It is possible, indeed, for someone who is neither a sceptic nor a proponent of the 'human world' thesis to accuse a position like Huxley's of hubris. Stephen Clark is recalling an old theological view—Philo of Alexandria's, for example—when he denies that it is 'humble' to suppose that science, or any other human enquiry, could, through its own efforts, attain to knowledge of the world. '[I]t would be ridiculous to expect a bunch of hairless primates on a ball of mud to possess the key to the cosmos—unless we were somehow united with the law by which it is made'—unless, that is, we have been *given* that key by God.[42]

Countercharges of hubris only assume a distinctively humanist form in the wake of the 'Copernican turn' that made 'full-blown' humanism itself possible. For Kant himself, the reason why philosophers like Leibniz were 'dogmatists', and 'without an ounce of epistemic humility',[43] was not that they dispensed with divine help or failed to appreciate the frailty of our mental faculties. It is because they credited human beings, impossibly, with the capacity to transcend the limits of understanding, to gain access to things in themselves and not just to phenomenal, mind-relative objects. For Kant, I argued (p. 68), the 'we' in whose absence there would be no empirical objects, were not we human beings: for the young Nietzsche, however, they were, and it is in his early writings where one finds, perhaps, the first 'full-blown' humanist accusations of hubris against the 'dogmatists'. It is 'arrogant and mendacious . . . pride' to suppose that we possess an 'organ of truth', a capacity for knowing or even thinking about things in themselves—a pride no less 'puffed up' and absurd than that of a gnat which took its perspective faithfully to represent reality.[44]

After the mature Nietzsche ended his flirtation with transcendental idealism, his criticism was directed, not at the pretence of access to things in themselves—for there aren't any—but at the 'conceit' of scientists and others to attain to a 'non-perspectival' knowledge, a 'contemplative',

[42] *God's World and the Great Awakening* (Oxford: Clarendon Press, 1991), 116.

[43] Rae Langton, *Kantian Humility: Our Ignorance of Things in Themselves* (Oxford: Clarendon Press, 1998), 68.

[44] *Philosophy and Truth*, 79–80.

'innocent' standpoint free from any intrusion by human evaluations and interests. The arrogance of supposing that any such standpoint could be adopted was to become a familiar theme among later writers of a broadly humanist persuasion. Thus Dewey, stung by the charges of 'impiety' levelled against pragmatist humanism by Russell and Santayana, retorts that the truly 'presumptuous' attitude is that of philosophers like these who imagine that human beings are capable of so 'isolating' themselves from the world as to obtain a detached, objective view.[45] Max Scheler, persuaded by Dilthey's and Husserl's account of the inextricable embroilment of the scientific enterprise in 'life-interests', denounces the misplaced 'intellectual pride' in supposing that reality could be 'reached *via* its "human" object-aspect'—the only aspect available to enquiries whose understanding of the world is shaped by a concern with 'practical modifiability'.[46]

The countercharge of lack of humility against realism continues to the present. In Chapter 1, I cited Crispin Wright's reference to 'the presumptuous thought . . . that, while such fit as there may be between our thought and the world is determined independently of human cognitive activity, we are nevertheless . . . capable of conceiving the world aright, and, often, of knowing the truth about it' (p. 12 above). And here is how two authors, rather glumly, summarize the drift of much recent literature:

Inchoately, perhaps, modesty has played a large role in debates over realism . . . [T]he critic of realism asks whether an appropriately modest view of language and enquiry would show this conception of 'the world' to be plagued with problems of semantic or epistemic access—at best excessive, at worst incoherent or inexpressible.[47]

Now that my chronicle of charges and countercharges is complete, it is time to consider whether, as that passage perhaps suggests, the whole exchange is 'inchoate'. What, if anything, is at issue when humanists and their opponents swap these apparent insults?

---

[45] John Dewey, *A Common Faith* (New Haven, Conn.: Yale University Press, 1934), 25 and 54.

[46] *On the Eternal in Man*, trans. B. Noble (London: SCM Press, 1960), 76–7, 97.

[47] Peter Railton and Gideon Rosen, 'Realism', in J. Kim and E. Sosa (eds.), *A Companion to Metaphysics* (Oxford: Blackwell, 1995), 437.

Two Modes of Humility

There are those who would argue that the charges and countercharges of hubris just chronicled are indeed either 'inchoate' or, at best, philosophically irrelevant. A reply to their argument, as well as diagnosis of the charges of hubris, requires prior discussion of notions like humility and modesty 'for their own sake'.

The argument that needs addressing goes like this. It makes no literal sense to accuse philosophical doctrines like humanism and its rivals of lack of humility. It is individual people who possess or lack humility, and they do so in virtue of their reflexive opinions about, for example, their own abilities. Humanism is not a person, nor does it make a claim about itself. It may be that the charges and countercharges are intended to impugn the characters of individual philosophers who embrace some doctrine or other, as when Fichte announces his 'disrespect' for the 'servile' character of his rivals. But not only is it implausible to suppose that a certain character pairs off with a certain doctrine, it is irrelevant to the truth of the doctrine whether it appeals to people of a certain temperament. It is hard to see, therefore, that charges of hubris against a doctrine are anything but rhetorical devices for denouncing it as false. If so, the charges are redundant, adding nothing to the barer claim that the doctrine is mistaken. All the philosophically relevant work goes into showing it is mistaken, not into making out a charge of hubris that contributes nothing but figurative emphasis.

With some components in this argument, one can be brief. Granted that, in 'central' or 'paradigmatic' cases, humility or its lack is ascribed to an individual person on the basis of a belief about himself, it is clear that extensions beyond the 'central' cases are both familiar and intelligible. First, it is not only individuals, but collectives, which may lack humility: the French, say, may be accused of a hubristic view of their nation's history and achievements. Second, as that example suggests, hubris need not be strictly reflexive. Pierre, or the French, may be boastful, not about their achievements, but about those of people, long dead and buried, with whom they 'identify'. As Hume points out, softening his assertion that "tis always self' which is the object of pride and humility, the object can be anything which is 'in the least ally'd or related to us'.[48] 'In the least' needs stressing here: it is not just the

---

[48] David Hume, *A Treatise of Human Nature* (Oxford: Clarendon Press, 1960), 279–80.

achievements of one's family, dog, or country—to cite Hume's examples—
that may be objects of pride. Someone can be proud of the achievements of
mankind, *his* species, remote as most of its members are from him, when,
for example, he is comparing these achievements with those of God, animals, or Martians. Finally, it is a harmless extension of the vocabulary of
humility to apply it, not to people—whether individuals or collectives—but
to more 'abstract' subjects: beliefs, doctrines, attitudes, and so on. A belief,
say, will be hubristic when it is hubristic to hold it.

It matters little whether we decide that 'humility' is being employed literally when, for instance, a belief about the importance of mankind is charged
with lack of humility. Even if we decide it is not, we can sensibly ask what is
meant by the charge. 'Extended' or figurative talk can be as worthy of
investigation as literal talk, and certainly it need not be 'merely' rhetorical, if
that means redundant or irrelevant.

There is something else wrong with the argument I rehearsed. It assumes
that charges of hubris are always levelled against someone on the basis of
some *belief*—estimate, opinion—about himself. But in many cases of hubris,
it is infelicitous to describe the target of the charge as a belief. We should distinguish between what I shall label 'hubris (humility) of belief' and 'hubris
(humility) of posture'. The distinction is not sharp. Someone with an
immodest opinion of his prowess can usually be expected to manifest this in
various ways—in his bearing, attitudes to other people, readiness to accept
challenges, and so on. Equally, someone whose posture is hubristic will
typically have certain immodest beliefs about his abilities. Nevertheless, the
distinction, while not sharp, is genuine: sometimes it is a person's beliefs,
sometimes a person's posture, which is the prime target, and neither is
reducible to the other.

By 'posture', I do not have in mind someone's physical bearing—though
that may well be an indicator of a certain posture. (One might note that the
Greek, Sanskrit, and Latin for humility have their word 'ground' or 'earth' as
the root: hence the associations of 'humble' with 'lowly' or 'crawling'.)
What I have in mind is illustrated by that exemplar of hubris, our old friend
Prometheus. Let's recall some earlier remarks about him. As portrayed by
Aeschylus and Goethe, various beliefs can be attributed to the Titan: for
example, that 'all human skill and science was [his] gift'. But even without
identifying these, we know that Prometheus is a hubristic figure from the
proclamations he makes. In Goethe's poem, he addresses Zeus thus: 'You

must leave my earth to me . . . Here I sit, forming men after my own image,
a race which is like me in . . . not having any regard for you and yours.'[49]
Aeschylus's Prometheus scorns the Chorus's advice to 'fear Nemesis',
'assigns to these new gods [human beings] their honours', and expresses dis-
dain for the 'servile humility' of the messenger of the old gods, Hermes.[50]
Here one has the hubristic posture: excessive self-confidence, an 'Up yours!'
attitude to authority, pre-emptive dismissal of warnings and advice, taking
oneself as a model, and so on. The posture does not, of course, have to be as
dramatic as Prometheus's. Patrick Leigh Fermor writes admiringly of the
'spare, hawk-eyed' mountain shepherds of northern Greece. Yet their sense
of self-sufficiency, which he praises, begins to sound like excessive pride.
Perhaps they do 'spell . . . independence and inviolacy' and 'represent
exemption'.[51] But, to the extent that these qualities belong, as Fermor concedes, to 'an older and shaggier scene' than Arcadia, let alone twentieth-
century Greece, proclaiming them and pretending that they still belong
among the conditions of a viable modern life are postures. One can think of
still less dramatic illustrations: the attitude, say, of the ageing man who
refuses the support without which, in truth, he cannot function. Probably
no single word adequately captures the whole range of attitudes intended
by 'the hubris of posture'. But an expression that has cropped up several
times in this book suggests itself: in the posture of hubris, someone is refusing to 'lean upon', refusing to rely in any way on whatever it is—the gods,
other people, tradition, authority, help—that he cannot really do without. In
the hubris of posture, a person represents, to recall Fermor's term, an
'exemption' that must, to a degree, be illusory.

I return to hubris of posture in the next section, but I now switch attention to hubris of belief. Although I begin with the 'central' case of a person's
belief about himself, this is in order, eventually, to cast light on what it is for
a doctrine to be lacking in humility. On the way, we shall see that charging a
belief with lack of humility is never a matter simply of rejecting that belief
as false, as was suggested by the argument rehearsed at the beginning of this
section.

---

[49] See Chapter 3, n. 2.
[50] Aeschylus, *Prometheus Bound and Other Plays*, trans. P. Vellacott (Harmondsworth: Penguin, 1961), 48–9.
[51] *Roumeli: Travels in Northern Greece* (Harmondsworth: Penguin, 1983), 48–9.

It will help structure the discussion to set it in the context of an apparent paradox. This is sometimes referred to as 'the paradox of modesty'. (For certain purposes, no doubt, distinctions between modesty and humility, and immodesty and lack of humility or hubris, are important—but these purposes are not germane to my discussion.) The following three assumptions result in a contradiction:

a. Modesty is a virtue.
b. Ignorance is not a virtue, nor is anything which necessarily requires ignorance.
c. Modesty necessarily requires ignorance.

The reasoning behind (c) is that someone who believes he is the greatest is surely not modest, even if he is the greatest: modesty requires him to believe something less superlative, and hence to be mistaken about, ignorant of, his true prowess. (It's also been argued, though I shan't pursue this, that to be modest a person must be unaware of being modest.)[52]

The second and third assumptions entail that modesty is no virtue, which contradicts the opening assumption. So which assumption(s) should be rejected? The reasons for rejecting (a) that I have come across are either irrelevant, since they concern modesty or humility in a different sense from that under discussion, or uncompelling. If, by 'modesty', one meant what Montaigne did—something a woman lays aside with her skirt and puts on again with her petticoat—then it might be questioned, at least in our liberated times, whether modesty is a virtue.[53] Again, if one understood humility, like Hume, to be a 'painful sensation' attendant on recognizing one's 'deformities', there would be nothing to admire in its cultivation.[54] However, humility in the present context is not a sensation, but a quality of beliefs or of people in respect of their beliefs. Later in the *Treatise*, this is what Hume too has in mind when, uncompellingly, he argues that modesty is not a virtue. To be more exact, he distinguishes between an 'outer' humility or modesty, in speech and comportment, which 'good-breeding and decency require', and an 'inner', 'secret' humility of self-opinion. It is, he

---

[52] See Julia Driver, 'The Virtues of Ignorance', *Journal of Philosophy*, 86 (1989), 376.

[53] *The Complete Essays*, trans. M. Screech (Harmondsworth: Penguin, 1991), i. 21.

[54] *Treatise*, 286. Hume is wrong, incidentally, to suppose that recognition of one's 'deformities'— or limitations—is necessarily painful. Humble realization that one doesn't have the talent to win a Nobel prize might bring with it a sense of relief, of being disburdened of 'the duties of genius'.

holds, wrong to esteem the latter in the way one does the former. Indeed, people with 'any practice of the world' will not expect humility to 'go beyond the outside' and will approve 'hearty pride' and the 'propensity of men to over-value themselves' provided they retain 'the appearance of modesty'.[55] Here, surely, the urbanity of Hume's men with 'practice of the world' descends into cynicism, their 'indulgence' for simulations of modest self-appraisal symptomatic of a jaded view of human nature. Less jaded people, I suggest, regard 'secret' humility, and not just humility 'on the outside', as something to cultivate.

Some philosophers have rejected (b), arguing for the existence of so-called 'virtues of ignorance'—not only humility and modesty but, for instance, a 'charity of the heart' blind to the faults of others.[56] This position, I suspect, rests on a confusion. It may be, in certain contexts, 'a good thing' that people underestimate their abilities: they won't rest on their laurels and become complacent, for example. But it does not follow that such underestimation is a virtue. For one thing, a parallel argument would establish that *over*estimating one's abilities is a virtue, for in certain contexts it may be 'a good thing' that people have an inflated opinion of themselves. It gives them confidence, cheers them up, and so on. Second, it strains the notion of a virtue to suggest that it is virtuous to be ignorant. A virtue is something to cultivate: blindness to one's true abilities, however, is not something a person should try to promote. What a person should try to do, surely, is both to arrive at a proper estimate of his talents *and* to avoid complacency.

If the first two assumptions of the argument are retained, then it is (c) which must be abandoned if paradox is to be avoided, and this has become the preferred option among recent writers. It is perfectly possible, they argue, for a person's *true* belief about his abilities or achievements to be modest. Indeed, some of these writers *equate* modest belief with accurate belief. '[H]umility involves having an accurate opinion of oneself, one's abilities, and one's accomplishments.'[57] *In*accurate opinions are either immodest or over-modest.

This is too simple. While it is (c) which must go, the blunt equation of

[55] Ibid. 598.
[56] Driver, 'The Virtues of Ignorance'.
[57] Jeffrey Blustein, 'On Taking Responsibility for One's Own Past', *Journal of Applied Philosophy*, 17 (2000), 14.

humility with accuracy produces some strange results. To begin with, the virtue of humility becomes redundant, reducible to that of truthfulness, of trying to match one's beliefs to how things actually are. Second, the equation entails, 'just like that', that someone who believes he is the greatest boxer ever, the most profound philosopher in history, or the like, is *not* lacking in humility, provided only that his belief is *true*. And that is too quick. Such beliefs do not *sound* modest, and we want to enquire further before concluding that, even though true, they really are modest.

This point is recognized by Owen Flanagan. The world's fastest runner, he argues, 'might be modest' despite knowing he is the fastest. His modesty is indicated by his thinking, inter alia, that 'being the world's fastest human is not so important *sub specie aeternitatis*' and that his becoming such a fine athlete 'involves a significant amount of luck'.[58] The implication, of course, is that if the runner had very different concomitant beliefs—that, for example, luck played no role—he would not be modest, despite the truth of his belief that he is the fastest runner. Flanagan rightly directs us to enquire into a person's concomitant beliefs before judging whether the original belief, while true, is compatible with humility. But while his point suffices to spoil the bare equation of modesty with accuracy, it needs to be developed further, for it is incomplete on two counts.

First, it contains no hint of the relevance, when judging someone's modesty, of concomitant beliefs that the person has, not about his abilities, but about his entitlement to his assessment of these. It counts against someone's modesty if, in reply to the question 'Why do you think you're the greatest boxer in history?', he answers, 'It's self-evident! You only have to watch me fight for a few minutes to see it'—rather than, 'Well, in a recent poll of champions, 95 per cent voted me the best. Statistics show that I've knocked out more opponents than any one else', and so on. Second, the issue of how a belief, though true, may be immodest is only postponed by Flanagan's point. For suppose the concomitant beliefs, however 'hyperbolic', are, as it happens, *true*. Suppose, to revert to his example, that God is an athletics fan, who created the world in order to enjoy the spectacle of runners competing—so that being the fastest runner really is of great importance *sub specie*

[58] *Self Expressions: Mind, Morals and the Meaning of Life* (Oxford: Oxford University Press, 1996), 176.

aeternitatis. And suppose that luck played only a tiny role: even if he hadn't had all those breaks, he would still have been the world's fastest runner because of innate endowment.

On Flanagan's account, it follows from the truth of the runner's original belief that, if his concomitant beliefs are also true, he is not lacking in humility. That seems to me intuitively wrong. Someone who believes that he is the fastest runner and, to boot, that being so is of supreme cosmic importance, that his talent is almost entirely due to native endowment, and the like, is prima facie hubristic—even if each of these beliefs is true. What needs to be added to Flanagan's point is something like this: although, as it happens, the runner's concomitant beliefs are true, he has no warrant—not even spurious warrant—for thinking they are. I insert 'prima facie' and 'not even spurious warrant' in order to cater for the following sort of possibility: the runner's guru, in whom he has absolute confidence, has told him that God loves athletics, that luck doesn't exist, and so on. In such a case, the runner has, one might say, a spurious warrant for his concomitant beliefs, and because of that we should hesitate to brand him hubristic. With such possibilities excluded, the concomitant beliefs are ones for which the runner has no warrant unless he possesses cognitive powers that he in fact lacks—the power of insight into God's purpose, say, or to know the truth of countless counterfactuals of the form 'If X had not happened, I would still have been the fastest runner' (ones, that is, which deny the role of luck). Something similar can be said, it is worth noting, about the kind of concomitant belief illustrated by the boxer example: only someone with special cognitive powers that he does not in fact possess could just 'see', from watching a film clip, say, that he was the greatest of all boxers.

My suggestion, then, is this. Whether someone is modest or otherwise in his opinion about his abilities is never settled by the truth of that opinion. Its truth is compatible with modesty and immodesty. Nor is the matter settled by the truth of various concomitant beliefs he holds. In particular, it is possible for all these beliefs to be true, along with the original opinion, yet for the person to be hubristic. This will be the case when his concomitant beliefs, though true, are ones which only a creature with enhanced cognitive powers—not possessed by the person himself—would be warranted in holding. Crudely put, to be hubristic, you need not have an exaggerated opinion of your talent: it's enough that you have an exaggerated view of your powers to know certain things about that talent.

Diagnosing the Charges

In this section, I draw on the preceding discussion of the modes of humility to diagnose or 'reconstruct' the charges of hubris, chronicled earlier, that were exchanged by humanists and their opponents. The account will be schematic until, in following chapters, we turn to the substantiation of the charges.

The discussion had an important negative conclusion. At its outset, I rehearsed the argument that charges of hubris levelled against humanism and rival positions can only be rhetorical devices for branding them as false, and hence cannot have independent critical force. We now have reason to reject that argument. Charges of hubris are never equivalent to rejecting beliefs as false. In some cases, they are poorly construed if taken to be primarily targeted at beliefs rather than at 'postures'. But even where it is a belief which is targeted, the charge cannot be equivalent to rejection of the belief, since it is compatible with the truth of the belief. The fastest runner can be hubristic even though he really is the fastest runner.

So let's ask again about the point of charging humanism or its rivals with hubris. I suggest that there is an asymmetry between the main charges directed against humanism and the countercharges levelled by the humanist. The former are accusations of 'hubris of posture', the latter of 'hubris of belief'. I begin with these latter. Let us, first, recall my label for any doctrine which asserts that there is a discursable way the world anyway is independent of 'the human contribution'—'absolutist'. The two questions to then ask are: What is involved in charging absolutism with hubris? and, What philosophically relevant, critical force could such charges possess? To answer these questions, we first describe what, according to the humanist, is the *typical* form taken by absolutist doctrines.

These doctrines subscribe to what I called the 'independence' thesis: there is a discursable way the world is independent of 'the human contribution'. As the humanist sees it, however, the substance and even the sense of that thesis are typically furnished by claims that absolutists make about human abilities. To begin with, they claim that human beings have the capacity to arrive at an absolute account of the world—one which captures the way the world independently is. That claim, in turn, is given substance or sense by the claim that human beings have the capacity to arrive at an account of the world which is both 'acceptable' and 'clean'. An account is

'acceptable' if it is true by criteria of truth that the humanist is not concerned to challenge (see the opening section of Chapter 9 for elaboration).
(Whether an 'acceptable' account is also true in the sense of corresponding
to the way the world independently is will, of course, depend on whether
the 'independence' thesis can be made out.) An account is 'clean' if it is suitably untainted by 'the human contribution', if it does not bear the stamp, in
a sense to be explained, of a human perspective or form of life. Finally, the
claim that human beings have the capacity to produce an 'acceptable' and
'clean' account of the world is typically supported by the further claim that
this capacity has been at least partly realized—that some people (physicists,
say) have already arrived at an account which approximately describes how
the world independently is.

The humanist recognizes that some absolutists are not typical and demur
from the description of absolutism just sketched in different ways. Some
demur from associating the 'independence' thesis with claims about human
capacities. They may even deny, as transcendental idealists do, that there is a
human capacity to arrive at an absolute account of the world. Others reject
the thought that the capacity to arrive at an 'acceptable' and 'clean' account
of the world should only be postulated if it has already been partially realized. This is the view of absolutists who think that we may be quite in the
dark as to the nature of the independent world, but that the light might one
day dawn. The humanist will argue that such demurrals, while 'modestly'
prescinding from certain claims about human capacities, divest absolutism
of substance or even sense. We can, he thinks, only 'get a handle on' the
'independence' thesis when this is understood in terms of claims about
human capacities and their realization.

But what, in his view, makes these claims hubristic? To be sure, they are
ones that, if true, mean that human beings are set above all other creatures
in being able to escape the constraints which their creaturely condition
might be thought to impose. After all, no one, to recall Nietzsche's example,
imagines that the gnat can rise above the gnat-perspective on the world. But,
as we saw in the previous section, claims about capacities may, even if true,
be hubristic when they are ones that only creatures with enhanced cognitive
powers, not enjoyed by the claimants themselves, could have any warrant
for making. The humanist's charge against the 'typical' absolutist is that the
latter's claims are of precisely this kind. The claim on which 'typical' absolutism rests—that human beings can already provide an approximately

absolute account of the world—is one for which the absolutist can provide no warrant. (One is reminded of the point made by early critics of Kant, to the effect that Kantian humility *ought* to have taken the form, not of denying that we are acquainted with things in themselves, but of denying that we could have any warrant for supposing we are.)[59] The humanist's first task, then, will be to secure the charge of hubris against the absolutist's claim that human beings have partially realized their capacity to provide an absolute account of the world.

But what is the exact critical force of such a charge? I have stressed that justified charges of hubris against people who hold certain beliefs do not entail that these beliefs are false. The fastest runner's hubris was compatible with the truth of his various beliefs, including the belief that he is the fastest runner. So how does one impugn the absolutist's claims by showing him to be hubristic? In the case of the fastest runner, *his* lack of warrant did not impugn his belief about his prowess, but only because *we* were in a position to judge it true. In the case of the absolutist's claims, there is no 'we' in that privileged position. Indeed, there is, in a good sense, no 'he' either. 'The absolutist' is a fiction: to say that 'he' has no warrant for his claims means that *there is* no warrant for them. So although his claims might, conceivably, be true, there can be no reason to suppose that they are, and given the style of argument the humanist will adopt, there is good reason to suppose they are not .

This criticism of absolutism falls short of holding that no sense can be made of the 'independence' thesis. As the humanist sees it, 'typical' absolutism—which devolves into claims about human capacities and their realization—is intelligible, but wrong. At any rate, there is good reason to reject it. Not all absolutists, the humanist agrees, are typical: they uncouple the 'independence' thesis from claims about capacities in the ways mentioned. In doing so, however, the thesis is divested of sense. That is where the humanist's charge of lack of intelligibility enters in.

So much, until the following chapter, for the humanist's charges of a hubris of belief against absolutism. I conclude the present chapter by considering, again schematically, the charge of a hubris of posture levelled against humanism. Why do I say that it is posture, rather than doctrine,

---

[59] See, for example, Nietzsche, *Philosophy and Truth*, 32.

which is the primary target when critics complain of humanism's lack of humility? Before answering, we should recall the point made when introducing the two modes of humility, that no sharp distinction is intended. In particular, a hubristic posture will typically be associated with beliefs that are themselves perceived as lacking in humility. Nevertheless, it is often more perspicuous to regard a posture as the real locus of hubris, with the associated beliefs counting as immodest through inheriting the hubris discerned in the posture.

That it is hubris of posture at issue is suggested, to begin with, by the rhetoric which both humanists (or close relatives) and their critics indulge in (pp. 156–60 above). When Fichte recommends his idealism for the 'full feeling of . . . absolute self-sufficiency' it inspires, or when Rorty extols a pragmatism which induces a sense that we owe 'obedience [only] to our own conventions', the idiom recalls that of the various figures used to illustrate the hubris of posture. And when humanism's critics complain of a refusal of the 'objective stance', of 'cosmic impiety' and 'intoxication of power', it sounds to be a certain posture which is the target.

A more decisive reason for taking hubris of posture to be the issue is the difficulty of seeing which doctrine or thesis of humanism could, as such, be an appropriate object for charges of lack of humility. It is, to be sure, possible to characterize the thesis of 'the human world' in ways that make it sound immodest—as 'cutting the world down to size' or 'making the world dependent on us'. Such characterizations, however, cite a Promethean, 'sculptural' rhetoric to which the existential humanist, at least, is just as opposed as the critics of humanism. When the 'sculptural' rhetoric is abandoned, and when the 'human world' thesis is viewed in contrast with the absolutism schematically discussed earlier in this section, the thesis emerges as an essentially negative one: a denial that human beings have the capacities imagined by absolutists. That denial may be mistaken, but it is hard to see how, per se, it is lacking in humility.

One is drawn to the thought, therefore, that if the 'human world' thesis is hubristic at all, it inherits its hubris from that of a posture which, for humanists, is the appropriate one to adopt when that thesis is absorbed. We know what this posture is: that of the 'dis-incumbenced', 'authentic' life, one whose 'tone' the existential humanist explained in the opening section of this chapter. But why should it be presumed that this posture is hubristic? Characteristic of the posturally hubristic figures I earlier introduced—

Prometheus, the Greek shepherds, and others—was their pretence of enjoying a self-sufficiency, an 'exemption' from authority and other constraints, a lack of answerability, that they do not in fact enjoy. An analogy with dis-incumbence is not, I hope, strained. The dis-incumbenced life, to echo James's and Sartre's words respectively, is pervaded by the sense that our experience, beliefs, and values finally 'lean on nothing', that they are 'without foundations' to support the forms of life to which they are inextricably bound. For his critics, the existential humanist preaches a posture of 'exemption' which is no more feasible than the kind pretended to by the Roumeli shepherds portrayed by Fermor.

The precise target of criticism may vary. The charge might be, for example, that the humanist exhorts us to abandon those traditional concepts (and constraints) of truth, objectivity, and knowledge without which, in fact, intelligent thought and action are impossible. The general critical point, however, is constant. The posture, the tone to life, which for the existential humanist is 'vitally' enjoined by appreciation of the 'human world' thesis, is a pretence. It is marked by a hubris which is then inherited by the thesis itself: for, if that thesis really does enjoin the posture, it is one with which life cannot be in accord.

So the lines of battle are drawn up. If the humanist's charge of a hubris of belief against absolutism is made out, then there is no reason at all to accept absolutism. If the absolutist's charge of a hubris of posture against humanism is secured, humanism cannot be embraced, because no one could live who genuinely tried to embrace it. An interesting situation, to anticipate, emerges if *both* charges are secured. For it would then seem that the choice is between a thesis there is no reason to believe and a thesis that no one could live with. By the end of Chapter 10, just that situation will have been reached.

The Hubris of Absolutism

Ascent and Descent

The situation referred to at the end of the previous chapter will transpire only if the humanist can secure a charge of hubris against his absolutist rivals. The present chapter sympathetically describes his attempt to do this. Before that, it will help briefly to reprise some earlier results.

First, we should remind ourselves of what the existential humanist takes himself to have achieved in Chapter 5. There he argued that the world as we ordinarily encounter and describe it—the world of hammers, chairs, trees, and winds—is a 'human world', as intimately related to those who move about in it as a language is to those who speak and use it. Indeed, the items in that world may be compared to the words of a language in several respects: the former, like the latter, are what they are—enjoy the criteria of identity they do—through an 'operative' knowledge embedded in practices that are integrated in a 'form of life' in virtue of which alone they 'light up' so as to permit access to them. The existential humanist considered the objection that, while there is indeed no access to things except through concepts which may well be shaped by purposive practices, the 'human contribution' is thereby exhausted—for it is the world which then dictates the application of those concepts. The reply to this 'concept-bound realism' was that applications of concepts are themselves 'moves' in a 'form of life' in the absence of which no sense is to be made of whether such applications are correct or not. His real enemies, the existentialist humanist recognized, are those who concede his claim about our everyday, 'engaged' encounter with and description of 'the human world', but who insist that it is possible to ascend to or descend from these to an 'absolute account' of the world from which the human contribution has been excised.

His response is that the conception of an absolute account of the world is hubristic. So let us remind ourselves, second, of the form of this charge, as sketched in Chapter 7. For the 'typical' absolutist, we have the capacity, already approximately realized, to provide an account of the world that is both true (by criteria the humanist is not concerned to challenge) and 'clean' (free from 'contamination' by the interests, purposes, and values to which our 'engaged' descriptions of the world inevitably owe). This claim, in the humanist's view, is lacking in humility because it is one that someone could only have reason to accept if he or she were possessed of enhanced cognitive powers they in fact lack. Implicitly and illegitimately, therefore, absolutism pretends to an exalted cognitive capacity.

A further preliminary is required before examining how the humanist secures his charge. A little earlier, I referred, in the plural, to his enemies, and it is indeed the case that he must deal with different styles of absolutism. Not only is there the distinction, flagged in the previous chapter and revisited later in the present one, between 'typical' and 'atypical' forms, but, cutting across that distinction, a further one indicated by my metaphors of ascending and descending from our everyday, engaged account of the world. I shall speak of ascending and descending types of absolutism.

For the ascending absolutist, the reason that engaged accounts describe a merely 'human world', not an independent one, is that they are insufficiently theoretical. An absolute account would, so to speak, have to rise above engaged accounts on a number of scales familiarly used to measure the degree to which an account is theoretical. It would need to be more sophisticated, more abstract, and wider in explanatory scope. For the descending absolutist, on the contrary, the trouble with our engaged descriptions is that they are *too* theoretical, the products of projections and constructions that go well beyond what is actually *given* to us in our experience of the world. We need, as it were, to get below the relatively theoretical level at which even our ordinary concepts operate. What is required of an absolute account is not sophistication, but renewal of a more innocent perception; not further abstraction, but a return to that from which all abstraction begins; not explanatory sweep, but retrieval of the basic materials on which all explanation—including that implicit in descriptions of 'the human world'—is built.

There is no single form ascending absolutism must take, but it is hardly in question that, in recent times, the favoured version has been 'scientific realism'. Here is a robust statement of this position by Wilfrid Sellars:

speaking as a philosopher, I am quite prepared to say that the commonsense world of physical objects . . . is unreal—that is, there are no such things . . . [I]n the dimension of describing and explaining the world, science is the measure of all things, of what is that it is, and of what is not that it is not.[1]

The absolute account of the world, it is clear from this parody of Protagoras, is the one provided by science. It is fitting that Sellars's remarks come from a piece best known for its attack on a rival, descending form of absolutism—what he calls 'the myth of the given'. But as a specimen of the descending approach, one might cite an author Sellars does not discuss, Husserl. For him, the ascent from commonsense description of the 'life-world' to scientific theory is precisely the wrong direction to take. This is not simply because, scientists being no less human than the rest of us, science is inevitably 'pulled . . . into the—merely "subjective-relative"—life-world' and so represents 'but *one* among the many practical hypotheses and projects which make up the life of human beings'.[2] It is also because science adds another layer of theoretical postulates on top of those already lurking in the 'natural' attitude of actors in the life-world concerning the reality of the things belonging to it. What is required is a 'bracketing' of all such 'opinions about "the" world' so that what is 'first in itself', 'things themselves', may be laid bare before the purely 'spectating' consciousness. What is 'itself given and therefore has its own evidence' must 'come into view', untainted by the interests and theoretical predilections with which even our 'naive' conception of the world, let alone the scientific one, is marked.[3] Where such a descent ends up is a matter for dispute. More popular, historically, than Husserl's stopping-point—the 'pure' ego and its *cogitationes*—have been the immediate data of sensory experience, and it is with this conception of the absolute given that we shall be concerned in the following section.

Corresponding to the ascending and descending styles of absolutism are two different ways of understanding 'cleanliness', the criteria an account must meet in order to be, in a relevant manner, untouched by the human contribution. Certainly that notion calls out to be understood. It won't do,

---

[1] 'Empiricism and the Philosophy of Mind', in his *Science, Perception and Reality* (London: Routledge & Kegan Paul, 1963), 173.

[2] Edmund Husserl, *The Crisis of European Sciences and Transcendental Phenomenology*, trans. D. Carr (Evanston, Ill.: Northwestern University Press, 1970), 130–1.

[3] Ibid. 152; Husserl, *Cartesian Meditations*, trans. D. Cairns (The Hague: Nijhoff, 1977), 11 and 25.

as remarked earlier, to define a clean account as one which captures the way
the world independently is, since the absolutist's strategy is to explicate
independence in terms of cleanliness. An account portrays the way the
world anyway is just in case it is true and clean. We need to know, moreover,
what is the 'relevant manner' in which a clean account must be 'untouched'
by the human contribution. Is it, for example, simply a matter of its not
being motivated by characteristically human purposes?

As the passage quoted from Sellars suggests, the ascending absolutist
looks for cleanliness in the direction of explanatory power. The thought
here is that an account of the world is uncontaminated, in the relevant manner, by any human contribution—by any peculiarly human perspective—if
it has the resources to explain, or perhaps explain away, any such contribution or perspective. As Bernard Williams puts it, 'the absolute conception
should explain, or at least make it possible to explain, how more local representations of the world can come about'.[4] The guarantee that an account is
clean is that it has so risen above any 'local' or perspectival account as to
show, in its own terms, how these—and indeed itself—have emerged.

If, for ascending absolutism, the key to understanding cleanliness is the
explanatory power of an account, then, for descending absolutism, it is to be
sought, rather, in the neutrality of an account. As Husserl explains, the phenomenologist, in seeking a 'pure' account of what is 'given' or 'evident', is
trying to identify 'what is identical through variation of subjects and their
practical interests'—to describe items of experience with, as Heidegger put
it, their cultural 'skins off'.[5] Indeed, I only encounter the 'given' when the
content of my experience is neutral as to the actual physical existence of
anything corresponding to it. The 'given' lies beneath all possible 'life-
worlds', the neutral basis on which they are founded. The guarantee that an
account is clean, for the descending absolutist, is that it confines itself to
describing what we encounter in terms that are neutral between all subsequent interpretations of what is encountered—in terms upon which all
subjects can agree, whatever cultural skins are subsequently stretched over
these directly encountered items when they are taken up into various life-

---

[4] *Descartes: The Project of Pure Enquiry* (Harmondsworth: Penguin, 1978), 245.
[5] Quoted in Hubert L. Dreyfus and John Haugeland, 'Husserl and Heidegger: Philosophy's Last
Stand', in M. Murray (ed.), *Heidegger and Modern Philosophy* (New Haven, Conn.: Yale University
Press, 1978), 232–3.

worlds.

The proposals to understand cleanliness, and thereby absoluteness, in terms, respectively, of the explanatory power and the neutrality of an account of reality are not new. There are, for example, intimations of both in Plato's theory of Forms. The absolute is the Form of the Good, and one reason for this is that the philosopher who knows this Form knows, inter alia, *why* we perceive, experience, and conceive of things in the various ways we do. The Form of the Good is the explanation of everything, including the philosopher's capacity approximately to know it. At the same time, a Form is what is common to, participated in by, a number of objects under all variations in the ways these objects are experienced by we denizens of a world of change and illusion. Though we may not know it, we all encounter the same Form, neutral between our differing experiences, when, for example, we see trees, albeit from our 'local' perspectives.

Both proposals, certainly, have their appeal. To someone with the prior conviction that the 'independence thesis' must be true—that there must be a way the world anyway is—it is not unnatural to construe independence in terms of an account of the world which proves its freedom from human contributions either by rising above and explaining these contributions or by digging beneath them to a common, neutral stratum. It is the humanist's claim, however, that it is hubristic to imagine that an account of either kind can be forthcoming. Let's begin with his view of the prospects of descending absolutism.

'The Myth of the Given'

Descending absolutism as such does not entail any particular view of the contents of the clean descriptions to which, on this approach, we should get down to. When descending absolutism is combined with a certain plausible thought, however, it is not surprising that the favourite candidates should be those canvassed in the empiricist tradition—the simple data of sensory experience. The plausible thought is that the given or 'evident' is that with which encounters are entirely 'passive'. The more a mode of encountering objects requires 'activity' on our part, the more the suspicion sets in that 'subjective' factors are so involved that the encounters are no longer with what is just there before us, with what is neutrally presented prior to interpretation and regimentation. Doubtless, this plausible thought does not by itself force an identification of the given with the impressions, sense-data, or the like of empiricist pedigree: but this is the version I, like most critics, will discuss, with some confidence that the central observations also apply to other versions.

Parenthetically, there is a confusion to avert. By many empiricists, given items of experience are held to be 'mental'—Berkeley's simple ideas, say, or (in some of his writings) Russell's sense-data. As such, they are 'mind-dependent'. It is important to recognize that this is not the dependence on human beings asserted by humanists and denied by absolutists. The humanist rejects the claim that there is a discursable way reality anyway is, independent of human agency. It makes no difference if this claim comes from an empirical idealist like Berkeley: the claim that reality as it anyway is consists of ideas and minds is, from the humanist's standpoint, no better than the claim that it consists of material substances or sub-atomic particles.

With two groups of friends of the given, it's also worth remarking, the humanist does not have a quarrel germane to the issue of absolutism. In the first group are those for whom the given is ineffable. 'We cannot', wrote C. I. Lewis, 'describe any particular given' since in the attempt to do so we would, inter alia, have to relate it to other particulars and hence fail to specify 'it as such'.[6] These friends do not, therefore, regard the given as constituting a *discursable*, articulable realm, and hence do not fall under the humanist's hammer. (Some humanists, indeed, such as Nietzsche, happily talk of a 'chaos of sensations' which, since they resist description, cannot therefore figure in any account of the world.) In the second group are those who are simply not interested in whether experiences or descriptions of the given are of the world as it anyway is—for their interests are not in ontology or metaphysics, but in epistemology alone. For these friends, the given is a requirement of knowledge, providing the basic, 'foundational' evidence against which all statements are to be tested. Only ones that pass the test are knowably true. To the extent that friends of the given prescind from any claims about the ontological status of descriptions of the given, their position is not, directly at least, in the humanist's line of fire.

That said, it is hard to divorce these friends' view of the epistemological

---

[6] *Mind and the World-Order* (New York: Dover, 1929), 52.

role of the given from a view of how we relate to objects of experience that the humanist certainly does reject. Certainly it is true of the most celebrated attack on 'the myth of the given'—Sellars's—that its scope is not narrowly epistemological: for it impugns the picture of intentionality, of our experience of objects, which seems required if the given is to play the evidential role ascribed to it by its epistemologist friends.[7] As such, humanist critics of descending absolutism can invoke Sellars's discussion, skewing it, where necessary, in the direction of the issue which concerns them.

There are three linked points belonging to that discussion which the humanist is especially happy to invoke, for they conspire to spoil the thesis, required by absolutist friends of the given, that there is available, for description of the given, 'an autonomous fragment of a language—one that might be understood though no others are'.[8] Only if the fragment were autonomous in that sense could it be clean, uncontaminated by the human contributions which shape our engaged descriptions of the world. The first point is that, if there are such autonomous terms, they could not, as empiricists traditionally imagine, be grasped by first 'noticing' the sorts of items to which they are then applied. 'To have the ability to notice a sort of thing is already to have the concept of that sort of thing, and cannot account for it.'[9] Meaningfully to judge 'This is red', I am relating the item to other like items, exercising a concept under which they fall.

The further points ensue from reflection on the conceptual abilities required even for such simple judgements. The first of these is the 'holistic' one that concepts are not acquired and exercised one by one, 'atomistically'. Meaningfully to judge 'This is red', I must be able to judge, inter alia, that the object is coloured, not green, darker than another, and so on. As Sellars puts it, 'one could not have observational knowledge of *any* fact unless one knew many *other* things as well'. A judgement belongs 'in the logical space of reasons': it, and the concepts it deploys, owe their sense to inferential relations with further judgements and concepts.[10] Hence, to cite a follower of Sellars,

---

[7] John McDowell makes the point well: Sellars's discussion concerns 'not only a picture of the credentials of empirical knowledge, a topic for epistemology in the narrow sense, but also a picture of what is involved in having one's thought directed at the world at all, the topic of reflection about intentionality'. *Having the World in View: Sellars, Kant, and Intentionality* (The Woodbridge Lectures, 1997), *Journal of Philosophy*, 9 (1998), 436.

[8] Robert B. Brandom, *Making It Explicit: Reasoning, Representing, and Discursive Commitment* (Cambridge, Mass.: Harvard University Press, 1994), 90.

[9] Sellars, 'Empiricism and the Philosophy of Mind', 176.

'the idea of an autonomous . . . set of practices of applying concepts . . . consisting entirely of noninferential reports (even of purely mental happenings) is a radical mistake'.[11] But while traditional empiricists have been guilty of that mistake, they might perhaps concede the point, provided that the inferential network of judgements to which a report of a given item belongs consists only of propositions at that same level, that of the given. Can't the language of the given be both holistic and autonomous?

Sellars's final point is a negative answer to that question. 'It cannot be emphasized too strongly', he writes, 'that the particulars of the common-sense world are such things as books, pages, turnips, dogs'—not sensory impressions.[12] True, one can focus on, say, the colour of the book or the texture of the turnip and report what one observes—'This is red', 'That is soft'. But the intelligibility of such reports is parasitic on reference to the physical particulars. Someone who judges 'This is red' is, at a minimum, claiming that the colour he sees is what is common to particulars which are or look a certain colour, and that his current experience is a 'reliable symptom' of the object's being that colour. As McDowell, developing Sellars's argument, puts it, the exercise of even the simplest perceptual concepts, like red, 'depends . . . on having the world in view, in a sense that goes beyond glimpses of the here and now'.[13] Put differently, the inferential network, or logical space of reasons, to which concepts like red belong, is not an autonomous one, but includes as well such 'wordly' concepts as those of books, turnips, and dogs. But this is to deny that terms like 'red' belong to the vocabulary of the given at all—and to deny, therefore, that they are clean. Inferentially tied to terms like 'book' and 'dog', they are no less contaminated by the human contribution than these latter are.

While the existential humanist concurs, as anticipated, in rejecting an autonomous vocabulary of the given, he will want not only to render it in his own idiom, but to suggest that Sellars's points have a foundation in the account of human ex-istence developed in Chapter 5. Thus the first point—that 'noticing' presupposes a conceptual repertoire—does not record some 'primitive' fact about perception, or follow from the meanings of 'notice' and 'concept'. Rather it reflects the existential humanist's thought that for

---

[10] Ibid. 168–9.
[12] 'Empiricism and the Philosophy of Mind', 191.
[11] Brandom, *Making It Explicit*, 91.
[13] *Having the World in View*, 435.

items—including sensory data—to 'light up', to be accessed, so as to figure in judgement, they must be significant for human practice. It is through our dealings that items show up or get noticed as this or that, and hence as falling under concepts. It would be wrong to suppose that this emphasis on deal-ings reduces noticing an item as this or that to a bare behavioural response. As Heidegger remarks, the kind of dealings we have with items we encounter 'has its own kind of "knowledge"'.[14] An important reason for speaking of knowledge or understanding here is that we do not deal with items one by one, atomistically, but in the context of wider dealings, pur-posive and intelligent, with an array of things to which any particular item is related.

As that suggests, the existential humanist accepts Sellars's second point about the 'holistic' character even of observational concepts. Again, how-ever, he will treat the claim that all concepts are 'inferentially articulated', occupants of a 'logical space of reasons', not as 'primitive', but as reflective of the holistic character of ex-istence. The human world in which we ex-ist is a 'referential totality', to recall Heidegger's words, in which the things we encounter and deal with refer to one another, and refer *us* to a form of life in which our various practices are integrated. That is why the concepts applied to different sorts of things allow for inferences back and forth.

The final point—that the use of an observational vocabulary is 'world-involving'—is one the existential humanist has already stressed. A much-quoted passage from Heidegger, comparable to Sellars's books-and-turnips remark, makes the point explicitly:

What we 'first' hear is never noises or complexes of sounds, but the creaking wag-gon, the motor-cycle . . . .. It requires a very artificial and complicated frame of mind to 'hear' a 'pure noise'. The fact that motor-cycles and waggons are what we proximally hear is the phenomenal evidence that in every case Dasein, as Being-in-the-world, already dwells *alongside* what is ready-to-hand within-the-world; it certainly does not dwell proximally alongside 'sensations'.[15]

---

[14] *Being and Time*, trans. J. Macquarrie and E. Robinson (Oxford: Blackwell, 1962), 95. I may have misunderstood Brandom, but his remarks on p. 90 and p. 666 n. 35 of *Making It Explicit* seem to sug-gest both that the only (and wholly inadequate) alternative to his own 'inferential' account of con-cepts is the behavioural response model and that Heidegger is in effect employing that model. Both suggestions, if I am right, are mistaken.
[15] *Being and Time*, 207.

For the existential humanist, as for Sellars, our 'language of sensations' is parasitic on talk of the world. Once more, however, he will emphasize, in a way the latter does not, the human contribution. One consideration emerging from that emphasis surfaced in Chapter 5, in connection with our colour vocabulary. There, it was argued that aspects of our application of colour terms are explicable only in terms of certain general interests, notably in prediction of the behaviour of the things which have this or that colour. One could at least imagine people with very different interests— inveterate aesthetes, perhaps—whose application of the terms significantly deviates from ours. There is a further reason, articulated by Merleau-Ponty, for tying the language of sensations to that of things. Which phenomenal properties of a thing I see (hear, smell . . .) typically depends on what I take it to be. When I see my pen as black under the sun's rays, I am not *inferring* that it is black from the shimmering surface before me, even though someone who thought the pen was a courgette or a cigar-tube would see it as green or silver. Again, 'the blue of the carpet would never be the same blue were it not a woolly blue'.[16] Merleau-Ponty's point is that our sensory experiences, hence their descriptions, are responsive to our understanding of the world in which we move. In many cases, moreover, there is a clear connection between the experiences and the roles things play in activities. The toast feels warm even though it is several degrees less than the cool piece of coal I take from a recently dead fire. The strawberry feels hard even though it is easier to compress or puncture than the soft football. Such uses of our kinaesthetic vocabulary are explicable by reference to our purposive dealings with things. The strawberry is hard because it doesn't 'melt in the mouth' as this fruit 'ought to', while the football is soft because it won't bounce as it 'should' when kicked about.

But what has happened to the charge of hubris? The criticisms of the given levelled by Sellars, and amended or 'deepened' by the existential humanist, have not invoked it. So should we say, contrary to expectations I raised, that the issue of humility is irrelevant to assessment of descending absolutism? No, for it comes into play when friends of the given attempt a certain reply to the above criticisms. These, they hold, show that our *actual* observational language is not autonomous, neutral, or clean, but do not

---

[16] Maurice Merleau-Ponty, *Phenomenology of Perception*, trans. C. Smith (London: Routledge & Kegan Paul, 1962), 305 and 313.

entail the impossibility of a pure sense-datum language which, though too cumbersome and too detached from ordinary purposes of communication to be practicable, might nevertheless capture the contents of experience as directly given to us. Encouragement for this possibility might come from the refined vocabularies developed by people with, so to speak, a professional interest in the phenomenology of experience—wine-tasters, parfumiers, and so on.[17]

The trouble with our actual observational language, the defence continues, is that, as Sellars et al. have demonstrated, its concepts are not only inferentially tied to other terms, but 'world-involving', intelligible only in relation to our talk of things. The concepts of the possible language envisaged will be neither. This means that its terms must be ones understanding of which *suffices* to distinguish correct from incorrect applications. Only then will their application be immune to the influences and revisions to which that of our actual terms 'red', 'warm', etc., is subject in virtue of their inferential relations with a whole array of other terms. This, in turn, means that the sense of the new terms is fixed demonstratively.[18] Whereas 'red', on Sellars's account, is understood by means of definite descriptions—'the colour blood looks under normal conditions', and the like—'red*' is understood simply as the name of *that* visual datum. 'Red' and 'red*' will, of course, differ significantly in their extension. The blood remains red as dusk falls, but a red* sense-datum turns into a red** one the moment it 'looks darker'. The visual datum is no longer *that* one—the one 'red*' was coined to name. But, for defenders of the given, such differences constitute no obstacle to envisaging a *-ed language.

Doubtless, there are many difficulties with imagining the construction of such a pure, *-ed language, but I shall set most of these aside and focus on objections which invoke the notion of hubris. To the question whether we could have reason to suppose, of a putatively pure, *-ed language, that it provides an absolute account of what is given to us, the humanist's answer is:

---

[17] Laurence BonJour cites such cases in limited support of his claim that there is 'no reason why it would not be possible for us to have the conceptual resources to provide . . . a phenomenological description of experience to any level of precision and accuracy desired' in 'something like [a] pure sense-datum language'. 'Foundationalism and Coherentism', in J. Greco and E. Sosa (eds.), *The Blackwell Guide to Epistemology* (Oxford: Blackwell, 1999), 135.

[18] For something like this account of what the language of the given must be like, see A. J. Ayer, 'Basic Propositions', in M. Black (ed.), *Philosophical Analysis* (Englewood Cliffs, N.J.: Prentice-Hall, 1950).

only if we possessed cognitive capacities which we in fact lack. Hence to announce the possibility of this language is implicitly to pretend to enhanced powers. That answer rests on two arguments—concerning, respectively, the truth and cleanliness of a putatively pure, *-ed language— to the effect that we could have no reason to suppose the descriptions afforded by such a language were true and clean unless, impossibly, we could share the standpoint of a 'super-spectator'.

In order for 'This is red*' to be true, red* must be a genuine concept— applicable to an indefinite number of items, and capable of being correctly or incorrectly applied to them. This, in turn, requires that a user of 'red*' can recognize that newly experienced items are qualitatively the same as the datum which served, supposedly, to fix the reference of the term. These requirements spawn a familiar problem. Since the reference of 'red*', if it is a genuinely conceptual term, cannot be restricted to the single sensory item it originally named, there must be some criterion for its correct application to further items. But since it refers, in any user's lexicon, to data of his or her sensory experience, and not to publicly available objects, what could this criterion be? Only, it seems, a conviction, reliant on personal memory, that these new items are qualitatively the same as the original one. And that, surely, is no criterion at all, for it allows no workable distinction between its seeming to someone that he is correctly applying the term and his actually doing so.

That point, of course, is made by Wittgenstein in the course of his remarks on 'private language'. The conclusion he draws is that the idea of such a language is incoherent: for where we cannot distinguish being right from seeming to be right, the notion of being right evaporates—and with it, the claim of the 'private language' to be a genuine language at all.[19] The humanist may be happy to accept that conclusion, but is aware that, for many philosophers, it is too strong. That neither we nor the experiencer himself can distinguish between his applying 'red*' correctly and his conviction that he is doing so does not, in their view, entail that the distinction has lost sense. Surely, these philosophers continue, we can imagine a 'super-spectator', equipped with an infallible memory and 'direct access' to the sensory experiences of more humble spectators. He, at least, can tell

---

[19] Ludwig Wittgenstein, *Philosophical Investigations*, trans. G. E. M. Anscombe (Oxford: Blackwell, 1963), §§ 244 ff.

whether I am now applying 'red*' to items qualitatively the same as the original one.

Whether we can imagine this, the humanist will say, hardly matters: for even if we can, it is apparent that none of us are, or could be, 'super-spectators'. Hence, we could never be in a position to judge, of any putatively pure, *-ed language, that it was being used to provide true descriptions. Only if we shared the remarkable cognitive powers of the 'super-spectator' could we have any warrant to suppose that a set of *-ed descriptions were true descriptions of what is given to experiencers. The idea that we might, with sufficient patience, develop a 'pure sense-datum language' which constituted an absolute account of the given is, therefore, hubristic: it pretends that our cognitive powers might be so 'super' as to enable a discernment of its correct and incorrect uses without which its credentials as a language are bogus.

Even if the above argument is waived and it is allowed that 'This is red*' could correctly describe experiences, the question of the cleanliness of a putatively pure, *-ed language remains. To count as a language of the given, it must be intelligible in isolation from the 'world-involvement' of its speakers. This is tantamount to saying that it is one which all subjects of experience could conspire to employ whatever their 'life-world', form of life, or practical interests. Put differently, it would be the language of a 'super-spectator', distinguished this time by his complete abstraction from a life of engagement and agency—the language of a 'mere witness'.

The pertinent question is whether we could have any reason to judge, of a putatively pure language, that it even approximates to that of the 'super-spectator'. We could only if we were able approximately to place ourselves in his position. And there is every reason to think we cannot. Certainly, as we have seen, our actual observational vocabulary—'red', 'warm', etc.—is 'world-involving' and not that of a 'super-spectator'. Nor should one think that this 'world-involvement' is overcome by people like Raphael, of whom it is reported that he could focus so intently on the colours of things as to be unaware of what the things were. (Jean Cocteau tells the story of a woman who, asked what Debussy's corpse looked like at his funeral, replied 'I don't know. I didn't see *him*. *I* see nothing but colours'.)[20] For, of course, such

---

[20] Quoted by André Gide, *Journals 1889–1949*, trans. J. O'Brien (Harmondsworth: Penguin, 1978), 305.

people describe colours using terms whose sense is formed through involvement in a wider vocabulary employed for talking about the world in which people act and move.

The main reason we cannot place ourselves in the 'super-spectator's' position is that we have no idea what would 'show up' for him—what items, and what recurrences of items, would be salient—so as to be 'picked out' from a 'chaos of sensations' and linguistically registered. There can, for example, be no presumption that 'red*' will figure in his language: for it is illegitimate to assume that, in isolation from all worldly interests, monochromatic patches—rather than, say, 'fusions' of bits of those patches with bits of neighbouring ones—would 'stand out' for him. The fact is that guesses about the experiential processes of this 'pure witness', and of the language which registers them, would be wild.

The existential humanist is willing to go further than this: to deny the coherence of the idea of this 'super-spectator'. How, he asks, *could* any items of experience 'show up' except in a context of practices? But, just as he recognized that Wittgenstein's charge of incoherence against 'private languages' has no unanimous support, so he concedes that this latest charge of incoherence may be too strong for some stomachs. Again, however, that won't matter, for the charge of hubris remains in reserve. The claim that we could develop a pure, clean sense-datum language is idle unless we could tell of any candidate that it at least approximated to the language of a 'super-spectator' or 'pure witness'. But we never could have reason to suppose it thus approximated, because we do not have the capacity so radically to disengage from involvement in the world as to imagine what the experience and language of a 'pure witness' might be like. It is hubristic to suppose that we could attain the experiential standpoint of that being.

Science and Society

With 'the myth of the given' judged to be just that, a myth, the humanist can turn his attention away from the descending style of absolutism to the ascending one. There can be no absolute account of how things anyway are in terms which purport 'neutrally' to underlie the conceptual repertoires embedded in forms of life. But perhaps the criterion of absoluteness should be sought, not in 'neutrality', but in the explanatory power of an account.

Such, we saw, is the *idée mère* of ascending absolutism. The idea goes back at least to Plato, though it was, perhaps, Hegel who first elaborated it. The reason that knowledge of the Notion (*Begriff*) is 'absolute knowledge' is that this 'self-moving Notion . . . takes its determinations back into itself'.[21] The Notion is absolute because it explains, makes intelligible, the viewpoints or 'determinations'—such as religion—which offer partial glimpses of the 'unity' articulated by the Notion. Moreover, one thing in particular which it explains is its own coming to self-consciousness—how, that is, conscious beings (Hegel himself, at least) have come to know it.

The form, though hardly the content, of Hegel's position is inherited by those contemporary champions of ascending absolutism for whom it is the natural sciences which promise to provide an absolute account of the world. It is with scientific realism, in this sense, that the remainder of the present chapter is concerned.[22] Before turning to the existential humanist's rejection of the position, on grounds of its lack of humility, a more careful characterization of it is required.

The *locus classicus*, in recent times, of a statement of ascending absolutism is Bernard Williams's book on Descartes. An 'absolute conception', he writes, is one which, if true, provides 'knowledge . . . of what is there *anyway*'. As such, it is no merely 'local representation', not just one more 'perspective' from which the world may be described. Indeed, the descriptions it provides must use 'concepts which are not peculiarly ours, and not peculiarly relative to our experience'.[23] But what guarantees that a conception is not local, perspectival, or peculiarly ours? Williams's answer, already cited on p. 176 above, is that 'the absolute conception should explain, or at least make it possible to explain, how the more local representations of the world can come about', how peculiar or local perspectives can yet be 'perspectives on the same reality', one judiciously captured by the absolute account itself.

---

[21] G. W. F. Hegel, *Phenomenology of Spirit*, trans. A. V. Miller (Oxford: Oxford University Press, 1977), 37.

[22] There are other senses of 'scientific realism' from which the one I am discussing needs distinguishing. Thus it is not the anti-instrumentalist thesis, though it entails it, that the theoretical entities of science are 'real'. Nor is it the anti-sceptical thesis that much of contemporary science is knowably true—though, in its 'typical' form, it does require that we have good reason to suppose that science offers at least an approximately true account of reality. On the different senses of 'scientific realism', see David Papineau's editorial introduction to *The Philosophy of Science* (Oxford: Oxford University Press, 1996).

[23] *Descartes*, 244.

The conception's claim to absoluteness would, of course, be threatened if it could not account for its own possibility, for then there would remain something opaque about the world it purports to describe. Hence, says Williams, the absolute conception 'must make it possible to explain how it itself can exist'.[24] In my terminology, Williams is holding that an account is clean only if it is able to explain or explain away—and in that respect rise above—all those perspectives and vocabularies bearing the mark of peculiarly human contributions.

Like Sellars (see p. 175 above), though more hesitantly, Williams holds that natural science is capable of providing an absolute account. While the concepts of physics are, of course, 'ours', they are not 'peculiarly ours', and 'the picture . . . offered by natural science, would explain the phenomena . . . *even as they present themselves in other, more local, representations*'. A paradigm of such explanation is that of our perception of secondary qualities in terms of the effect on us of the primary qualities that 'characterize the material world as it really is'. Williams does not require that physics just as it is constitutes an absolute account. He is, however, a 'typical' absolutist in holding that the scientific realist 'conception of an absolute conception . . . would look too pale' if we 'have no conception at all of what an adequate physics might look like'. As it is, happily, some scientific theories we already have surely 'could not fail to represent in some way how the world really is'. Nor does scientific realism require that the only knowledge we have is that provided in the scientific conception: but it does require that 'things we know must . . . be comprehensibly related to that conception'.[25]

That final remark reflects Williams's further view that 'if knowledge is possible at all . . . the absolute conception must be possible too'.[26] Unless this were so, he reasons, it would be impossible to reconcile what would otherwise be irreconcilably rival claims to knowledge—a situation incompatible with regarding any of those claims as legitimate. This further view does not by itself entail any particular version, such as the scientific one, of the abso-

---

[24] Ibid. 246.

[25] Ibid. 244–8. Another scientific realist who is a 'typical' absolutist is Richard Boyd: '[T]he [scientific] realist must be able to defend a historical thesis regarding the recent history of relevant sciences according to which their intellectual achievements involve *approximate* theoretical knowledge . . . approximations to the truth'. 'Realism, Approximate Truth, and Method', in D. Papineau (ed.), *The Philosophy of Science*, 216.

[26] Williams, *Descartes*, 65.

lute conception. It is a view, I shall suggest, with a grain of truth to it that threatens, moreover, to grow into a real problem for the humanist. But this is a topic for Chapter 10.

Let us return to the scientific realism defended by Williams as the most plausible version of ascending absolutism. It is a position nowadays subscribed to by many people, philosophers and non-philosophers alike. Indeed, it is often passed off as the merest educated common sense.[27] This is surely both questionable and irrelevant. While most educated people accept that various scientific descriptions of the world are true, I doubt that many of them have a considered opinion on the status of those truths—as corresponding, say, to how reality is independently of human conception. Consider, by way of analogy, the implausible attribution to young people today of a commitment to 'moral realism' on the basis of their enthusiastic allegiance to 'anti-racist' and 'anti-sexist' policies. (If Allen Bloom is right, their teachers can be confident that, despite such allegiance, these young people nearly all sign up to 'moral relativism'.)[28] Moreover, to the degree that it might be legitimate to attribute a philosophical world view to a general public, it surely has not been, and still is not, the common sense—the *sensus communis*—of some publics to accept a view of which scientific realism could be an educated extension. It is often said, for example, that the predominant conviction of India is the Vedāntic one on which the physical realm is *maya*, an 'illusory' manifestation of *brahman*. Few scientific realists are likely to regard the conviction of hundreds of millions of Indians as a relevant objection to their position—in which case it is hard to see how it could be relevant to appeal, by way of relevant support, to the alleged common sense of their own societies. As Socrates taught, the relevant convictions, when it comes to philosophically weighty matters, are not those which are untutored, but those which are tried and tested in philosophical dialogue.

So let us see how scientific realism, in particular its claim to provide a clean and absolute account of the world, stands up to the trials and tests conducted by its humanist critics. In the remainder of this section, I glance at some familiar considerations, of a broadly sociological and historical kind, that are sometimes thought to militate against scientific realism. The upshot

---

[27] See, for example, Michael Devitt and Kim Sterelny, *Language and Reality: An Introduction to the Philosophy of Language* (Oxford: Blackwell, 1987), 187 f.

[28] *The Closing of the American Mind* (New York: Simon & Shuster, 1987), 25.

will be that, while the scientific realist should not be unduly perturbed by these considerations, they do hint at the more serious charges of hubris examined in the following section.

The familiar considerations are used to impugn the cleanliness of science by demonstrating the complicity of scientific enquiry and its theoretical products with wider, extraneous dimensions of human life and endeavour. While not sharply distinct, these considerations can be roughly ordered on a scale measuring the particularity and generality of the alleged complicities. At the most particular level, sociologists of knowledge study the production of scientific theories as specimens of social activity, subject to the same influences, motives, and pressures to which interpersonal enterprises generally are—jealousies, ambition, 'peer pressure', and institutional interference, as well as high-minded dedication and respect for criticism. The slant of such studies is, frequently, to stress the 'constructed' character of scientific theories. A theory does not, any more than a building, come out of the blue, ready-made, into the mind of an individual contemplator: rather, it emerges, typically, from a process of negotiation and cooperation no more immune than is the process of building to factors 'all too human'.[29]

Next, there is the thought—something of a received idea among contemporary critics of scientific culture—that, whatever the particular influences at work in specific enquiries, the enterprise of modern natural science conspires in the wider one of technological progress and control of nature. There is, wrote Heidegger, 'nothing independent in science' since it is only an 'offshoot of a . . . proliferation of tool-preparation', while for Max Scheler science is thoroughly 'human' in that it is 'primarily inspired by a will to *master . . . to order* the whole of nature'.[30] For some writers, this consideration suggests that it is only by narrowly pragmatic criteria of technological success that modern scientific theories have any greater claim to truth than, say, the belief-system of voodoo. The example is Paul Feyerabend's, who uses it, however, less in order to harp on the complicity of science with technological control of nature than to urge the wider consideration that 'history, not

---

[29] Oft-cited examples of such studies are Andrew Pickering, *Constructing Quarks* (Chicago: University of Chicago Press, 1984), and Bruno Latour, *Science in Action* (Cambridge, Mass.: Harvard University Press, 1987).

[30] Martin Heidegger, *Contributions to Philosophy (From Enowning)*, trans. P. Emad and K. Maly (Bloomington: Indiana University Press, 1999), 50; Max Scheler, *On the Eternal in Man*, trans. B. Noble (London: SCM Press, 1960), 97.

argument undermined the Gods', voodoo, and other traditional cosmologies. Scientific enquiry owed its emergence, legitimation, and 'shape' not to its rational credentials, but to 'idiosyncratic historical developments'. As with any other world view, the scientific picture is 'only partly determined by research; the basic moves which establish it consist in asserting a certain form of life' with which it resonates.[31]

Feyerabend is not alone in holding that the history of science is not the story of an autonomous intellectual development, but of one made possible by shifts in vision that science, which presupposes them, did not itself legitimate. For Husserl, the crucial shift, Galileo's, was one away from the world as 'actually given through perception' to a 'mathematically substructured world of idealities' which, henceforth, prescribes the concerns and methods of science.[32] Heidegger, as we shall see, speaks of a 'ground-plan', prepared in advance, governing the direction and possible results of scientific enquiry. Even if these thinkers have misidentified the 'basic moves', 'shifts in vision' or 'ground-plan' to which science owes, there would remain, finally, the very broad consideration that science is the work of scientists—of men and women whose original home is not the laboratory or observatory, but the 'life-world'. As Husserl puts it, 'science is a human spiritual accomplishment which presupposes . . . for each new student, the intuitive surrounding world of life, pregiven as existing for all'.[33] The ship of science cannot fail to be caught in the currents that flow through the life-world, simply because it is manned by human beings who themselves sail in them. That, for Husserl, this presupposition of the life-world impugns the cleanliness of science is apparent from his constant tirades against an age which has 'forgotten' that the life-world is the 'meaning-fundament of natural science'.

The familiar considerations just rehearsed are, doubtless, important. Certainly they do something to spoil a sanguine image of scientific enquiry that scientists, or their philosophical spokesmen, have—at least until recently—liked to promote. Those considerations make Huxley's image of the scientist humbly sitting, in childlike innocence, before the facts which he

---

[31] *Conquest of Abundance: A Tale of Abstraction versus the Richness of Being* (Chicago: University of Chicago Press, 2000), 57, 138, 79.

[32] *The Crisis of European Sciences*, 48.

[33] Ibid. 121.

obediently records look naive. On the other hand, it is hard to see that any of them, as they stand, genuinely impugn the cleanliness, in our sense, of the scientific picture of reality. For a scientific realist and ascending absolutist like Williams, a main charm of understanding cleanliness in terms of explanatory scope is that an account's claim to be clean and absolute is rendered immune to sociological, historical, and 'genealogical' considerations. As one defender of Williams's approach explains, we need to distinguish between an account's 'betraying' a point of view or perspective and its *being* a 'merely' perspectival one. That personal ambitions, general human interests, and 'shifts in vision' may have 'inform[ed] the production of a representation' entails nothing about 'the role the representation can play' in explaining and integrating all 'local' perspectives.[34]

The scientific realist can accept that theories, like buildings, are human 'constructions', but deny that this diminishes the explanatory power of the constructions—and resist, as well, the bland inference of which some 'constructivists' are guilty that the entities postulated by the theories are themselves constructions.[35] He might accept, too, that the origins and development of the natural sciences are interwoven with Baconian ambitions technically to master and exploit the natural world. But he will resist the conclusion that it is only by pragmatic criteria of technological success that natural scientific theories can be held true. He will also resist the suggestion, Nietzsche's, that the very 'utility' and practical 'advantages' yielded by the sciences are 'a sign that truth is not involved at all'—that these benefits are the sole reason for our embracing the sciences which produce them.[36] It is, he will reply, less the 'practical' superiority of natural science over other accounts of the world than its capacity to explain (away) those accounts, which is a main reason for crediting it with a truth which they lack.

Nor, finally, need the scientific realist challenge the observations that science is an activity that 'grows' out of the 'meaning-fundament' of the lifeworld, that the possibility of scientific enquiry owed to a 'shift in vision' or 'basic move' in human history, and that science executes a 'ground-plan'

---

[34] A. W. Moore, *Points of View* (Oxford: Clarendon Press, 1997), 88–9.

[35] Ros Driver, *Changing Conceptions: Adolescent Development and School Science* (London: King's College, 1987), 6, for example, is guilty of this.

[36] F. Nietzsche, *The Will to Power*, trans. W. Kaufmann (New York: Random House, 1968), § 455. For criticism of Nietzsche's suggestion, see P. Poellner, *Nietzsche and Metaphysics* (Oxford: Clarendon Press, 1995), 145 ff.

which could not, therefore, itself have been the result of scientific enquiry. None of those observations, as they stand, entail that what grew and got executed was not an account of the world with the power to explain, not only what goes on in that world, but the different views of what goes on that preceded and, in some cases, still flourish alongside, the scientific account.

In short, the scientific realist can concede the many human contributions which have gone into the production of the scientific account of the world, but without conceding that it is therefore a 'peculiarly' human account, that it is anything less than an absolute one. Put differently, the human contribution he happily admits is not the relevant kind of contribution—the kind which spoils the putative cleanliness of an account and which, the humanist insists, infects every possible account. To recall an earlier distinction, the human contributions discussed over the last few pages have been relevant only to 'the production of a representation': what they need to be, if the scientific realist's absolutism is to be threatened, are contributions relevant to 'the role that the representation can play'.

Scientific Realism and Humility

On several occasions in the previous section, I emphasized that the considerations noted there do not *as they stand* impugn scientific realism. In the present section, I argue that they may be elaborated and exploited in a manner which exposes that version of absolutism to three related, but distinguishable, charges of hubris. The earlier considerations can be viewed as having softened the enemy up in preparation for a more final assault.

The softening up preparatory to the first charge was done by drawing attention both to the historical contingencies at work in the current entrenchment of the scientific vision and to science's execution of a 'ground-plan'. Nobody doubts that, in the contemporary west at least, it is the scientific account of how reality anyway and ultimately is that is most entrenched—and not the accounts provided by, *inter alia*, Leibniz's monadology, Berkeley's idealism, Advaita Vedānta, or Schopenhauer's metaphysics of a cosmic will. Two things should be noted about that entrenchment. First, it might never have happened. Descartes's fear that the fledgling science of his day might never fly could have been confirmed. Intellectual fashion, political or religious climate, economic catastrophe—

these and much else might have prevented the full emergence and domi-nance of the scientific image. Maybe Leibniz's monadology would come to have set the 'research agenda' for future enquiry into the nature of things. Second, the failure of any rival to the scientific image to become our entrenched view was not due to the recognition, after patient and prolonged investigation, that the entities and processes postulated by the rivals did not pass muster in comparison with those proposed by physics. Monads with their 'appetites', the dark gurglings of the Schopenhauerian will, and so on, were ruled out in advance by the 'ground-plan' of science, on which only those entities amenable to mathematical characterization get admitted for consideration. The fact is that no one has ever tried, in detail, to develop the 'research programmes' indicated by such rival images of reality, or to com-pare them, in terms of explanatory scope, with those of the natural sciences.

Neither point shows that scientific descriptions of the world are anything less than true (by criteria of truth not in contention), or that various 'local' perspectives (including perception of secondary qualities) do not find an explanation in the scientific scheme. But the claim that it would be 'mad' to 'go outside' this scheme is an arrogant one.[37] For no serious attempt has been made to examine rival accounts of how things anyway are for their capacity to generate true descriptions and plausible explanations of what, by their lights, are also 'local' perspectives. It is worth noting, here, that, according to many of these rivals, science itself is one such 'local' perspec-tive: not a fundamental account of reality but, say, a set of useful devices for predicting our 'ideas', as Berkeley held, or descriptive of a certain level at which a cosmic will manifests itself, as Schopenhauer thought. Such specu-lations have never been put to the test, for we have never, so to speak, lived with and worked with the metaphysical schemes which inspire them. To assume that they could never have successfully been worked and lived with, and that no satisfying placement of scientific enquiry within their terms could have been possible, is arrogant preemption. As Christine Korsgaard observes, the insistence that science provides absolute or fully objective 'knowledge of what the world is really like' is no more than a 'statement of confidence' in science that will cut no ice with someone—Leibniz, Berkeley, Śaṃkara, Schopenhauer—who is unpersuaded that wavelengths have any

[37] Colin McGinn, *Problems in Philosophy: The Limits of Inquiry* (Oxford: Blackwell, 1993), 16.

more to do with what the world is really like than colours have on the scientific account.[38]

The accusation of 'madness' against departures from scientific realism sounds still more arrogant when one reflects that some rival metaphysical schemes, including those I mentioned, offer at least some promise of addressing what all but the most bull-headed of scientific realists recognize to be a problem for their position—the domain of the mental. The blithe conviction that 'mental ontology' can be accommodated within a 'naturalistic picture of the world' must strike many people, as it does Tyler Burge, as 'having more in common with political or religious ideology than with philosophy that maintains perspective on the difference between what is known and what is speculated'.[39] The idea that, in order to accommodate the mental at all, an adequate metaphysics must, as it were, build in the mental at the most fundamental level—as the systems of Leibniz, Berkeley, Śaṃkara, and Schopenhauer indeed do—may be wrong, but scarcely mad.

The thrust of the first charge of hubris, then, is against the immodesty of holding that the scientific account of the world has any edge over rival accounts with respect to truth and cleanliness. Only a creature able to survey such rivals, to work out their implications, to compare them with one another and with our entrenched scientific account, could have good reason to conclude that the last of these has the edge. None of us could even approximate to such a creature, and to pretend that we not only could, but actually do, is to be lacking in humility.

The second charge was prepared for by the reminders that scientific theories are achievements of human beings who participate in a 'surrounding world of life' and that they owe their entrenchment, as Feyerabend puts it, to their 'receiving a response' within that world. Scientific realists are themselves likely to issue such reminders when addressing the point, just made, that historical contingencies have played their part in the entrenchment of science. The response to that point is apt to be that, while we can imagine that history should have gone differently, it is not an accident that the natural sciences have come to provide our 'best theory' of the world. For not only do these sciences extend and lend sophistication to what has anyway become the shared common sense of modernity—the conviction, for

---

[38] Christine Korsgaard, *The Sources of Normativity* (Cambridge: Cambridge University Press, 1996), 71.

[39] In J. Heil and A. Mele (eds.), *Mental Causation* (Oxford: Clarendon Press, 1993), 117.

instance, that we live in a world of material objects subject to causal laws—
but they visibly engage with central 'projects' of modernity, such as the
amelioration of life through technological intervention. It is for reasons like
these that the postulates of science, but not those of Greek theogony or
Hindu cosmology, now 'receive a response' and 'resonate' with us.

The scientific realist who points all this out will quickly, and rightly, add
that the truth and cleanliness of the scientific image are not thereby
impugned. The step from the 'rootedness' of science in the 'surrounding
world of life' to its failure to furnish an absolute account cannot, *pace*
Husserl, be an immediate one. On the other hand, Husserl's and
Feyerabend's reflections serve to prepare for a real objection to scientific
absolutism.

The objection emerges when we ask about the scientific realist's attitude
towards forms of life in which the postulates and theories of science would
not and could not 'receive a response'. Let us recall what is supposed to render the scientific account of the world an absolute one. It is the alleged fact
that all other descriptions of the world are either false or 'local' perspectives
on the world which is canonically captured by scientific theories. Now it
may not be entirely implausible so to treat other descriptions when these
occur within a form of life already receptive to science, one already shaped
by scientific enquiry and its authority. Bible-belt creationists and flat-
earthers have got things wrong by the very evidential criteria to which they
themselves for the most part subscribe. Talk of things as red and sweet, or
even as good, is perspectival talk, explicable (away) in terms of physics or
evolutionary biology. But once attention shifts to forms of life in which the
postulates of science could have no more resonance than the pantheon of
Greek gods or Leibnizian monads have in ours, the idea that other descriptions of the world must be false or merely perspectival looks dogmatic and
arrogant.

I am imagining forms of life within which, while various scientific
hypotheses may be accepted, their status—as mere tools for prediction,
say—would be quite different from that which they currently enjoy among
ourselves: forms of life in which it would strike people as *incredible* to suppose that these hypotheses tell us anything about the world as it basically is.
It would, as Korsgaard argues, be misplaced confidence to suppose that our
descriptions or 'ways of cognizing the world' must be so 'shareable' with
these people that their ways can be seen as 'local' perspectives on the same

world that science canonically describes.[40] As for dismissing their descriptions and ways of cognizing as just false, since irreconcilable with scientific wisdom, this would amount to nothing more than the bald 'statement of confidence' in science to which Korsgaard earlier alluded.

The scientific realist's reply to this argument must be that the forms of life I am imagining are impossible. If he concedes that they are possible, then there may be accounts of the world which cannot be explained (away) as merely perspectival or, without begging questions, dismissed as false. In that event, science can no longer pretend to provide an absolute account. But to deny the possibility of the imagined forms of life is hubristic. It would 'require us to get some overview of the totality of ways life could be intelligibly be lived'.[41] Our inability to imagine, in any detail and in a way which 'brings them to life' for us, forms of life whose possibility the absolutist denies strikes me as a *failure* of our imagination—and perhaps of our historical sense: a failure which owes, no doubt, to the entrenchment of the scientific image itself. But this failure is poor reason to conclude that these forms of life are impossible. That conclusion would require an 'overview' of the intelligible ways in which life could be lived to which no one could actually attain. In denying the possibility of forms of life of the kind imagined, the scientific realist implicitly pretends to the capacity for such an 'overview'. It is that pretence which invites the second charge of hubris.

A third charge was prepared for by Heidegger's remarks on both the complicity of science with technology and its proceeding according to a 'ground-plan'. Let's first remind ourselves that, as Williams puts it, the 'possibility . . . of forming the absolute conception . . . depends heavily on the notion of explanation'.[42] It is science's alleged capacity to explain, not only how the world works, but our various 'takes' on the world, which elevates it to an absolute conception. In a significant footnote, Williams remarks that explanation in science is of a particular kind, one 'associated with the idea of *that representation of an event which enables one reliably to produce it*'. This is why, he adds, it is mistaken 'to separate radically a theoretical from a "merely

---

[40] *The Sources of Normativity*, 71.

[41] Jane Heal, *Fact and Meaning: Quine and Wittgenstein on the Philosophy of Language* (Oxford: Blackwell, 1989), 159–60. Here, Heal is expressly criticizing Bernard Williams and endorsing what she reasonably regards as Wittgenstein's view.

[42] Bernard Willams, *Ethics and the Limits of Philosophy* (London: Fontana, 1985), 139.

technological" level of scientific explanation'.[43] His point, I take it, is that, in science, we explain an event in terms of regularities of the form 'Whenever A then B' which are established, typically, by experiments which show that the B-events are (only?) producible by first producing the A-events. Production (*techne*) is therefore integral to scientific method and explanation.

These remarks are consonant with Heidegger's. For him, too, 'nature reports itself' to science as containing such-and-such objects and events only in relation to the methodology of scientific explanation, which proceeds through establishing 'causalities' that are 'strictly speaking . . . "if-then" relationships in the form of when-then'. And the reason why it is shallow to think of technology as 'applied science', why technology is 'historically earlier', is that the methodology is an experimental one requiring the ability to 'order' and produce events.[44] This is the real import of his remark that science is an 'offshoot of tool-preparation', not the cynical thought that scientists prostitute themselves in the service of industrial technology.

For Heidegger, however, in contrast with Williams, such considerations are a prelude to rejection of the absolute status of science, of its claim to provide a representation of the world independent of human interest and purpose. He wants, to begin with, to disabuse us of the idea that there is anything *substantial* in the claim that, because of its explanatory power, science should be regarded as descriptive of 'nature as such'. Rather, it is due to 'stipulation in advance', to 'the projection . . . of a fixed ground-plan', that only those events and objects which figure in the calculable 'when-then' regularities that constitute scientific explanations count as belonging to 'nature as such'. It is, then, the trivial consequence of a stipulated 'ground-plan' that 'spatio-temporal magnitudes of motion', but not colours or emotions, belong in the scientific conception of reality.[45] Second, Heidegger maintains that the notion of explanation which defines the scientific enterprise is not only just one among many notions, but that it is privileged for contingent reasons related to human purposes and interests that have become paramount in the modern world. It is a privileging which, for example, has

---

[43] *Descartes*, 248 n. 21.

[44] Martin Heidegger, *The Question Concerning Technology and Other Essays*, trans. W. Lovitt (New York: Harper & Row, 1977), 23; *Contributions to Philosophy*, 102; *The Question Concerning Technology*, 22.

[45] *The Question Concerning Technology*, 118–19.

required the atrophy of all but one—the *causa efficiens*—of Aristotle's 'Four Causes': of, for example, the concern of the Greeks with how something is possible in terms of its form.[46]

If Peter Poellner is right, Heidegger's second point was anticipated by Nietzsche. The latter, Poellner plausibly argues, would have been unimpressed by the idea that science, in virtue of its explanatory power, describes what is 'objectively real . . . independently of our . . . interests and concerns'. For

what, according to [Nietzsche], we have *de facto* come to regard as 'explanation' in science . . . is itself . . . dependent on fairly obvious interests of subjects like us. It is only in so far as we have a vital interest in predicting and manipulating various events and 'objects' which figure . . . in the course of our experience that we consider certain universal propositions enabling us to do so to be 'explanatory', that is, to be answering the questions we desire to ask.

To suppose that 'objects', like colours, which do not play a role in explanations of this kind are, for that reason, not 'objectively real', is, Poellner continues, 'evidently to introduce a criterion of reality which is dependent upon certain interests of subjects like us'.[47] In short, it is illegitimate to regard a conception as absolute in virtue of the explanations it yields if the privileging of that style of explanation—the conviction that it alone is 'really' explanatory—is itself bound to discernible human purposes and interests.

Williams is aware of the objection, which he attributes to Wittgenstein, that explanation is relative to human interests and perspectives, so that the scientific conception of the world only 'wins' relative to science's favoured notion of explanation. His reply is that it is merely 'quixotic to deny that a transcultural idea of explanation' is the one central to scientific methodology, one 'associated with the idea' of being able 'reliably to produce' the events explained.[48] But, even if we grant that, in every culture, this idea of explanation is to be found, Williams's reply is quite insufficient to secure the absolute character of the scientific conception. For what need not be—and, arguably, *is* not—true across all cultures is the privileging of the scientific style of explanation that is required if the success of that style is to entail that

---

[46] Ibid. 7.
[47] *Nietzsche and Metaphysics*, 95–7.
[48] *Descartes*, 248 n. 21.

science alone captures the world as it objectively, independently is. It is possible to imagine, or indeed actually locate, cultures in which, while 'when-then' explanations are accorded their worth for certain purposes and in certain contexts, they are no more regarded as fundamental than, in our culture, are explanations of puzzling phenomena through analogies with more familiar phenomena. In these other or imagined cultures, the questions people most desire to ask are not of a kind to invite answers in the scientific style.

Owing to the grip which science's model of explanation now exerts, there is a tendency to regard alternative styles—teleological ones, say—as primitive or confused stabs at doing what modern science so consummately does. But only ignorance, vanity, or both could make one think that Aristotle was being simple in elevating enquiry into final and formal causes over one into efficient causes; that Spinoza and Hegel were 'confusing' logical and causal necessity when insisting that nothing is properly explained until it is shown how it could not conceivably have been otherwise; that Leibniz was just eccentric to hold that an event remains unexplained until it is understood why it was 'for the best'; or that Bradley 'misunderstood the logic of relations' to propose that explanation of anything is a matter of grasping the whole reality in which it has its place. It would be more accurate to say that, for these thinkers, different questions from those we tend to pose were in the foreground, ones that invite explanations in different styles. There is no obvious reason to deny that there have been whole cultures for which these philosophers' questions, not ours, were in the foreground. Wittgenstein asked why there should not be, as perhaps there have been, forms of life which 'culminate in . . . belief in a Last Judgement', ones in which that belief is always 'before [the] mind' and in which, we might suppose, proper explanation of the vicissitudes of the world is deemed to await a final summation that makes everything fall into place.[49]

It matters little whether there have been, or only might have been, forms of life in which different styles of explanation are central. The point will remain that explanatory adequacy is relative to human concerns and interests. And if that is so, the scientific conception loses its title to absoluteness,

---

[49] *Wittgenstein's Lectures and Conversations on Aesthetics, Psychology and Religious Belief*, ed. C. Barrett (Berkeley & Los Angeles: University of California Press, 1967), 58 and 53.

for this was understood in terms of the cleanliness of the conception, a notion defined in terms of an explanatory power now seen to depend on just those interests and concerns from which a clean, absolute conception was supposed to be free. The postulated entities of science have no more claim to constitute objective reality, what there anyway is, than those which figure in world views that answer to very different styles of questioning.

What has this to do with the hubris of scientific realism? The point I have been arguing might be expressed as follows: there is no reason to think that a 'pure' or 'super-explainer' would embrace the scientific style of explanation and, hence, the kind of world view inextricably tied to that style. This figure—a cousin of the 'super-spectator' envisaged earlier—is without any of the less exalted human interests and purposes: he simply aims, and successfully so, to understand the whys and wherefores of everything 'for its own sake'. Now it may be that, as with his cousin, it is impossible to form a genuine conception of this 'super-explainer'. But suppose we can. Suppose, in particular, that we can get an overview of the whole range of styles of questions he would ask. We might then speculate that all but the scientific style strike him as secondary, that, rather like Laplace's observer, he is fully satisfied when he can spell out the totality of 'when-then' relations. Or we might speculate that he arrives at a scientific account of the world so sophisticated, so far in advance of our own, that—in a manner we cannot now envisage—he deploys it to answer all the questions, in all the styles, which he has posed. But these, of course, are the merest speculations. None of us could even begin to put ourselves in the position of the 'super-explainer' so as to confirm those speculations. Yet this is what we would need to do in order to warrant the absolutist claim of scientific realism and to have reason to suppose that the scientific conception of the world alone yields explanatory answers to all the questions people might seriously and legitimately ask. According to the third charge of hubris, then, the scientific absolutist is guilty of implicitly pretending to approximate to a 'super-explainer'.

A good deal of ground has been covered in the discussion, over two sections, of the scientific realist's claim that the natural sciences constitute, at least approximately, an absolute account of reality. A brief summary may be useful. Many people, existential humanists among them, have argued that reflections of a broadly sociological, 'genealogical' kind are sufficient to impugn scientific realism. Although they are mistaken in this, their reflections did serve to prepare the way for a more decisive criticism in the form of related charges of hubris against the absolutism of the scientific realist. The basis of the three charges made was that scientific absolutism is guilty of several illegitimate exclusions: those of (a) rival accounts of the world, (b) intelligible forms of life in which science could not 'receive a response', and (c) the centrality of styles of explanation quite different from the kind which defines scientific enquiry. These exclusions would be legitimate only if the scientific realist was blessed with insights or cognitive powers that he patently lacks—those required for, respectively, (a) a complete survey and critique of rival accounts of the world, (b) an overview of all the ways life might intelligibly be lived, and (c) a 'super-explainer's' pronouncement on the inadequacy of all but science's style of explanation. It is because the scientific realist, while lacking any such powers, must implicitly pretend to them if he is to have reason to suppose that science provides an absolute account that he is open, on three counts, to the charge of hubris in the sense specified. I conclude that science, at least as we know it, should be seen as existential humanists and others have always urged—as providing a conception and explanation of the world important in relation to certain human purposes and concerns, but no more independent of 'the human contribution', no less perspectival, than any number of other accounts that human beings have, or might have, advanced.

'Atypical' Absolutism

If, as argued, the central objection to scientific realism and the kind of absolutism it exemplifies is its hubristic pretence that human beings possess cognitive powers or capacities that they in fact lack, it is clear what type of manoeuvre champions of absolutism must make. They must dissociate absolutism from the offending claims about human capacities. They must, to recall the terminology of Chapter 7, shift to a position of 'atypical' absolutism. The typical absolutist discussed in the previous section holds that we not only have the capacity to arrive at a true, clean account of the world, but that this is already in our approximate grasp—in the form, say, of a natural scientific description of reality. Atypical absolutists come in two grades, according to which of the typical claims they retreat from. The lesser move is to concede that no current account of the world deserves to be regarded as even approximately absolute, while still insisting that human beings possess the capacity, in principle, to attain to an absolute account. The greater move is to reject that insistence, to concede that, while there is a discursable way the world anyway and independently is, this is not something human beings could ever articulate. (That move needs to be distinguished from the view—Kant's, Schopenhauer's, and Scheler's, for example—that independent reality is necessarily opaque to any discursive intelligence at all. On the former view, it is allowed that God, say, can represent and articulate the independent order of things, but that we never can—perhaps because God wants to keep it to himself.)

Although the distinction between the lesser and the greater retreats is real enough, there are atypical absolutists who either are not sure which retreat to effect or attempt manœuvres that involve elements of both. Thomas Nagel is not sure whether the world contains simply 'what we *can't yet* conceive' or, as well, 'what we *never could* conceive'. 'It *may*', he thinks, be 'largely incomprehensible to us . . . because of our nature'.[50] Colin McGinn likewise rejects the rationalist 'dogma' that 'human reason . . . [can] penetrate to the objective nature of every part of reality'. But given his serene confidence that 'we are natural objects' and that it would be 'mad' to go outside naturalistic explanation of the world, his position seems to be that it is only the ambition to articulate *some* ingredients in an absolute conception of the world—the nature of consciousness, say—from which we must fully retreat.[51] Hesitation between, or combinations of, the two retreats need not debar us from considering them separately.

Those who make the lesser retreat often say that they do so in a spirit of humility. As one defender of absolutism, A. W. Moore, puts it, 'true modesty means focusing not on the distinction between what we can know and what we cannot, but on the distinction between what we do know and what we do not. There is more than enough in this latter distinction to check our hubris'.[52] To sidestep the charge of hubris, it is enough to concede that no current account of reality may approximate to an absolute one: there is no need to deny, as well, our capacity eventually, or in principle, to provide such

---

[50] *The View From Nowhere* (New York: Oxford University Press, 1986), 108. My italics.

[51] *Problems in Philosophy*, 135.

[52] *Points of View*, 251. John McDowell, similarly, identifies lack of humility with supposing that 'the world is completely within the reach of a system of concepts . . . as it stands at some particular moment': *Mind and World* (Cambridge, Mass.: Harvard University Press, 1994), 40.

an account. Indeed, for the philosophers I have in mind, that denial is disastrous, a retreat into obscurantism. For Moore, 'there *is* no unknowable beyond' outside of our cognitive reach, and the idea of one is incoherent.[53] C. S. Peirce agreed. The 'ideal limit towards which endless investigation would tend to bring scientific beliefs', and 'concordance' with which is truth, may never in fact be reached and might look very different from current scientific wisdom. Still, 'contrite fallibilism' requires no further concessions than these, for the notion of truth beyond possible investigation by us, of truth necessarily inaccessible to scientific enquiry, is 'a fiction of metaphysics'.[54]

What prospects does the lesser retreat hold out for salvaging absolutism? I begin with a problem indicated by Williams's remark, cited earlier, that unless we know what an adequate physics might be, the 'conception of an absolute conception . . . would look too pale'. One thing he means to imply is that the approximation of physics as we know it to an absolute account of reality constitutes a strong argument for the possibility of our ever arriving at such an account. If he is right, the problem for atypical absolutists who effect the lesser retreat is that they are left without a good reason for thinking that human beings might ascend to an absolute conception.

A typical absolutist need not hold, of course, that physics as it stands provides an absolute account. But the moderate 'fallibilism' which allows that contemporary physics is not sacrosanct and is open to improvement is insufficient to deflect the charges of hubris levelled in the previous section. For there to be any chance of deflecting those charges, there must be a retreat to the view that science as we know it is only remotely related to a possible future account with any title to being absolute. The trouble is that we cannot then point, by way of an argument for absolutism, to current science as an approximation to an absolute account. As much is conceded by Moore. His 'picture of an absolute representation' cannot, he explains, 'be obtained by any known methodological strategy' from any 'extant scientific theory'. Hence, he cheerfully adds, in saying that physics can furnish an absolute rep-

---

[53] *Points of View*, 251.

[54] C. S. Peirce, *Collected Papers* (Cambridge, Mass.: Harvard University Press, 1931–58), vol. 5 § 564 and vol. viii § 13. This characterization of truth may sound idealist or anti-realist, but Peirce's many unequivocal statements of realism contradict that impression. He is not reducing the notion of truth—of which he provides a correspondence account—to ideal consensus, but denies, nevertheless, that we could intelligibly regard a theory on which there is consensus, at the ideal limit, as false.

resentation, 'physics' is a virtually 'vacuous' term. The conclusion he then draws is that reference to physics adds nothing, by way of argument, to the bare claim that 'absolute representations are possible'. This conclusion does not worry Moore since, while he thinks the absolutist assumption—that there is a discursable way the world anyway is—is true, he 'does not think that it can be justified'.[55] This is admirably honest, but cuts no ice, of course, with those, like the existential humanist, for whom that assumption is far from evident and requires a justification which, by effecting the lesser retreat, Moore debars himself from offering.

But am I not ignoring another argument for absolutism, briefly alluded to on p. 188, to the effect that all claims to knowledge presuppose a standpoint from which, when they conflict or seem to conflict, they may be adjudicated? This is a point to which I return in Chapter 10. For the present, I simply remark that, even if sound, it cannot be employed so as specifically to favour the lesser retreat. Depending on how it is construed, the argument either favours typical absolutism or is neutral between the two forms of atypical absolutism. If it is construed to require the actual availability of an (approximately) absolute standpoint from which competing claims may be adjudicated, in order for any of them genuinely to count as knowledge, then it is an argument for typical absolutism. If, alternatively, it requires only that there be an absolute standpoint, even though it may or must be forever unavailable to us, it cannot matter which of those disjuncts—'may be' or 'must be'—is opted for. For once it is allowed that there can be genuine knowledge in the absence of any actually accessible absolute standpoint, it becomes irrelevant whether our attainment of an absolute standpoint is a distant possibility that may never be realized or an impossibility.

The main objection, however, to the lesser retreat is that the atypical absolutism in which it results remains open to the same charges of hubris of which the typical form was convicted. I said above that, for there to be any hope of deflecting those charges, a science with absolutist pretensions would have to be remote from science as it stands. But that was to hold out false hope. It was not, after all, the sociological or genealogical considerations that are sometimes thought to impugn the truth or cleanliness of science which were crucial. Such considerations as the complicity of science with technology or the historical contingencies responsible for the

---

[55] *Points of View*, 75–6 and 188.

entrenchment of science served only to prompt the reflections which issued in the charges of hubris. Nor, it was apparent, did those charges rest on the thought that current scientific theories are insufficiently sophisticated or confirmed to inspire confidence in the accuracy of their depiction of the world. The charges did not, in fact, rest on any considerations that apply to science as it stands but might not apply to an ideal physics of the possible future, to a scientific consensus at Peirce's 'ideal limit'.

The thrust of the charges was that science's account of the world could only pretend to absoluteness if one were entitled to exclude, without invidious question-begging, various possibilities: those of rival accounts of the world with no less pretension to absoluteness, of forms of life in which science could not 'resonate', and of the centrality for people of styles of explanation unlike that which informs scientific enquiry. The charges took the form of accusing these exclusions of hubris in the following sense: only a creature possessed of cognitive powers far beyond our human capacity could have any warrant for making the exclusions.

It matters not a whit for this argument whether 'science' refers to science as it stands, to a future extension of current science, or to a science so remote from what we currently possess that, like 'physics' for Moore, the term has become virtually 'vacuous'. In fact, it does not matter for the argument if 'science' is replaced by some dummy term. For the point of the argument is that *any* account of the world that pretends to absoluteness will be guilty of the hubristic exclusions referred to. No human being could be warranted in thinking that he or his fellows possess the cognitive capacity to exclude the possibilities that must be excluded if some one candidate account of the world, whatever that is, is reasonably to be regarded as an absolute account. If this is right, the lesser retreat goes nowhere, for while it may be additionally hubristic to suppose that science as it stands approximates to absoluteness, the hubris identified in the charges levelled in the previous section was not of a kind from which modesty about what we presently know can rescue the absolutist. *Pace* a remark cited earlier, the relevant sort of modesty *does* require focusing on the distinction between what we can and cannot know, and not primarily on that between what we do (now) know and what we don't.

In order to win immunity from the charges of hubris, the absolutist must make the greater retreat to the position that, while there is a discursable way the world anyway is, it is impossible for human beings to arrive at an account of this way. Hubristic pretension about our cognitive capacities is thereby abandoned. The greater retreat is sometimes explicitly motivated by humility. In Nagel's case, for example, it is humility that requires the admission that the world may be 'largely incomprehensible' to us. What is common to those who urge the greater retreat is the conviction that there is an independent, discursable reality combined with a refusal, whether firm or tentative, to regard this reality as within our compass. Different reasons get offered for that refusal. For writers of a Pascalian persuasion, it is simply incredible that such a finite, 'weak reed' of a creature as man could, at least without divine aid, penetrate to the nature of reality.[56] For others, like Benjamin Lee Whorf, entrapment within local linguistic schemes that organize our access to the world entails that we live only on the 'skin' of an 'unknown, vaster' world.[57]

While the greater retreat wins immunity for absolutism against the charges of hubris, it does so only by paying several prices. To begin with, it deprives absolutism, even more emphatically than the lesser retreat did, of a supporting argument in the shape of actually or potentially available accounts of the world with an initially plausible title to be absolute ones. Relatedly, once an absolute account is held to be forever and necessarily out of our reach, it cannot play the role that made it seem an attractive prospect—that of enabling us to explain (away) our competing perspectives on the world. A final price is scepticism. It was not the intention of the typical absolutist to impugn everyday, perspectival claims to knowledge. Provided such claims— about a thing's secondary qualities, say—could, in a suitably generous sense, be 'translated' into the vocabulary of the absolute account, they may count as true. Once, however, the absolute account is placed beyond human reach, this strategy for saving everyday knowledge-claims collapses. In no tolerable sense of 'translate' may concepts and terms that we do understand be translated into ones which, ex hypothesi, we never could. In that case, the discursable reality that is truly described by the absolute account is one that our accounts of the world can only distort and falsify. The one way that our ordinary knowledge-claims could be saved—

[56] Blaise Pascal, *Pensées*, trans. A. Krailsheimer (Harmondsworth: Penguin, 1980), nos. 200, 75, for example. See, for a similar point, S. R. L. Clark, *God's World and the Great Awakening* (Oxford: Clarendon Press, 1991).

[57] *Thought and Reality: Selected Writings of Benjamin Lee Whorf*, ed. J. Carroll (Cambridge, Mass.: MIT Press, 1965), 258.

their being 'taken up' or 'translated' into the idiom of the absolute account—is now blocked.

These are heavy prices to pay by those who advocate the greater retreat. Is there the still heavier one of a lapse into incoherence? Many critics think so. The absolutism arrived at through that retreat is, after all, a radical version of the 'metaphysical realism' condemned by Putnam and his many followers as senseless, incoherent, vacuous, and the like. Whether this form of absolutism is senseless or not, it is certainly a distinctly uncomfortable position to occupy. Putnam is right to distinguish the 'metaphysical realism' he dismisses from an idea that he is 'not inclined to scoff at'—that of a 'noumenal ground behind the dualities of experience' which is 'the concern of religion'.[58] Perhaps, as he remarks elsewhere, in a nod to Kant, 'we can't help thinking that there is *somehow* a mind-independent "ground" for our experience even if attempts to talk about it lead to nonsense'.[59] In effect, Putnam is making the distinction, drawn at the start of this section, between the atypical absolutist thesis of a discursable, though humanly inaccessible, world and the 'ineffabilist' thesis that reality in itself is not discursable at all. I agree with Putnam that the former thesis is more problematic than the latter.

Crudely put, our atypical absolutist tries to have things both ways. He wants to retain the idea of an independent *world*—of something structured and replete with objects and properties to which concepts and words apply, of something apt for conceptual, linguistic representation. Yet he wants to sever the connection between an absolute representation of this world and our human, all too human, conceptual and linguistic repertoire. Richard Rorty deftly identifies an 'archetypal philosophical fantasy' in these desires: the dream of 'cutting through all [human] description, all [human] representation, to a state of consciousness which, *per impossibile*, combines the best features of inarticulate confrontation with the best features of linguistic formulation'.[60] This is a 'dream', since it is indeed hard to see how the combination Rorty refers to is possible. If confrontation with reality as such is of a kind necessarily unattainable by us humans, why suppose it to be

---

[58] *Realism and Reason: Philosophical Papers, Vol. 3* (Cambridge: Cambridge University Press, 1983), 226.

[59] *Reason, Truth and History* (Cambridge: Cambridge University Press, 1981), 61–2.

[60] *Consequences of Pragmatism: Essays 1972–80* (Brighton: Harvester, 1982), 194.

more than an 'inarticulate' one, a 'direct' intuition of the noumenal 'ground', of which some supra-human being is deemed capable? If, on the other hand, it is insisted that the confrontation takes the form of structured, conceptually informed experience of a world apt for representation, why suppose it to be of a kind from which we are necessarily debarred?

Indeed, what could that supposition amount to? We are invited, by our retreating absolutist, to entertain the idea of concepts and terms—those figuring in the repertoire of some supra-human knower—that not only operate outside of any context of human practice, speech, and enquiry, but are totally remote from any that we might understand. It is difficult not to sympathize with those many writers—'internal' realists, 'concept-bound' realists, existential humanists, and so on—who deny that we can even comprehend what we are being invited to entertain. But there is no need, perhaps, to decide on the senselessness of the invitation, for it is enough to record that the idea of a conceptual, linguistic access which could never be ours is at once obscure and groundless. The only possible ground would be the absolutist's convicion that there *must* be a discursable way the world anyway is. But the effect of the greater retreat is to render that conviction itself obscure and groundless. For it was the notion of an absolute account—of a true, clean account of the world—and of the feasibility of arriving at such an account that was supposed to lend some precision, substance, and support to the absolutist's conviction. We were asked, recall, to understand the independence thesis in terms of that notion. Once that notion becomes the atrophied one it does after the greater retreat, it is incapable of casting any light on the nature of the absolutist conviction itself.

With the two styles of atypical absolutism rejected, the case against absolutism is complete. Typical absolutism, of both descending and ascending kinds, stands convicted of hubris, of positing cognitive capacities that there is good reason to suppose human beings could never possess. The lesser retreat from the typical position proved incapable of deflecting the charges of hubris, while the result of the greater retreat is that absolutism becomes an obscurantist, if not strictly senseless, doctrine bereft of all supporting grounds.

CHAPTER 9

The Hubris
of Humanism (1)

Truth and Objectivity

In Chapter 7, I showed that, when it comes to charges of lack of humility, the traffic is two-way. While humanists accuse their absolutist rivals of hubris, they in turn are accused of the same. The reciprocal charges were, however, different in character. In the terminology of that chapter, humanists accuse their rivals of a 'hubris of belief', an accusation I supported in Chapter 8. It is, by contrast, a 'hubris of posture' of which humanists stand accused by their many critics. I characterized the posture advocated by the humanist as 'dis-incumbence'. It is the posture of those who, accepting the thesis of 'the human world', aspire to live in the recognition that, ultimately, their beliefs and values 'lean on nothing' beyond themselves, that they are 'exempt from', not 'answerable to', control by a discursable world that is independent of human thought, perspective, and interest. Accusations of lack of humility are unsurprising, I suggested, in the face of proclamations that extol, say, a 'full feeling of [our] absolute self-sufficiency' or 'obedience to our own conventions' alone. It is not, however, these proclamations per se, which are anyway overdramatic, that are the critic's target, but the pretence that the dis-incumbenced life they extol is one of which human beings are capable. It is in this pretence that the humanist's lack of humility resides.

In this section, I examine one form that a charge of hubris takes. Its thrust is that the humanist precludes himself from employing a number of concepts without whose exercise thought and rational discourse are impossible. No one, therefore, who aspired to a dis-incumbenced life would be aspiring to a human life, for that is one to which thought and rational discourse are integral. This charge fails, but it prepares the way for a different form of argument, discussed in the following section. The exchange of views considered there turns out to be indecisive, and this is for a reason explained in the final section of the chapter. There I argue that the issue of the hubris of humanism requires restatement, or at any rate a fresh angle of vision. With that achieved, I proceed in the following chapter to suggest that the charge of hubris may indeed be secured.

For thought and discourse of any serious, informative type to be possible, it is necessary that people can appraise one another's beliefs, assertions, and arguments along certain dimensions. They must be able sensibly to raise such questions as 'Is that assertion true or false?', 'Does he really know that?', 'Is her argument sound?', or 'Is that judgement of his only subjective?'. People who lacked concepts of truth, objectivity, knowledge, soundness and the like would be incapable of appraising the thought and talk of one another, and hence be incapable of characteristically human thought and talk themselves.[1] If it is shown, therefore, that no space can be made for these concepts within a humanist conception, it would follow that the posture advocated on that conception is not one that human beings could seriously adopt. (I have already alluded to one attempt to demonstrate this sort of point: Bernard Williams's contention that, unless one entertains the possibility of an absolute conception, one is not entitled to make any claims to knowledge.)

The concepts mentioned are, no doubt, intimately related, to the point, possibly, of interdefinability. (Maybe, for instance, knowledge = objectively established true belief.) For the purposes of the present discussion, there is no need to consider them all, and I confine my remarks to truth and objectivity. It will be convenient to consider these concepts in relative isolation, even if they are mutually involving.

The idea that humanists and their relatives cannot accommodate a concept of truth suitable for the appraisal that thought and talk presuppose is a familiar one. As one writer puts it, relativists, anti-realists and their ilk 'have lost sight of the point of the notion of truth', which is precisely to register the gulf between how things really stand and how they are taken to stand. With that point registered, the answer to the question 'How could there fail to be a reality independent of what people happen to believe?' is obviously

---

[1] For this line of argument, see Donald Davison, *Inquiries into Truth and Interpretation* (Oxford: Clarendon Press, 1984), especially essay 7, pp. 155–70.

'There couldn't'.[2] The humanist's response to this and similar arguments is that they illegitimately import into the concept of truth—into the meaning of 'true'—some conception, some theory, of truth. We should, he continues, confine our concern, in the present context, to the concept and to the humanist's ability to accommodate it—and set aside conflicting theories as to what makes beliefs true.

It is especially important, the humanist urges, not to confuse certain platitudes or truisms about truth, acceptance of which is required of anyone deemed to grasp the concept of truth, with substantial and contestable claims about the relation of true beliefs to the world. It is platitudinous, for example, that a true statement is one which corresponds with the facts, 'tells it as it is', and says how matters actually stand. These platitudes must not be confused with any traditional correspondence *theory* of truth according to which, say, truth is a 'picturing' relation between a statement and some structurally isomorphic fact in the world. The humanist is surely right here: when the jury decides that the witness's description corresponded with the facts, it is not deciding on a metaphysical issue. It decides, simply, that the witness was speaking truly.

For the humanist, the platitudes are vernacular ways of expressing the generalization more formally expressed by the schema:

It is true that P if and only if P.

Indeed, he would be happy to accept the 'minimalist' or 'deflationary' account of truth according to which there is no more to our usual 'understanding of the truth predicate' than our decision or willingness 'to accept any instance of the [above] schema',[3] such as:

It is true that snow is white if and only if snow is white.

That account seems, after all, adequately to explain the *point* of the concept of truth, of the expression 'is true'. When I know what a given proposition is, I do not need to call it true in order to inform you that things are as it says they are: it is enough for me just to assert the proposition itself. Plain 'P!', rather than '"P" is true', will do. Often, however, I want to inform you that a

    [2] Robert Kirk, *Relativism and Realism: A Contemporary Introduction* (London: Routledge, 1999), 45.
    [3] Paul Horwich, 'Truth, theories of', in J. Dancy and E. Sosa (eds.), *A Companion to Epistemology* (Oxford: Blackwell, 1992), 512. Horwich defends his 'deflationary' account at length in *Truth* (Oxford: Blackwell, 1990).

proposition is true when I do not know (the content of) the proposition—as when I assure you that, whatever she told you about her evening with me, she was being truthful. Given your acceptance both of my assurance and the above schema, you can now infer that the evening was innocent if 'The evening was innocent' was—as you know, but I don't—what she said.

That the 'deflationary' approach caters for the platitudes and for the point of the term 'true' makes it an anyway attractive option. Its further attraction for the humanist is, as a contemporary champion of the approach explains, that it is *neutral* between realists and anti-realists, absolutists and relativists, and related rivals.[4] Perhaps true beliefs do picture a world, as Sartre puts it, 'already fully constituted before us', or perhaps, as he himself thinks, 'there is only truth in relation to [the human] point of view that makes a world exist'.[5] That is not an issue that could be settled by consulting our understanding of the concept of truth if this understanding reduces to willingness to accept all instances of the 'It is true that P iff P' schema. Precisely because the concept is, on this approach, neutral, the humanist does not preclude himself from using it as a result of advocating the thesis of 'the human world'. Like anyone else, he can use it in its one *essential* role of appraising propositions of whose content he is unaware. Certainly the 'deflationary' option is more attractive, if less swashbuckling, than the implausible attempts made by some humanists to offer revisionary defini-tions of 'true' in the pretence that these capture our familiar understanding. Thus, *pace* Rorty, there is no such thing as 'the homely use of "true" to *mean* "what you can defend against allcomers"'.[6]

The 'deflationary' account is not without its critics. A common com-plaint is that it fails to build into the concept of truth anything to indicate why truth is something at which our assertions and beliefs normally aim. It is insufficient, critics allege, to embed the account within a wider story that explains why true belief is a desideratum: its being a desideratum, they hold, is integral to the very notion of truth.[7] This complaint will not disturb the humanist, provided that the fault is rectified by a strategy compatible with

---

[4] Horwich, *Truth*, 8.

[5] Jean-Paul Sartre, *Truth and Existence*, trans. A. Van den Hoven (Chicago: University of Chicago Press, 1989), 56 and 59.

[6] Richard Rorty, *Philosophy and the Mirror of Nature* (Oxford: Blackwell, 1980), 308. My italics.

[7] The *locus classicus* of this complaint is Michael Dummett's article 'Truth', in his *Truth and Other Enigmas* (London: Duckworth, 1978), where he compares accounts of truth which do not

'the human world' thesis. For example, the equation of 'true' with Dewey's expression 'warrantedly assertible'—which indicates why truth is desirable, since we like what we do to be warranted—would be congenial. For the idea that an assertion is warranted does not, per se, carry a commitment to a way the world anyway and independently is. It may well be that this equation is untenable: we do not, for one thing, regard the truth of a proposition as something that changes over time, whereas people's warrant for asserting it can come and go. But that problem, arguably, may be solved by a beefed-up notion of assertibility—'robustly warranted assertibility', 'superassertibility', or whatever—which is not similarly sensitive to time and which therefore comes closer in sense to truth.[8]

It *may* be that there are features of our ordinary, if hardly everyday, talk of truth which presuppose convictions rejected by the humanist. I am thinking, especially, of a tendency to consider true or false propositions that we could never, even under the most favourable conditions, have reason to regard as one rather than the other. Even if there are such features—and matters here get highly technical—the humanist need not be unduly concerned. If, as anti-humanists are the first to insist, their position is 'commonsensical', it would be unsurprising if symptoms of this common sense showed up in ordinary talk of truth. The humanist will want rid of these symptoms, but it would be exaggerated to conclude that, in doing so, he also rids himself of the concept of truth. If, by taking the 'minimalist' approach, boosted perhaps by a beefed-up notion of warranted assertibility, he is able to accommodate the platitudes about truth, to characterize the understanding of 'true' implicit in our everyday use of the term, to explain the role of 'true', and to indicate why truth is a desideratum, he surely has the right to entertain and deploy the concept of truth. (Notice that 'true' plays no role in *appraising* propositions which, ex hypothesi, we could never have any reason to regard as true rather than false. Hence, to deny that they are true or false—if that is the route taken by the humanist—is not to divest 'true' of

incorporate an indication of why we aim at truth with definitions of 'winning a game' which fail to bring out that winning is the aim of playing games.

   [8] For 'superassertibility', see Crispin Wright, *Truth and Objectivity* (Cambridge, Mass.: Harvard University Press, 1992). A statement is superassertible if and only if 'it is, or can be, warranted and some warrant for it would survive arbitrarily close scrutiny of its pedigree and arbitrarily extensive increments to or other forms of improvement of our information' (48). He goes on to argue that, for at least some discourses, 'superassertibility is a model of the truth predicate' (60). A humanist, perhaps, would hold that it is a model in the case of all discourses.

this function.) To suppose that the humanist is debarred from employing the concept is somewhat like supposing that the concept of democracy cannot be used by someone who, perhaps rightly, detects in our usual talk of democracy elements inherited from older and discredited conceptions of politics. Removal of some stains from one's clothes does not entail having to go about naked.

If the humanist's posture is to allow for the appraisal, and indeed possibility, of thought and rational discourse, however, is it sufficient to establish an entitlement to employ the concept of truth? A further requirement, it will be urged, is that he also makes room for the idea of *objectivity* of judgement. Indeed, perhaps this is not a *further* requirement, for it is, arguably, one of those platitudes about truth, which any respectable account must honour, that in appraising a judgement as true a workable distinction is presupposed between objective judgement and subjective impression.

The question of whether humanists can entertain the concept of objectivity is complicated by the realization that there is no one concept. Writers on this topic typically distinguish between an 'epistemic' and an 'ontological' notion.[9] When we refer to people, methods, and opinions as objective, the contrast is with ones that are biased, partial, prejudiced, and the like. Objectivity of this kind is, one might say, an epistemic virtue, something to be striven for if knowledge is to be effectively and reliably acquired. But we also speak—the philosophers among us, at any rate—of entities, properties, and values as being objective. Here, the rough intent is that something is objective if it exists or obtains independently of what people may think, experience, or feel. Expressions like 'objective judgement' and 'objective proposition' are therefore ambiguous. The former, for example, may refer to a judgement arrived at in a suitably impartial, detached manner, or to one that concerns an objective state of affairs—the price of a wine, say, as opposed to its quality.[10]

A natural move for the humanist is to argue that the concept of objectivity required in appraisal of thought and discourse is the epistemic one, and that to this he is perfectly entitled. For the existential humanist,

---

[9] See, for example, the articles on 'Objective/Subjective' and 'Objectivity', by Robert Audi and David Bell respectively, in Dancy and Sosa (eds.), *A Companion to Epistemology*.

[10] Thus, for both Hume and Kant, aesthetic judgements may be objective qua the judgements of impartial or 'disinterested' judges, but are necessarily subjective qua judgements which register our responses rather than describe properties that belong to the world independently of feeling.

admittedly, experience and description of the world cannot but register interests and purposes embedded in a form of life. But such general constraints do not entail that judgements must always be subject to the prejudices, biases, and intrusions of emotion that the objective person aims to avoid. The constraints do not obliterate the familiar distinction between, say, the fan's rose-tinted assessment of his team's prospects and the pundit's coolly detached one. In the previous chapter, the existential humanist stressed, indeed, that the embroilment of scientific enquiry with technological interests, or its operating according to a pre-established 'ground-plan', did not per se impugn the truth and cleanliness of scientific theories or imply that the theorists must be swayed by 'subjective' considerations.

It is not uncommon, certainly, for a philosopher to introduce a notion of epistemic objectivity so exacting that the possibility of objective judgement is no longer one that a humanist could countenance. One writer, for example, characterizes 'objectivism'—the view that objectivity is possible—as the 'conviction that there is . . . some permanent, ahistorical . . . framework to which we can ultimately appeal in determining the nature of rationality, knowledge, truth, reality . . . or rightness'.[11] The humanist's reasonable response is that objectivity so characterized is remote from the familiar, less demanding notion employed in everyday appraisal of judgements as objective rather than partial or prejudiced.

The strategy of confining attention to epistemic objectivity is threatened, however, if, as is sometimes insisted, this concept requires that of ontological objectivity. The thought here is that 'in the final analysis, the objectivity of a belief is to be explained by appeal to the independent existence of the entities it concerns'.[12] In support of this, it gets argued that there would be no point to, or virtue in, epistemic objectivity except on the assumption that, by practising it, the odds on arriving at what is independently—objectively—the case are improved. What would be the purpose, it is asked, of striving for impartial, unbiased judgement if it were decided in advance that there were no independent facts to get right or wrong?

If this line of thought is intended to show that epistemic objectivity requires 'the independence thesis' of a discursable way the world anyway is,

[11] Richard Bernstein, *Beyond Objectivism and Relativism: Science, Hermeneutics and Praxis* (Philadelphia: University of Pennsylvania Press, 1983), 8.
[12] Bell, 'Objectivity', 311.

the humanist must, of course, resist it. For it is to that thesis that his own thesis of 'the human world' is opposed. Resistance is encouraged by the reflection that the virtue of impartiality and the like is not rendered nugatory in areas of discourse, like that of humour, to which it is generally agreed that 'the independence thesis' fails to apply. Objective appraisal of a joke is not a waste of time just because, 'in the final analysis', funniness is dependent on human attitude and response. More generally, for the humanist, the attempt to explain epistemic objectivity in terms of its ontological cousin moves in the wrong direction. It is talk of things' independence or objectivity that needs explication, and in terms of the possibility of our arriving at certain sorts of judgement. This, recall, was the humanist's strategy with respect to absolutism. To the degree that the notion of an absolute conception was not explicable in terms of its cleanliness—which one may think of as a demanding form of epistemic objectivity—that notion remained opaque. As absolutists like Bernard Williams are the first to insist, the claim that science, say, provides an absolute account gets its substance from the idea that, through providing a clean explanation of our partial perspectives, it delivers epistemically objective, non-perspectival knowledge.

The suspicion will linger, however, that humanists cannot do justice to the distinction between how things are and how they are taken to be that gives point to the concept of epistemic objectivity. Once that concept is in place, the thought goes, it can play an attenuated role in areas, like that of humour, where this distinction, 'in the final analysis', dissolves. But its original place is in areas, like that of factual, empirical discourse, where the distinction must not be allowed to dissolve.

But is it true that, in these areas, the humanist cannot honour the distinction—as much of it, at least, as is required for familiar appraisals of judgements as objective? An argument for supposing he cannot is implied by Robert Brandom in the course of criticizing a position akin to the humanist one.[13] Humanists or their relatives are, Brandom argues, able to draw the

---

[13] *Making It Explicit: Reasoning, Representing, and Discursive Commitment* (Cambridge, Mass.: Harvard University Press, 1994), 53. Brandom is criticizing what he takes to be Crispin Wright's endorsement of a position that Wright, in turn, takes to be Wittgenstein's. Almost certainly, Brandom misunderstands Wright's position, for the latter does not equate correct application with communally agreed application. He argues, rather, that no workable distinction could be made between the two *if* the 'contractual' account of concept application, discussed in Chapter 5 above, were right. Whether Wright would reply to Brandom along the lines I proceed to do, I do not judge— just as I do not judge whether Wright's and/or the humanist's position is that of Wittgenstein.

obvious distinction between correct application of a concept and what an individual takes it to be, but only by *identifying* correct application with what a *community* takes it to be. For these philosophers, 'the community is incorrigible about what is a proper application of a concept'. This, Brandom holds, is mistaken and obliterates the '*objective* commitments' that our understanding of concepts carries. It is apparent, he continues, that our use of a term like 'dog' is such that 'the facts settle' whether dogs will, say, always be carniverous, 'independently of what we, even all of us and forever, take those facts to be'.[14] If so, we 'could all be treating as a correct application of . . . concepts . . . what is objectively an incorrect application of them'. And that conclusion seems at odds with the existential humanist's view that application of concepts is not settled in isolation from agreement among people.

There are at least two things wrong with this argument, if construed as an attack on the humanist. To begin with, the humanist does not, like those Brandom takes himself to be criticizing, identify a correct application of a concept with one on which there is general consensus. It is not the humanist's view that everyone's saying or judging that something is F makes it correct to count it as F. Recall, here, from Chapter 5, some of the ways in which, for the humanist, application is dependent on human agreement. An application 'reverbrates with the characteristic structures of our form of life'; it is a 'move in one sort of life rather than another', in a whole 'context of interactions' among, inter alia, 'practices and interests'; and 'compressed' into it are those 'fundamental activit[ies]' whereby people 'project' themselves towards their world. With these remarks recalled, it is clear that the humanist would reply to Brandom in the manner Wittgenstein famously replied to a similar objection:

'So you are saying that human agreement decides what is true and what is false?'—It is what human beings *say* that is true and false, and they agree in the *language* they use. That is not agreement in opinions but in form of life.[15]

---

14 This is not Brandom's own example, which concerns the terms 'mass' and 'gravitational collapse'. I amend it in order to make the following discussion simpler. The amendment makes no difference, I think—not, at least, if one agrees with the argument of Chapter 8 that 'ascent' to scientific concepts does not enable the humanist's opponents to attain to a level from which 'the human contribution' has been cleaned away.

15 Ludwig Wittgenstein, *Philosophical Investigations*, trans. G. E. M. Anscombe (Oxford: Blackwell, 1963), § 241.

Since it is upon 'agreement in form of life', not in 'opinions', that correct application of concepts depends, the humanist, like Wittgenstein, can allow the possibility of a mistaken consensus and, hence, of the maverick who rightly persuades the rest of his fellows that their opinion on some matter contradicts deeper-seated 'structures of their form of life'.[16] Maybe, for example, the 'structures' of Greek life and thought did *not* permit classifying certain people as 'natural slaves', even if that is how nearly all Greeks did classify them. The humanist, then, is not committed to the implausible claim that correct equals communally agreed application.

There is something more subtly wrong with Brandom's argument. He argues that, if dogs' remaining carniverous is independent of what we, 'all of us and forever', may say or think, then application of the relevant concepts or words is an objective matter, similarly independent of human practice. But this move from a claim about dogs to one about concepts like 'dog'— from the canine to the meta-canine—is unwarranted. How things stand with dogs and their relation or lack of one to human practice does not entail anything about how things stand with our concepts and their relation to practice and form of life. Because the canine claim does not entail the meta-canine one, the humanist's denial of the latter—his denial of the objectivist, 'contractual model' of concept application (p. 128 above)—does not require him to deny the former, to deny that the future carniverousness of dogs is independent of human conceptual practice. Consistent with his account of concept application, therefore, the humanist can allow sense to the thought that whether dogs will always be carniverous is not a function of what humans may come to say.

But *what* sense, the critic will press, can this be? If dogs of the future belong to 'the human world', how can they and their habits be independent of human conception? Well, the humanist has no difficulty in specifying *some* senses in which 'the facts' are independent of human conception. He is not, for a start, claiming that the linguistic and conceptual practices embedded in a form of life somehow, and magically, cause it to be the case that dogs will remain carniverous. Nor, of course, does he subscribe to the

---

[16] This is true even in those 'special' cases where, according to Brandom, communal consensus *does* determine correctness of application—for example (his own), where tribesmen agree to count a certain gesture as one of greeting. Even here, surely, the maverick might persuade his fellow tribesmen that they are wrong— that, say, they are overlooking an ancient, honoured tradition which would be violated if this gesture were to become a form of greeting.

hyper-Promethean idea that we make it the case that dogs remain carniverous by some stipulative convention.

If the critic insists that admission of these senses still fails to do justice to a further sense of the objective independence of 'the facts', the humanist can only ask what this further, viable sense might be. If the critic, in response, invokes the 'contractual model'—arguing that application of our concepts, once in place, is solely determined by the world, so that people who fail to apply them in the manner determined are simply mistaken—the humanist can only repeat his objections to that model. Who knows what possible shifts in constellations of purposes and interests, in form of life, may render it natural and compelling for people to apply concepts in ways that, from our present standpoint, seem odd and deviant, but which it would be invidious to brand as mistaken? Who knows what shifts may lead to a conception of the world in which there is no room for many of the concepts that we currently deploy—and who is to say that a conception where there is no room for judgements such as 'There are carniverous dogs' has got the world wrong?

It is true, of course, that if I watch a futuristic movie, I unhesitatingly describe the bone-gnawing creatures portrayed as carniverous dogs—just as I describe the similar ones living on my street. That is, I project on to a future world the concepts I project on to the present one. But this unsurprising phenomenon no more counts in favour of the independence, from forms of life, of how the world is than a similar projection of my sense of humour on to joke-tellers of an imagined future counts in favour of the independence of humour from human response and attitude. What matters is not how we, as we are now, describe an imagined world of the future, but how the participants in that world, as they will be, describe it. For the humanist, there is no reason to assert that, where the descriptions differ, either we or they must be getting things wrong. If, as the humanist anyway doubts, the familiar notion of objectivity requires us to assert this, then it is a notion to dispense with.

'Dis-incumbence': Some Rival Approaches

I have looked at only two of the notions important in appraisal of thought and talk that, according to critics, the humanist's position debars him from employing. But I take it that he would approach all of these in the general manner that he approached truth and objectivity. If his arguments are well taken, the thesis of 'the human world' is consistent with the notions of truth and objectivity familiarly deployed in appraisal, for these are neutral between rival metaphysical visions. Even if they have become infected with convictions of an absolutist kind, it is possible to remove the infected areas and be left with viable concepts recognizable as truth and objectivity.

If, therefore, the posture of dis-incumbence that the humanist urges is hubristic—one impossible to adopt—this is not because the dis-encumbenced person is denied the use of notions essential to the appraisal of thought and talk. If the posture is shown to be hubristic, this will not be through analysis of such notions. The matter does not turn, as Rorty remarks in a related context, on 'what the word "true" means . . . [and] the requirements of an adequate philosophy of language'.[17] Considerations of a less 'technical', more 'vital', kind are at work.

'Dis-incumbence' was my coinage for the posture that other writers, with greater drama, have sought to identify when speaking of the mood of *Angst*, the sense of 'absurdity', or the 'ironic' attitude which, in their view, ought to be induced by appreciation that the world is a human world, that our conceptions and norms 'lean on nothing' absolute. The dis-incumbenced person succeeds in living with or resolving a certain tension. He or she lives 'in the midst' of the world—in 'the stream of life', to use Wittgenstein's phrase—replete with beliefs and commitments, and not in the state of suspended animation that, on the surface, might seem to be the corollary of denying that these have 'foundations'. It is a dis-incumbenced posture that is urged by, among others, Nietzsche, (early) Heidegger, Sartre, Camus, and Rorty. Nietzsche's 'free spirit', for example, has his 'table of values' and beliefs, despite a recognition that there are 'only interpretations'. In the moral domain, as Iris Murdoch observed (p. 154 above), it is a posture advocated, too, by a host of 'analytical' philosophers for whom our moral judgements—'prescriptive', 'emotive' or 'projective' as they are—need not be abandoned in the face of the realization that they have no grounding in a 'reality separate from ourselves'.

The charge of hubris against humanism is that the dis-incumbenced life

---

[17] Richard Rorty, *Consequences of Pragmatism: Essays 1972–80* (Brighton: Harvester, 1982), p. xliii.

cannot be lived, that the posture which informs it is one that men and women are incapable of adopting. A predictable rejoinder to this charge is that there plenty of people—including, presumably, the philosophers just mentioned—who *are* dis-incumbenced. They subscribe to a thesis of 'the human world' and their lives are not thereby paralysed. To be sure, there may be people—familiar, for example, from the pages of Dostoevsky—who go to pieces when their absolutist convictions are punctured: people of the 'servile' sort despised by Fichte, who cannot function without the prop of a 'reality separate from ourselves' on which to lean. But the existence of such people impugns neither the possibility nor desirability of the dis-incumbenced posture. *Pace* the words put into Plato's mouth by Iris Murdoch, it is not generally true that 'the spirit must have something *absolute*, otherwise it goes crazy'.[18]

To this rejoinder, the humanist's critic has his own predictable counter. People who seem to maintain the dis-incumbenced posture are not really doing so. Either they do not genuinely embrace the beliefs or moral commitments that would place them 'in the midst' of the world or they do not genuinely internalize their humanist proclamations. The thesis of 'the human world', when it is not a 'fashionable "put on"',[19] is nevertheless one to which only people who are self-deceived or blind to its implications could sign up. Resolution of this dispute will require reflection on what it means for the dis-incumbenced life to be livable or not. But it will be useful, in preparation for that, to rehearse some fairly familiar views, both pro and con the possibility of dis-incumbence. In my judgement, the exchanges between these views are indecisive, and a main reason for that, as will emerge, is a failure to attend to *experiences* of a kind that should figure centrally in reflection on the livability issue.

The familiar views all accept that there is at least a prima facie tension between life 'in the midst' of the world and adoption of the 'human world' thesis. All of them concede that there is a temptation to suppose that serious commitment to beliefs requires the assumption that these are finally answerable to something independent of human interest or perspective. I

---

[18] 'Above the Gods: A Dialogue about Religion', in her *Existentialists and Mystics: Writings on Philosophy and Literature*, ed. P. Conradi (Harmondsworth: Penguin, 1997), 520.

[19] Hilary Putnam's verdict on the 'linguistic idealism' he associates with Derrida and other 'postmodernists': *Pragmatism: An Open Question* (Oxford: Blackwell, 1995), 75.

begin with two views on which that temptation can and should be resisted, ones which, therefore, endorse the feasibility of dis-incumbence. These two approaches—the 'heroic' and 'serene', as I dub them—are, however, strikingly different.

On the heroic approach, the tension described above is increased almost to breaking-point and the possibility of dis-incumbence is explained in terms of an individual's strength in bearing that tension. The hero succeeds, where most fail, in maintaining or forging beliefs and commitments despite a vivid sense of their ultimate groundlessness and of the threat this poses. The inspiration for this approach is, of course, Nietzsche. As one commentator puts it, 'Nietzsche . . . feels very keenly . . . that the realization that a belief is held for pragmatic purposes is halfway to its abandonment . . . "Nihilism stands at the door", and to accept nihilism and overcome it calls for a degree of inner strength far beyond the normal'.[20] But perhaps the most uncompromising version, to which many others approximate, is found in Albert Camus's *The Myth of Sisyphus*.

Camus poses the issue of livability in its starkest form: how is it possible for someone with a lucid appreciation that the 'appetite for the absolute' can never be satisfied not to commit suicide? How can this person bear the 'absurd' predicament of commitment to beliefs despite his recognition that the only world we can understand is one 'reduc[ed] to the human, stamp[ed] with his seal'?[21] In Camus's judgement, his fellow existentialists have, to a man, sold out, for they surreptitiously import the prospect of some 'transcendental', typically religious, grounding for our beliefs—thereby obliterating the real absurdity of our situation. Not so Camus's hero, 'the absurd man'. This man succeeds in living at once 'without appeal' to grounds and 'without resignation' from commitment. Through 'daily effort, self-mastery [and] *ascesis*', the 'absurd man' manages not only to keep afloat, but to celebrate the absurdity of his situation. Indeed, it is his achievement in seeing that 'man's sole dignity' rests in the capacity to bear the tension that enables him to keep afloat.[22] It is, for Camus, in 'the absurd man's' strength

---

[20] Edward Craig, *The Mind of God and the Works of Man* (Oxford: Clarendon Press, 1987), 281.

[21] *The Myth of Sisyphus*, trans. J. O'Brien (Harmondsworth: Penguin, 1975), 23 f. Camus boasted that he was no philosopher, and it is perhaps presumptuous to ascribe to him the thesis of 'the human world'. He veers between humanist remarks, like the one quoted, and sceptical ones about the 'silence' and unknowability of reality.

[22] Ibid. 54 and 104.

to 'create' beliefs, or make them his own—to 'take up his bets'—that 'majesty' is brought to his life.[23] Sisyphus has the last laugh: by endorsing the absurdity of his situation, he confers sense, indeed 'majesty', on the fruitless task to which the gods condemned him.

For proponents of the 'serene' approach, dis-incumbence does not require the Promethean heroism of Camus's 'absurd man' and similar figures from the existentialist pantheon. It is not the feat of bearing an extreme tension, but the release of tension, that makes possible the dis-incumbenced stance. Advocates of serenity agree with Nietzsche and Camus that, once the 'appetite for the absolute' is seen to be unsatisfiable, people experience a loss of an authority for their beliefs. The solution, however, is not to replace this authority by that of heroically authentic commitment, but recognition that the appetite or yearning for the authority of an independent order was always misplaced. This recognition calls, not for heroism, but for the discrediting of a bad philosophical tradition that has whetted this appetite. With that achieved, the tension with which the dis-incumbenced person must live turns out to have been only a prima facie one.

One such serene strategy is followed by Richard Rorty's 'ironist'. He or she is aware of an 'intellectual tradition' in which there exists a truth 'out there' to which we 'must try to be adequate'. But they are also aware that this tradition 'has not paid off', and that a culture is both possible and desirable where some people, at least, cheerfully dispense with hope of 'a criterion for telling whether we are in touch with reality'.[24] Freed from such useless hopes, the ironist 'faces up to the contingency' of even his 'most central beliefs and desires', but without any automatic loss of confidence in these. He will still accept the claims of, say, physics and the pronouncements of liberal morality against cruelty and injustice. It's just that he does so in ironic mode, seeing them as no more than 'descriptions' that 'work', at least for the culture in which they are current. He must, moreover, regard them, not as belonging to any 'final vocabulary', but as ones he should feel free constantly to challenge by offering 'redescriptions' that—who knows?—may 'work' better and fulfil more of our 'hopes'.[25]

---

[23] Ibid. 54 and 60.

[24] *Consequences of Pragmatism*, pp. xxxvii–xxxviii and xxxix.

[25] *Contingency, Irony and Solidarity* (Cambridge: Cambridge University Press, 1989), pp. xv and 80 ff.

For some philosophers, the accommodation of the Rortyan ironist to the dis-incumbenced stance, though less gruelling than that of Camus's 'absurd man', is still insufficiently serene. Indeed, for these 'quietists', as I shall call them, no new accommodation is necessary since, so to speak, dis-incumbence is our default position.[26] Admittedly, it is one from which we can, for a time, be displaced when in the grip of bad metaphysics. Rorty is right, therefore, that the way to dis-incumbence is through relief of a tension for which philosophizing has been responsible. But, for the quietist, this is a way *back*—to the ordinary, familiar relationship to our beliefs and commitments that we enjoyed before being knocked off course. Once we recognize how misguided it is to seek a grounding for our beliefs and commitments in an independent reality that we could compare them with, 'from sideways on', we may serenely return to our ordinary, 'participant' style of justifying our commitments (citing evidence, proving consistency, and so on). To speak in Wittgenstein's terms, our reflections will have shown us that everything is in order as it is. Dis-incumbence, so understood, is less a matter of welding together continuing commitments with acceptance of a philosophical thesis—that of 'the human world'—as one of appreciating that philosophical theses cannot touch or impugn the former.

Whereas the ironist was first and foremost a philosopher, quietist man or woman is a participant. The challenge for the ironist was to accommodate his attitude towards his beliefs to his philosophical position. The challenge for the quietist is simply to eschew the 'old philosophical problems'. With these eschewed, there is then no call to cultivate a new attitude of irony, to regard one's beliefs as nothing but provisional 'descriptions' that have so far 'worked', and that we should 'play with' in a non-stop game of 'redescription'.

The difference between the ironist and the quietist may seem to be in emphasis and rhetoric rather than in substance, but it can be sharpened by considering their respective responses to the existence of *alternative* beliefs and commitments to our own. Both agree that, sometimes, an alternative

[26] The quietism considered here is akin to the quietism, discussed in Chapter 5, that is advocated by philosophers—including John McDowell and Cora Diamond—who take to heart Wittgenstein's remark that philosophy leaves everything as it is. I do not, however, cite these authors in the present context, since it is their tendency strongly to resist labels like 'anti-realist' or 'humanist'. I have already expressed puzzlement at this tendency (pp. 123 ff).

belief can and should induce us to reconsider our own convictions: maybe the foreigners' way of looking at such-and-such a matter is better than ours. Suppose, though, the envisaged alternative—the code of the Samurai, say, or the world view of animists—is not one that could seriously induce revision to our prevailing beliefs or principles. For the ironist, nevertheless, such alternatives should indeed remind us of the sheer contingency of our convictions, and that our only possible response is along the lines, 'We are liberals, with a scientific Weltanschauung. Our "central beliefs and desires", therefore, cannot be theirs'. Reaffirmation of our beliefs can only take the form of affirming that they are ours, that they belong to our form of life.

This response, in the quietist's view, surrenders to a relativism that is surely harder to live with than the ironist imagines. If, for example, 'the last word in moral discussion is the same as the last word in etiquette . . . this is how we do it' then, as Simon Blackburn argues, there can be no 'authentic sense of the authority of [our] position'.[27] This does not mean, however, that, to keep nihilism from the door, authority must be sought in an order of reality independent of human sensibility and attitude. 'Faced with different vocabularies and voices, we compare theirs with ours', not theirs and ours with something beyond all 'vocabularies'. In doing so, we are indeed 'working from within [our] own framework . . . as of course [we] must do'.[28] This is not to say, however, that our reason for regarding the Samurai code as obnoxious is 'this is not how we do it'. Our reason is that this code exalts death, wildly overvalues physical prowess, and so on. Rejection of such alternatives, therefore, requires neither 'incumbenced' submission to an 'authority' beyond the attitudes that are contingently ours, nor ironic ascent to a position that allows us to reaffirm those attitudes solely on the grounds that they are ours. What it requires, simply, is that we remain, serenely undisturbed by philosophy, as participants in moral and other norms—for it is these alone that furnish grounds for criticism of those whose practices, beliefs, and desires differ.

I now turn to two familiar views on which the dis-incumbenced posture is not a feasible one. It is a mark of the uncertainties that surround the issue that defenders of the first of these—the 'rationalist' one—adduce considerations similar to those raised by quietists in their defence of dis-incumbence.

---

[27] Ruling Passions: A Theory of Practical Reasoning (Oxford: Clarendon Press, 1998), 279 and 304.
[28] Ibid. 294 and 306.

The main statement of the rationalist approach, in recent years, is Thomas Nagel's *The Last Word*. I have already cited, on several occasions, Nagel's charge of hubris against humanism for its attempt to 'cut the world down to size'. In the present context, it is a different charge of his that is relevant, to the effect that the humanist's posture of dis-incumbence is a 'put on', one that cannot seriously be sustained. In all but name, it is dis-incumbence he targets when complaining of those who 'accompany the continuation of substantively realistic thought and judgement with ritualistic metacomments declaring . . . allegiance' to positions of a humanist, anti-realist kind.[29] Those metacomments, were someone to make them non-ritualistically, would make it impossible for him seriously to continue holding beliefs and advancing arguments.

Like the quietist, Nagel insists that 'external' or 'meta' observations on our beliefs and processes of reasoning cannot, in general and per se, impugn or weaken our confidence in them. Judgements we make 'inside' our mathematical, moral, or whatever thinking must, in the end, 'dominate', since even to challenge their rational credentials by regarding them as 'perspectival' or 'parochial', 'one has to rely . . . on judgements . . . which one believes are not themselves subject to the same challenge'. When engaged, therefore, in 'inside', participant justification of judgements, 'the last word' belongs to the justifications themselves, not to the affirmation that 'this is how *we* do it' or 'this is my form of life'.[30]

The difference between the rationalist and the quietist emerges when Nagel writes that the process of 'outside' reflection on our beliefs and commitments must 'lead eventually to thoughts that we cannot think of as merely "ours"', ones whose 'validity' is entirely 'impersonal', and which we must view as obeying, in a 'Platonic harmony', 'the order of logical relations'.[31] Nagel would surely sympathize with Martin Buber's remark—directed against Nietzschean and Sartrean talk of 'choosing' one's commitments— that 'I can believe in and accept' something, especially something that has a 'direction-giving value' in my life, only if I regard it as 'revealed to me in my

---

[29] *The Last Word* (New York: Oxford university Press, 1997), 142.
[30] Ibid. 10–11 and 34. See also David Wiggins's criticisms of a 'naive non-cognitivism' in moral philosophy whose account of moral judgement is contradicted by 'the inner view' which 'participants' necessarily take. 'Truth, Invention, and the Meaning of Life', in his *Needs, Values, Truth*, 3rd ed. (Oxford: Blackwell, 1998), 98 ff.
[31] *The Last Word*, 142–3 and 129.

meeting with Being', not something 'freely chosen for myself', albeit in accord with 'some fellow-creatures'.[32]

What matters in the present context is not whether the rationalist's 'Platonic' or 'Kantian intuition' of an order transcendent to 'our' thought is correct. The relevant point, rather, is the insistence that it is 'unintelligible' for anyone who claims to be thinking and reasoning at all *not* to assume such an order. For if that point is correct, then the acceptance by the *soi-disant* disincumbenced person of the thesis of 'the human world', continuing as he does with his 'inside' commitments, is indeed 'ritualistic'.

The impossibility of dis-incumbence is, for the rationalist, a matter of logic: the price of the attempt to maintain it is unintelligibility. The rationalist's view differs, therefore, from an older, perhaps less sophisticated, one on which the impossibility is due to human psychology or culture and the price of adopting the posture is mental or social collapse. This is the objection to dis-incumbence implicit in the assertion by Murdoch's Plato that 'the spirit must have something *absolute*, otherwise it goes crazy'. Let's call it the '*mens sana*' objection.

Confirmation for this approach might be sought in a figure like the poet and playwright, Heinrich von Kleist, whose suicide partly owed to the 'shattering' effect on him of Kant's transcendental idealism. By restricting our understanding to mind-dependent phenomena and placing things in themselves behind 'a veil of appearances', Kant made a nonsense of our 'every effort' and 'highest goal', which is precisely knowledge of Truth, absolute and independent.[33] Kant himself, one suspects, would have sympathized with Kleist's despair, for despite his strictures on the legitimate scope of reason, Kant was sensitive that reason is 'burdened by questions' that it is not 'able to ignore', though it is 'not able to answer' them either.[34] A similar despair, resulting if not in suicide then in a kind of mental paralysis, overwhelms several of Dostoevsky's characters when it is brought home to them that reality may have no 'formula' for us to discover. Before he stiffens himself with the Camusian reflection that human dignity may be regained in the

[32] Martin Buber, *The Eclipse of God: Studies in the Relation between Religion and Philosophy* (Atlantic Highlands, N.J.: Humanities Press International, 1988), 70.

[33] Quoted by Nietzsche, *Untimely Meditations*, trans. R. Hollingdale (Cambridge: Cambridge University Press, 1985), 141–2.

[34] *Critique of Pure Reason*, trans. W. S. Pluhar (Indianapolis: Hackett, 1996), A vii.

performance of *actes gratuits*, the narrator of *Letters from the Underworld* had concluded there was nothing to do but 'subside silently . . . relapse into inertia and the blowing of soap-bubbles', for one's previous convictions have turned out to be 'airy trifles'.[35]

The humanist perception, even if not literally fatal, is, according to this objection, destructive of a healthy human existence, of *mens sana*. For it is impossible, in Leszek Kolakowski's words, 'to eradicate from the human mind the desire . . . to know what is . . . true without qualifications, true quite apart from our thinking and perceiving, from our practical considerations'. There is a 'mental compulsion', a 'drive', to seek absolute truth—which is why the news that 'the Absolute is nothing' can result only in a paralysing 'metaphysical horror'.[36] Kolakowski is non-committal on the question whether this compulsion is 'a structural part of culture or of human minds'. The compulsion is 'ineradicable' because—whether by nature or through civilization—human beings suffer from a sense of their own 'fragility', one that may only be overcome by confidence in the answerability of our beliefs and commitments. The desire for that confidence 'cannot be satisfied with anything less than the Absolute'.[37] For one thing, without the prospect of such satisfaction, our tendency would be a 'tolerant generosity' towards perspectives that differ from our own, and that would make it impossible to 'stick to' our own, for all confidence in our 'privileged cognitive prowess' would evaporate.[38] Quietists may be right that *if* we stick to our own beliefs we can, indeed must, continue robustly to reject incompatible ones. What they ignore is the corrosive impact on our own beliefs that must accompany the 'generosity', or indifference, towards rival ones which follows in the wake of 'metaphysical horror'. (Dostoevsky's narrator had made this point, too: one cause for the relapse into inertia is that one could never '*really* be angry with anyone' if there is no 'formula' for them to have got wrong.)[39]

Proponents of the *mens sana* approach are aware of the predictable, empirical objection that people *do* manage to eradicate the 'compulsion' to seek 'truth without qualifications', but without relapsing into inertia, horror, or Kleistian despair. Various responses to this objection are offered.

---

[35] *Letters from the Underworld*, trans. C. Hogarth (London: Dent, n.d.), 17 and 23.
[36] *Metaphysical Horror* (Oxford: Blackwell, 1988), 4, 13, 32, 21.
[37] Ibid. 16 and 33.
[38] Ibid. 102–3.
[39] *Letters from the Underworld*, 17.

People's claim to have eradicated the compulsion is merely 'ritualistic', a 'put on'. Or they are self-deceived: like Plato's interlocutors in Murdoch's dialogue, they may deny that they hold anything to be absolute, but 'all their life proves' otherwise.[40] On the 'cultural' version of the *mens sana* approach, it may even be conceded that people perhaps once were, and perhaps in the future will again be, capable of eradicating the compulsion. Maybe Nietzsche was right: the early Greeks really could remain 'courageously at the surface', unconcerned about the answerability of their beliefs to something 'deep'.[41] But we—the products of two millennia of Abrahamic religion and much else—are not the Greeks. For us, with our now ingrained 'fragility', to 'stick to' anything without confidence in a 'real world beneath the surface', to be 'satisfied with anything less than the Absolute', is beyond our capacity.

In rehearsing these various approaches to the possibility of dis-incumbence, I mentioned some critical points that the interlocutors raise against one another, and thereby indicated some arguments that would have to be clinched for the issue to be resolved in favour of any one approach. One thing to have emerged is that the structure of alliances is complex. While the heroic and serene (whether ironic or quietist) approaches, unlike the rationalist and *mens sana* ones, endorse the possibility of dis-incumbence, on some matters there is more in common between positions on opposite sides of that division than between ones on the same side. For example, the hero and the ironist are alone in urging a new stance towards one's beliefs and commitments in the face of the 'human world' thesis. On the other positions, that thesis either destroys the possibility of belief and commitments or leaves them serenely undisturbed. Again, advocates of the two serene approaches are alone in denying that our absolutist aspirations are inerad-icable. Champions of the remaining approaches differ as to why they are ineradicable and over the appropriate response to their being so, but they agree in rejecting the serene view that it is only bad philosophy, a played-out intellectual tradition, which is responsible for those aspirations. In their view, the serene person is guilty of an ostrich-like refusal to acknowledge both the depth of those aspirations and the powerful impact that abandon-ment of them must have.

---

[40] 'Above the Gods', 519.
[41] *The Gay Science*, trans. W. Kaufmann (New York: random House, 1974), Preface § 4.

Philosophical Moods

The approaches discussed have all construed the issue of dis-incumbence in a similar and, no doubt, natural way: as one concerning the possibility of a posture in which a person continues 'in the midst' of the world—replete with beliefs and commitments necessary for an engaged life—despite subscribing to philosophical propositions that at least prima facie threaten any such continuation. On some of the approaches, the threat was both real and insurmountable, whether for reasons of logic, psychology, or culture. On others, it was genuine but could, either heroically or ironically, be surmounted. And on one approach, the quietist, the threat was illusory: the philosophical propositions in question 'leave everything as it is'.

I now want to suggest that, on all these approaches, the issue is misconstrued. But how can that be? Did I not describe it as that of combining life 'in the midst' of the world with embrace of the thesis of 'the human world'? I did, but without due attention, as yet, to what is involved in this 'embrace'. It will emerge that it is poorly or insufficiently characterized as assenting to a number of philosophical propositions, such as 'There is no way the world anyway is, independent of human perspective and form of life'.

To develop this suggestion, I invoke one of the discussions that, in Chapter 7, inspired introduction of the notion of dis-incumbence— Heidegger's account, in *Being and Time*, of *Angst* and authenticity. The form that dis-incumbence takes in this work is that of authentic *Dasein* (human being), a 'way of existing' whereby *Dasein* attains its 'ownmost potentiality-for-Being' and which Heidegger explains in terms of 'anticipatory resoluteness'.[42] What matters in the present context is not this explanation, but Heidegger's perception of what 'calls' for authenticity, of the 'threat' to which the authentic person responds. This threat, in my terminology, is an embrace of 'the human world' thesis—in effect, an understanding of *Dasein* and the world that Heidegger himself articulates in his account of our being-in-the-world. This is so despite the fact that, on the surface, Heidegger gives a very different description of the threat to which authenticity is a response. What 'hold[s] open the utter and constant threat to [*Dasein*] . . . is

---

[42] *Being and Time*, trans. J. Macquarrie and E. Robinson (Oxford: Blackwell, 1962), §§ 54 and 62.

Angst', which is a 'mood' or 'attunement', something belonging to our 'affectedness'.[43]

To grasp the import of this remark requires attention to Heidegger's wider strategy. The 'fundamental ontology' on which he embarks in *Being and Time* takes the form, he explains, of the 'analytic of *Dasein*'—the attempt to render explicit and salient *Dasein*'s own understanding of itself and its world. A central component in 'fundamental ontology', therefore, is examination of 'affectedness' and mood. This is because it is in moods that *Dasein* and its world are 'disclosed . . . *prior to* all cognition and volition, and *beyond* their range of disclosure'.[44] It is only in virtue of an 'attunement', a proneness to be 'affected' in certain ways, that a person is 'open to' the world in a certain manner, so as then to register the things that become objects of his cognitive attention.

Like any mood, *Angst* is 'disclosive', but it has a special 'existential-ontological' significance: for what *Angst* opens up for us is not a range of objects in the world, but the very phenomenon of 'worldhood' itself. Indeed, in *Angst*, 'entities within the world . . . *sink away*', leaving exposed 'the world as such', 'the world as world'.[45] The world for Heidegger, recall, is 'the human world', the world as a 'relational totality' of 'significance', of things that owe their identity to their relations, finally, to *Dasein* and its 'projects'. *Angst*, in short, is the 'uncanny' mood in which one's ordinary involvement with things whose place in the fabric of reality is unquestioned evaporates in favour of a disturbing, 'oppressive' experience of a world inseparable from human interpretation—from, in particular, the 'average', 'public' interpretations of the anonymous 'Them' (*das Man*).

I return to Heidegger's description of *Angst* in the next chapter. For the present, the point to emphasize is that, for him, the primary threat to which the authentic or dis-incumbenced posture responds is not an explicitly articulated set of philosophical propositions, but a mood or attunement. The 'embrace' of the thesis of 'the human world' that threatens our capacity to continue 'in the midst' of the world has, as its 'primordial' form, a state of

---

[43] Ibid. 310. 'Affectedness' is Hubert L. Dreyfus's suggested translation of 'Befindlichkeit'. See his *Being-in-the-World: A Commentary on Heidegger's* Being and Time, *Division I* (Cambridge, Mass.: MIT Press, 1991), p. x. Certainly this is an improvement on Macquarrie and Robinson's 'state-of-mind'.

[44] *Being and Time*, 34 and 175.

[45] Ibid. 230 ff.

'affectedness'. The issue of dis-incumbence is indeed posed by the 'human world' thesis, but only when it is appreciated that embrace of this thesis has an indelibly affective dimension.

It would reflect misunderstanding of Heidegger's point to retort that, if the tension allegedly resolved by the dis-incumbenced posture is between continuing commitments and a mere mood, then the feasibility of the posture is of interest only to psychology. Perhaps, it will be said, people in that mood can, perhaps they can't, continue with or arrive at commitments: either way, there is no philosophical issue at stake. But this retort ignores Heidegger's insistence that *Angst* is no 'mere' mood, not some 'inner disturbance' or 'feeling' that may happen to accompany our cognitions. It is itself 'disclosive', a 'primordial disclosure . . . in which *Dasein* is brought before its Being'.[46] It would equally miss the point to suppose that we can simply partition *Angst* into its affective and cognitive components, with the latter then construed as assent to certain philosophical propositions. This overlooks Heidegger's insistence that such 'theoretical cognition' could not be the 'primordial' mode in which the disclosure of 'the world as such'—the embrace of the 'human world' thesis—occurs. The 'theoretical cognition' articulated in philosophical propositions 'reach[es] far too short a way compared with the primordial disclosure belonging to moods', which is 'beyond the range' of the former.[47]

For Heidegger, moods, including *Angst*, are, so to speak, seamless and primitive. It is bad philosophical psychology that forces partition of a mood into subsequently stitched-together elements—a psychology that locates understanding solely in 'representations', propositions or cognitive 'mental acts', while simultaneously viewing the affective as the realm of 'inner disturbances' and the like, devoid of any disclosive capacity. Moods are primitive, moreover, in that our attempts at propositional articulation, which anyway reach 'too short a way', are attempts to thematize and render explicit what is already disclosed through moods. This does not mean that there is no point to such attempts: *Being and Time*, after all, is just such an attempt. But it does mean that understanding and embrace of a philosophical disclosure, like that of 'the human world', is never a matter, simply, of registering and asserting certain propositions. Genuinely to absorb and hold true those propositions is to be attuned to the world in a way to which they

---

[46] Ibid. 173.   [47] Ibid.

attempt to give voice.[48] The propositions reach 'too short a way', not because they distort what is disclosed in *Angst*, but because they cannot communicate the 'uncanniness', the mood, that is the original mode in which 'the world as world' rises up—the original mode, that is, of the embrace of the thesis of 'the human world'.

It is not surprising to find Heidegger adopting this view of the relationship between mood and theoretical cognition. For it represents an application to philosophical discourse in particular of the general existential humanist conception of language. Philosophical talk is too far removed from the rough-and-tumble of life for its intelligibility to owe to any direct involvement with our practical activities. But, to speak with Wittgenstein, unless it is simply an instance of language gone on holiday, it must, to engage our understanding at all, participate in 'the stream of life'. What that means, I suggest, is that for theses like that of 'the human world' and its rivals to be embraced, they cannot be prised off—as so many propositions to 'stop and stare at'—from the moods in and through which the world figures for us and that vitally shape our stance or comportment towards that world.

It should not occasion surprise, either, that Heidegger is by no means alone in his attitude, for it is one bound at least to suggest itself to philosophers alert to the problematic status of philosophical propositions. It is in this light, perhaps, that one should understand Fichte's point in the passages—already cited as putative examples of a triumphantly hubristic anti-realism—in which he announces his 'disrespect' for the 'spiritual servitude' of 'dogmatists' (p. 156 above). His main aim, arguably, is not to impugn the character of his rivals, but to identify exactly what is at issue between them and idealists like himself. 'The dispute', he writes, is 'actually' one over 'the self-sufficiency of the I', and the idealist is someone who 'shoulders his own self-sufficiency'. As such, Fichte continues, the nature of the dispute confirms that, more generally, 'a philosophical system is not a lifeless household item' but something 'animated by the very soul' of those who embrace it.[49]

---

[48] In his later writings, which I will discuss further in Chapters 11 and 12, Heidegger goes further than this. '[T]he thinking-saying of philosophy . . . does not describe . . . explain' or state at all. Rather, it facilitates a 'grounding-attunement', helps prepare for the 'transformation of the man who understands' that 'takes place' in 'philosophical knowing'. *Contributions to Philosophy (From Enowning)*, trans. P. Emad and K. Maly (Bloomington: Indiana University Press, 1999), §§ 1 and 5.

[49] *Introductions to the* Wissenschaftslehre *and Other Writings*, trans. D. Breazeale (Indianapolis: Hackett, 1994), 17 ff.

His point, in Heideggerean terminology, is that embrace of a philosophical position is a matter, primarily, not of a 'theoretical cognition', but of a mood or attunement to the world that the propositions registering that cognition struggle to convey.

Perhaps this is the way, too, to understand some of William James's apparent excursions into the psychology of philosophers—his division of them, for example, into 'tender-' and 'tough-minded'. If, as he puts it in prag-matist spirit, 'there can *be* no difference . . . that doesn't *make* a difference',[50] there arises a real question concerning the character of the differences that divide philosophical positions apparently remote from the practices to which more mundane thought and talk makes a difference. James notes, for instance, that it is difficult to discern what substantially, and not just rhetoric-ally, distinguishes monists from pluralists. A distinction, he goes on to say, may however be observed at the affective level, in the tone, as it were, that the world takes on for these rivals. The monist is one who 'sees the All-Good in the All-Real' and for whom, perhaps—as for religious people more gener-ally—the world is a 'Thou', rather than an 'It', and so something to relate to in the manner suggested by that perception.[51] For James, too, then, it seems that the mood of someone who embraces a philosophical position is not a bolt-on, psychological extra, but the very form of that embrace.[52]

These views of the intimate relationship between philosophical theses and affectivity should be distinguished from that of a group of philosophers whose central tenet indeed rendered the status of the former problematic. I refer, of course, to the logical positivists. In their hands, the relationship between philosophical—at any rate, 'metaphysical'—claims and affective phenomena takes the form of a *reduction* of the first to the second. Rudolf Carnap, for instance, argues on verificationist grounds that metaphysical utterances are devoid of 'literal' or 'cognitive' meaning. Since they are not, however, meaningless in the manner of a mere jumble of words, we can

---

[50] *The Writings of William James* (Chicago: University of Chicago Press, 1977), 379.

[51] Ibid. 268, 733.

[52] John McDowell should be added to this list of thinkers for whom embrace of philosophical positions is more than a matter of assent to certain propositions. In Chapter 1, I cited his character-izations of the competing positions of 'philosophical realism' and humanism in its 'virulent' form of 'social pragmatism'. Built into those characterizations, it seems, are references to the moods of those who embrace these positions—to, for instance, a sense of 'terror' or 'vertigo'—and to further 'vital' dimensions of embracing them.

allow them the same sort of meaning that, say, laughing has. They have 'expressive' meaning, registering emotions, rather as poetry, in Carnap's view, has.[53]

The Heideggerean approach will, to be sure, have little sympathy for at least one motive behind Carnap's conclusion. For this is rooted in just that bad philosophical psychology discussed above: the dichotomy between thoughts or propositions as the sole vehicles of understanding and feelings or emotions as 'inner' episodes bereft of epistemic import. It is because metaphysical utterances, in Carnap's view, cannot register the former that they are reduced to expressions of the latter. Still, there is no need to object to the characterization of philosophical claims as expressive or even poetic, provided these notions are not relegated to the second-class status Carnap plainly intends. The idea that 'poetic' talk inevitably belongs outside the language in which people try to convey understanding must strike all but the most philistine as comical. Nor, of course, can it be seriously contended that, in being 'expressive', philosophical talk must therefore be akin to laughing. When, for example, Merleau-Ponty speaks of language as expressive, he means that it is the speaker's way of 'project[ing] himself towards "a world" . . . [of] taking up a position in the world of his meanings'.[54] To call attention to the way in which certain philosophical utterances may indeed be 'expressive' and 'poetic' is not to treat them as ejaculations prompted by 'inner disturbances'. Rather it is to emphasize, once more, that such utterances are our attempts to give voice and articulation to the disclosive moods in which understanding and embrace first take place.

This chapter began with a reminder of the issue of the hubris of humanism. This was the issue of whether a certain posture—dis-incumbence—could be 'lived': for if it cannot, there is hubris in the humanist's claim that it could and should be adopted. We should have to have powers or capacities that we do not possess. In the first section, I considered and rejected the charge that the dis-incumbenced posture is impossible because anyone trying to adopt it would deny himself the use of notions, like that of truth, without which intelligent engagement in the world and with one's fellows could not proceed. In the following section, I rehearsed a number of views,

[53] *Philosophy and Logical Syntax* (London: Kegan Paul, 1935), 29.

[54] Maurice Merleau-Ponty, *Phenomenology of Perception*, trans. C. Smith (London: Routledge & Kegan Paul, 1962), 191 f.

pro and con the feasibility of dis-incumbence, that turned out, in my judgement, to be indecisive—for a reason I have tried to expose in the present section.

Those views construe the tension that would have to be resolved by the dis-incumbenced person as one between the beliefs and commitments necessary for life 'in the midst' of the world and assent to certain philosophical propositions—those that articulate the humanist's thesis, the 'human world' thesis. With the help of Heidegger's discussion of affectedness, mood, and attunement, I have proposed that this tension be viewed differently: as one between beliefs, commitments, etc. and the mood or attunement that discloses the world in the way to which philosophical articulation of the 'human world' thesis attempts to give voice.

To restate the issue of dis-incumbence, of the hubris of humanism, in this way is not, of course, to settle it. The question remains: can the dis-incumbenced posture be adopted and maintained? What the restatement does achieve, however, is to open up the issue to a range of considerations—concerning the mood of the humanist vision—that have so far remained out of view. In the next chapter, these considerations are let into the picture.

CHAPTER 10

The Hubris
of Humanism (2)

Dis-incumbence and 'Compensation':
Three Experiences

My purpose in this chapter is to secure the charge of lack of humility against existential humanism and its close relatives. The strategy is to establish the unlivability of the dis-incumbenced posture. This is equivalent to establishing the impossibility of embracing the thesis of 'the human world' unless—a point I shall come to—that embrace is 'compensated'. It will emerge that the claim that uncompensated embrace of humanism would be unendurable is something of a tautology. For the notion of this embrace—of the 'mood' that reveals 'the human world' (see pp. 232 ff)—will have been so packed or invested that its unendurability becomes evident. William James wrote of certain ideas 'growing hot and alive within us', so that 'everything has to re-crystallize about' them.[1] My objective is to suggest that when the 'human world' thesis becomes 'hot and alive within us'—and not simply a set of propositions coolly stared at and assented to—then, indeed, matters 'crystallize' in a certain way, one that human beings cannot take.

Tautologies, being 'true by definition', do not, in a sense, need arguing for. What may require argument and, in our case, certainly does, is the way of understanding of crucial notions which implies the tautologous character of various claims in which they figure. So work must be done to motivate a certain understanding of what it is to embrace uncompensated humanism. If this work is well done, it follows that the appropriate response to the

---

[1] *The Varieties of Religious Experience* (New York: Longmans, Green & Co., 1923), 197.

thesis of 'the human world' cannot be one of exhilarating frisson, of Foucauldian celebration at the passing of the 'danger' of 'constraints' on our 'transgressive activity'.[2] Nor can it be a 'serene' one, whether an ironic hovering above our beliefs and commitments or a quietist confidence that everything remains where it was, without 're-crystallization'.

It is, I said, 'uncompensated' embrace of humanism that would be unendurable. Let me explain this qualification by recalling some remarks from Chapter 1 on the Indian philosopher, Śaṃkara. If humanism is the thesis that there is no discursable way the world anyway is, independently of human perspective and interest, then Śaṃkara was a humanist. For while he thinks there is an independent, absolute reality, *brahman*, this is not discursable. We might, I suggested, mark the difference between his position and the humanism whose development was charted in Chapters 2–5 by saying that his is not a 'raw' humanism. That is just a matter of labelling. The important point in the present context is that the doctrine of *brahman* is a good example of one that 'compensates' for the thesis of 'the human world'. Śaṃkara's view is that that thesis *would* be unendurable *without* the further compensating doctrine. By uncompensated embrace of humanism, I mean an embrace *not* complemented by the embrace of some further thesis whose effect, putatively, is to render humanism endurable. It is clear that the forms of humanism on which I have focused— Prometheanism, for example, and existential humanism—are *not* thus complemented. Raw humanism comes without compensation. That is why, in these forms, the only available way of accommodating to humanism is adoption of the dis-incumbenced posture. It is why, therefore, to demonstrate that dis-incumbence is unlivable is equivalent to showing that uncompensated embrace of humanism is impossible.

In this section, my tactic is inductive in style: I pile up testimonies to the unendurability of uncompensated humanism. These are the testimonies of thinkers who have at once embraced the 'human world' thesis, as something 'hot and alive', and recognized that, uncompensated, it is unendurable. Although I cite only a selection of testimonies, their scale, like the stature of many of the testifiers, is impressive. But it is not primarily weight of numbers or reputation that is intended to prepare for acceptance of the charge of

---

[2] David Owen, *Maturity and Modernity: Nietzsche, Weber, Foucault, and the Ambivalence of Reason* (London: Routledge, 1994), 207.

hubris against humanism. The citations will, I hope, serve to support both my earlier proposal that the primary vehicle of the embrace of humanism is a mood or attunement, and my present proposal that this mood incorporates an appreciation of the unlivability of uncompensated humanism. Taken together, the testimonies serve to enrich the depiction of the mood of embrace. This is because they are not monochromatic, and indeed fall into distinguishable 'ranges', within which, moreover, interesting differences are discernible.

I shall speak of 'ranges of experience' that these ranges of testimony evoke. The experience(s) in a given range might be called a 'modality' of the mood of embrace of humanism. The term 'experience', as I intend it, is invested with a similar force to that of 'mood'. An experience, like the mood of which it is a modality, is a revelatory state of 'affectedness', an attunement in the light of which matters 'crystallize' in a distinctive way. Only in the second section of this chapter do I attempt to distill, so to speak, the essence of these ranges of experience, of the mood to which they belong, and to argue—no longer in inductive style—that the charge of hubris against humanism may indeed be secured. For convenience, I label the three ranges of experience and testimony now chronicled the 'Asian', 'aphasic', and 'unheimlich' ones. These are not to be thought of as exclusive: indeed, they lend themselves to the kind of 'distillation' attempted in the next section.

(a) The 'Asian' Experience

By this label, I do not mean to imply that testimonies of the type cited are unique to Asian thought, although the traditions on which I draw are certainly rich sources for such testimonies. Those traditions are Advaita ('non-dualist') Vedanta and the 'schools' of Mahāyāna Buddhism that owe inspiration to the *prajñāpāramitā* ('perfection of wisdom') literature—for example, the Ch'an or, in Japanese, Zen school.[3] In both traditions, there is

---

[3] Advaita Vedānta is so-called because, according to its main representative, Śaṃkara (8th century CE, probably), the Vedāntic ('end of Veda') texts—notably the Upaniṣads and the Bhagavad-Gītā—teach that there is nothing but a single Self (ātman) which is identical, therefore, with the absolute, brahman. Mahāyāna Buddhism is a broad church. The tendency within that tendency on which I focus is that found and inspired by the Prajñāpāramitā-sūtras and given its main philosophical expression by the 2nd-century monk Nāgārjuna. That tendency 'travelled' to China in the 6th century with

subscription to the 'human world' thesis, and on grounds familiar to western subscribers. Like other Asian traditions, however, these have an expressly 'practical', even soteriological, ambition to facilitate a certain serenity or
mental peace—for example, the Buddhists' 'cessation of craving'. As such, it
may seem odd to cite these traditions in support of the view that embrace of
humanism is unlivable. The explanation is that, in both cases, there are further compensating doctrines that neutralize the vital implications of 'raw'
humanism.

In another respect, it is natural to appeal to these traditions: for it is their
assumption that the primary vehicle of philosophical understanding is
experience or mood. According to the Buddha, his own articulated philosophical propositions are only 'skilful means' for facilitating and recording
the embrace of this understanding. When one 'sees' things for what they
are, writes a Hua-yen Buddhist, 'the mind is as calm as the sea . . . one issues
forth from one's bonds and . . . hindrances'. Similarly, for the Advaitin,
Śaṃkara, to 'grasp the truth' of *brahman* is inseparable from a 'whole practical view of the world' and a sense of 'release' from 'bondage'.[4] It is for this
reason that the traditions emphasize the cultivation of meditative moods
and certain modes of comportment towards the world: for it is in these, not
the mere assertion of philosophical formulae, that the embrace of right
understanding occurs. It is worth noting—in response to the modern western proclivity to regard 'realism' as plain common sense (p. 189)—that these
Asian spokesmen take themselves to be testifying to experiences that are
perfectly common or, at least, would be if people were less absorbed in daily
life. We are all, as Zen has it, *already* 'Buddha-mind'.

Advaita Vedānta and the relevant Mahāyāna tradition (see n. 3) are often
set poles apart. After all, the central doctrine of the former is that there exists
'one universal Self', *ātman*, identical with *brahman*, while that of Buddhism
is that there is only 'not-self'. However, as the accusation of 'closet
Buddhism' against Śaṃkara, and the great Mahāyānist, Nāgārjuna's, strenu-
ous efforts to put clear water between himself and the Vedāntins suggest,

the monk Bodhidharma, afterwards spawning such schools as Ch'an or Zen and Hua-yen or Kegon
(whose central text was the late *Avataṃsaka-sūtra*).

[4] Fa-tsang, 'The Golden Lion', in W. Baskin (ed.), *Classics in Chinese Philosophy* (Totowa, N.J.:
Helix, 1984), 390–1; Śaṃkara, *Brahmasūtrabhāsya*, trans. E. Deutsch and J. van Buitenen, excerpted in
D. E. Cooper (ed.), *Metaphysics: The Classic Readings* (Oxford: Blackwell, 1999), 78.

the substantial distinction between the traditions may be subtle. Certainly some commentators find it elusive.[5]

Whatever the distinction, it becomes relevant only at the level of compensation. In their embrace of the 'human world' thesis, and their appreciation that the thesis, unless compensated, is unlivable, the two traditions are at one. Śaṃkara expresses the thesis when he writes that the empirical, discursable world is the result of an 'ignorant' yet 'natural procedure . . . on the part of man' to 'superimpose' form and structure upon seamless, indescribable *brahman*. For the Buddhists, there is no such being on which to superimpose the empirical world, but it remains that, as the Sixth Patriarch of Ch'an put it, 'all things were originally given rise to by man'.[6] Some reasons given for this relativity of the world to human beings echo those familiar from earlier chapters. It is because of the pursuit of our interests that we 'grasp' at things, whose identity then depends on the place they occupy in relation to those interests. The differences between things, says one Zen master, are due to our 'seeking' these things.[7] Again, it is a familiar theme that the existence and identity of things is not independent of how they are described. '"Seizing upon a material object"', according to the *Diamond Sūtra*, is 'a convention of language'; while, for Śaṃkara, 'the fiction of Nescience'—the empirical order, that is—'originates entirely from speech only'.[8]

When it comes to depiction of the experience or mood of the embrace of humanism, the vocabularies of the two traditions reflect their dispute over the existence of a 'universal Self'. In the Vedāntic texts, the empirical world is experienced as *māyā*—as a 'dream', an 'illusion', or, to quote a contemporary Advaitin, a 'puppet show' and the happenings on a cinema screen.[9] While Buddhists sometimes use the same imagery, their rejection of a reality of which the empirical world could be an illusory or fictional version usu-

[5] David Loy goes further, writing that 'the nondualist denial of self (as in Buddhism) is equivalent to asserting that there is only the self (as in Vedānta)': 'Wei-wu-wei: Nondual Action', *Philosophy East and West*, 35 (1985), 84.

[6] Śaṃkara, *Brahmasūtrabhāsya*, 71 ff.; *The Platform Scripture of the Sixth Patriarch*, trans. P. Yampolsky (New York: Columbia University Press, 1967), 151.

[7] *The Zen Teachings of Huang Po: On the Transmission of Mind*, trans. J. Blofeld (London: Buddhist Society, 1968), 84.

[8] *The Diamond Sūtra: With Supplemental Texts from the Final Teachings of the Buddha* (New York: Concord Grove Press, 1983), 27; Śaṃkara, *Brahmasūtrabhāsya*, 88.

[9] Shantanand Saraswati, *The Man who Wanted to Meet God* (Shaftesbury: Element, 1996), 59.

ally prompts a more 'nihilistic' rhetoric. 'There is really nothing at all', wrote Huang Po, inspired presumably by Nāgārjuna's remark that, given 'universal relativity', 'There is nothing disappears, nor anything appears . . . Nothing moves'. In a famous passage, to which I shall return, the eighth-century Zennist, Ching Yuan, records how, after years of Zen meditation and study, 'I saw that mountains are not mountains, and waters are not waters'.[10]

Despite the difference in imagery, there is agreement that the experience of the world as *māyā* or 'nothing' is one that, uncompensated, would be unendurable. Śaṃkara makes this point in writing that, only when 'the soul cognizes that *brahman* is the Self of all' could a person renounce his conception of the world as something 'fixed and distinct'.[11] For as a western admirer of Vedānta, Arthur Schopenhauer, was to insist, were there only the 'veil of *māyā*', the world would, unbearably, 'pass us by like an empty dream'.[12] The Mahāyanists, too, emphasize that naked, uncompensated recognition that all is 'void' or 'empty' would be one of 'primeval awfulness', the embrace of a doctrine that frustrates the human need for 'something really affirmative and . . . soul-supporting'. By producing a 'rage against the world of the senses', it would cripple intelligent engagement in that world.[13]

Fortunately, on both traditions, compensation is at hand. In the Advaitin case, as we know, compensation comes in the shape of the doctrine of *brahman*. In appreciating that 'all that we see . . . is not real in itself', the enlightened person also enjoys a sense of 'the reality behind everything'. While this reality is strictly ineffable, he or she knows it to be, if only in extended senses of the terms, 'truth, consciousness and bliss' (*satcitānanda*).[14] Life then has its point—the effort to identify with this reality—and the world is saved from being merely a dream that passes us by.

It is more difficult to summarize the compensating doctrine advanced in Zen and related Buddhist schools—not least because of their predilection

[10] *The Zen Teachings of Huang Po*, 64; Nāgārjuna, *Madhyamaka-Kārikā*, trans. T. Stcherbatsky, in Cooper (ed.), *Metaphysics: The Classic Readings*, 64.; Ching Yuan, quoted in Alan W. Watts, *The Way of Zen* (London: Arkana, 1990), 146.

[11] *Brahmasūtrabhāsya*, 89.

[12] *The World as Will and Representation*, trans. E. Payne (New york: Dover, 1969), i. 99.

[13] D. T. Suzuki, *Essays on Zen Buddhism: III* (London: Luzac, 1934), 240 and 250; Seng Ts'an (the Third Patriarch), 'On Trust in the Heart', in E. Conze (ed.), *Buddhist Texts Through the Ages* (Boston, Mass.: Shambhala, 1990), 297.

[14] Saraswati, *The Man who Wanted to Meet God*, 72.

for paradoxical forms of expression. Having told us, in seemingly nihilistic vein, that 'whatever is form [a material object, say], that is emptiness', the *Heart Sūtra* then informs us that 'whatever is emptiness, that is form'[15]—thereby, it seems, retrieving the empirical world whose existence was apparently denied. This certainly seems to be Ching Yuan's point when, having, as we noted, come to see that mountains are not mountains, he goes on to say that, after further Zen meditation, 'I am at rest . . . I see mountains once again as mountains, and waters once again as waters'. It is tempting to construe such remarks in quietist fashion (p. 225 above): as suggesting, like McDowell, that 'recoil' to anti-realist rhetoric is due to previous attachment to a benighted 'metaphysical realism' from which further meditation frees us, thereby enabling us to view the world in the commonsensical way we did before bad philosophy knocked us off course. Ching, on this construal, simply and sensibly returns to where he started—'There are mountains'—so everything is left as it was. This is not, in my view, the right construal. I shall not pursue that claim here, since the Mahāyāna notion of emptiness becomes, after my turn towards the topic of mystery, a central one in Chapter 12.

(b) The Aphasic Experience

Asian texts sometimes indicate a further dimension, or modality, of the embrace of humanism. Chuang Tzu—the Taoist thinker to whom Ch'an Buddhism owed almost as much as to Buddhist thought itself—wondered if our words, since they do not delineate an independent reality, are any 'different from the chirping of chickens'.[16] Alan Watts, in the course of explaining what it is to 'get the feel' of the 'relativity' of the 'outside' world to human being, cites a modern Zen master who, attempting to convey the onset of that 'feel', reports how 'I spoke, but my words lost their meaning'.[17] For my main testimonies to this 'aphasic' experience, however, I turn to authors closer to home. I am not, of course, using 'aphasic' in its literal mod-

---

[15] In Conze (ed.), *Buddhist Texts Through the Ages*, 152.

[16] *The Chuang Tzu*, in Wing-Tsit Chan (ed.), *A Source Book in Chinese Philosophy* (Princeton, N.J.: Princeton University Press, 1969), 182.

[17] Watts, *The Way of Zen*, 141.

ern sense, to describe the medical condition, presumably a brain disorder, of which one symptom is a failure to recall the meanings of perfectly familiar words. But, understood in an extended way, the term is a convenient one for the kind of experience intimated in the following testimonies.

Before turning to these, it is worth remarking that, in the view of some critics of humanism, an aphasic experience of language is precisely what *ought* to follow in the wake of subscription to the 'human world' thesis. Unless a certain metaphysical, indeed theological, realism is true, maintains Stephen Clark, then the vocabulary of science, for example, 'must in the end be merely verbal music'[18]—as devoid of reference, and so meaning, as a toot on a flute. McDowell, in the course of defending the 'contractual' view of meaning that we saw the existential humanist earlier reject (pp. 128 ff and pp. 217 ff), holds that, unless the application of concepts, once established, is determined by the world alone, our speech would be nothing but a 'brute meaningless sounding-off'.[19] In earlier chapters, my sympathies were with the existential humanists. They were right, I suggested, to maintain, as against McDowell, Brandom, and other 'concept-bound realists', that applications of words are 'moves in one sort of life rather than another'. What the aphasic experience suggests, however, is that this conception of language, unless compensated, is not one with which we can live. Taking that experience seriously will not reinstate the realist conception, but it will lead to an apparent impasse: realism is unacceptable, but if the humanist conception were right, then . . .. Well, let's hear what the authors of the following testimonies think would ensue.

Especially vivid testimony is provided in two short stories—'Colours' and, still more, 'The Letter of Lord Chandos'—by Hugo von Hofmannstahl, the Austrian poet and essayist and, among much else, Richard Strauss's librettist. 'The Letter' purports to be written by a brilliant playwright and scholar, Philip, the young Lord Chandos, to Sir Francis Bacon, explaining why he has given up writing. The reason, bluntly, is that he has 'lost completely the ability to speak of anything coherently'.[20] In 'Colours',

---

[18] *God's World and the Great Awakening* (Oxford: Clarendon Press, 1991), 18.

[19] 'Wittgenstein on Following a Rule', in A. W. Moore (ed.), *Meaning and Reference* (Oxford: Oxford University Press, 1993), 269.

[20] Hugo von Hoffmanstahl, *Selected Prose*, trans. M. Hottinger and T. and J. Stern (Bollingen: Pantheon, 1952). Quotations are from pp. 133–6 of 'The Letter' and from pp. 143–8 of 'Colours'.

too, a young man, returning to Europe from working in the East, has this unnerving experience of his language losing coherence. Hofmannsthal was not writing philosophical treatises, so it is perhaps presumptuous to ascribe to him—or rather to his two protagonists— conversion to a humanist thesis as the catalyst for their aphasic experiences. Still, Chandos describes the atrophy of his earlier conviction that, when perceiving and speaking, he was doing so in the direct 'presence of Nature', never 'suspecting mere appearance' in the world about him. And when he goes on to report that, now, concepts seem to be 'concerned only with each other', to be 'eyeless statues' that do not look out onto an independent reality, it seems reasonable to credit him with an embrace of something like the 'human world' thesis.[21]

It is an embrace in which loss of a sense of nature's 'presence' is co-extensive with an experience of words 'crumbl[ing] in my mouth like mouldy fungi'. At first, only abstract terms, like 'soul', become 'hollow', but soon the 'corroding rust' extends even to words like 'dog' or 'table', whose failure to designate solid items of reality prompts 'nausea'. Although Chandos and the expatriate continue, at a certain level, to 'function' and communicate, they do so as sleepwalkers during a nightmare—their words 'flowing by' them, 'floating round' them like 'whirlpools which gave [them] vertigo and, reeling incessantly, led into the void'.

Both young men, fortunately, manage to find compensation, indeed salvation—at least during 'good moments'—that rescues them from total breakdown or worse. The compensation, however, is not of a kind that returns to language its former solidity and links to reality. In 'Colours', it comes through looking at the paintings of Van Gogh, before which the narrator enjoys a sense of a 'more exalted' and direct form of language than words—that of colours—able to 'lift' him out of 'the frightful chaos of Non-Living' towards a renewed experience of the presence of 'Being'. In 'The Letter', it is the most ordinary objects—a pitcher, a small dog—meditatively viewed, that, for Chandos, 'become the vessel of my revelation', ciphers of a 'Presence' that words remain incapable of communicating.

Some of the expressions used by Hofmannsthal will remind readers of

---

[21] One is reminded of McDowell's imagery in *Mind and World* (Cambridge, Mass.: Harvard University Press, 1994), where he says that the effect of the 'coherentist' conception that he attributes to Donald Davidson is to render the exercize of concepts a 'self-contained game', with the concepts themselves in 'frictionless' spin. See e.g. pp. 5 and 14.

other testimonies to the aphasic experience. Compare, first, his 'words as whirlpools' simile with these lines from the first of T. S. Eliot's *Four Quartets*:

> Words strain,
> Crack and sometimes break, under the burden,
> Under the tension, slip, slide, perish,
> Decay with imprecision, will not stay in place,
> Will not stay still.[22]

The philosophical context of the experience of language evinced here is not spelt out by Eliot. But we know that he was an admiring student of Vedāntic thought and there are sufficient indications in the poem that the lines on language are set against a contrast, of the kind drawn by Śaṃkara, between the 'silent', ineffable and eternal realm, 'the still point', and the 'dancing', 'twittering world' that 'turns' around that point. Eliot's claim, one might propose, is that our words, since they cannot gain any purchase on the former realm, indeed 'perish' and refuse to 'stay in place': for, not only is the 'twittering world' transient and unstable, but it is lacking in that independence from our thought and talk which alone could confer on words the significance that we ordinarily invest in them. To embrace the thesis that the world we familiarly encounter is only the 'turning', 'dancing' one is inevitably, therefore, to experience erosion of meaning, to hear speech as so much 'shrieking' and 'chattering'.

Hofmannstahl's mention of the 'nausea' that goes with the experience of words' failure to designate solidly independent items must also remind readers of Sartre's novel of that name. It recalls, in particular, the famous description by the novel's narrator, Roquentin, of his 'nauseous' experience in a park when staring at the roots of a chestnut tree. Sartre installs more philosophical stage-setting than do Hofmannstahl and Eliot, although commentators differ as to exact point he is making. But here is one plausible interpretation.

As a good humanist, Sartre holds that we ordinarily encounter objects only in their 'relationship' to ourselves, as belonging to 'the human world of measures'.[23] *That* this is so, however, is only brought home to us in

---

[22] 'Burnt Norton', in T. S. Eliot, *Collected Poems 1909–1962* (London: Faber & Faber, 1963), 194.
[23] Jean-Paul Sartre, *Nausea*, trans. R. Baldick (Harmondsworth: Penguin, 1965). Quotations are from pp. 182–93.

extra-ordinary experiences—when, as in the park, a person experiences the world in its 'obscene nakedness', with the 'veneer' of human measure melted away. Sartre is quite clear that it is experience, not detached thinking, that is necessary to bring this home. Naked existence cannot be 'thought of' from a distance; it has to invade you suddenly, pounce upon you'.

The important aspect of this 'invasion', in the present context, is the aphasic one on which Roquentin dwells. He feels each word— 'root', 'black', and so on—'empty itself of meaning'. 'It was no use my repeating: "It is a root"', for *that* naked lump, abstracted from its role in 'the human world of measures'—as a suction-pump, say—has fallen 'beneath all explanation' and description. It helps to explain Sartre's point to recall the existential humanist account of language from Chapter 5. It was argued, there, that words are meaningful through referring us to objects that are themselves meaningful in virtue of their place in a human world of purposeful engagement. When Sartre writes that 'words had disappeared, and with them the meaning of things, the methods of using them', he is exploiting precisely that argument. Roquentin's aphasia in the face of 'naked' existence is the recognition that when things lose the individuality, diversity, and identity they possess in the 'the human world', our concepts and words are revealed as devoid of the significance—the pointing towards an independent order— with which we invest them when engaged in ordinary thought and talk. Words indeed function and communicate solely through their role in our purposive activities in a human world: but a genuine embrace of that thought—of the thought that our language is 'arbitrary', something 'without any grip on' an independent, determinate order of things—is nauseous.

Sartre and Roquentin seek no compensation for this thought. They would be unimpressed, too, by the quietist proposal that we need only liberate ourselves from a bad, 'metaphysical realist' theory of meaning—from an ambition to obtain a 'sideways on' view of the relation between language and reality—in order to regain confidence in our words. Sartre agrees that this is a bad model, but Roquentin's nausea demonstrates that when appreciation of its bankruptcy becomes 'hot and alive', a perception of language is induced with which we cannot live, unless that perception is either compensated by some further doctrine or, as in Roquentin's own case, one simply waits for it to 'leave' one, to 'pass off', so that one may get on, at least for a while, with the business of life. By the time Roquentin leaves the park, the trees and bushes—and our words for them—once again '*meant* something'.

He is back in the world of human measure: but only because his embrace of 'the human world' thesis has itself passed off, cooled down, for the time being.

(c) The Unheimlich Experience

The translators of *Being and Time* render 'unheimlich' as 'uncanny'. The term indicates a mood to which several writers in the existentialist trad- ition—Kierkegaard, Jaspers, and Gabriel Marcel, for example—draw our attention, as indeed do authors not usually placed in that tradition. Simone Weil, for example, describes an uncanny, unnerving experience of floating in a 'void' when a person becomes 'detached' from established, public 'points of view' that serve as forces of 'gravity', keeping his or her beliefs and convictions on terra firma.[24] But it is to Heidegger's discussion of *Angst* that one naturally turns for a primary testimony to the *unheimlich* aspect of the dis-incumbenced mood. When remarking on that discussion in Chapter 9, my main concern was with *Angst* as a paradigmatic illustration of mood in the intended, Heideggerian sense—a 'seamless', 'primitive' vehicle of 'revelation' or 'disclosure'. In what follows, concern shifts to the specific character and object of *Angst*.

It is, Heidegger remarks, precisely 'in anxiety that one feels "uncanny"'.[25] However, he invests the term 'unheimlich' with a pathos not indicated by the English word, for this fails to register the connection between *Unheimlichkeit* and 'homelessness'. In anxiety, Heidegger therefore writes, one experiences 'not being at home'. A person is 'at home' in the world when living, thinking and talking under 'the protecting shelter' of *das Man*—the anonymous 'They' whose 'average interpretation' of things, events, and their significance the person ordinarily and unreflectingly just 'goes along with'. *Angst* sets in precisely with the recognition that this is indeed the condition of our ordinary being-in-the-world. In *Angst* we come 'face-to-face with [our] being-in-the-world', or as Heidegger also puts it, with 'the world as such', the world recognized as 'Their' world, dependent

[24] See, especially, *The Notebooks of Simone Weil*, trans. A. Wills (New York: Putnam's Sons, 1956).
[25] All quotations over the next few paragraphs are from § 40 of Martin Heidegger, *Being and Time*, trans. J. Macquarrie and E. Robinson (Oxford: Blackwell, 1980).

upon 'Their' ways of comportment and interpretation. With this 'disclosure', 'everyday familiarity collapses'—rather as when the young hero of a *Bildungsroman* finds that the moral or religious certainties in which he was brought up leach away once his travels take him beyond the boundaries of his parish, his *Heimat*.

Several ingredients in Heidegger's description of *Unheimlichkeit* recall testimonies cited earlier in this chapter. Someone in that mood will, like Chandos, experience 'aphasia'. Words are no longer heard as referring one, and thereby linking one, to things as they are: instead, one hears only 'what-is-said-in-the-talk', the 'chatter' (*Gerede*) through which 'They' 'pass along' their interpretation of things. In *Unheimlichkeit*, as in Roquentin's 'nausea', things go by 'floating unattached', since 'the world has the character of completely lacking significance' for the person now 'set free' from the 'They' who are the arbiters of meaning. And echoing the nihilist rhetoric of some Buddhists, the person in *Angst* is described as experiencing 'nothingness'—no thing-ness—for he has, so to speak, floated free from the schemes of interpretation relative to which things possess their identity.

Heidegger, however, emphasizes a dimension of dis-incumbence that was not explicitly attested to in the earlier testimonies. *Angst*, he says, 'individualizes': it discloses the person who experiences it as 'solus ipse'. Like the hero of the *Bildungsroman* who looks back towards the family home he is leaving, so the anxious person experiences solitude once outside the 'protective shelter' of 'Them', his extended family, as it were. The human situation that, for Heidegger, is disclosed through *Angst* is not, however, solipsism: my *Unheimlichkeit* is not a dreadful suspicion that I might be all there is. What is disclosed, rather, is an individual freedom and responsibility that cannot be 'delegated'. My interpretation of the world cannot be dictated by the way the world, independently of human interpretation and comportment, really is—for there is no such way. Hence, I must 'choose' between 'inauthentically' going along 'under the dictatorship' of 'Them', and 'authentically' taking a stance of my own. Either way, the buck stops with me.

In *Being and Time*, Heidegger offers no further doctrine that could compensate for the 'stifling', 'oppressive', and *unheimlich* mood of *Angst* in which the truth of the 'human world' thesis is disclosed and embraced. (That it *is* oppressive and unsettling, says Heidegger, is shown by its comparative rarity: for this indicates a need to 'flee' in the face of *Angst*, back to the 'tranquillization' afforded by 'Their' protective shelter.) While what is revealed through *Angst* must be taken on the chin, without compensation, the Heidegger of *Being and Time* does, however, allow for the possibility of *Unheimlichkeit* modulating into a 'sober', even 'joyful', appreciation of one's capacity for authentic decision. In the 'anticipatory resoluteness' of authentic existence, a person is at least sufficiently free from 'Them' to look to the past or 'heritage' of his culture to identify, and perhaps resolve upon, interpretations alternative to the 'average everyday' ones dictated by *das Man*.[26]

By the late 1930s, however, Heidegger had come to reject any such possibility of authentic individual 'coping' with the condition disclosed through *Angst*. As Herman Philipse accurately remarks, Heidegger now regarded 'the burden of authentic resoluteness as . . . in principle unbearable', and expressed a 'longing to shake off the burden of existence, which he so penetratingly described in *Sein und Zeit*'.[27] It is not simply that Heidegger came to think that human beings, unaided, do not possess the resources to rise above the prevailing, engrained understanding that dominates their 'epoch'—that, in his words, 'we are never capable of stepping-out on our own'.[28] In addition, as Philipse again explains, the humanism of *Being and Time* entailed that a person 'cannot rely on *any* ideas or principles in making his authentic choices'.[29] He cannot rely on any supposedly independent order of things, and reliance on any given interpretations of the world, including those drawn from one's 'heritage', would be reliance on something that, with the onset of *Angst*, is seen to be without grounds. In Heidegger's later writings, then, there is clear testimony to the unbearability of uncompensated disincumbence. How he attempts to provide a compensating doctrine that was precluded in *Being and Time* will engage our attention in later chapters.

---

[26] See *Being and Time*, § 74.

[27] *Heidegger's Philosophy of Being* (Princeton, N.J.: Princeton University Press, 1999), 222 and 265.

[28] Martin Heidegger, *Contributions to Philosophy (From Enowning)*, trans. P. Emad and K. Maly (Bloomington: Indiana University Press, 1999), 339. It has been suggested to me that here I, and presumably Philipse, exaggerate the distance between 'early' and 'late' Heidegger. Does he not already, in *Being and Time*, speak of *Dasein* as a 'clearing' and of its responsiveness to Being? Yes, but such talk sits, however uncomfortably, alongside a more 'activist' and 'decisionist' rhetoric. Despite Heidegger's own attempts to minimize the distance between his earlier and later philosophies, it is only in the latter that confidence in man's ability to 'step-out' on his own is abandoned.

[29] *Heidegger's Philosophy of Being*, 264.

Answerability

The testimonies cited in the previous section attest to something for which, in this chapter, I aim to argue: that the dis-incumbenced posture is unendurable. To argue for this is, as explained, tantamount to maintaining that uncompensated embrace of the 'human world' thesis is not a human possibility. Humanism lacks humility because it supposes this is a possibility. The experiences recorded in the testimonies serve, one might say, to confirm the hypothesis that the moment uncompensated humanism is genuinely embraced, it must also, like some electric eel, be let go. They confirm that the mood of an embrace in which the humanist thesis becomes 'hot and alive'—in which, as Buddhists say, it is 'deeply cultivated'[30]—precludes life 'in the midst' of the world. As such, the testimonies support that investment of the embrace of humanism which makes it a virtual tautology that no such embrace is finally feasible.

Mere recitation of supporting testimonies cannot, of course, clinch the case. A critic will ask what reason there is to take the testimonies seriously. Granted that the mood of many people who embrace uncompensated humanism may also be 'nauseous', 'anxious', 'unheimlich', 'aphasic', or 'nihilistic', why not regard this as the symptom of neurosis, weakness, or plain misunderstanding? This objection, already anticipated in Chapter 9, will be considered in the course of addressing a further question. The testimonies cited, while compatible with respect to what is 'disclosed' by the experiences, attested to different aspects or 'modalities' of the mood of embrace of humanism. The question arises whether it is possible to distil from them some essential component. Can one see the various 'Asian', 'aphasic' and 'unheimlich' experiences as revolving around a pivotal perception of what renders uncompensated humanism unlivable? In the remainder of this chapter, I identify and elaborate such a pivotal perception and argue—no longer by appeal to testimony—that this perception is warranted.

In earlier chapters, we came across various metaphors, employed by

---

[30] Tenzin Gyatso (The Fourteenth Dalai Lama), *Transcendent Wisdom*, trans. B. Wallace (Ithaca, N.Y.: Snow Lion, 1994), 35. He also distinguishes between mere assent to a doctrine and developing an 'instinct' for or 'experientially realizing' it.

champions and opponents of humanism alike, for characterizing—whether by way of congratulation or criticism—a general feature or effect of humanism. Most of them divide into two groups. First, there are the 'reliability' metaphors. For humanists, it is said, our concepts, beliefs, or whatever have nothing finally to 'lean on', no independent 'foundations' or 'grounds'. Second, there are the 'answerability' metaphors. Humanism entails, it is held, that we are 'responsible' to nothing beyond ourselves, that the world is an 'obsequious shadow' of our discourses, ones that are free of independent 'constraints'—and so on.

Previously, I was not concerned to distinguish these groups of metaphors, but in fact they are significantly different in import. In ordinary contexts, we certainly distinguish reliance on something or somebody from answerability or responsibility to it, him or her. A child, for example, may be answerable for its work to its teacher, and may also be able to rely on the teacher for help or support: but these are two different matters. More relevantly for what follows, wanting or needing to have something to rely upon is quite different from wanting or needing to be answerable. The child, in a spirit of independence, may want to be responsible to its elders, but without relying on their help—or, in a different spirit of independence, want to be answerable to no one, but nevertheless to be able to rely on their advice.

My proposal is that what is pivotally disclosed in the mood of embrace of uncompensated humanism is our lack of answerability. It is this, rather than a sense that we have nothing, finally, to rely or lean upon, that renders the uncompensated 'human world' thesis unendurable. The motto or slogan for this disclosure or perception might be, in the words of a commentator summarizing Heidegger's later position, 'Human life must answer to something beyond itself'.[31]

There may appear to be a certain irony in charging humanists with a denial of our answerability, since they are often accused by their critics of gross inflation of our degree of answerability or responsibility. Certainly some humanists invite that accusation: recall, for example, Sartre's boast that 'there is no legislator but [man] himself'. However, there is no contradiction in charging humanism with both denial and inflation. One needs,

---

[31] James C. Edwards, *The Authority of Language: Heidegger, Wittgenstein and the Threat of Philosophical Nihilism* (Tampa: University of South Florida Press, 1990), 111.

simply, to distinguish between answerability *to* and answerability *for*.[32] It may be precisely through inflating human beings' responsibility for the way the discursable world is that humanists diminish our answerability to something 'beyond' ourselves.

In what follows, I elaborate and defend the charge that humanism renders us unendurably unanswerable to . . . . In this chapter, I leave those blanks studiously unfilled. I do not, that is, speculate on what might satisfy our need to be answerable. Certainly it should not be assumed that the reply to the question 'What are human beings answerable to?' has to be something like 'The Facts', 'The way the world anyway is', 'The independent order of reality', and so on. Indeed, given the success of the existential humanist's attack on absolutism, of his accusation of hubris against the pretension to provide an absolute account of the world, any such reply is problematic. Only in the final chapters do I speculate on the prospects for replies of a very different kind.

To begin my elaboration of the perception of unanswerability, I want to remark on two pre-emptive attacks on the viability of my proposal. According to the first, it is just mistaken to suppose that the 'human world' thesis leaves us unanswerable. Was it not established, in Chapter 9, that the humanist is able to accommodate notions like truth and objectivity, and to respect such platitudes as that a true belief must correspond with the facts or that 'we should aim at making our . . . judgements conform to the way things are in reality'?[33] Again, the humanist is perfectly able to complain, as Sartre does, against any hyper-relativistic attempt to 'enclose the world' within a given, transitory scheme of beliefs and concepts.[34] That there is no discursable world independent of human perspective does not entail that, in exploring our human world, we never get things wrong and are immune to correction by future experience. Rather differently, the humanist is the first to emphasize the way that cognitive practices are constrained by the wider practices and 'projects' that are integrated in a form of life. In sum, the

---

[32] In the Preface to later editions of *Man's Responsibility for Nature*, 2nd ed. (London: Duckworth, 1980), John Passmore records his irritation at people who misquote the title by replacing 'for' by 'to', and thereby altering its sense completely, making it sound that the book will be about Nature's own, rightful demands on us—a notion Passmore rejects.

[33] P. F. Strawson, 'Echoes of Kant', *Times Literary Supplement*, 4657 (1992), 12.

[34] Jean-Paul Sartre, *Truth and Existence*, trans. A. Van den Hoven (Chicago: University of Chicago Press, 1989), 66.

humanist is surely entitled to speak of the answerability of people's beliefs and conceptions—of their answerability to facts, to future experience and inquiry, to the constitutive practices of a form of life, and so on.

For the critic of humanism, this rejection of the unendurability of disincumbence misses the point. One may concede that the humanist is entitled to speak of our answerability in the respects just mentioned. But what the testimonies that register the perception of unendurability indicated was precisely that these are not the respects at issue. As Kolakowski points out, the insistence that the humanist is entitled to distinguish truth from falsity by pragmatic criteria, or to employ criteria of meaning in terms of human intention, will hardly reassure those whose 'metaphysical horror', whose sense of our 'fragility', resides precisely in the fear that there can be no appeal to—no answerability to—anything beyond such criteria.[35] If, more specifically, it follows from any conception of truth acceptable to the humanist that 'true sentences do not . . . *do* anything except answer to the demands of our . . . true thoughts', so that the 'states of affairs' recorded by these sentences are 'no more than *shadows* cast by . . . our discourse',[36] the alleged answerability of our discourse and thought to states of affairs looks fraudulent. Certainly it is not the sort of answerability of language to the world whose absence was experienced by Chandos in his crisis and by Roquentin with nausea. As for the assurance that our thinking is constrained by, and answerable to, our form of life, Barry Stroud is surely correct to observe that, if the legitimacy of general ways of thinking may itself be legitimately questioned, that assurance is worthless—even if, one might add, the thinking embedded in our form of life is the only one that we can imagine. For that questioning will apply to the form of life itself. Once our thinking at large 'has been identified as something "subjective"'—or as bound to a form of life—'it will be too late to hope for anything we should recognize as success' in responding to the demand for legitimation.[37] In my terminology, it can do nothing to mitigate *Unheimlichkeit* to stress the

---

[35] Leszek Kolakowski, *Metaphysical Horror* (Oxford: Blackwell, 1988), 13 and 118.

[36] Crispin Wright, *Truth and Objectivity* (Cambridge, Mass.: Harvard University Press, 1992), 181–2.

[37] 'The Allure of Idealism', *Proceedings of the Aristotelian Society, Supp. Vol.*, 58 (1984), 258. Stroud himself argues, in 'quietist', allegedly Wittgensteinian vein, that we should not get ourselves into the position of asking for legitimation of 'our ways of thinking, in general'. The critic of humanism would hold that we cannot help but get ourselves in that position.

constraints imposed by a form of life, since at the root of that experience is precisely the perception that these—'Their'—constraints are the only ones there finally are.

According to the second pre-emptive attack on my proposal, while it is true that the 'human world' thesis renders us unanswerable, it is wrong to suppose that there is anything unendurable in this. At worst, our lack of answerability is something to be sanguine about: at best, it may even be something to celebrate. Horror, nihilism, *Angst*, *Unheimlichkeit*, and their relatives are inappropriate, if temporarily forgivable, 'recoils' on the part of people whose confidence in a bad, absolutist metaphysics has been shaken. If, say, Chandos had not been wedded to a bad picture of the relation between words and things, he would not have been thrown into crisis when the truth dawned.

We are familiar with this view from the 'serene'—'ironic' or 'quietist'— defence of humanism described in Chapter 9. I have already recorded misgivings about it. The quietist response sounds more like a refusal to engage with philosophical positions and their implications than a considered position of its own, and its denial that our moral beliefs, say, should be at all affected by the recognition that they can be answerable to nothing beyond themselves looks to be not just sanguine, but ostrich-like. But my present worry concerns the quietist diagnosis, shared by the Rortyan ironist, of the mood of the embrace of humanism as one in recoil from prior attachment to the 'independence' thesis. It is, in my view, more plausible to regard this attachment— the conviction that there is a discursable way the world anyway is—as an important symptom of a need for answerability than to explain people's sense of the unendurability of (uncompensated) humanism as the consequence of a severing of that attachment. It is worth remarking, in this connection, that the experiences recorded in the testimonies cited were *not* those of people necessarily wedded to anything so specific, and relatively sophisticated, as the independence thesis, 'metaphysical' realism, the viability of an absolutist account of the world, and so on. It is not clear, for example, that prior to their 'aphasic' experiences, Chandos and Roquentin entertained any particular doctrine about the relation of words to world, as opposed to some vague, unreflective conviction that our talk is answerable to something beyond itself. The experiences of the unendurability of unanswerability are not, therefore, confined to those in recoil from subscription to some exploded metaphysical doctrine.

It is also worth remarking, perhaps, that it is far from clear that Rorty's ironist, at least, has succeeded in severing all attachment to some such doctrine. One wonders, at least, what is responsible for the ironist's urge constantly to be in the business of 'redescribing'. Why does the person now convinced that no description of the world has foundations—that there can be answerability to nothing beyond our 'own conventions'—not just fatalistically go along with the prevailing descriptions? It is hard not to detect in the ironist's apparent compulsion to 'redescribe' a nostalgia for the thought that there is such a thing as getting it right, as being answerable to something more 'independent' than our own conventions.

But suppose the unendurable experiences of the embrace of humanism were always in recoil from prior attachment to some exploded metaphysical doctrine. Why should this show that they are 'misplaced', 'neurotic', and the like? Earlier I quoted Kant's remark to the effect that we are unable to ignore demands for knowledge that we are nevertheless unable to satisfy. It is hardly obvious that Kleist's despairing response to the unsatisfiability of his demand for knowledge of things in themselves—of the answerability of beliefs to something absolute—was 'misplaced'. Perhaps he accurately perceived that our situation, from which most of us avert our eyes, is a genuinely tragic one. After all, we do not always, or even generally, dismiss people's despairing responses to the unsatisfiability of their demands as 'neurotic', as something to just 'get over'. We do this, perhaps, when those demands are 'silly'—and there are those quietists for whom 'metaphysical' realism and the like are indeed silly. But they are wrong: absolutism, in the form, say, of the scientific realism discussed in Chapter 8, may be unacceptable, but it is not a nonsense, and it is surely appropriate that the news of its demise should be disturbing. It is a serious position, responding to serious aspirations. Again, one might start to regard as 'neurotic' a person's depression if he has long, and definitively, abandoned all possible prospect of satisfying his wants. But it is far from clear that the demand for the answerability of human life to 'something beyond itself' could be satisfied *only* by the independence thesis or some brand of 'metaphysical' realism. We would not be entitled, therefore, to brand as 'misplaced' the perception that the 'human world' thesis leaves us unendurably unanswerable until we have exhausted all possibilities of compensating for that thesis—including those explored in my final chapters.

It will help in the elaboration of my proposal to locate it in relation to two attempts, described in Chapter 9, to reject the possibility of the dis-incumbenced, humanist stance—those of the 'rationalist' and 'mens sana' approaches. On the former—Nagel's—approach, the dis-incumbenced stance is logically incoherent: giving 'the last word' to our practices, form of life, perspectives or whatever is incompatible with the giving of reasons for our beliefs, since these must be viewed as belonging to an 'impersonal order of logical relations'. I have already indicated that this understands the issue of dis-incumbence in an overly intellectualist manner. Granted that sub-scribers to the 'human world' thesis, having read their Nagel, may be unable to reconcile it with belief and commitment 'in the midst of the world', this would only make their dis-incumbenced stance *unlivable* on the implausible assumption that people can only live with a position to which they have given logical clearance. That not all people are like this is shown, for ex-ample, by the continuation of people's religious belief in the face of 'the problem of evil', whose intractability they concede. My strategy, instead, identifies the unlivability of dis-incumbence with the unendurability of a mood which pivots, so I propose, around a perception—'hot and alive'—of our unanswerability.

There is a further difference between my proposal and Nagel's approach. If he is right, then no rational creatures could subscribe to beliefs without giving 'the last word' to 'impersonal' reasons: if they did, they would not be rational. I do not know if he is right here. Maybe those critics are correct who urge that there can be rational creatures who give reasons for their beliefs whilst recognizing that any giving of a reason must be tacitly prefixed by 'We are so minded that . . .', 'By our lights . . .', or the like, so that 'the last word' does, after all, remain with 'us'.[38] Given the uncertainty here, pru-dence recommends retreat to a more modest claim than Nagel's: to the claim that, even if there could be rational creatures of the type imagined by the critics, we humans are not among them. Or rather, transposed into the idiom of my proposal, the claim would be that, however matters may stand with other possible creatures, beings of a human or human-like kind are incapable of belief, commitment, and reason-giving without a perception of

---

[38] See, for example, Christine Korsgaard's response to Nagel in *The Sources of Normativity* (Cambridge: Cambridge University Press, 1996), 246. She argues that reasons are always given from a 'perspective', but that they count as 'objective' provided that 'we have no choice but to occupy those perspectives'.

their answerability to 'something beyond themselves'. Movement to this more modest and transposed claim means, of course, that attention must shift from questions of logical coherence to considerations of human existence. What is it about *their* existence that renders the perception of unanswerability something that cannot be endured by human beings?

An answer to that question was offered by Kolakowski and other advocates of the *mens sana* approach. There is a fundamental and ineradicable human desire, urge or drive for absolute knowledge of what is the case 'quite apart from our thinking and perceiving'. It is humanism's affront to these aspirations that, on this approach, makes it unendurable. So is it in terms of an affront to a particular human drive that we should understand the unendurable character of the perception of unanswerability? That, I think, would be a last ditch position to which we should be reluctant to fall back.

To begin with, the postulate of a special drive in order to explain 'metaphysical horror' at the news that there is no 'truth without qualification' looks ad hoc. Indeed, in the absence of independent evidence for the existence of the drive, the postulate explains nothing, for it would amount to no more than redescription of the occurrence of 'horror'. It would not help, in this connection, to cite Aristotelian remarks on man as a creature who 'desires to know', or to catalogue man's dogged pursuit of scientific knowledge 'for its own sake', since these are desires and pursuits that might be explained without assuming that 'the spirit must have something *absolute*'. Second, it would be disappointing to discover that our need for answerability were just a contingent, hived-off feature of human beings, no more integral to a distinctively human existence than, say, our need for warmth. But reference to a special drive, if taken seriously, gives just that impression.[39] Were our need for answerability no more than this, moreover, it should be something that, submitting to an appropriate course of pills or mental training, we could suppress or exorcize—like some unwelcome sexual proclivity. I want to say that the need for answerability is more *interesting* than the depiction of it as a particular drive implies.

[39] Kolakowski, it is true, relates the drive to our 'fragility'. This suggests he would want to elaborate the drive in terms of a need for reliance upon . . .. If so, his approach is one with which my proposal, centred on the notion of answerability to . . ., is intended to contrast.

So, two desiderata for an account of the perception of unanswerability—ones not met by the *mens sana* approach—are that the postulation of a human need for answerability should not be ad hoc and that this need be displayed as integral to human existence. I now proceed to develop such an account.

Measure and Purpose

In this and the following section, I defend the thoughts, in a manner consonant with the desiderata just mentioned, that human beings need to be answerable, and that this answerability must be to 'something beyond' human life itself. While the discussion will proceed without any assumption as to what that 'something' may be—God, say, or an independent, discursable order of things—some elucidation is required of what I have in mind by answerability and, hence, of the condition anything must meet to satisfy a need for it. To want to be answerable to, I shall say, is to want the elements of one's life—one's actions, commitments, and so on—and perhaps the whole life they constitute to be subject to *measure*, to what Kierkegaard called a *Maalestok*, a 'qualitative criterion', that enables assessment.[40] The 'something' we need to be answerable to must be a source of measure.

To anticipate a later point, it is not essential—not obviously so, at any rate—that in order for people to experience satisfaction of that need they must know, in any detail at least, what that measure is and how their lives shape up by it. In many religious traditions, the idea of God as a source of measure is combined with a refusal to 'second guess' God, to pretend knowledge of how he measures us. There will be a day of judgement when everyone is allotted their due, but it is not for us to anticipate how the judgement will go. Confidence that there is a measure of how one's life has gone, unmatched by a similar confidence in one's capacity to divine it, is, for some people apparently, sufficient to satisfy the need for answerability.

The need to be subject to measure is rooted in precisely that dimension of human existence emphasized by the existential humanists. Human beings,

---

[40] Søren Kierkegaard, *The Sickness Unto Death*, in H. and E. Hong (eds.), *The Essential Kierkegaard* (Princeton, N.J.: Princeton University Press, 1997), 363.

one might say, are inveterately teleological creatures. This does not mean, simply, that they happen, for much of the time, to be engaged in purposive activity, in the pursuit of goals. That human beings *ex-ist*, that they are constantly engaged in purposive 'projects', is not some bolt-on extra ingredient in their lives: for, as we saw in Chapter 5, it is only as ex-isting creatures that anything 'lights up' for them at all, that experience and understanding of a structured world of identifiable objects is possible. But something further is intended by emphasizing people's inveterately teleological character: namely, that it is essential to them to *see themselves* as ex-isting, as engaged in 'projects'. Kierkegaard describes the life of the 'aesthetic' person—one who lives 'immediately', blows with the wind, subject to 'external' stimuli and conditions—as one of 'despair'. The saving aspect of the 'ethical' life to which, in despair, the 'aesthete' turns is precisely that it affords long-term, organizing purposes—a close and rewarding married life, say.[41] Kierkegaard is right: the perception that all or most of what one is doing is without point indeed induces despair. It is a perception which, as Nietzsche recognized, people go to great lengths to avert. 'If you have your *why?* for life, you can get along with almost any *how?*',[42] he wrote: his point being that people will grab at even the most unpromising purposes rather than remain in a goalless vacuum.

The purposes and projects that people need to see themselves as engaged in are not, of course, just any old activities that could be said to have a goal—running for a bus, say. Rather, they are like Bernard Williams's 'ground projects' that provide a person with a 'motive force which propels him into the future and gives him a reason for living'.[43] They must be projects of a

---

[41] *Either/Or*, trans. W. Lowrie (Princeton, N.J.: Princeton University Press, 1971), ii. 196 ff. The 'despairing' person, for Kierkegaard, need not be experiencing depression, since he or she may, at least in the short term, protect against this through, say, sensual indulgence or frenetic activity. Compare Peter Sloterdijk's analysis of that 'discontent' of (post)modern culture he calls 'cynicism'. The cynic, like the dis-incumbenced person, rejects the possibility of 'foundations' for values, and for that very reason is a 'borderline melancholic'. However, despite glimpses of 'the nothingness to which everything leads', cynics usually manage, under 'the force of circumstances' and for the sake of 'self-preservation', to 'keep their symptoms of depression under control'. *Critique of Cynical Reason*, trans. M. Eldred (Minneapolis: University of Minnesota Press, 1983), 5. These remarks are relevant to my discussion, in the following section, of the livability of the dis-incumbenced stance. Sloterdijk's view would be that this stance is possible, but only with the help of self-tranquillization and/or self-deception.

[42] *Twilight of the Idols*, trans. Duncan Large (Oxford: Oxford University Press, 1998), Maxim 12.

[43] 'Persons, Characters and Morality', in his *Moral Luck* (Cambridge: Cambridge University Press, 1981), 13.

relatively long-term type that serve to structure and integrate a range of more particular activities, ones with the prospect of guaranteeing that not too much of one's life is spent on things that one cannot see as mattering, as contributing to anything to which one can attribute worth. Putative examples of such projects might be raising a family, writing a book, and conserving the natural environment.

If the need for answerability and measure is 'rooted' in our inveterately teleological existence, then it is indeed integral to human life and there would be nothing ad hoc in appealing to it in explanation of 'metaphysical horror'. So to see the need as being rooted in this way would meet the desiderata mentioned at the end of the previous section. But why, quite, should our inveterately teleological character inspire this need?

Subjection to measure is sometimes portrayed as an unwanted, even begrudged, consequence of engagement in 'ground projects'. In keeping with this, some writers feel compelled to remind the reader that, since engagement 'carries with it ... standards of assessment, ... he cannot ignore those standards' if 'he truly wishes to be considered' as seriously engaged.[44] For two reasons, this distorts the relation between measure and project. Both reasons are indicated in Alasdair MacIntyre's characterization of that species of project he calls 'a practice'. By this term, he means a 'cooperative human activity through which goods internal to that form of activity are realized in the course of trying to achieve those standards of excellence which are appropriate to, and partially definitive of, that form of activity'.[45] This passage suggests, first, that the relation between a project and a measure is so intimate and salient that no one embarking on the former could only later, and grudgingly, discover that he is now subject to the latter. Not all projects are 'defined' by clear-cut standards of excellence in the manner of MacIntyre's practices, but all of them—raising a family, say—are subject to appraisal and quite plainly so. All of them can be engaged in more or less well.

The passage also suggests that subjection to measure figures in the very description of what a person wants—what he is 'trying to achieve'—from engagement in a project or practice. It is partly in virtue of affording

---

[44] Anthony Rudd, *Kierkegaard and the Limits of the Ethical* (Oxford: Clarendon Press, 1997), 95. Generally, Rudd's discussion of projects and human teleology is extremely illuminating.

[45] *After Virtue: A Study in Moral Theory* (London: Duckworth, 1981), 175.

measure for activities that 'ground projects' or practices satisfy a human need. For they are engaged in, not simply to fill the empty hours, to ward off boredom, but to lend point and a sense of worth to at least many of the things a person does. But 'point' and 'worth' are normative notions, and no one could see a project as conferring point or worth who did not regard what he is trying to achieve, and how, as subject to measure. Once, for example, an embryonic project is deemed to fail the relevant measure—is judged to be just frivolous, say—it can no longer lend point to the activities geared up for it.

So it is not so much that our inveterately teleological existence 'inspires' a need for answerability and measure as that this need is internal to such an existence. Our kind of teleogical existence, incorporating a requirement to view ourselves as projective, as constantly 'on the way' towards goals set by 'ground projects', is ipso facto one that stands in need of measure.

Should that requirement and need be taken as 'primitive', irreducible? Kierkegaard argued that it was based on a deeper necessity and ambition— that of 'becoming a self'. According to Judge William in *Either/Or*, the person without 'ground projects' is in despair because he is not a genuine self. In order for there to be a 'collecting of oneself', an 'emergence of a concrete personality in continuity', that person must become engaged in projects or 'ethical' practices.[46] Perhaps the judge is right, but it is not an issue I shall explore, beyond remarking that it seems equally plausible to reverse the direction of his argument. One might reason that it is not in order to 'become a self' that one engages in projects, rather that a 'collecting of one-self'—a continuity and integrity to one's life—is a precondition for projective engagement. Serious engagement in projects requires some cohesion among them, both synchronically and over time. One project can conflict with another; a later one may make nonsense of an immediately preceding one. For engagement to be viable, then, a person cannot be so splintered, so *staccato*—so little a self, a 'concrete personality'—that conflicts and erasures are par for the course of his life.

Reference to measure, in the singular, is not intended to elide the several ways—some already alluded to—in which projects are subject to measure. To begin with, any project may be assessed for the manner, the 'how', in which it is pursued. In the case of a MacIntyrean practice, for example, the

---

[46] *Either/Or*, 218 ff.

question can always arise as to whether this manner conforms to those standards of excellence that partially define the practice. Second, the purpose of the project, if it is to confer point or worth on activities, is itself subject to measure. Well-executed activities lose their point if the purpose to which they contribute itself gets perceived as a waste of time. Typically, if not always, the purpose is answerable to—receives its measure from—a still wider scheme for the conduct of a life. Finally, no project is pursued in a vacuum, but always in a context that includes a background of presuppositions. A well-intentioned project, skilfully pursued, loses point if the presuppositions relative to which it has sense or feasibility are themselves unwarranted. If the conservationist's assumption that a certain species *can* be saved is mistaken, his project to save it is one he should abandon.

It is worth remarking, for future reference, that such presuppositions may be of a very deep—'metaphysical'—nature. If Buddhists are right, for example, then many of the projects on which people embark with respect to their future well-being are misguided since they assume something false—namely, that they, the very same people, the same 'selves', will continue to exist.[47] If the humanist is right, the project of the sciences to provide an absolute account of an independent, discursable reality cannot be sensible, since there is no such reality.

Insistence on our inveterately teleological existence, and hence on our need for answerability, is compatible with at least some familiar observations that, on the surface, militate against it. It is a common observation that, especially in modernity, people are excessively obsessed with the pursuit of purposes or goals. They should take far longer 'time-outs' than they customarily do from this pursuit so as, for example, simply to enjoy—'for their own sake'—the sensory delights that their world affords.[48] Again there is the sentiment, inspired perhaps by Zen reflections, that people place too much weight on activities devoted to 'big' goals, with the result that those 'little', mundane deeds like eating one's rice or sweeping one's floor are hurried through without 'mindfulness' of the way that they, too, may express and cultivate a proper comportment to the world. As Zen masters put it,

---

[47] See Steven Collins, *Selfless Persons: Imagery and Thought in Theravada Buddhism* (Cambridge: Cambridge University Press, 1982), for a discussion of the implications of the 'not-self' doctrine for the conduct of life.

[48] See Passmore, *Man's Responsibility for Nature*, 188–9.

there is 'nothing special' in actions devoted to the fulfilment of ambitious goals.

These may be edifying sentiments, but they do nothing to challenge the inveterately teleological character of our existence, with its need for measure. It is compatible with that need that large chunks of life should be without self-conscious attention to the achievement of purposes. Moreover, it is apparent that advocates of 'experiences for their own sake' or of attentiveness to our humblest tasks are not without their own 'ground projects'. For them, too, sense, worth, and point are conferred on activities—the walk in the forest, sweeping the floor, or whatever—by a conception of how human life should go. Like any other project, the cultivation of receptivity to experiences or of 'mindfulness' is subject to the modes of measure outlined above. Our advocates, after all, are *advocating*—something that, in the absence of a perception of measure, they could have no business doing.

At odds with the observation that human beings are too intent on point and purpose is 'postmodernist' delight that, at long last, people are successfully dispensing with such notions. As the novelist Alain Robbe-Grillet put it, 'modern man no longer feels the absence of meaning as a lack, or as an emotional distress. Faced with this emptiness, he succumbs to no dizziness. His heart no longer requires a hallow place in which to take refuge'.[49] These remarks naturally tempt one to ask how Robbe-Grillet regards his own practice as an author. One doubts that he sees this as devoid of any significance, a way of passing the time incapable of lending point and worth to the various activities—the crafting of sentences, say—that belong to it. Moreover, that he has reflected, and felt sufficiently motivated to pronounce, upon the place or absence of meaning in the conduct of life already distances him from the Kierkegaardian 'aesthete' whose life of 'immediacy', of subjection to caprice and the call of the 'moment', is indeed devoid of purpose. As Kierkegaard himself observed, once the 'aesthete' begins to ponder the character of his life, he ceases to be an 'aesthete' and is viewing life under the categories of purpose, project, and measure.

Robbe-Grillet's celebration of the liberation of life from the constraints of meaning and purpose is, I suspect, a version of the familiar proposal that the only meanings and purposes are those that agents themselves confer on their projects and practices. This proposal is not a denial of our inveterately

---

[49] Quoted in Herbert R. Kohl, *Age of Complexity* (London: Greenwood, 1977), 232.

teleological existence, nor of our need for answerability, but a particular view of what our lives are answerable to: the commitments we ourselves make, or the imperative to live as 'authentic' beings who are the sole sources of value and meaning in their lives. Notice that, at one point, it is a 'hallow' refuge—an abode of meaning that human beings do not confer—which Robbe-Grillet says that we moderns do without. To do without that, however, is not to do without answerability: rather, it is to adopt the humanist view that answerability is compatible with the dis-incumbenced stance. Whether that view is coherent is precisely the issue to which it is now time to turn.

Beyond the Human

Well, almost time, for it will helpful, first, to review our enquiry. This has been into the viability of the dis-incumbenced posture, the stance of a person who, while continuing to live an engaged life, replete with epistemic and normative commitments, eschews the prospect of grounding these in an order independent of human perspective. Reformulated, the enquiry is into the charge of hubris against the humanist's supposition that human beings are capable of adopting this stance. In the previous chapter, some indecisive arguments pro and con the viability of dis-incumbence were rehearsed. One reason for their being indecisive was the failure properly to attend to the mood of the embrace of humanism, to what is involved when the 'human world' thesis becomes 'hot and alive' for a person. It was pertinent, therefore, to describe a number of testimonies to that mood, witnesses to the unendurability of embracing the thesis of 'the human world' when uncompensated by some further doctrine that could draw its sting.

The question arose whether the various testimonies reflected a common, pivotal perception. All of them, I suggested, evince the perception that uncompensated humanism is unendurable because it violates a need for the answerability of our commitments, beliefs, and norms. This need was elucidated as a need, rooted in the inveterately teleological character of human existence, for measure. To concede this need is not, ipso facto, to accept that it cannot be satisfied within the terms allowed by humanism. It has yet to be shown that Robbe-Grillet and others are wrong to suppose that its satisfaction is incompatible with the dis-incumbenced stance. Whether or not they are wrong is the present issue. Must we regard human life as answerable to something beyond itself—to a 'source' independent of human perspective, commitment, and choice—if our activities and projects, and the beliefs and conceptions they presuppose, are to be answerable? Should we, that is, move from the centrality in our lives of a need for answerability and measure to the embrace of a source 'beyond human life itself'?

It will be helpful to have on the table a specimen of this movement. Central to the philosophy of the neglected French writer, Gabriel Marcel— coiner of the term 'existentialism'—is the notion of 'fidelity'. Fidelity to something or someone other than oneself is necessary as an antidote to that 'self-adherence' or 'self-enclosedness' that Marcel calls 'unavailability', and hence as protection against the 'despair' to which the self-enclosed person, like Kierkegaard's 'aesthete', is liable once he reflects on the point or worth of his life. Fidelity cannot, however, take the form of commitments 'purely from my own side'—to principles, say, that I have 'invented' or 'chosen': for that would itself be a form of unavailability or 'sclerosis', a refusal to countenance the possibility of 'experiences' that, on critical reflection, display the 'accidental', hence ungrounded, character of those commitments. Fidelity, rather, entails a sense that something 'has a hold over me': it is always in 'response' to what is 'other' than my own 'invention'.[50]

What, then, might be the 'other' that exerts this hold, to which I owe fidelity and am therefore answerable? Other people? The norms of my society? Such candidates cannot, according to Marcel, be final ones. Once the question is raised—as it always can be by someone 'available' to reflection—concerning the legitimacy of other people's demands and of society's norms, the absence of any further measure of these can only be experienced with 'despair'. 'Despair', writes Marcel, is the 'shock' of recognizing that 'there is no more'—no more, one might say, than measures that a reflective, 'available' person cannot help but question. There is, for Marcel, only one respectable reply to the question 'To what, finally, does one owe fidelity and stand answerable?' It is 'Being'—'the place of fidelity', the 'absolutely given'—which, with 'a sense of stewardship', we should hold ourselves

---

[50] Gabriel Marcel, *Being and Having*, trans. K. Farrar (London: Dacre, 1949), 69, 71, 46. See also Marcel's criticisms of Sartrean commitment in his *The Philosophy of Existence*, trans. M. Harari (London: Harvill, 1948). Incidentally, I have preferred 'available' over 'disposable' as a translation of Marcel's term 'disponible'.

'responsible towards'. This, explains Marcel, is because Being is 'the principle of inexhaustibility'.[51]

Opaque as such remarks are, the idea that nothing short of Being provides measure is familiar. Heidegger, for example, writes that it is 'from Being' that there comes 'the assignment of those directives that must become law and rule for man'.[52] Familiar, too, is the thought that this is due to what Marcel calls the 'inexhaustibility' of Being and others refer to as its 'limitless', 'encompassing', or 'infinite' character. Unsurprisingly, some of these writers, including Marcel, identify the inexhaustible and encompassing with God, but not, typically, with the intention to clarify those notions, since it is in terms of them that the notion of God is to be understood rather than vice versa.

It is not my present aim to explore how Being, as a 'principle of inexhaustibility', might provide measure, but it is worth sketching the line of thought that inspires this suggestion. 'To see something's limits', remarked Robert Nozick, 'is to question its meaning.' Only, therefore, 'when something is all-encompassing and all-inclusive', so that there is 'nowhere else to stand from which to survey its limits', is a halt called to such questioning. Whether, as Nozick speculates, the limitless or inexhaustible must be 'its own importance and meaning', it must at any rate serve as a 'stopping-point' for such questions.[53] While, as limitless, there is nothing beyond it, this is not the 'no more' the 'shocking' experience of which Marcel described as 'despair'. Our 'finite'—contingent, even 'accidental'—practices and projects invite questioning from people sufficiently 'available' to reflect on them. This invitation prompts a search for somewhere to stand from which to survey the limits of those practices and projects as measures for our activities. 'Despair' ensues with the recognition that these limits are not surpassable, that there is 'nowhere to stand'. That there is 'no more' beyond Being, beyond the encompassing, induces no similar reaction, for built into such a notion is the aburdity of looking for a further place from which to survey limits. There *might have been* 'more' beyond our finite practices and, if not, that is our tragedy. There is nothing tragic in the absence of anything beyond the limitless.

---

[51] *Being and Having*, 69, 41, 15, 102.

[52] 'Letter on Humanism', in *Basic Writings: Martin Heidegger*, ed. D. F. Krell (London: Routledge, 1993), 262.

[53] Robert Nozick, *Philosophical Explanations* (Oxford: Clarendon Press, 1981), 597, 600, 603.

Our present concern, however, is not with the obscure idea of limitless Being as the source of measure, but with the movement from the need for answerability to the conviction that this must be answerability to something 'beyond human life'—beyond projects or interests and what is dependent on human perspective. Perhaps that movement cannot halt anywhere short of Being: but the more immediate task is to examine the style of argument for making that movement, postponing the issue of precisely where it comes to a halt.

Before that, however, it is important to dispel any impression that the movement concerns only answerability and measure in the sphere of our broadly 'moral' commitments, such as fidelity to friends. For it concerns, as well, the answerability of beliefs about the world. Or better, reflection on the point or worth of our activities and projects must, given the contexts of beliefs that they presuppose, encompass these as well. Thus many projects—in the educational sphere, for instance—presuppose not merely a body of scientific beliefs, but something like a world view that privileges scientific enquiry. For the significance of those projects to be sustained, it is arguable that those beliefs and that view must successfully answer to something 'beyond human life'. As one writer puts it—with Coleridge's line, 'in our life alone does Nature live', in mind—the idea that 'in his scientific activity man is meeting only himself' induces 'meaninglessness and futility'.[54] His point is that someone convinced by constructivists or other humanists that science is just one, not especially privileged, account of the world—reflective of practical interests and a pre-emptive 'ground-plan' (see pp. 197 ff above)—could not continue to invest scientific activity, and the projects that presuppose the scientific world view, with the significance or worth formerly ascribed to them. For they now answer to no measure, it seems, beyond ones that we ourselves, groundlessly, apply. Such a person could be compared to a religious believer now convinced, by 'demythologizing' theologians, that the religious world view is nothing but an expression of certain human needs and emotions.

The antidote to 'meaninglessness and futility', this argument implies, is a conviction that one's representation of the world, scientific or otherwise, is 'in harmony' with what is beyond human decision and perspective. In the case of science, at least, this harmony is typically sought in a correspondence with a discursable, independent order of facts. That is the wrong place to

54 T. F. Torrance, quoted in Clark, *God's World and the Great Awakening*, 3.

seek for those persuaded by the humanist that there is no such order. For these people, an understanding of harmony with 'something beyond'—one capable of compensating for, and rendering endurable, the thesis of 'the human world'—must take a different form, one couched perhaps in the opaque idiom of Being as a source of measure.

There is, it is worth remarking, a rather special class of beliefs, if not exactly 'about the world', upon which these remarks also bear. I refer to beliefs concerning the meaningfulness of the words employed to talk about the world. For beliefs of this type, too, are clearly presupposed by many, perhaps all, our activities and practices. In connection with these semantic beliefs, certainly, we find the movement towards the idea of answerability to something 'beyond the human'. If our speech is to be more than 'verbal music', if we are to overcome the 'aphasic' experience of language as merely a 'brute meaningless sounding-off', then, so the thought goes, the application of our words must be governed by something beyond human decision or judgement. For some philosophers, we have seen, this requires that the application of words, once they are in place, is 'contractually' dictated solely by how the world anyway and independently is (pp. 128 ff). If, however, the humanist critique of the 'contractual' model is correct, it must be in a different direction that one seeks something 'beyond the human'— harmony of our speech with the *logos*, say—to serve as the measure to which the application of words is answerable.

These are matters to which to return in later chapters after consideration of the style of argument that encourages the movement towards the idea of answerability to something 'beyond the human'. The movement executed by Marcel is of a very familiar sort, defended or criticized in almost any essay on 'the meaning of life'. Shorn of his particular terminology, the reasoning is as follows. As inveterately teleological creatures, human beings need to view substantial stretches of their activity as having significance. (I use 'significance' as a portmanteau term for what we want such stretches to possess—point, worth, meaning, importance, the distinction of mattering, and so on.) Typically, at least, to assign significance to an activity is to display its appropriate connection with—say, its contribution to—something beyond itself that then serves as a source of its significance: a wider project, perhaps, that provides measure for the activity. This is why an activity is typically regarded as devoid of significance when perceived as so limited and enclosed as to fail appropriately to connect up with anything beyond itself.

The problem is to judge how and where the chain of significance-conferring connections stops without rendering pointless the activities whose significance is originally questioned. For, as Nozick puts it, 'to be important for something which is itself unimportant is . . . to be unimportant'. When it is the significance of our lives that is at issue, we want it to go 'all the way down'.[55] If the chain stops with something that itself invites, but receives no answer to, Tolstoy's question 'And then what?', then not only it, but those activities and projects whose source it is are without significance. The truth would then be, as Tolstoy concludes, that 'life is meaningless'.[56] For Tolstoy himself, as for Marcel, the chain will indeed have stopped at this disastrous point if it stops with the human—with our practices, forms of life, traditions, personal commitments, social norms, repertoire of 'natural sentiments', or whatever. For, of each of these, one may ask—indeed, cannot help asking once reflection is underway—'And then what?' How can it matter, how can it confer significance, that our activities connect up with such sources if these fail to connect up with a further source—if, for example, our society's norms or our 'natural sentiments' are subject to no measure that shows how a life in accordance with them is worth something? If significance is to be conducted back along the chain, its source must be 'beyond the human', for whatever remains within the precincts of the human always inspires the question of its own significance.

As earlier remarks indicate, further chains extend from our activities—orthogonal, as it were, to the one just discussed—in the direction of beliefs about the world and about the meaningfulness of our talk about the world. Activities presuppose such beliefs and cannot have their assumed point unless these are warranted. Once enquiry into warrant begins, the problem of where the chain stops re-arises, for, to amend Nozick's remark, to be warranted by something that is itself unwarranted is to be unwarranted. One does not give a warrant to certain beliefs presupposed by an activity by appealing to some supporting conception of reality that itself dangles. If warrant is to be conducted back along this chain, its final link, the argument goes, cannot be anything human—conceptions, world views, perspectives, Collingwood's 'absolute presuppositions', or whatever. Any such candidate

55 *Philosophical Explanations*, 599.
56 Leo Tolstoy, *A Confession and Other Religious Writings*, trans. J. Kentish (Harmondsworth: Penguin, 1987), 29–30.

must be supposed to gets its warrant through a connection with something 'beyond the human'—through correspondence with an independent, discursable order of facts, harmony with the Tao, reflection of 'the divine ideas', illumination by the Form of the Good, or whatever. For whatever remains within the precinct of the human can always inspire the question of its own warrant, of the source that justifies the taking of it, and the practices which presuppose it, with the seriousness that our need for answerability dictates.

I find the above line of argument compelling in the only way, perhaps, that argument in this area can be compelling—a way compelling enough, at any rate, for demonstrating the unlivability of the dis-incumbenced stance. For it articulates and regiments the compulsion experienced, once the significance of activities is questioned, to extend the chains just discussed 'beyond the human'. Put differently, it articulates the compulsion, recorded in the testimonies from early in this chapter, to abandon the dis-incumbenced posture if our condition is not to be one of *Angst* or 'despair'. For to remain in that posture is to allow that the chains stop within the precincts of the human.

That most people do not execute the movement 'beyond the human' is no objection to its compelling character if this is due, as I suggest it is, to their generally undisturbed assumption that the significance of their activities, and the warrant for the beliefs these presuppose, *do* have a source and measure 'beyond the human'—to a dumb conviction that someone, somewhere could, with sufficient wits and energy, identify this source and measure. For such people, the issue of dis-incumbence to which the movement is a response is not an issue: they are not at the appropriate level of reflection, not sufficiently 'available', to recall Marcel's term. This is a point, presumably, that would be endorsed by those many philosophers who regard realism as our commonsense position. The assumption that our beliefs, etc., have a measure 'beyond the human' will indeed generally take the form of 'dumb conviction' if it resides at the level of everyday, unreflective common sense.

Not everyone's failure to make the movement can, however, be so explained. There are 'available' people, and not just among philosophers, who reflect on the significance of their activities without, it seems, experiencing a compulsion to extend the chains 'beyond the human'. In this connection, however, it is important to recall the mood of the embrace of the 'human world' thesis, for it is no objection to the claim that the movement is compelling if those who do not find it so are, crudely put, just 'sounding off' or guilty of a 'fashionable put-on'. My concern has been with those—the authors of my testimonies, for example—for whom that thesis has become 'hot and alive', 'deeply cultivated'.

But are there not people who fit that description yet resist any compulsion to appeal 'beyond the human'? Yes: people who find the argument which articulates the movement to be flawed. Three lines of resistance may be discerned among these critics. To begin with, it gets argued that the failure of the chains to stop at a point that does not invite a further 'And then what?' does not impugn the significance of the activities originally in question. Significance, on this view, must indeed be relative to a further context or source: but precisely because this *must* be so, the impossibility of closing the chain with something that could not invite 'And then what?' is nothing distressing—for there is no alternative. In practice, we content ourselves that certain activities are significant provided that we can travel a reasonable distance along the chain—connecting them to some wider projects, say, that in turn get their point from some further goal in life. That we can think of no further source for this goal, or for one a bit further along, should not occasion shock, since we know that provision of further sources must anyway, eventually dry up.

This is a puzzling view, for it offers as a panacea for our worries something that can only intensify them. If our need for answerability inspires a search for a source that does not invite another 'And then what?', the discovery that this search *could* never succeed is hardly comforting. Recognition that it is impossible in principle for that need to be satisfied is more 'despairing' than admission that the need remains as a matter of fact unsatisfied. That many people, in practice, rest content with travelling only a 'reasonable distance' along the chain is due, not to their appreciation that the journey could never have a final destination, but, on the contrary, to their assumption that it *does*, albeit a destination that they themselves need not locate since this has been, or could be, done by those with the sagacity, leisure, and professional credentials for the task.

A second line of resistance to the movement rejects the thought that in order for something to be significant, it must connect up with something further or wider whose own significance can in turn be questioned. Those who take this line invoke the case of linguistic significance or meaning.

When we ask what meaning an expression bears in a poem, we may certainly need to identify its contribution to the whole poem, but the question of what the poem as a whole means may not be a legitimate one. Indeed, according to today's literary critical wisdom, as taught by Archibald MacLeish, a poem should not mean, but be. The trouble is that, while this may be wise counsel in the realm of poetics, it does not carry over to the realm of life, and the analogy between the meaning of linguistic items and the significance of our activities is a poor one. The better analogue to the latter is not the words in a poem, but the acts of writing the words. These acts have their immediate point as contributing to the composition of a whole poem. Now the writing of poems, with the devotion of time and energy it requires, surely is something whose significance in their lives people may question, even if the poems themselves—according to MacLeish's dictum— cannot be said to have meanings. When it is a matter of the meaning of our lives, to recall Nozick's remark, we want meaning to go all the way down. That any such desire may be illegitimate in the case of linguistic meaning is beside the point.

A third line of resistance concedes that the significance attributed to the components of a life must indeed go all the way down the line, but it is held that the line ends, unproblematically, within the precincts of the human. The chain stops with something that no longer invites 'And then what?', but this something is not 'beyond the human'. If this is right, then my assertion that, once reflection is underway, one cannot help questioning the significance of anything still within the precincts of the human was mistaken. There is a source within those precincts that one can and should absolve from further questioning. For some writers, the source is found in the region of human will. In a manner recalling Camus's strategy for saving Sisyphus's exertions from absurdity, Richard Taylor argued that there is 'no need to ask questions' about projects for which people have 'bent their backs', even if these seem to 'get nowhere', provided that the projects are 'just what it is their will to pursue'. For it is this will or commitment 'from within us' that is the 'whole justification and meaning' of the projects and of the activities which contribute to them.[57] But it seems to me obvious that,

---

[57] Richard Taylor, 'The Meaning of Life', in O. Hanfling (ed.), *Life and Meaning: A Reader* (Oxford: Blackwell, 1988), 47.

while busy, back-bending people may rarely question the significance of the projects which it is their will to pursue, it is open to them to do so—and once they do, they cannot be satisfied by Taylor's answer. For to question one's project for its significance is also to question the worth of one's commitment to it, of one's willing to pursue it. To be told 'Look at how resolutely you have willed to pursue it!' is useless: the problem is whether all that resoluteness was wasted.

For other writers, the human source at which the chain stops is something like a whole form of life, for while any activity or project has its significance in relation to such a form, it cannot itself be interrogated for its significance. The thought behind this claim is one we encountered earlier, in Chapter 7, when introducing the notion of dis-incumbence. There I rejected the view that, simply because engagement in a form of life is a precondition of intelligibility, it is impossible for a participant to gain a reflective distance from it. Hence my sympathy for Putnam's claim, inspired by remarks of Wittgenstein, that one may question 'whether the form of life . . . has practical and spiritual value'. That sympathy, in the present context, becomes antipathy towards the attempt to regard a form of life as the human 'something' at which the chain could stop. It might be replied that, since no form of life is monolithic, questioning practices that belong to it should be understood as questioning 'some particular sub-set' of practices from the critical standpoint of people engaged in a different sub-set, but one which still belongs to the same form of life.[58] But this 'internal' questioning must be of a relatively limited and conservative kind unless the notion of a form of life is to become hopelessly distended and hence incapable of playing a strategic role in resisting the extension of the chain 'beyond the human'. Certainly it could not be of the 'radical' kind that questions the worth of, for example, all projects in pursuit of improved material conditions of life, or, in the manner of Kierkegaard, that queries the credentials of social morality as a whole. These, surely, are not questions addressed from a standpoint *within* a form of life recognizably like our own.

There is, then, no effective line of resistance to the compulsion to extend the chain of significance conferring sources or measures 'beyond the

---

[58] Sabina Lovibond, *Realism and Imagination in Ethics* (Oxford: Blackwell, 1983), 109. For a critical, Kierkegaardian response to her position, see Rudd, *Kierkegaard and the Limits of the Ethical*, 119–20.

human'. Nor is there, I suggest, to a similar extension of that other, warrant-conferring chain earlier discussed. 'Available' human beings, once they question the beliefs about the world presupposed by their activities, cannot find their need for answerability satisfied by, for example, the proposal that the final source and measure of those beliefs is the form of life in which they are embedded. There is little doubt, surely, that a final source is sought, or simply assumed to reside, 'beyond the human'—in, say, an independent, discursable order of facts. That is one reason why constructivist and other humanist conceptions receive short shrift, not only in the scientific community, but among a more general public.

The upshot of this chapter is that the dis-incumbenced stance cannot be maintained. The thesis of 'the human world', once 'deeply cultivated', turns out to be one with which human beings cannot live. If our need for answerability is to be satisfied, human life must indeed answer to something beyond itself. The charge of hubris against uncompensated humanism is therefore secured: for this was precisely the lack of humility in the conviction that human beings are capable of the dis-incumbenced stance, of living with 'the human world' thesis. Answerability, it has emerged, entails what Marcel calls 'ontological humility', the antithesis to a hubris that 'consists in drawing . . . strength'—measure, one might say—'solely from [ourselves]'.[59]

---

[59] *Being and Having*, 132; *The Philosophy of Existence*, 20.

CHAPTER II

Mystery

Impasse?

On a number of occasions, I have anticipated an apparent impasse that would ensue if the charges of hubris exchanged by humanists and their opponents were both secured. With those charges now secured, or at any rate rendered plausible, it is time to identify this impasse and to consider how it might be escaped.

If the arguments of the last few chapters are accepted, then the choice between absolutism and humanism is one between something unbelievable and something unlivable. There could never be reason to suppose of any account that it describes the world as it anyway, independently is; yet to suppose that there is only the human world requires a 'dis-incumbenced' stance which cannot be sustained, since it precludes satisfaction of an ineliminable need for answerability and measure 'beyond the human'. The 'independence' thesis cannot be believed: the 'human world' thesis cannot be lived with. If humanism and absolutism are our only alternatives, then, we indeed find ourselves in an impasse. And so far, no other genuine alternatives have presented themselves. Attempts to steer between the two alternatives, in the manner, for example, of allegedly 'modest' versions of realism, failed—or so I argued, for these versions collapse into forms of humanism or absolutism, depending on how they are elaborated.

In retrospect, there was a premonition of this impasse right at the beginning of the story I told early on in this book. The 'Ockhamists', in their rejection of the 'Augustinian heritage', struggled to combine a continuing faith in an independent reality created by God with an insistence that any world knowable and describable by human beings must, so to speak, be 'their world'. It was always unlikely that any attempted resolution of a perceived tension in this combination could satisfy all aspirations. Preservation of the faith in independence would threaten the conviction that the world can be *known* by us: securing that conviction would threaten faith in independence. The growing complaint against increasingly robust forms of humanism was that independence—hence answerability—was being dissolved. The charge against rationalism and later forms of absolutism was that their proclamations of an independent order were at best without any warrant, at worst unintelligible: either way, our thought and talk could not be deemed to engage with such an order.

In retrospect, too, one can see that, right from the start, the currency of debate between the opposing factions would be that of hubris and humility. This is because the debate was, for centuries, linked to reflection upon the relationship—the (un)likeness—of human beings to God. For the 'Ockhamists' and the earlier cohorts of humanists, there was impiety in the pretence of their opponents to emulate God's understanding and knowledge of the reality he created. For those opponents, however, it was to the very creativity of God—his responsibility for a world—that the humanists, in their impiety, were aspiring.

I am not the first author to note the parallels between the recent charges of hubris and the earlier ones of impiety or blasphemy that were swapped between humanists and their rivals. Adrian Moore has described the aspirations of those I have labelled humanists and absolutists as different modes of an 'aspiration to be infinite', one that is, in effect, 'a craving for God'. If absolutism is the aspiration to be like God in one's unconditioned knowledge of reality, then humanism (of the Promethean ilk, certainly) reflects a 'temptation to proceed as if . . . our representations constituted reality', a rebellion against constraints on our creativity, and hence an urge to emulate the unconditioned will of God.[1]

Moore dramatizes our competing aspirations in these ways partly in order to prepare the ground for what he sees as the only sensible way out of the impasse for which they are responsible. We cannot just eliminate these aspirations, but we can 'come to terms' with them by 'learning how to be finite'.[2] I interpret that to mean that, first, we should recognize both that the world is not 'constituted' by us and that we cannot achieve that knowledge of how the world anyway is which would satisfy a yearning for final answer-

---

[1] A. W. Moore, *Points of View* (Oxford: Clarendon Press, 1997), 259 f, 277.
[2] Ibid. 276.

ability: and that, second, we should just learn to live with this situation. Injured pride and despair are reactions that we must learn to overcome.

But I do not see this as a way out of the impasse as I have characterized it. To begin with, if the humanist's objections to absolutism are correct, the world is, in a tolerable sense, 'constituted' by us: hence we should recognize that it is. Second, if the humanist's critics are right, the demand for answerability 'beyond the human' is not something that can be 'overcome'. Perhaps one can survive with a lack of final answerability, but not by 'coming to terms', or 'learning to live', with it: rather, one would have, as it were, to take tranquillizers, or otherwise prevent the movement of thought that leads 'beyond the human' from getting underway.

There is, I suggest, only one way out of the impasse available, at least as a formal option. Recall that absolutism is the thesis that there is a *discursable* way the world anyway is independent of 'the human contribution'. Humanism is the denial that there is any such way the world is. Put like this, it is clear that the two positions are contraries, not contradictories. They cannot both be true, but they might both be false. And this is because of the availability of the following thesis: there is a way the world independently is, but this way is not discursable. (In case the words 'the world' strike you as too obviously referring to something discursable, substitute 'reality' for them—as I shall often do.)

Put differently, a doctrine of *mystery* would provide a formal alternative and an escape from the impasse. This doctrine is admirably even-handed towards the competing '-isms'. Humanists are right to say that any discursable world is a human one, but wrong to equate reality with a discursable world. Absolutists are right to say that reality is independent of 'the human contribution', but wrong to suppose that it is discursable. Humanists are wrong to suppose that our beliefs and commitments can answer only to what is within the precincts of the human. Absolutists are wrong to suppose that what is 'beyond the human', to which they are answerable, is anything discursable. So even-handed is the doctrine that one could, if one wished, describe it as a radically amended humanism—one that provides the 'compensation' for 'raw' humanism discussed at the beginning of Chapter 10. Or one could describe it as a radically amended absolutism: absolutism without the idea that the world as it anyway is must be discursable. Or, of course, one could abandon such labels, and simply speak of a doctrine of mystery.

It is clear from these remarks, I hope, that 'mystery' is to be taken in a strong sense. The claim that there is mystery is not the one encountered earlier, when discussing some allegedly 'modest' forms of absolutism, that there may be—or even probably are—aspects of reality that will be forever beyond our ken. These, after all, are forms of *absolutism*: the possibility in principle is allowed that there could be warrant for regarding an account of the world as an absolute one. To hold that there is mystery, in my sense, is to maintain that what there anyway is is undiscursable, ineffable, since any discourse inevitably captures only a 'human world'. 'Mysteries', wrote the Sūfi poet, Rūmi, 'are not to be solved.'[3] There is no 'solution' to, no 'explanation' of, what is mysterious, since the terms of solutions and the categories of explanation are applicable only to that from which the human contribution has *not* been weeded out.

But is the doctrine of mystery more than a merely formal option—one articulated in sentences that are well formed, syntactically pukkah, but at which we can only blankly stare? Is the idea of mystery, as Rorty says of an ineffable *être-en-soi*, a 'purely vacuous' one that we can do nothing with?[4] If it is, then a number of philosophers will be disappointed: those who, like myself, expressly invoke this idea in the hope of escaping the impasse described above, of honouring the requirement of humility, and of satisfying the need for answerability and measure.

One such disappointed philosopher, whose position is not untypical, would be Max Scheler. As a good phenomenologist, Scheler holds that any account of the world is only a description of it under its '"human" object-aspect'. So in hock to human interests and purposes are scientific and other accounts that they register, Scheler hyperbolically puts it, a perception of everything as 'friend or foe'. But if there is a false 'intellectual pride' in supposing that reality itself is 'reached' by such descriptions, there is also a lack of humility in remaining at a level of 'life-engrossment and anthropomorphism'. Reflective human beings should surrender to that 'movement' or 'upsurge' which, if their lives are to strike them as more than 'contingent' ones with a merely 'relative' justification, takes them towards the 'absolute', towards 'the kind of participation demanded by . . . [a] primal essence' that Scheler compares to the *brahman* of Vedāntic thought.[5]

[3] *The Essential Rūmi*, trans. C. Barks (Harmondsworth: Penguin, 1999),107.
[4] Richard Rorty, *Consequences of Pragmatism: Essays 1972–80* (Brighton: Harvester, 1982), 15.
[5] Max Scheler, *On the Eternal in Man*, trans. B. Noble (London: SCM Press, 1960), 75–7, 86, 92, 95.

Talk of 'primal essence' and *brahman*, and of the 'act of humility' which is 'free sacrifice' to 'participation' in these, is unlikely, presumably, to persuade those who impugn the idea of mystery as purely vacuous to change their minds. Their dismissal of the doctrine of mystery as no more than a formal option for escaping the impasse calls for closer attention.

Impugning Mystery

Mystery has not enjoyed favour with modern 'mainstream', Anglo-American philosophy. While some writers, notably Russell, respected the mystical spirit—the urge to 'so enlarge our interests' as to secure 'a form of union of Self and not-Self'[6]—the more common verdict has been harsher. The idea of the undiscursably mysterious is 'purely vacuous' or, in Putnam's phrase, 'quite empty'.[7] But what lies behind such summary verdicts? Not, one hopes, a failure to note a possible ambiguity in expressions like 'idea of mystery'. If what is mysterious is undiscursable, then I cannot have a genuine idea of it in the way that, to speak in seventeenth-century idiom, I have the idea of gold or snow—for that implies my ability to apply concepts or descriptions to particular objects. But it will not follow from this, of course, that I cannot have the idea of mystery in the sense of intelligibly supposing that there *is* mystery, that there *is* the undiscursable.

The thinking behind Rorty's and, one suspects, many similar verdicts is indicated when he remarks that an ineffable *être-en-soi*, noumenon, or whatever, would be so 'aloof' that appeals to such notions 'do . . . not get us anywhere' and just 'have not worked'.[8] Still, this leaves the exact objection unclear. Has Rorty examined the many cultures in which a notion of mystery has not only been widely entertained, but has seemingly played a central role in moral or religious practice, and then discovered that this notion never really 'worked' for these societies, never 'got them anywhere'? If so, he does not record his investigations. But, predictably, when one looks more closely at Rorty's point, it becomes clear that he would not regard any 'work' done by the notion in such cultures as relevant anyway. For his point is the

---

6 Bertrand Russell, *The Problems of Philosophy* (Oxford: Oxford University Press, 1980), 91 ff.
7 Hilary Putnam, *Pragmatism: An Open Question* (Oxford: Blackwell, 1995), 29.
8 *Consequences of Pragmatism*, pp. xx, xiv.

one made by Putnam when explaining why noumena and the like cannot be the concern of 'rational philosophy'. There could not, Putnam says, be a *theory* of noumena, and there is 'nothing in the history of science' to suggest that we should 'aim at' the kind of absolutism associated with a doctrine of noumena.[9]

The objection to the idea of mystery, in short, is that it can play no role in empirical, scientific enquiry. It does 'not get us anywhere' when where we are trying to get is an optimally explanatory science: it does not 'work', because it cannot facilitate prediction and control of events, or any other outcomes criterial for the success of the scientific enterprise.

Even to other pragmatists who share the view that ideas or beliefs must 'work' in order to possess genuine content or truth, Rorty's and Putnam's construal of that view will appear stunted. It is a far cry, certainly, from William James's 'genial' version of pragmatism which allowed, for example, that 'if theological ideas prove to have a value for concrete life, they will be true'.[10] It is simply arbitrary to dictate that, for the idea of mystery to 'get us anywhere', it must do so—in the manner of such notions as anti-matter or quarks—by conveying us towards a comprehensive, explanatory science. And that, of course, is not the kind of 'role' that people attracted to the idea of mystery have envisaged it playing. In my account, for one, the idea emerged in order to play the role of enabling an escape from a philosophical impasse. *Pace* Putnam, consideration of the idea of mystery does belong within 'rational philosophy'. To be sure, in order to play that role, a doctrine of mystery must offer some promise of catering to our need for answerability and measure. But if it fails to do so, its not 'working' is nevertheless a very different matter from its 'failure' to fit into the fabric of empirical science.

Lurking in some remarks by both Rorty and Putnam, however, there seems to be a further, less pragmatic objection to the idea of mystery. To enquire into Kant's ineffable things in themselves, says Putnam, is to 'ask how the world is to be described in the world's own language', not in ours—but there is, he adds, simply 'no such thing' as that language.[11] Rorty is simi-

---

[9] *Realism and Reason: Philosophical Papers, Vol. 3* (Cambridge: Cambridge University Press, 1983), 226, 228.

[10] *The Writings of William James* (Chicago: University of Chicago Press, 1977), 387. Elsewhere, in *The Varieties of Religious Experience* (New York: Longmans, Green, & Co., 1923), James expresses great sympathy with mystical thought.

[11] *Pragmatism*, 29.

larly dismissive of a reality in itself that could be captured, not by 'our' representations, but in such terms 'as it would describe itself, if it could'.[12]

I agree that there is no mileage in the notion of a language that accurately describes reality, but is beyond any possible comprehension by ourselves. If reality could speak, we *could* understand it. But to agree on this is not to concur in rejecting the idea of mystery. We can see this by noting that Putnam's point is ineffective against its alleged target, Kant, and this is because Kant himself was insistent that things in themselves are undiscursable, not only by us but by any 'discursive intelligence'. Ironically, Putnam himself, in the earlier *Reason, Truth, and History*, clearly distinguished 'metaphysical realism', which does entail the possibility of a discourse beyond our reach, from Kant's doctrine of noumena, which does not. Indeed, I congratulated him on that distinction in Chapter 8.

To invoke the terminology used in the final section of that chapter, the objection of Rorty and (the later) Putnam is not against a doctrine of mystery, but against a version of 'atypical' absolutism. According to that version, there is a structured, discursable way the world anyway is: it's just that this way cannot be articulated by us. That version, as I put it, has made a 'greater retreat' from the original, 'typical' version of absolutism—Bernard Williams's, for example—according to which an approximately absolute account of reality is actually within our reach. Ironically, once more, it was precisely arguments culled from Rorty and Putnam that I commandeered when criticizing that 'greater retreat'. For example, I cited with approval Rorty's point that the resulting version of absolutism illegitimately tries to combine the thought of our 'inarticulate confrontation' with reality in itself with that of reality in itself being sufficiently structured to be conceptually and linguistically represented, albeit not by us.

My present aim is not to repeat the Chapter 8 criticisms of the 'greater retreat', but, first of all, to emphasize that this retreat leads not to a doctrine of mystery—of what is mysterious or undiscursable *tout court*—but to a version of atypical absolutism on which it is only mysterious 'for us'. Second, however, I want to draw an important lesson from this discussion for the prospects of a doctrine of mystery.

The fact that Putnam's and Rorty's criticism is effective against a certain

---

[12] *Consequences of Pragmatism*, 194.

kind of position should discourage proponents of mystery from allowing their doctrine of mystery to slide into that position. This is not, unfortunately, a lesson heeded by some *soi-disant* proponents of mystery. Readers of the vast literature of, or on, mysticism will be familiar with the tendency of many authors, first to announce the mystery or ineffability of something— God, *brahman*, the *Tao*, or whatever—and then to say so much about it that the original announcement is undermined. In some cases, the result is not even an atypical version of absolutism, for the loquacious authors supply just that discourse whose availability to us they have earlier denied. So, to take an example almost at random, one authority on Sūfi mysticism tells us that the Sūfi's God can 'never be the theme of thought and discussion', yet in the following paragraph describes this God as active, omniscient, not a *prima causa* but still the creator of the world, far removed from this world, the God of the Koran, the source of all love, and so on.[13] Indeed, by the end of the chapter, this being beyond 'thought and discussion' ends up sounding barely more mysterious than some rather grand and remote earthly potentate.

Even much less loquacious proponents of mystery often employ a vocabulary that invites a conception of mystery that makes it sound at least *apt* for familiar linguistic and conceptual articulation. This is a worry that some critics have expressed concerning Kant's talk of things in themselves. It was almost certainly not Kant's intention to hold that, corresponding to each phenomenal object, there exists a noumenal doppelgänger. Yet, as Schopenhauer noted, the very reference to thin*gs* (in themselves) suggests the image of a reality structured into discrete entities, with all that this implies by way of the applicability of criteria of identity, of a *principium individuationis*. Such an image is already close to the incoherent picture of reality in itself attacked by Rorty—one that allows only for 'inarticulate confrontation', yet is apt for linguistic articulation.[14]

The incoherence of the resulting picture, and the effect of undermining an initial announcement of mystery, are not the only problems with the loquacious tendencies just noted. The strategic role of mystery, as it

---

[13] Annemarie Schimmel, *I Am Wind, You are Fire: The Life and Works of Rumi* (Boston, Mass.: Shambhala, 1992), 73.

[14] See also Donald Davidson, 'On the Very Idea of a Conceptual Scheme', in his *Inquiries into Truth and Interpretation* (Oxford: Clarendon Press, 1984), who notes a similar incoherence when criticizing philosophers who build a degree of structure and articulation into what, they allege, precedes and awaits any conceptual framing.

emerged in my discussion, is to provide measure for our beliefs and activities, concepts and norms—something to which these are answerable.
Clearly mystery cannot play that role, except circularly, if, built into the conception of mystery, are ingredients of just the sort for which measure is
sought. Now the belief that there is a God who is a loving creator is, rather
obviously perhaps, one that is not independent of 'the human contribution',
of human perspective. The belief and the terms in which it is couched are
ones for which measure is sought, and no such measure can be provided by
a 'mystery' defined by that belief and its terms. Again, our conception of the
world as consisting of *things*—our 'thingly' ontology—must, if it is to be
more than the pragmatic, though potentially dangerous, convenience that it
was taken to be by Nietzsche, be answerable to . . ..[15] For that to be possible,
the mystery to which it is to be held answerable cannot already be invested
with an 'all-too-human' ontology of things.

   Should we say, then, that the lesson to be learned by proponents of mystery from the problems encountered by the over-loquacious among them is
one of just shutting up? Should someone hoping for intimations of the
nature of mystery avoid words and listen instead to, say, babbling brooks,
the Late String Quartets, or the wind gusting through Tintern Abbey? This
would be, for a start, a premature conclusion to draw. Clearly it will be a *delicate* matter to speak 'about' mystery without running into the problems outlined. But I will suggest, in the following section, that the matter might
nevertheless be handled. Blank silence is not the only option. Indeed,
secondly, blank silence can hardly be an option at all if mystery is to play the
strategic role indicated just a few lines earlier. If mystery is to provide any
effective measure, we cannot be content simply to announce 'There is mystery' and then go away, tight-lipped. Something further needs to be said
'about' it, something to connect mystery with 'the human world', conceptions of which and activities within which are to be held answerable to . . ..
This saying of 'something further' must, to be sure, be compatible with the
constraints indicated by terms such 'ineffable' and 'undiscursable'. Let's proceed, then, to this, as already remarked, delicate matter.

   [15] Dangerous because, for Nietzsche, this ontology at once reflects and reinforces a conception
of minds, selves, or persons as persisting objects or 'substances'. See my 'Schopenhauer and
Nietzsche on Self and Morality', in C. Janaway (ed.), *Willing and Nothingness: Schopenhauer as
Nietzsche's Educator* (Oxford: Clarendon Press, 1998), 196–216.

Ineffability and Mystery

We might begin the approach to this matter by repeating, and elaborating, why what is mysterious or ineffable *is* ineffable and so cannot be talked about, even if it can be talked 'about'. I shall sharpen the distinction intended by 'about' versus '"about"' in due course. For the moment, it may be put in this vague way: to talk about mystery is, impossibly, to describe what cannot be described, whereas to talk 'about' it is to say something in connection with it that may not be similarly impossible.

Any number of reasons have been offered for why something or other is ineffable: for example, that what it is cannot be communicated to someone who does not personally experience it. Lorca wrote of the *duende*, the 'mysterious power' apparently discerned by aficionados of flamenco and bullfighting, that 'no philosopher has explained' it, since explanation, besides being unnecessary for the aficionados, is incapable of conveying its essence.[16] Or the suggestion might be that the ineffable *is* a certain sort of experience or feeling, one so deep and private as to lack those connections with overt behaviour and other 'outward' criteria that are prerequisite for communicating one's psychological states. A very different reason has been suggested by many mystical philosophers in line with Plotinus's remark that since 'understanding proceeds by concepts and the concept is a multiple affair, the soul misses the One when she falls into number and plurality'.[17] To talk about something is to apply concepts to it, but concepts serve to distinguish things from one another, or some aspects of a thing from other aspects. Hence neither they nor our words have purchase on a One than which there is no other and which is, so to speak, internally seamless.

None of these suggestions, however, identifies the reason for regarding the mystery introduced at the beginning of this chapter as ineffable. The mysterious was not identified with an experience or feeling, nor was any commitment made to its being 'the One', whatever that might mean. A better indication of that reason is provided, whatever its author's own intention, by Wittgenstein's remark that 'Perhaps what is inexpressible . . . mysterious . . . is the background against which whatever I could express has

---

[16] *Lorca: Selected Poems*, ed. J. Gili (Harmondsworth: Penguin, 1960). Goethe said something similar about the quality of Paganini's playing and Louis Armstrong about jazz.

[17] *The Enneads*, trans. S. MacKenna (Harmondsworth: Penguin, 1991), VI. 9.

its meaning'.[18] According to the doctrine of mystery with which we are concerned, whatever we can meaningfully express requires an inexpressible, mysterious 'background' as the 'measure' of what we say and believe. There is no discursable way things stand independently of 'the human contribution' to provide this measure, and the thought that 'the human world' may provide it is unlivable. Any attempt to describe what gives measure by using terms and concepts applicable to 'the human world' will impugn its status as a measure: for the employment of those terms and concepts is answerable to . . . just as much as the use of any others is. One might read Wittgenstein's remark as registering the sense, recorded in the 'aphasic' testimonies of Chapter 10, that the meanings of our words 'crumble' unless, somehow, our language successfully answers to something 'beyond the human'.

This type of reason for entertaining the ineffable has a long pedigree, in the East if not the West. It was articulated, for example, by Chuang Tzu. In the other Taoist classic, the *Tao Te Ching*, it is taken for granted, from line 1, that 'The Way that can be spoken of is not the constant Way'. Chuang, however, concludes that 'the Great Way is not named' after arguing for the 'relativity' of the discursable world to language. 'Things become what they are called'. Although our words are 'not just hot air', since they 'work' for practical purposes, they would, in the absence of further measure, be no different from 'the chirruping of chicks'. The sage, therefore, 'looks beyond the confines of this dusty world' to a 'Guiding Light', the indescribable Tao, to which his own words and actions might answer.[19]

It will prove useful, as we turn to the issue of what may be said 'about' the ineffable, to bear this long pedigree in mind, for we may have something to learn from thinkers like Chuang, who were well aware of the problem of the status of their remarks. An early formulation of that problem, indeed, illustrated it by reference to the *Tao Te Ching*. A ninth-century Chinese philosopher wondered how, if 'Those who know do not speak' and Lao Tzu 'knew', 'could it be that he wrote no less than 5,000 words?'[20] How, more generally, can it fail to be self-stultifying to proclaim the ineffability of something and then proceed to talk about it? The answer, of course, is that it can't.

---

[18] *Culture and Value*, trans. P. Winch (Oxford: Blackwell, 1980), 16.

[19] *The Book of Chuang Tzu*, trans. M. Palmer (Harmondsworth: Penguin, 1996), ch. 2.

[20] Po Chui, cited in Chang Chung-Yuan, *Creativity and Taoism* (New York: Julian, 1963), 30.

What cannot be said cannot be said. But it does not follow that it is similarly self-stultifying to talk 'about' the ineffable. That we need the sort of distinction gestured at by my typographical device is clear from the following consideration. There is surely nothing absurd in saying 'The ineffable can't be described'. And that, arguably, is because the sentence is not about *what* is ineffable, but about the concept of ineffability. It tells us what is meant by 'ineffable'. It is, if you like, 'about' ineffability through being about the concept of ineffability. (Compare 'Heroes are rare', which is 'about' heroes through telling us something about the class of heroes—it has few members.)

Despite the possibility of exploiting an 'about'/'"about"' distinction, many commentators are dismissive of writers in mystical traditions who claim that their utterances are innocent of talking about what they allege to be ineffable. William Alston, for example, thinks that this alleged ineffability is 'blown out of all proportion'. Given how fulsomely mystics *do* report their experiences, 'one can hardly take literally the claim that the experiences are *ineffable*'. All that needs to be conceded is that some experiences cannot be 'specified literally in terms taken from common experience', a concession 'by no means peculiar to mystical experience'.[21] W. T. Stace is no less dismissive: 'In saying that no language can express his experience', the mystic is 'making a mistake'. This is because he confuses 'the paradoxicality of mystical experience with ineffability'. In fact, the mystic's words may be 'the literal truth' about his experience: it's just that this is something 'contradictory'—that of a Godhead which is 'everywhere and nowhere', perhaps. As a 'logically minded man', the mystic is 'embarrassed' to ascribe contradictory properties to something, and so prefers to think he has said nothing about it.[22]

Ironically, considerations of the kind raised by Alston and Stace are used by other writers to *defend* mystics against the charge of self-stultification. In conceding that 'recourse must be had to metaphor, analogy, symbols', they ask, is Alston not in effect agreeing that some mystical experiences are ineffable? To be ineffable, they insist, is to be *literally* indescribable: mystical utterances can be 'about' the ineffable, without being about it, precisely

---

[21] William Alston, *Perceiving God: The Epistemology of Religious Experience* (Ithaca, N.Y.: Cornell Univesity Press, 1991), 32.

[22] W. T. Stace, *Mysticism and Philosophy* (London: Macmillan, 1961), 304–5.

because their status is necessarily that of metaphor, analogy, or whatever. Again, in allowing that mystical utterances describe experiences with a paradoxical character, is Stace not conceding that *what* is experienced—the 'object' of the experiences—remains undescribed? The mystic's words, precisely because they are only about his experience, are merely 'about' what is experienced: hence his claim that this object is itself ineffable is not violated.

My sympathies, suitably qualified, are with these retorts to the charge of self-stultification. That the mystic has recourse to non-literal language is a reason for, not against, his claim not to be talking about mystery. Certainly it is a reason advanced by many ineffabilists: by Rudolf Otto, for example, who held that the 'numinous' is incapable of conceptualization precisely because it can be described only in metaphorical terms. Certainly, too, one familiar objection to this reasoning is a weak one. Stace writes that 'metaphorical language is only meaningful . . . if it is . . . translatable into literal language'.[23] If that is right, the mystic never *needs* to have recourse to non-literal language, and if he *could* put things in straight, literal terms, then he does after all 'eff' the allegedly ineffable. But it isn't right. Once we pass beyond established, conventional metaphors with an agreed interpretation, there is no reason to suppose that metaphors are 'translatable' or paraphrasable by literal terms.[24] Again—to turn to the other retort—it surely does not follow from the fact that someone is describing an experience or feeling that he or she is thereby describing its object. 'What I experienced' is doubtless ambiguous: but, in one perfectly acceptable sense, a report of what I experienced—fear, joy, spookiness—need not even purport to provide information about the object of the experience. So we should not jump to the conclusion that the mystic is telling us about the object of an experience from his reporting of that experience.

My sympathies with these retorts, however, require an important qualification. As I have presented them, the retorts share with the rejected positions—those of Alston and Stace—an assumption that should be challenged. This is the assumption that the mystic's utterances are descriptions or assertions. That assumption remains alive and well in the claims that these utterances are only metaphorical descriptions or assertions and that

---

[23] Ibid. 293.
[24] I have argued this point at length in my *Metaphor* (Oxford: Blackwell, 1986), inspired in large part by Donald Davidson's 'What Metaphors Mean', in his *Inquiries into Truth and Interpretation*.

they are about experiences, not about the objects of the experiences. This assumption has, perhaps, already come into question. To hold, as I just did, that many metaphors are not 'translatable' into literal terms is already, arguably, to resist categorizing them as descriptive or assertoric. The role of such metaphors is, rather, to 'hint at', to 'intimate', to 'inspire' or 'evoke' a way of seeing or thinking about something. Be that as it may, I now propose that the reason mystical utterances are not about, but only 'about', what is ineffable is that they do not describe or assert at all.

Of course, just as I have been using 'about' as a loaded term of art, so 'description' and 'assertion' must be understood in rather special ways in order for the above proposal to look plausible. At an everyday, vernacular level, just about any utterance of the form 'A is F' can be said to describe, assert, and be about something. Philosophers, however, who are familiar with the distinctions drawn by some of their number between, say, 'deep' and 'superficial' grammar, or between 'logical' and 'grammatical' form, will also be familiar with more restrictive uses of terms like 'description'. Think, for example, of the claim made by many moral philosophers of a 'non-cognitivist' bent that where 'A is F' is a moral judgement, like 'Abortion is evil', the utterance does not describe or assert anything about abortion, but serves rather to express an attitude or prescribe certain conduct. Or think of the Wittgensteinian suggestion that 'I am in pain' does not self-describe, but is better construed as a piece of pain behaviour, a cry for help, as it were.[25] Or think again of the idea already mooted that a fresh metaphor, like 'Architecture is frozen music', does not describe something, but invites or intimates a way of viewing it.

Doubtless the philosophical motives for withholding the terms 'description' and 'assertion' in the various cases just mentioned are themselves various. Nor is it easy to spell out with precision the intended and restricted senses of these terms that the withholdings reflect. But the rough idea is presumably this: in a paradigmatically descriptive assertion, a property referred to by a predicate is truly or falsely predicated of something referred to by the subject of the sentence. Where, therefore, this is a poor account of what a

---

[25] Other familiar examples would be: 'You are free to go', in certain contexts, is not an assertion about you, but the granting of a permission; 'The whale is a mammal' describes nothing, but provides an 'inference ticket' enabling one to travel from 'Moby Dick is a whale' to 'Moby Dick is a mammal'.

sentence of the (grammatical) form 'A is F' is doing, there is reason not to regard it as describing or asserting. The account would be a poor one if, inter alia, it is thought that 'A is F' is incapable of truth or falsity, 'A' is wrongly construed as a logical subject, or the purpose of uttering it is remote from that of conveying information about something's properties.

Although its application in particular cases might sometimes be questionable, this rough idea is a good one: it reflects a worthy determination to mark the significantly different roles that superficially similar sentences may perform. Applied to our present area of concern, the idea is that utterances which may seem illegitimately to be describing the allegedly ineffable need not be doing so, since they are not describing anything. Their relation to the ineffable, in virtue of which they are 'about' it, is not one of making assertions. Maybe they are 'untranslatable' non-literal utterances—metaphorical, analogical, or symbolic in force—that 'evoke' or 'intimate'. Or, consistently with that possibility, maybe they are *Äusserungen*—the 'expressions' of which Wittgenstein wrote in his very late works—that people feel impelled to mouth when required to 'put into words' their experiences. An *Äusserung* does not describe the experience but, as it were, exhibits it: the words are the result of the experience, those 'prompted' by it or that 'just come to' the person called on to articulate it.[26]

My proposal accords with a long tradition of mystical writers who have reflected on the tension between their urge to speak and their appreciation of unsayable mystery—the tension Rūmi records when he writes that 'There's no way to ever say this . . . and no place to stop saying it'. When this poet himself compares his words to the sounds of a reed flute, or to 'old chaperones' that, having brought the lover (the mystic) and the beloved (God) together, may be sent home, he indicates the way to resolve the tension. Considered as 'traditional' descriptions, the words are 'just babbling': considered as conduits or expressions of experience, or as devices for bringing others to that experience, they are not.[27] That words may be 'expedient devices' with a role quite different from description is familiar, too, from

---

[26] Compare A. W. Moore's suggestion that 'A is shown that *x*' means that 'A has ineffable knowledge, and when the attempt is made to put what A knows into words, the result is: *x*'. *Points of View*, 157. His point, like mine, is that uttering '*x*', which may be a nonsensical sentence, does not violate the speaker's claim that his knowledge, or experience, is ineffable.

[27] *The Essential Rūmi*, 89, 138, 198.

Buddhist reflections on religious language. The wise man, explains the Zen master, Huang Po, 'eschews thought' about Nirvāṇa, but may, nevertheless, utter as 'temporary expedients', designed to attune people to this conception, such phrases as 'the void [that] is both one and manifold'.[28] Rūmi's musical analogy is also employed by many other proponents of mystery, for whom their own words are more akin to a song that wells up than to assertoric propositions. Chuang Tzu, for whom the Tao is indeed indescribable, combines the musical analogy with that of 'expedient device' to explain how his own words do not violate that conviction. 'I have spoken without art, naturally, according to . . . impulse . . .. Preliminary to all discourses, there pre-exists an innate harmony . . .. From the fact of this pre-existing harmony, my speech, if it is natural, will make others vibrate'.[29]

One could go on citing testimonies from ancient tradition, but I turn instead to a much more recent set of reflections on the status of the language of mystery, those which punctuate the later writings of Heidegger. (Here, the focus is on his account of this status, not—as in the following chapter—on his proposals for an appropriate vocabulary.) In those later writings, Heidegger is an unequivocal proponent of a doctrine of mystery. We should cultivate an 'openness to the mystery', appreciate that 'we have come to confront something ineffable', and recognize that there is a world— that 'things are things'—only in virtue of a 'mysterious wellspring'.[30] Yet Heidegger does not counsel a relapse into silence. On the contrary, it is the mystery that is the proper concern of what he calls 'thinking' (sometimes qualified as 'meditative thinking'), and thinking in turn is inseparable from a certain form of 'saying', of seeking the appropriate language of mystery. Hence his frequent use of the compound 'thinking/saying'.

The names Heidegger uses for what is mysterious and ineffable are various. They range from mere place-holders, like 'Being' and 'It', to ones indicative of the dependence of the world on the mystery, such as 'wellspring' and 'source', to a bewildering array of apparently bizarre terms— 'the Enowning' or 'Appropriating event' (Ereignis), 'that-which-regions', 'the

---

[28] *The Zen Teachings of Huang Po: On the Transmission of Mind*, trans. J. Blofeld (London: Buddhist Society, 1968), 48, 53.

[29] Chuang Tzu, ch. 27a, in *Wisdom of the Daoist Masters*, trans. L. Wieger (Lampeter: Llanerch, 1984).

[30] Martin Heidegger, *Discourse on Thinking*, trans. J. Anderson and E. Freund (New York: Harper & Row, 1966), 55, 88, 76.

Giving', 'the nearing nearness', and so on—any illumination of which demands a delving into Heidegger's thought that is not our current business. The apparent tension between employment of this vocabulary and appreciation that we 'confront something ineffable' is relaxed by Heidegger's insistence that, when employing this vocabulary, his remarks 'about' the mystery are far from 'ordinary' ones. Unlike 'ordinary' subject–predicate sentences, they do not 'describe' or 'represent' some object as having certain properties, for 'it is no longer a case of talking *about* something and representing something objective'. They do not make statements or assert propositions, for 'thinking can never be said in a proposition'.[31]

For some critics of Heidegger, his denial that Being can be 'expressed in propositions' is enough to hang him. '[I]f Heidegger did not assert anything, there is nothing to discuss either', writes one critic: there is only 'an empty play with words', since nothing is offered by way of 'meaningful description'.[32] But this is too impatient. Would one conclude that there is 'nothing to discuss', only an 'empty play with words', in the countless poems whose authors would not, any more than Heidegger, regard themselves as making statements or asserting propositions? The criticism reflects a peculiar blindness to the sensible idea, rehearsed a few paragraphs back, that it may be quite wrong to assimilate certain sorts of utterance to paradigmatic cases of propositional assertion, and that a reasonable way to resist that assimilation is to withhold such epithets as 'statement', 'description', 'representation', and 'propositional assertion' itself. When the same critic adds that 'it is up to the Heideggerians to explain what kind of speech acts Heidegger is performing if he does not make assertions', that may sound a just demand—except that we do not have to turn to 'the Heideggerians' for this, since their mentor himself offered explanations.

At any rate, he certainly offered a whole battery of terms to characterize the roles played by his talk 'about' the mystery. These 'sayings' serve to 'attune' us to the mystery, and are the words of 'intimators'; they expound no doctrine, but are 'directives', and acts of 'projecting-open'. In 'thinking/saying', we 'call' or 'name', but not in the ordinary—and, for Heidegger,

---

[31] *Contributions to Philosophy (From Enowning)*, trans. P. Emad and K. Maly (Bloomington: Indiana University Press, 1999), 3, 45.

[32] Herman Philipse, *Heidegger's Philosophy of Being* (Princeton, N.J.: Princeton University Press, 1999), 302.

derivative—sense of 'coordinating' a linguistic object with another object. Rather, to call, in the relevant sense, is to 'commend, entrust, . . . to call into arrival; to address commendingly', just as 'by naming, we call on what is present to arrive'.[33] So there is no shortage of 'speech acts' quite different from assertion and description that, according to Heidegger, the language of mystery performs. Whether or not his own sayings succeed in such a performance is a different question, one we postpone. The present point has been to explore how we can talk 'about' the mystery when this 'confronts us as something ineffable'. We can do so without self-stultification, Heidegger reasonably suggests, provided that such talk is heard in the performative roles just cited. 'Being enowns', for example, will not be illegitimate talk about Being if it is an attunement or directive.

What cannot be similarly postponed is the question of the purpose of the attunements, directives, intimations, commendings, and so on that Heidegger's sayings—and talk 'about' the ineffable more generally—are supposed to effect. At first glance, Heidegger proposes two different and barely compatible answers to that question. On the one hand, he speaks of this purpose as cultivation of a certain 'comportment' (*Haltung*) to the world and to what is mysterious.[34] To this answer belong such opaque characterizations of whence the sayings 'direct' us as 'the composure of releasement', 'letting-oneself-into-nearness', and 'offering an abode'. On the other hand, he speaks of the sayings as attuning us to an 'experience'—of 'the full non-ordinariness of be-ing over against all beings', or of 'the essential swaying of th[e] unknown'.[35] On closer inspection, however, there is no conflict between these answers. 'Comportment' is not simply some form of behaviour, but involves a way of seeing, 'revealing', and experiencing things. (In technological comportment, for example, the world is 'revealed' as so much 'equipment'.) At the same time, Heidegger emphasizes 'the non-ordinariness' of the 'experiencing' referred to. It is not simply that such experiencing is 'seldom': we must, as well, be on our guard not to construe it on the model of a person experiencing some object, as in the perceptual experience of hearing or seeing a car. Experience, in the relevant sense, is not, moreover, 'an act of illumination' that a mystic might suddenly enjoy, for it is not an act or occurrence at all—more, as Heidegger puts it, a kind of 'dwelling'.[36] In short, to experience the mystery and to comport oneself in a certain way towards it are two sides of the same coin.

We shall return, in the final two chapters, to the comportment/ experience to which Heidegger deems that his thinking/saying attunes or directs us. It is not, in my judgement—and Heidegger's, too, perhaps— something so very different from what another vocabulary, belonging to a much older tradition, also strives to evince. When, in the following chapter, we turn to considering that vocabulary and tradition, it will prove useful to heed both Heidegger's proposals for how a vocabulary of mystery may avoid self-stultification and his warnings concerning the construal of the experience of mystery.

[36] *On Time and Being*, trans. J. Stambaugh (New York: Harper & Row, 1972), 53.

CHAPTER 12

Emptiness

'The World is Empty'

Securing the charges of hubris against both absolutism and raw or uncompensated humanism, it was argued in the previous chapter, results in an impasse, whose only resolution would have to be a doctrine of mystery. But if that option is to be more than a merely formal one, and to have any prospect of indicating a 'measure' to which beliefs, concepts, and commitments may be answerable, one cannot just stammer out 'There is mystery' and then shut up. Since what is mysterious, in the relevant sense, must be ineffable, the delicate problem is thereby posed of speaking without self-stultification, without illegitimately 'effing' the ineffable. That problem, it was suggested, can be overcome by a distinction between talking about and talking 'about' the mysterious. With Heidegger's help, I tried to motivate the idea of a language, a 'thinking/saying', that talks 'about' mystery through 'attuning' or 'directing' its hearers towards a 'comportment' with an 'experience' of mystery.

But what might such a language or vocabulary be? The history of mysticism and, more broadly, of traditions of thought that entertain the idea of mystery, is replete with suggestions—Taoist talk of 'the Way' and its 'virtue', neo-Platonic talk of 'the One' and its 'emanations', transcendental idealist references to things in themselves, Heidegger's own verbal concoctions, and so on. Rather than debate the merits of these and other proposals, however, I shall explore the particular vocabulary that, in my view, is the most promising vehicle of 'thinking/saying'. It is not self-stultifying; it indicates how what is mysterious may serve as a measure; it does not populate mystery with entities—things, minds, God, or whatever—that, if humanists are right, are confined to 'the human world'; and it does minimal violence to 'common sense', for unlike many doctrines of mystery, it does not require dismissing our ordinary thought and talk about the world as so much error or illusion.

The vocabulary I have in mind is that of 'emptiness', a notion I touched upon early in Chapter 10 when sketching the 'Asian experience' of 'uncompensated' humanism. The obvious place to look for this vocabulary is, as I there indicated, the philosophical literature of Buddhism, especially that of the Mahāyāna ('Great Vehicle') schools in which the notion of emptiness has been pivotal. Nevertheless, one does not have to 'be a Buddhist'—to sign up to the Four Noble Truths and follow the Eightfold Path—in order to deploy the notion and find it illuminating. Many writers have noted, for example, the affinities between Buddhistic emptiness and the 'pure nothingness' of all creatures, things, and their 'ground', the 'godhead', spoken of by the medieval Dominican, Meister Eckhart.[1] These affinities may be found, as well, in Sūfi literature: for Rūmi, we, and presumably all other creatures and things, 'are emptiness' and come 'out of emptiness'.[2] Still, it is upon the relevant Buddhist traditions that I focus. In this and the following section, I first briefly trace the development of the Buddhist vocabulary of emptiness, then consider the conflicting interpretations of this vocabulary by both adepts and commentators, and then—before finally going on to sing its praises—I explain how, at least for my strategic purposes, it needs to be understood.

The inspiration for Buddhist talk of emptiness is the Buddha himself. Why, asks a follower, 'is the world called "empty"?' Because, replies the Buddha, 'it is empty of self and of what belongs to self'.[3] 'Self' (Pali: ātma) here applies not just to persons but to almost anything—material objects, minds, bodies, sensory impressions—that may be taken to have substantial, independent existence. In calling the world 'empty', therefore, the Buddha is restating the central Buddhist doctrine of 'not-self' according to which persons, material objects and so on do not have 'intrinsic' reality or identity, are without 'own being'. This doctrine is derived from that of 'dependent

---

[1] These writers include Keiji Nishitani, *Religion and Nothingness*, trans. J. van Bragt (Berkeley & Los Angeles: University of California Press, 1983), 61–7, and John D. Caputo, *The Mystical Element in Heidegger's Thought* (Athens, Ohio: Ohio University Press, 1984), 203–18.

[2] *The Essential Rūmi*, trans. C. Barks (Harmondsworth: Penguin, 1999), 20 and 28.

[3] *Samyutta-nikaya* IV 54, in E. Conze (ed.), *Buddhist Texts Through the Ages* (Boston, Mass.: Shambhala, 1990).

origination' (or 'conditioned arising', *pratityasamutpāda*), which holds that all such entities are dependent for their 'relative' reality and identity on further conditions.

The authors of the early *Abhidharma* ('pure doctrine') school understood the Buddha's declaration of emptiness to apply only to complex entities, since these are dependent on and reducible to the fleeting atomic constituents of reality (*dhammas*). 'Complexes have no inner might, are empty in themselves.'[4] (One is reminded of Russell's view that material objects and people are 'fictions', 'constructed' out of the 'logical atoms' that are the only real constituents of the world.)[5] With the emergence, around the first century BCE, of the 'Perfection of Wisdom' (*prajñāpāramitā*) discourses, however, the doctrine of emptiness took a more radical form. In these 'Great Vehicle' sutras, it is now maintained that *'all dhammas* are empty', that 'form (*rūpa*)'—an all-purpose term for what we ordinarily take to populate the world—'is emptiness (*Śūnyatā*) and emptiness is form'.[6] There are no atoms or constituents of reality with 'intrinsic' identity or 'own being', for everything is interdependent in the 'process' of dependent origination. Not that this 'process' should itself be 'reified', for it has no reality apart from the empty forms. Indeed, 'perfect wisdom' consists in recognizing a triple equation between form, emptiness, and 'suchness' or 'ultimate reality' (*tathatā*).[7] The ultimate truth about reality is that it is nothing but 'selfless' or empty form. This entails, moreover, a further equation. If nothing is non-empty, Nirvāṇa—the soteriological goal of Buddhists—must also be empty: it cannot therefore be some realm disjoint from the mundane world of empty, interdependent form (*saṃsāra*). So the wise man will no longer 'discriminate' between *saṃsāra* and Nirvāṇa, appreciating instead that both are emptiness.[8]

These obscure equations were more systematically made, and subtly defended, by the second-century monk, Nāgārjuna. Oversubtly, perhaps, since while many prominent Buddhist philosophers in the Mahāyāna trad-

---

[4] *Lalitavistara* XIII 98, in Conze (ed.), *Buddhist Texts Through the Ages*.

[5] Bertrand Russell, *The Philosophy of Logical Atomism*, Lecture VIII, in *Logic and Knowledge: Essays 1901–50* (London: Allen & Unwin, 1956).

[6] *The Heart Sūtra*, in Sangharakshita, *Wisdom Beyond Words: Sense and Non-sense in the Buddhist Prajñāpāramitā Tradition* (Glasgow: Windhorse, 1993), 23.

[7] *The Large Sūtra on Perfect Wisdom*, trans. E. Conze (Delhi: Motilal Banarsidass, 1979), 349.

[8] Ibid. 650.

ition have appealed to Nāgārjuna's authority, there has been no consensus either among them or among modern commentators on the interpretation of the equations. What, in particular, can it mean to hold that 'suchness is emptiness'? Three interpretations seem to have thrived most, which I label the 'transcendental', 'nihilist', and 'downbeat' ones respectively.

The transcendentalist takes that equation to mean that in addition to, or behind the illusory façade of, the conditioned world of form, there is an absolute, unconditioned realm—that of emptiness. For him, in effect, 'empty' is ambiguous. Applied to forms, objects, and persons, it indicates that these, as conditioned, are without 'self' or 'own being'. But applied to suchness or Nirvāṇa, it points to a realm with 'nothing in it of conditioned existence',[9] one devoid of samsaric processes and ingredients. The sage's refusal to 'discriminate' between form and emptiness, or saṃsāra and Nirvāṇa, is legitimate in so far as there are not two *things* or *entities* to be set apart, but not if he denies the reality of a transcendent realm of emptiness/suchness. Robert Thurman captures the kernel of the transcendental, or as he calls it 'monist absolutist', position: it treats 'emptiness' and 'suchness' as 'referring "mystically" to an inexpressible Absolute, utterly beyond all human faculties, expressions, and reasons . . . [an] object of "mystic", . . . non-rational or trans-rational, contemplation'.[10]

The nihilist does not hear 'Suchness is emptiness' as elevating emptiness to the status of absolute reality, but as reducing the very notion of reality to empty illusion, and Nirvāṇa to samsaric 'play'. The ultimate truth is that of realitylessness, for there is nothing but form and form is empty. His view is again well captured by Thurman, under the label of 'existential relativism': 'the goal is to realize that there is no "Goal", to still the over-reaching aspirations of human reason, and to settle in the absolute relativity of the everyday, making the best of it.' It is, Thurman continues, an 'antinomial' position that treats language and thought as 'ultimately meaningless', for there exists nothing—objects, persons, right and wrong, causes and effects—to which these can genuinely refer.[11]

Few contemporary scholars, it seems, accept that Nāgārjuna's message,

[9] Sangharakshita, *Wisdom Beyond Words*, 232.

[10] Robert Thurman, *The Central Philosophy of Tibet: A Study and Translation of Jey Tsong Khapa's Essence of True Eloquence* (Princeton, N.J.: Princeton University Press, 1984), 150.

[11] Ibid. 150 and 153.

and that of the *Prajñāpāramitā* discourses, was either a transcendental or a nihilistic one. Was it not precisely Nāgārjuna's rejection of these extreme positions that made of his own a 'middle way' (*Madhyamaka*), the name of the school associated with him? On the prevailing 'downbeat' interpretation, transcendentalism and nihilism are overwrought reactions, in opposite directions, to the correct perception that all forms are empty. Adherents of both those tendencies take this perception to imply that the familiar world is illusion, but whereas the former react by identifying 'suchness' with an 'inexpressible Absolute', the latter take it on the chin, concluding that there is no 'suchness', nothing for our words, thoughts, or intuitions truly to relate to. For the downbeater, these reactions are unwarranted. Properly considered, equations like 'Suchness is emptiness' leave everything as it is. Neither the truth of our ordinary beliefs and descriptions, nor the reality of the familiar world, is impugned. They are simply seen for what they are: truth as conventionally agreed-upon description of a world of objects that, 'dependently originated', have no 'intrinsic identity', for they are independent neither of one another nor of the human practices, interests, and conventions that are themselves part and parcel of the 'chain' of dependent origination.

As Nāgārjuna reiterates, the doctrine of emptiness just *is* the doctrine of dependent origination.[12] And that doctrine has none of the dramatic implications drawn by transcendentalists and nihilists. Their problem is fixation on the idea that truth and reality require independence from dependent origination, from merely 'conventional' designation. The sensible person will strive to rid himself of that fixation, in the manner of the Ch'an (Zen) Buddhist, Ching Yuan (pp. 243 f above), who, recall, at first reacted to the atrophy of his naively realistic belief in mountains by denying their existence, but goes on to explain how, after further meditation, he became able to 'see mountains once again as mountains'. On the downbeat interpretation, recognizing that mountains could *not* be other than empty, conventionally designated items, and no longer, therefore, hankering after a more absolute, independent status for them, Ching Yuan serenely accepts that our language and thought, rightly viewed, are perfectly in order as they are.

---

[12] 'The "originating dependently" we call "emptiness"': Nāgārjuna, *Mulamadhyamakakārikās: Fundamentals of the Middle Way* 24.18, trans. Frederick J. Streng in his *Emptiness: A Study in Religious Meaning* (Nashville, Tenn.: Abingdon, 1967), 213.

It is time to make explicit some parallels, partly touched upon early in Chapter 10 and doubtless already apparent to many readers, between the present discussion and my previous remarks on humanism and dis-incumbence. The first thing to emphasize is that all three positions on emptiness are humanist ones in my sense: on each of them, there is no dis-cursable reality independent of 'the human contribution'. As an early Ch'an patriarch expressed it, 'all things were originally given rise to by man'. For the transcendentalist, there is, to be sure, a realm of absolute 'suchness' or 'emptiness', but it is 'inexpressible'. The humanism of these positions owes not only to the conviction that, as the *Diamond Sūtra* puts it, 'seizing upon' material objects and other forms is 'a convention of language', but to the role played by human factors in 'dependent origination'. In the Buddha's many rehearsals of the 'twelvefold chain' of dependent origination, factors such as human desire are among the links. In their absence, nothing would figure for us as material objects or other forms, and with their cessation, these forms are seen to be without 'own being'.

The second thing to emphasize, however, is that the three positions pair off with very different attitudes, earlier described, to the thesis of 'the human world' which they share. The downbeat position corresponds to the 'quietist' version of a 'serene' welcome both to that thesis and to the dis-incumbenced stance advocated by the humanist (see pp. 224–5 above). The quietist argued, recall, that once we appreciate how misguided it was ever to seek grounding for our thought and talk in an independent order, viewable from 'sideways on', we can serenely settle for our ordinary ways of justify-ing beliefs—citing evidence, ensuring consistency, and so on. Certainly there is no call for dramatic talk of the world as illusion or for 'deconstruct-ing' notions like truth and objectivity. Such dramatic responses, those of the 'antinomial' Buddhist nihilist, recall what I called the 'heroic' embrace of the 'human world' thesis (see pp. 223–4 above). The humanist hero, like Camus's, takes seriously the tension between our ordinary commitments and the dis-incumbenced stance, but with 'daily effort, self-mastery [and] *ascesis*' manages to reaffirm the former despite their 'absurdity', their lack of any objective grounding. Or maybe the Buddhist nihilist pairs off with a rather different figure encountered earlier—the person who recognizes that uncompensated humanism is unlivable, but then manages, as it were, to tranquillize himself, to put all such philosophical positions and their im-plications out of mind. (Buddhism is not without its texts in which a no-nonsense, anti-philosophical stance is advocated.) Such a figure is described by Nishitani Keiji: since he 'can neither abide in existence nor abide being away from it', he faces the prospect of being 'torn in two from within'.[13] His solution is not the quietist one of coming to see that his nihilistic fears are misplaced, nor the heroic one of turning those fears into a celebration, but simply to stun the urge to philosophize that threatens to tear him apart—perhaps, in a manner recommended by Zen, by just sleeping, eating, and raking the gravel.

The transcendental position, naturally, pairs off with that of those figures, from Chapter 10, who, having discerned the unlivability of an uncompensated humanism, look for compensation in the form of something 'beyond the human'—those for whom, like Iris Murdoch's Plato, 'the spirit must have something *absolute*, otherwise it goes crazy'. The Buddhist transcendentalist is someone who, within the context of his tradition, looks for the same kind of escape from the impasse described at the beginning of Chapter 11 that I proposed—the impasse, that is, which ensues when the charges of hubris against both humanism and absolutism (in my sense of subscription to the thesis of a discursable reality independent of 'the human contribution) are secured.

Unsurprisingly, therefore, I have greater sympathy, if not for the transcendental position itself, then for the spirit behind it, than do champions of the more entrenched downbeat interpretation of the meaning of emptiness in the Mahāyāna texts. My primary purpose in registering both this sympathy and my reservations with regard to the downbeat position is not, of course, one of Buddhist exegesis—of establishing, for example, what Nāgārjuna or the authors of the *Heart Sūtra* 'really meant' by their equations. It is to see what help we may get from talk of emptiness for attuning us to mystery. Still, it will be useful to record my reasons for doubting that the downbeat interpretation does justice to that talk and to the role that emptiness plays in Buddhist thought and soteriology. This will facilitate, in particular, an appreciation, exploitable for my purposes, of how emptiness is intended to play a role akin to the provision of measure, of something for us to answer to.

[13] *Religion and Nothingness*, 137.

Problems of Interpretation

Whatever my sympathy for the spirit that inspires the transcendental under-standing of emptiness, the prevailing view that this misrepresents the rele-vant Mahāyāna texts is surely correct. For those texts preclude treating emptiness as a reality 'behind' and disjoint from an illusory empirical world. Emptiness or 'the unconditioned' cannot 'be conceived separately from the conditioned': it is not to be 'differentiated' from saṃsāra.[14] This denial of 'duality' is encapsulated in the ubiquitous slogan 'Emptiness itself is empty'. On the matter of the illusoriness of the empirical realm, there is some oscil-lation in both the classic texts and later commentaries. Suzuki, for example, veers between saying of the equation of suchness with emptiness that it shows ordinary things to be but 'passing shadows' and claiming that it in no way implies that 'the solid earth has . . . vanished. Mount Hiei stands before one even more solidly'. But he goes on to explain, in a manner that is fairly standard, that calling things 'shadows' or māyā ('illusion') is not to treat them as anything like a dream, but simply to draw attention to their lack of 'self-subsistence', of 'own being'.[15]

The prevailing message that emptiness does not entail the illusoriness or 'nothingness' of the empirical, conditioned world also militates, of course, against the nihilist understanding of the doctrine of emptiness. So, too, does the view, despite a good deal of further oscillation on the issue, that the doc-trine does not threaten our everyday speech with meaninglessness or persis-tent falsity. Although one comes across such remarks as 'the way of names and words (which gives rise to phenomena) is terminated',[16] the more set-tled view appeals to the distinction that Nāgārjuna, following the Buddha himself, draws between the 'two truths'—'world-ensconced' or 'conven-tional', 'relative' truth and truth in the 'highest sense'.[17] The nihilist's mis-take is to assume that, in order for words or statements to be meaningful or true, they must correspond to an independent, unconditioned realm. Correctly recognizing that they don't, he then adopts his 'antinomial'

---

[14] *The Large Sūtra on Perfect Wisdom*, 94; Nāgārjuna, *Mulamadhyamakakārikās*, 25. 19.

[15] D. T. Suzuki, *Essays on Zen Buddhism: III* (London: Luzac, 1934), 242, 250, 274.

[16] Fa-tsang, 'The Golden Lion', in W. Baskin (ed.), *Classics in Chinese Philosophy* (Totowa, N.J.: Helix, 1984), 387.

[17] *Mulamadhyamakakārikās*, 24. 8.

attitude to language. (The nihilist's realist or 'eternalist' rival makes the same mistaken assumption. Correctly recognizing that our language is in order as it is, he then concludes that it must after all reflect an independent, unconditioned reality.)

So the transcendentalist and the nihilist both misconstrue the doctrine of emptiness. Are we compelled, therefore, to concur in the downbeat interpretation? An initial remark to make in response is that Buddhists who subscribe to that interpretation should surely be worried by some of their co-religionists' oscillations, just noted, over the issues of the illusoriness of the empirical world and the capacity of ordinary language meaningfully to express truths. The tendencies to respond to the doctrine of emptiness by regarding the world as illusory and language as senseless should be considered alongside some of those chronicled in the first section of Chapter 10. There I noted the testimonies of Buddhist thinkers to the 'primeval awfulness' of a raw recognition that all is void or empty, to that recognition's producing a 'rage against the world of the senses'. I did so in the context of assembling testimonies to the unlivability of an uncompensated humanism once the thesis of 'the human world' becomes 'hot and alive'. Now, on the downbeat interpretation, the doctrine of emptiness *is* a form of uncompensated humanism. All that there is is a human world, one of conditioned, empty things that are what they are only in relation, inter alia, to human perspective and desire. It is entirely understandable, therefore, if my perception of the unlivability of uncompensated humanism—of the dis-incumbenced stance—is right, that Buddhists should recoil, in nihilist fashion, against the form that this humanism takes in their own tradition, against a downbeat doctrine of emptiness. And understandable, further, if that recoil should engender another recoil, this time in the direction of a transcendentalism that seeks 'compensation' in what is 'beyond the human'.

We already know the downbeater's line of reply to this point: it is the 'quietist' one of the 'serene' humanist. While the recoils just mentioned are indeed *understandable*, they are nevertheless unwarranted, for they are the product, in effect, of fixation on a bad metaphysical model. While people still 'grasp' at 'own being'—while, that is, they assume that language and truth require correspondence with an independent order of substantial entities—they will indeed react to the news that there is no such correspondence in a nihilistic fashion, and then perhaps proceed to seek compensation in 'another' world beyond the human. They stand in need of cure, of being shown that they 'grasp' after the impossible. Isn't this just what happened to Ching Yuan with the help of Zen meditation? When he finally comes to see mountains as mountains once more, he has got over the metaphysical fixation that had earlier caused him to deny that there are mountains at all.

If my arguments in the preceding two chapters are well taken, then people should not, indeed cannot, 'get over' a conviction that there is 'something beyond the human'. The attempt genuinely to embrace a 'hot and alive', uncompensated humanism must fail. More to the present point, I do not think that this is what Ching Yuan 'got over'. At the very least, there are serious problems with construing his progress in that way—problems, therefore, for a downbeat construal of what it is to embrace the doctrine of emptiness.

The first problem concerns the place of emptiness in Buddhist soteriology. There is an unbroken tradition linking such remarks of the Buddha's as that reflection on the emptiness of everything confers 'unshakable freedom of mind' to recent pronouncements like Masao Abe's 'liberation is realized in Emptiness'.[18] Appreciation of emptiness, it seems, is the central component in Buddhist enlightenment, awakening, or liberation, a 'happening' that brings in its train a transformation of a person, 'release' from subjection to 'craving', and a new and compassionate stance towards all living beings. Now the difficulty is to see how something so apparently momentous as Ching Yuan's, or any other Buddhist's, awakening could consist in accepting a doctrine of emptiness that, on the downbeat reading, is equivalent to the doctrine of dependent origination—to a version, in effect, of the 'human world' thesis.

Or the difficulty might be put in the following way. One downbeat commentator claims that the realization that *saṃsāra* is empty is the 'insight' attested to by Nāgārjuna's phrase 'True emptiness, wondrous being'.[19] But what, one asks, could be so 'wondrous' about *saṃsāra* if it is simply a human world of interdependent, conditioned things? Suzuki strikes me as correct to insist that there is a 'gap' between the doctrine of 'relativity' or dependent origination and that of emptiness: the former is only a 'premise' for the

[18] *Majjhima-nikāya* I. 297–8, in Conze (ed.), *Buddhist Texts Through the Ages*; Masao Abe, *Zen and Western Thought* (Honolulu: University of Hawaii Press, 1985), 131.

[19] Joel R. Smith, 'Masao Abe on Negativity in the East and the West', in D. W. Mitchell (ed.), *Masao Abe: A Zen Life of Dialogue* (Boston, Mass.: Tuttle, 1998), 289.

latter, which involves an 'experience' not indicated by the reduction of emptiness to dependent origination.[20] The downbeater will reply, reasonably enough, that acceptance of dependent origination is not a matter, simply, of assenting to certain philosophical propositions. But it remains hard to see why the experiential embrace of the doctrine, whatever that might be like, should be the momentously life-transforming one that Buddhist soteriology requires of the appreciation of emptiness. (Indeed, if my earlier arguments are correct, the embrace of such an uncompensated doctrine is more likely to induce 'despair'.)

To turn to a second problem, Suzuki is also right to query the equation of the doctrines of emptiness and dependent origination by recalling the tradition according to which one who 'sees into emptiness' sees into something 'unthinkable'.[21] As one sūtra explains, the 'perfection of wisdom'—that is, the realization of emptiness—is 'inaccessible to . . . discursive thought', 'signless', 'inapprehensible', and only 'to be felt'.[22] Or, as the great Sōtō Zen philosopher, Dōgen, puts it: reflection on emptiness shows that the universe is not 'my possession', but 'something ineffable coming like this'.[23] The problem is to understand the warrant for such references to the ineffability and inapprehensibility of emptiness if 'Everything is empty' simply means 'Everything is dependently originated'. Indeed, if the empty objects that populate the empirical world depend upon human language and perspective for their 'relative' existence, it is difficult to know where the downbeater could locate anything ineffable and unconceptualizable in the realm of emptiness, since this, for him, just is the empirical world of 'relative' existence. If sense is to be made of the literature's references to 'signless' and 'inapprehensible' emptiness, it is hard to resist the impression—already registered by the transcendentalist—that 'empty' indicates one, perfectly effable thing when applied to the empirical world, and something rather different when used to evoke the character of 'suchness' or 'ultimate reality'.[24] To the downbeater's predictable reply that one must 'experience', and not simply say, that the world is one of dependent origination in order to grasp

[20] Suzuki, *Essays on Zen Buddhism: III*, 227.
[21] Ibid. 228.
[22] *The Large Sūtra on Perfect Wisdom*, 349 and 359.
[23] *Shobogenzo*, trans. G. Nishijima and C. Cross (London: Windbell, 1996), vol. ii, ch. 22. 3.
[24] See John Hick, 'The Meaning of Emptiness', in Mitchell (ed.), *Masao Abe*, 143–50.

the doctrine, the counter-response can only be to challenge him to explain why an experience that seems eminently to lend itself to propositional articulation nevertheless defies it.

The final problem confronting the downbeat position is how to accommodate a tradition of speaking of emptiness as, in Suzuki's words, the 'font and source' of the empirical world.[25] If *saṃsāra* and its 'forms' just are emptiness, it would seem to make no sense to regard the latter as a 'source' of the former. The tradition goes back to the Buddha himself. 'There is', he says, 'that plane where there is . . . no coming or going', and 'were it not for this unborn, not become, not made' plane, there would not be 'what is born, has become, is made'.[26] A later Mahāyāna sūtra tells us that 'all [beings] have been brought forth from the Unconditioned'; Dōgen remarks that 'all rely' on the 'Buddha-nature' (emptiness, that is); and Nishitani is happy to speak of emptiness as 'an elemental source'.[27] None of these authors are transcendentalists, and each immediately guards against the impression such remarks may create that emptiness is some hidden cause of the manifest, empirical world. It is not, says Nishitani, 'some point recessed behind the things we see with our eyes', and Dōgen insists that there is no Buddha-nature that does not 'manifest . . . itself before us'.

The downbeater will seize on such caveats and treat the talk of the empirical world 'relying' on emptiness or having it as a 'source' as a way—misleading perhaps—of recording the truth that, without emptiness, there would be no world. That is indeed a truth, since there is no 'differentiation' between world and emptiness: the world is empty. The trouble with this treatment is that, in the senses of 'rely' and 'source' proposed, emptiness would just as much rely on *saṃsāra* and have it as its source as vice versa. For, given the identity of emptiness and *saṃsāra*, there could not be the former without the latter. Now it is plain from the texts I cited that the direction of dependence or reliance is supposed to be one way—of the empirical upon emptiness—and not a two-way one. (This, too, is surely the point—despite his apparent refusal to 'differentiate'— of Nāgārjuna's verse, 'When emptiness "works", then everything in existence "works". If emptiness does *not*

---

[25] Quoted in Mitchell (ed.), *Masao Abe*, 43.

[26] *Udāna* 80–1, in Conze (ed.), *Buddhist Texts Through the Ages*.

[27] *The Large Sutra on Perfect Wisdom*, 519; Dōgen, *Shobogenzo*, ch. 22. 6; Nishitani, *Religion and Nothingness*, 123.

"work", then all existence does *not* "work"'.)[28] It may, to be sure, be difficult to grasp how emptiness, if it is not disjoint from the conditioned world, can be its 'font or source'. But that is a difficulty that needs to be faced, not spirited away, by a downbeat reading that is unfaithful to the texts.

That difficulty is akin to the others discussed. In each case, it is accepted that the transcendental and nihilist interpretations of the Mahāyāna equations are unacceptable, but the remaining downbeat interpretation fails to do justice to an aspect of emptiness attested to in the texts. Specifically, it fails to illuminate the soteriological role assigned to the appreciation of emptiness, the conviction that emptiness is ineffable and 'inapprehensible', and the conception of the world as relying on emptiness as its 'source'. The question, then, is how to do justice to these aspects without repeating the errors of the transcendentalist.

Metaphors of Emptiness

Progress can be made with this question—and so with my enterprise of seeking a viable doctrine of mystery in the vocabulary of emptiness—if more attention is paid than it usually is to the several resonances of the metaphors of emptiness that thinkers in the Mahāyāna tradition have intended us to hear. One is especially deafened to these resonances by commentators, of an ecumenical bent, who regard 'emptiness' as just one more word—alongside 'Tao', '*brahman*', 'godhead', and so on—for labelling that 'ultimate, ineffable, formless reality' that, deep down, is supposedly the common concern of all religions.[29] To treat 'emptiness' as if it might as well be replaced by 'X' or 'It' is not only to be deaf to its particular resonances, but to pre-empt the possibility that the vocabulary of emptiness might better attune one to mystery than rival ones.

Metaphors of emptiness resonate in at least five ways, each of which exploits some familiar association of our everyday use of 'empty'. Myopic concentration on one or a few of these ways fails to reveal the richness and potential of the metaphor. To begin with, the slogan 'Things are empty'

---

[28] *Mulamadhyamakakārikās*, 24. 14.
[29] Hick, 'The Meaning of Emptiness', 147. This paper exemplifies the ecumenical approach I am criticizing.

exploits the association of emptiness with lack. An empty fridge, like an empty head, is lacking in what it is supposed to contain. So heard, 'Things are empty' conveys the message that things are lacking in the independent 'own being' or 'self' that, according to Buddhists, we ordinarily take them to have. This, of course, is the way downbeaters primarily receive the metaphor.

But a second resonance of that slogan relies on the associations of emptiness with transparency and freedom from obstruction. An empty glass is one you can see through, while an empty road presents no obstacles. These associations are exploited when a Mahāyāna text speaks of 'look[ing] through each being' to 'suchness', when Dōgen alludes to emptiness as a 'bare, transparent state', and when Masao Abe writes that 'there is no hindrance between any one thing and any other thing'.[30] They are exploited, too, in the figure of 'Indra's net'—especially favoured by the Hua-Yen school—where objects are compared with jewels whose surfaces, free of obstructing dust, so reflect one another that to see one is to see all. The role of 'Things are empty', heard in this way, is to evoke the experience of the world enjoyed by someone in whom the doctrine of dependent origination is 'deeply cultivated'. That person will 'see through' each thing to the whole web of relations of which, so to speak, it is an intersection.

When the metaphor is heard only in the ways just mentioned, it is unsurprising if it inspires a nihilistic response: for it seems that the familiar occupants of our world are being bleached of more than 'intrinsic' reality, that each object is being dissolved into relationships. *Really*, one feels like saying, there is no 'it'—no jewel in the net, only the net. That this response is unsurprising is one reason why downbeat assurances that the equation of *saṃsāra* with emptiness brings liberation and peace sound unconvincing.

But there is a third resonance of 'Things are empty' that serves to check the nihilistic reaction. Here the associations exploited are those of places or spaces that, because empty or open, allow for entry—perhaps an 'open house', where people may come and gather. When received in this way, the image is of a thing as enjoying a unique and palpable identity through serving, as Nishitani puts it, to 'con-centrate' or 'gather' a world 'within itself',

[30] *Ratnogatravibhāga*, in Conze (ed.), *Buddhist Texts Through the Ages*, 217; Dōgen, *Shobogenzo*, ii. 10 (translator's gloss); Abe, *Zen and Western Thought*, 18.

to be 'the home-ground of everything else' where a 'world worlds'.[31] The thought, here, is that while each thing indeed depends for its identity on the web or world to which it belongs, that world is no less dependent on each thing. The 'entire universe', wrote Dōgen, 'manifests itself in . . . a tall bamboo'.[32] Just as a language would not be the one it is if it did not contain—or, at any rate, permit—the presence within it of just *this* word with just *that* meaning, so the world would not be what it is if it could not be 'concentrated' in just this bamboo.

It is important to stress, as many Buddhist thinkers do, that the two kinds of experience evinced by 'Things are empty' when heard in the second and third ways are to be had *together*. There must, it gets said, be a 'double exposure', a 'seeing' of a 'phenomenon's conventional and ultimate nature simultaneously', a conjoining—as Tsong Khapa puts it—of two 'perceptual habits'.[33] In such a vision, one experiences the bamboo as a bamboo, but at the same time 'sees through' it to the whole web of relations on which it depends. It is a vision encouraged, perhaps, by those Japanese paintings where a contorted tree, say, is depicted against an almost blank background, seemingly abstracted from any context. Yet, on closer inspection, the almost empty scene (a mist in the valley) and a few further strokes of the brush (the hint of a crag and a crow) succeed in rendering salient the environment of the tree in a way that a more crowded canvas by Constable or Claude might not. At the same time, that environment—the crag on which the tree is precariously rooted, the crow that perches on it, the mist swirling through its branches—serves to bring out the uniqueness and palpable presence of the tree.

[31] Nishitani, *Religion and Nothingness*, 123 and 149. Note the Heideggerian terminology of 'gathering' and 'worlding'. See in this connection, Simon P. James, '"Thing-Centred" Holism in Buddhism, Heidegger and Deep Ecology', *Environmental Ethics*, 22 (2000), 359–75. The second and third resonances of 'Things are empty' correspond, in James's terminology, to 'two moments of holism'—those of 'dissolution' and 'condensation', respectively. The ideas indicated by these terms are not, of course, an eastern monopoly. A. N. Whitehead, in particular, speaks of a thing or event 'infecting its environment with its own aspects' and he congratulates Wordsworth on 'grasp[ing] the whole of nature as involved in the tonality of the particular instance': *Science and the Modern World* (New York: Macmillan, 1925), 96 and 84.

[32] *Shobogenzo*, ii. 89.

[33] Lobsang Gyatso, *The Harmony of Emptiness and Dependent-Arising* (Dharamsala: Library of Tibetan Works and Archives, 1992), 124; Tsong Khapa, in Thurman, *The Central Philosophy of Tibet*, 342. Compare 'If you can see clear what is before your very eyes, it is what fills the ten directions: when you see what fills the ten directions, you find it is only what is before your eyes', from *Sayings of Daikaku*, in T. Leggett, *Zen and the Ways* (London: Routledge & Kegan Paul, 1978), 61.

So far, it is the resonances of the slogan 'Things are empty' that I have identified. But, as we have seen, Buddhists speak as well of emptiness itself. Consider, first, the depictions of emptiness as a 'reservoir of possibilities', a 'field of the possibility of the existence of things', a 'cosmic sky' through which things have their being.[34] These characterizations exploit the image of what is empty as something uncluttered that, for this reason, offers possibilities which what is choked up cannot. Think, for example, of the empty canvas (another of Suzuki's images) that affords possibilities for any number of figures to be painted.

The thought indicated by these metaphors of emptiness is that of something (not 'some *thing*') which enables there to be a world for us, a totality of objects that figure for us, but which, precisely as enabling this, cannot be something that either is or is *like* any entity within the world. That which allows anything to stand out for us, as something to which we can refer, cannot itself be such a thing. One is reminded of Wittgenstein's remark that 'no existing thing could be what we have meant by God'[35]—not if we have meant what allows for the existence of a world—and of Heidegger's refrain that Being as a source of beings cannot itself be a being. It is as intimating this thought that we might take Nāgārjuna's words 'True emptiness, wondrous being'. Emptiness is 'wondrous' not because it is an amazingly grand and impressive phenomenon, but because it is the necessarily inexplicable source of the possibility of a world, and hence that to which the being of the world and of ourselves owes. Again, one is reminded of Wittgenstein: 'it is not *how* things are in [or 'out' of] the world that is mystical, but *that* it exists', and it behoves us to appreciate 'the miracle . . . that the world exists', to experience 'wonder at the existence of the world'.[36] This is to wonder at the very possibility of there being a world and hence, for Buddhists, at the emptiness which, uncluttered by things found within the world, allows there to be a world in a way that necessarily resists explanation and understanding.

---

[34] D. T. Suzuki, *Zen and Japanese Culture* (Princeton, N.J.: Princeton University Press, 1959), 298; Nishitani, *Religion and Nothingness*, 151 and 98.

[35] Ludwig Wittgenstein, *Tractatus Logico-Philosophicus*, trans. D. Pears and B. McGuinness (London: Routledge, 1988), 6. 432. Think, too, of his remark that the 'ancients', with their appeal to 'God and Fate' were 'clearer' than modern science, since they recognized that explanation has a 'terminus', while the latter 'tries to make it look as if *everything* were explained': ibid. 6. 372.

[36] Ibid. 6. 44; *Notebooks 1914–16*, trans. G. E. M. Anscombe (Oxford: Blackwell, 1961), 86; 'Lecture on Ethics', *Philosophical Review*, 74 (1965), 8.

A further and final resonance is intended by some metaphors of emptiness. Those just considered evoked, one might say, a 'static' image of emptiness, as a reservoir or field of possibility, but there is also a more 'dynamic'
rhetoric. Dōgen wrote that reality 'has never been hidden': there is no transcendental suchness 'behind' the familiar world. But, as if anticipating a
nihilistic or downbeat reaction, he adds, as we saw earlier, that the world is
not 'my possession'. Rather, suchness or emptiness is 'something ineffable
coming like this' at us, an 'advancing' by 'all things'. The Buddha-nature
(that is, suchness or emptiness) is as 'a body manifesting itself'.[37] This more
dynamic conception is sometimes expressed by reference to emptiness as
not merely empty (non-substantial), but as empty*ing*. '*Śūnyatā* . . . is *emptying itself* and making everything alive . . . a dynamic activity constantly emptying everything, including itself.'[38]

These are opaque remarks whose point, if I understand it, I take up in the
following section. Whatever the exact import of the talk of empty*ing*, it
surely exploits the familiar metaphor of clouds or the heavens emptying
when it rains. No more than Dōgen's Buddha-nature is the emptying cloud
'hidden' or disjoint from the rain that 'advances' towards us. Rather it *is* the
rain 'coming like this', in the sense that there are not two things going on.
Likewise, in Nishida Kitaro's words, emptiness or 'the truly Absolute' is
'opposed to nothing': instead, it 'transforms itself' through 'self-emptying'
or 'self-negation' into 'the dynamic world' that confronts us.[39] But while the
emptying cloud is nothing 'hidden', it is, typically, recessive. When raindrops strike our faces, it is upon these that attention is confined, to the exclusion of the emptying which enables them. The perception of someone who
attends both to the drops and to the 'dynamic activity' of the emptying of
the cloud, who experiences the drops as the vanguard of an 'advancing' process, is akin to that of 'the eye of wisdom' (*prajñā*-eye). For someone with
that eye, in a further feat of 'double exposure', 'takes in . . . at a glance as one
Reality' both 'the realm of *Śūnyatā*' and 'the world of particulars'.[40] And, in
a final exploitation of the cloud metaphor, just as the emptying

[37] Dōgen, *Shobogenzo*, ii. 3, 19.

[38] Masao Abe, 'Epilogue', in Mitchell (ed.), *Masao Abe*, 382.

[39] Nishida Kitaro, *Last Writings: Nothingness and the Religious Worldview*, trans. D. Dilworth
(Honolulu: University of Hawaii Press, 1993), 68–9, 73.

[40] Suzuki, *Essays on Zen Buddhism*, 256.

cloud/falling rain brings life to the earth, so *Śūnyatā* or suchness, in its 'self-emptying', makes a world alive for us.

The metaphors of emptiness, then, resonate in many directions: the rhetoric is a rich one. At least five images conjured by our familiar uses of 'empty' and its cognates are called upon and exploited by the Buddhist rhetoric. These are the images of the empty as, respectively, lacking in, transparent to, open to, and uncluttered, and of (self-)emptying as a release-ment. When the resonances of the metaphors that exploit these images are harmonized, the rhetoric of emptiness serves to prompt or attune to a way of experiencing our world. This is the complex experience of a world as one whose ingredients are not the independent, substantial entities 'convention-ally' imagined, but things that depend on a network of relations in which we too are essentially embedded—things that do not, however, thereby lose identity, but retain it as unique 'places' at which the world as a whole 'gathers'. That world, in turn, is experienced as a 'wondrous' emergence from an inexplicable 'field of possibility', as an 'advancing' towards us that is the manifestation of an ineffable 'source'.

'*Śūnyatā*', writes Suzuki, 'is not an abstraction, but an experience.'[41] The above sketch of that experience, culled from the metaphors of emptiness, is only a sketch. I try to say something fuller and perhaps more helpful in the following section. I close the present one by recalling the difficulties con-fronting the downbeat equation of the doctrine of emptiness with that of dependent origination, and by briefly indicating why these are not diffi-culties for the richer understanding of the doctrine that has emerged over the last few pages. On p. 308, I summarized the difficulties faced by the down-beat interpretation as follows: it fails to illuminate the soteriological role assigned to the appreciation of emptiness, the conviction that emptiness is ineffable and 'inapprehensible', and the conception of the world as relying on emptiness as its 'source'.

It would take me too far from my own present concerns to explore, in any detail, why, for Buddhists, the way of experience to which the rich rhetoric of emptiness attunes should constitute 'liberation' and a 'crossing over' to Nirvāṇa—why, for example, it should put an end to 'craving' and induce universal 'compassion'. I confine myself to two remarks. First, while it may be that, as Zennists put it, there is 'nothing special' in experiencing

---

[41] Ibid. 257.

emptiness—no 'Eureka!' vision of the divine—and that it cultivates, rather, a 'celebration of the ordinary and everyday',[42] the experience is surely of a profound and transforming kind. When enlightened, Ching Yuan is once again aware of the mountains as genuinely present, but in a quite different register of awareness from his original one. It is not simply that he appreciates their dependent status: rather, he is capable of those 'double exposures' through which a mountain both 'dissolves' into and 'condenses' a world, and is both a unique, palpable particular and an integral expression of a 'wondrous', inexplicable 'advancing'. To borrow from Wittgenstein, the 'effect' on Ching Yuan is that his has 'become an altogether different world'.[43] That it has does not, by itself, explain the appositeness of terms like 'liberated'; but it is not hard to surmise how such a transformation in experience of and comportment towards the world might invite such terms. Second, the thought that appreciation of emptiness 'liberates', induces 'compassion', and ends 'craving' implies that a doctrine of emptiness provides measure for one's life, something for life to be answerable to. How it might provide measure—or, rather, how, more generally, a doctrine of mystery might provide this—is the topic for Chapter 13. So I say no more about it here.

As for the remaining aspects of the Mahāyāna texts for which the downbeat understanding of emptiness failed to cater, I take it as obvious that, in intent at least, justice is done to them by the richer rhetoric of emptiness. That emptiness is a 'font or source' of the things we encounter and speak of is explicit in the final two metaphors of emptiness I rehearsed. While emptiness as an open 'field of possibility' and a 'self-emptying' activity is not disjoint from the world—not a transcendental cause—it is that on which the world depends in a way that it does not similarly depend on the world. (When the doctrine of emptiness is equated, as by the downbeater, with that of dependent origination, the mutual dependence of emptiness and saṃsāra is entirely symmetrical. See p. 307 above.) No emptying cloud without raindrops, and vice versa: nevertheless, the former is a 'source' of the latter, and not vice versa. Finally, that emptiness is, as the sūtra had it, 'signless' and 'inapprehensible'—mysterious—is made explicit by Dōgen, Nishitani, and others on whose rhetoric I have drawn. 'Suchness is self-emptying', 'The bamboo con-centrates the world', 'The eye of wisdom takes in both Śūnyatā

---

[42] Nishida, *Last Writings*, 109.   [43] *Tractatus Logico-Philosophicus*, 6. 43.

and the world of particulars at a glance'—such utterances are *Äusserungen* and 'attunements', not assertions in which properties are predicated of subjects. Emptiness as the source of all that is sayable is not itself sayable, and none of the authors cited envisage that the way of experiencing the world that their words intimate or prompt is describable in terms from which figure or metaphor can be eliminated.[44]

Doctrines of Mystery: Desiderata and a Failed Attempt

We have on the table, then, a vocabulary of mystery—something more to go on than sealed lips or stuttering in response to the very idea of mystery. The vocabulary or rhetoric of emptiness is, moreover, a rich one that intimates or attunes in a distinctive key. It is not, of course, the only vocabulary of mystery on offer, but I suspect that only those alternatives that may be brought into alignment with it offer as much promise. One vocabulary—or range of vocabularies—with which it can certainly be aligned is that of Heidegger in his later writings, and this is a bonus, not because it automatically confers authority on the rhetoric of emptiness, but because it enables me, in what follows, to draw on more than one lexicon, confident of 'intertranslatability'. (Indeed, Heideggerese—'gathering', 'a world worlds'—already crept in during the account of emptiness in the previous section.)

We have it from the horse's mouth that this alignment is feasible. Writing of the Japanese equivalent of 'Śūnyatā', 'ku', Heidegger remarks that, far from 'naming' a merely 'negative nothing', it is the 'loftiest name' for what he himself has tried to 'say with the word "Being"'—one unsaddled, moreover, with 'the patrimony of [western] metaphysics'.[45] It is not difficult to

---

[44] This doctrine of ineffability, incidentally, should be distinguished from one that Zen thinkers are often credited with holding, to the effect that we can and should cultivate a 'direct', conceptless awareness of objects. The idea that we can experience *this* object, but not *as* a bamboo or anything else, strikes me as incompatible with the Buddhist view that there only *are* objects for us in virtue of 'conventions' of conceptualization and language. For effective criticisms of the idea, see Dale S. Wright, 'Rethinking Transcendence: The Role of Language in Zen Experience', *Philosophy East and West*, 42 (1992), 113–38, and Simon P. James, 'Awakening to Language in Zen and Heidegger', *International Journal of Field Being*, 4. 2 (2002).

[45] Quoted in Julian Young, *Heidegger's Philosophy of Art* (Cambridge: Cambridge University Press, 2001), 148. This book, incidentally, not only brings out some parallels between Heidegger's and East

locate Heideggerian points corresponding to those indicated by the several metaphors of emptiness just discussed. That things are empty, since dependently originated, pairs off with his claim that things depend upon a 'relational totality of significance'. That they are empty, since they 'dissolve' into a whole web of relations, yet also serve as 'places' where the world 'concentrates', compares with Heidegger's view that, simultaneously, 'things bear world' and 'world grants things'—that 'they penetrate one another'.[46] That suchness or emptiness is a 'self-emptying' that is an 'advancing' of the world towards us recalls Heidegger's talk of Being as a 'presencing' or 'giving' that bears 'presents' or 'gifts', and as a 'nearing'. Emptiness as a 'font or source' is Heidegger's Being or *Ereignis* as a 'mysterious well-spring'—and so on. Let us recall, as well, that for Heidegger and the spokesmen of emptiness alike, the vocabularies of mystery do not provide 'information', do not make assertions about the properties of emptiness/Being. They speak only 'about' mystery with the ambition of 'directing' us towards a way of experiencing, 'dwelling' in, or 'revealing' the world—one that, to repeat Heidegger's words, is replete with a sense of 'the essential swaying of th[e] unknown'.

In what follows, although I shall freely draw upon Buddhist and Heideggerian vocabularies wherever this proves useful, generally I put matters in my own terms, inspired as these are by those vocabularies. What follows, in effect, is a prolegomenon, thus inspired, to a doctrine of mystery. The aim is not to provide a full-blown metaphysics in which a notion of mystery plays a leading role—one replete with accounts of space and time, body and mind, objects and properties, and whatever else a total metaphysics might be expected to incorporate. More modestly, I indicate some main desiderata or conditions of adequacy of a decent doctrine of mystery, and suggest, in the next section, that the rhetoric of emptiness contains the resources for satisfying them. If I am right, then a doctrine of mystery offers more than a merely 'formal' solution to the impasse between humanism and absolutism arrived at in Chapter 11.

On pp. 296–7, I announced that the vocabulary of emptiness was 'the most promising vehicle of "thinking/saying"', of a doctrine of mystery, and

Asian thinking, but offers a clear and generally enlightening account of the place of mystery in Heidegger's later philosophy.

[46] Martin Heidegger, *Poetry, Language, Thought*, trans. A. Hofstadter (New York: Harper & Row, 1975), 202.

briefly listed some of its merits. I need to justify that announcement, to show that the doctrine of emptiness does have these and other merits—and indeed to show or remind you that these *are* merits. There are, I suggest, at least six desiderata of a doctrine of mystery, each of which the idea of emptiness (and those alignable with it) has the resources to satisfy. With three of these, I can be brief: about two of them, I have already said enough, about the third I say nothing until the next chapter. First, a doctrine of mystery must not be self-stultifying: it must not 'eff' the ineffable, say things about (as opposed to 'about') what it claims to be beyond propositional articulation. If the Buddhists and Heidegger are right to view their utterances as 'attunements' that cannot be cashed into literal propositions, then this first condition is met. Second, the doctrine must honour the truth in humanism, the thesis of 'the human world', to the effect that there is no discursable world independent of 'the human contribution'. It is clear that the doctrine of emptiness does honour this. For its champions, as for Heidegger, 'only where there is language is there world'[47]—a language inextricable, moreover, from human purposes, practices, and interests. Finally, the mystery appealed to by the doctrine must be capable of providing measure of our lives—our concepts, attitudes, comportment to the world. This is a desideratum, at any rate, of any conception of mystery inspired, as it is in this book, by the need for measure 'beyond the human'. How the idea of emptiness and its relatives might satisfy this condition is a topic set aside until the final chapter.

The remaining desiderata require more immediate and fairly prolonged treatment, not least because they are linked in a quite complex way. More precisely, they are desiderata whose simultaneous satisfaction is problematic, since moves that might naturally be made to satisfy the first create difficulties for satisfying the others. A decent doctrine of mystery should contain the resources, to begin with, for indicating the character of a 'compensating experience' to complement that of the world as a human world. But, second, it must do this in a way that does not violate the thesis of 'the human world'. Finally, the conception of mystery invoked should not be a 'transcendent' one. In sum, a doctrine of mystery should, without tension, intimate a 'compensating experience', reconcile the notion of mystery with that of 'the human world', and eschew a dichotomy between mystery and

---

[47] Martin Heidegger, *Existence and Being*, trans. W. Brock (London: Vision, 1949), 299.

the world. All of this needs elaboration before indicating how the rhetoric of emptiness and its allies is able to meet the desiderata.

Chapter 10 chronicled various testimonies to the unendurability of the 'dis-incumbenced stance' and hence of the raw, uncompensated thesis of 'the human world' once that thesis becomes 'deeply cultivated', 'hot and alive'. The mood or experience, in the various modalities chronicled, that the thesis then induces is one with which, according to those testimonies, human beings cannot live. The world 'dissolves', become 'uncanny', and the words we use to speak about it 'crumble' like 'mouldy fungi'—to cite some of the more dramatic testimonies. I then 'diagnosed' such responses to the raw, uncompensated humanist experience of the world as registering an insuperable need for an 'answerability to' and 'measure' that humanism precludes. Hence, a search for measure 'beyond the human' implies, given the unbelievability of absolutism—of 'the independence thesis'—a search for a doctrine of mystery.

There is the danger that that diagnosis portrays the predicament of those unable to endure uncompensated humanism in too purely an intellectual manner—as that of people requiring measure for their beliefs and commitments, finding that this demand is unmet by humanism, and so looking elsewhere. Thus portrayed, we are liable to forget the affective, experiential dimension of unendurability and the consequent need for compensation in a doctrine that, in offering the prospect of measure, also inspires an experience of the world and language no longer liable to dissolution and crumbling. One might say that a decent doctrine of mystery should, to recall Wittgenstein's words, enable the world to 'become an altogether different world' from the one confronted in the dis-incumbenced humanist posture. It cannot merely be a doctrine to recall and lend cheer at those occasional, dark moments in one's study when the enormity of raw humanism strikes one.[48]

---

[48] An analogy suggests itself with Descartes's view that the merit of his proof of a non-deceiving God is that it is there to recall when doubts strike people about their knowledge of things. They need only remind themselves that 'the intellectual faculty which He gave them cannot but tend towards the truth': René Descartes, *Selected Philosophical Writings*, trans. J. Cottingham, R. Stoothof, and D. Murdoch (Cambridge: Cambridge University Press, 1988), 142. Other religious writers—Pascal and Kierkegaard, for example—understandably criticize this doggedly intellectual conception of the role of religious certainty. For them, the world of the religious person indeed becomes an altogether different one from that of the atheist, and it is not just that the former has a 'measure' to fall back on when the philosophical going gets hard.

That it is a delicate matter to satisfy the desideratum of inspiring a compensating experience without flouting the other desiderata mentioned
three paragraphs earlier is seen by reflecting on the problems that one
prominent doctrine of mystery runs into. I refer to the transcendental idealism advanced, if not by Kant, then by Schopenhauer and, on some interpretations—including Schopenhauer's own—by Advaita Vedānta. We noted
earlier (p. 243) that, for Schopenhauer, if there were *only* 'the veil of *māyā*',
only 'appearances', then the world would, unendurably, 'pass us by like an
empty dream', a phantasm of the mind or brain. As these words suggest,
Schopenhauer's compensating doctrine of a noumenal 'will' underlying
'appearances' is intended to go deep with us. In particular, the tone of our
lives should be constant appreciation of the superficiality of a world of distinct, individual objects and persons. Otherwise, we shall not *feel* full 'compassion' towards the suffering of other creatures, human and non-human:
for that requires the sense that only superficially are they distinct from ourselves.[49] The Vedantic texts make similarly plain the vital, experiential
dimension of recognition of the mysterious 'reality behind everything'.
Indeed, for Śaṃkara, the philosophical *statement* of Advaita merely prepares
for a soteriological experience of the world as an appearance of *brahman*, as
something no longer 'fixed and distinct' (see p. 243 above).

This transcendental idealist doctrine of mystery sounds, to begin with, to
violate the desideratum of compatibility with the thesis of 'the human
world', for it was not the intention of that thesis to impugn the reality of the
world, to treat it as 'mere appearance', *māyā*. True, I was sympathetic to
those who reacted to the raw thesis with the feeling that it *does* impugn that
reality, but diagnosed this reaction as calling for a compensating doctrine
that would *remedy*, not *validate*, that feeling. Yet it is precisely validation that
Schopenhauer and the Advaitins, with their talk of *māyā*, provide. But is
there a substantial issue here? Given that there is a discursable world only in
relation to 'the human contribution', does it matter whether we deny reality to that world or, instead, speak of its really existing, though only, of
course, in relation to us? The answer is that there is a real issue here. For
Schopenhauer, a world underpinned by the thing in itself, the 'will', may not

---

[49] Arthur Schopenhauer, *The World as Will and Representation*, trans. E. Payne (New York: Dover,
1969), ii. 601–2.

be an *empty* dream, but it is still a dream, *māyā*. This is because it is so 'conditioned by the subject' as to have little or no resemblance to the thing in itself.[50] For the Advaitins, 'ignorance' (*avidyā*) is responsible for our 'mistaking' the everyday world for what is real, *brahman*. The model is that of the familiar world as the joint product of an underlying reality and human subjects or minds, a product so 'conditioned' by the latter as to bear little or no correspondence to the former. For the existential humanist and 'concept-bound' realist (see Chapter 5), this is a bad model, uncomfortably close, in structure at least, to the myth of an unconceptualized 'given' that the mind then knocks into shapes of its own. For these philosophers, the familiar, discursable world is as real as it gets, for there is no underlying realm, filtered through human subjectivity, of which it is a gross distortion. They are right: hence, if there is mystery—a 'beyond the human'—this should not be portrayed as something behind which 'the human world' comes in a poor, dreamlike second.

The same model that puts transcendental idealism at odds with the 'human world' thesis also violates the desideratum that a doctrine of mystery should eschew a dichotomy between world and mystery, that the mystery postulated should not be 'transcendent'. While it may not do so in the stark manner of some other doctrines of mystery—those, say, which treat the world as the creation of a mysterious God—Nietzsche was right to include it as one more chapter in his 'fable of "the true world"'.[51] Schopenhauer's thing in itself, like *brahman*, indeed constitutes 'another' realm, logically independent of the world of 'appearances'. There might not have been 'subjects'—brains, on Schopenhauer's unhappy account [52]— and if there had not, there would not have been a phenomenal world either, for that is a 'representation'. In Śaṃkara's account, that world is the product of 'play' (*līlā*) on the part of *brahman* in its personified form [53]—a metaphor

[50] Ibid. i. 3.

[51] Friedrich Nietzsche, *Twilight of the Idols*, trans. Duncan Large (Oxford: Oxford University Press, 1998), ch. 4.

[52] Unhappy, since Schopenhauer is invoking an object in the phenomenal world—the brain—to explain how there is such a world. See *The World as Will and Representation*, vol. ii, ch. 18. Recall my and Nietzsche's comments on this in Chapter 4.

[53] *Brahmasūtrabhāsya*, as summarized in Karl Potter, *Encyclopedia of Indian Philosophies* (Delhi: Motilal Banarsidass, 1991), iii. 141.

indicating that there might not have been a world. *Brahman* might not have got playful.

This treatment of what is mysterious as 'transcendent' to the familiar world has a further, unwelcome implication. Despite, or rather because of, erecting a dichotomy between world and 'another' realm, it in effect treats the latter as an item akin to worldly ones—a *thing* in itself, a will, a Self. True, those terms come with warning labels: nevertheless, if the world of *māyā* is the product of the impact upon mind of will or *brahman*, these latter must be conceived of as sufficiently like familiar causal items or processes for talk of 'impact'—for the whole model of a 'conditioned' world—to have any sense. But now, not only will the charge of self-stultification, of 'effing' the ineffable, arise, so too will the old worry that what is (allegedly) mysterious cannot provide measure. For the scheme of concepts for which measure is sought *includes* those of thing, will, self, activity, process, cause, condition, and so on.

Transparency, Grace, and Epiphany

Transcendental idealism, then, in its provision of a compensating experience—itself a flawed attempt, given its endorsement of the illusoriness of the world—sits uncomfortably with the thesis of 'the human world' and engenders a dichotomy between world and mystery. It fails, therefore, to satisfy the second trio of desiderata of a doctrine of mystery. By contrast, the rhetoric of emptiness and its Heideggerian cousin contain the resources to satisfy these desiderata. These resources are three notions that I label *transparency*, *grace*, and *epiphany*. They do not neatly pair off with the three desiderata, for they come as a tight package.

To open the package, we should first record the hostility of champions of emptiness to the 'bad model' of mystery, mind, and world employed by the transcendental idealists I discussed. On that model, the familiar world is the subjectively conditioned product of will, *brahman*, or whatever impacting upon mind. Rejection of that model goes in two stages (the second will take some time to reach). On the doctrine of emptiness, to begin with, there is no mysterious, unconceptualizable thing, force, substance, process, or whatever that impacts upon subjectivity so as to engender the familiar world. To speak with John McDowell, there is no thing, force, process, etc. to which our concepts do not 'reach out'. Hence, for the champions of emptiness, there is nothing for the familiar world to be a distorted, illusory version of. As Nishida puts it, reality is empty, 'a place of nothingness', because it is 'without underlying substance', and 'the path to truth' is not to impugn or 'negate' our ordinary perception of the world.[54] We may continue to 'celebrate' ordinary things: the mountain is once again a mountain.

So the doctrine of emptiness does not violate the 'human world' thesis in the manner of transcendental idealism—by treating the world as *māyā*, a veil masking reality in itself. Nevertheless, as Nishida reminds us, when 'the human standpoint' is 'maximized' in a 'purely secular direction . . . the world negates itself'.[55] In other words, as the testimonies in Chapter 10 indicated, raw humanism—uncompensated by mystery—depicts a world that, while not a veil of illusion, threatens to dissolve or collapse, to seem a fiction. We are already familiar, in outline, with the compensating experience—one that will counter the sense of dissolution—to which the rhetoric of emptiness attunes. It was the one gestured at by the talk of 'double exposure', by what I now call the notion of transparency. In effect, there are two experiences involved, since there were two 'double exposures'. First, there was that of 'seeing through' something—a tree, say—to the network of relations, the 'relational totality of significance', on which it depends, whilst also 'seeing' that whole 'gathered', 'con-centrated', in the tree. Then, second, was the experience of seeing things as ordinary particulars, while also 'seeing through' the world as a whole, a sense of which is cultivated in the first experience, to . . . Well, to what? I will try to say something in response when I reach the notion of epiphany. For the moment, let's simply recall some earlier terminological stabs and add a couple for good measure. As the Buddhists put it, we see through to 'self-emptying', to 'something ineffable coming like this', to an 'advancing'. In Heideggerese, we see through what 'comes to presence (beings)' to their 'presencing (Being)', which is thereby 'brought to the fore'.[56] In Max Scheler's extravagant prose, one 'looks

---

[54] *Last Writings*, 62 and 114. Nishida was the acknowledged 'leader' of the famous Kyoto school, and in his *Last Writings*—which owe as much to Heidegger as to Zen—he articulates a position as close to the one developed in this section as any I have encountered. Hence the liberal references to this work in what follows.

[55] Ibid. 119.

[56] Martin Heidegger, 'On the Question of Being', in *Pathmarks*, trans. W. McNeill (Cambridge: Cambridge University Press, 1998), 298–9.

through the web' of 'relativity' in 'the direction of . . . a miraculous repealing' of 'nothingness'.[57] Let's opt, for the time being, for 'presencing'. In the
second double exposure, one experiences the world as what is present *and* its
'presencing', its coming to be present.

I return to this after considering a problem that the image conjured by
such talk poses. This problem is that the picture one is tempted to fit to talk
of the world as coming to presence before us, or advancing towards us, no
longer looks that of 'the human world'. How can it be 'our world', dependent on us, if it is just 'comes to presence' before us? It looks as if, in characterizing the compensating experience, the champions of emptiness are, in their
own way, violating the thesis of 'the human world' that they purport to
accept.

However, this problem can be resolved, and no violation occurs. To
appreciate why, we need to consider the second stage in the rejection of the
'bad model' of mystery–mind–world. At the first stage, recall, it was the idea
of some unconceptualizable thing, stuff, process, or whatever impacting on
our subjectivity that was rejected. At the second stage, attention shifts to
that model's conception of subjectivity—of mind, of *us*. Now talk, on that
model, of a subjective 'conditioning' of the world might be, as it is sometimes intended to be, construed in a 'Promethean' way. We 'shape' or
'sculpt' an unconceptualized 'porridge' into a structured world. So construed, the model falls victim to the criticisms levelled against
Prometheanism by existential humanists way back in Chapter 5. While
'shaping' and 'constructing' may be appropriate terms for certain classificatory practices, the idea that we are generally engaged in such 'decisional'
business is, at the very least, phenomenologically absurd. As Merleau-Ponty
put it, while the world is 'inseparable from subjectivity', it is not 'constructed or formed' in obedience to a 'law' of our own making (see p. 103 above).

Existential humanists denied, naturally, that rejection of Prometheanism
threatened the 'human world' thesis: the world remains dependent on 'the
human contribution', even if that contribution is poorly described as a 'shaping' or 'constructing'. They were right to deny this. Nevertheless, water has
passed under the bridge since Chapter 5, and champions of emptiness are
equally right to think that both the 'bad model' *and* raw humanism—even

---

[57] *On the Eternal in Man*, trans. B. Noble (London: SCM Press, 1960), 101.

when Promethean rhetoric is eschewed—remain uncomfortably close in spirit to Prometheanism. For what is missed or 'forgotten' by their proponents is, in Heidegger's terms, that the 'disclosure' of a world—the fundamental ways in which things are 'revealed'—is a 'self-disclosure', not 'our handiwork'.[58] Or, as Nishida puts it, while we may 'transform' the world about us, we do so only as 'transformative elements of the world's own self-expression'.[59] Put poetically, that we 'disclose' the world in its most basic structures as we do is a matter of *grace*, not an achievement of ours.

Or better, there is no 'us', no subjectivity, that is in place and remains constant through different possible disclosures, for a disclosure to be an achievement *of*. The image of mind or subjectivity as some determinate conditioning agency from which a shaped and structured world emerges needs abandoning. Nishida is urging this when he complains that 'every subjectivistic interpretation, by taking its point of departure from an abstractly imagined, pre-existent conscious self, beclouds our vision'. Instead, we should recognize that 'self and other are co-originating through mutual interexpression'.[60]

The point at issue here is more sharply made in Heidegger's discussion of language, and is encapsulated in his remark that, in the first instance, it is not 'man' who speaks, but *language*.[61] This is directed against the raw humanist argument that since language is a tool of our making, and since there is no world without language, the world is therefore of our making. Heidegger concurs in the second premise, endorsing Stefan George's line, 'Where word breaks off no thing may be'. But he rejects the first, for two related reasons. First, the idea of language as a tool does no justice to the *intimacy* of the relation between human being and language. Language is not some bolt-on extra, a tool without which our kind of being would still have been distinctively human: rather, it is in and through language that we have that kind of being. Second, while human beings have of course concocted the words that belong to the various natural languages they speak, this is only

---

[58] Martin Heidegger, *The Question Concerning Technology and Other Essays*, trans. W. Lovitt (New York: Harper & Row, 1977), 18. See the helpful discussion of this remark in Young, *Heidegger's Philosophy of Art*, 130, esp. n. 6.

[59] *Last Writings*, 98.

[60] Ibid. 109 and 103.

[61] Martin Heidegger, *On the Way to Language*, trans. P. Hertz (San Francisco, Calif.: Harper & Row, 1982), 124.

possible through something that is not at all of their making. This is their 'receipt' of the fundamental categories, structures, and perspectives that organize and find voice in their languages. But it is, to recall Heidegger's first objection, a very special 'receipt': one that makes the 'recipients' what they are.

These remarks on language testify to Heidegger's 'turn' away from the Kantian spirit of *Being and Time*. There, *Dasein* was understood in terms of certain necessary features ('existentialia') that dictate how anything can 'show up' or 'light up' for it—dictate, that is, how *Dasein's* world will be. In his later rhetoric—close to that of emptiness—*Dasein* or 'man' is characterized as the 'clearing' or 'open space' where things 'light up' and 'gather'.[62] There are not, so to speak, two terms: 'man' as some determinate being that then discloses or 'projects' a world. Rather, there is simply the presencing of a world, an 'event' that is at the same time the coming to be of 'man'. As Buddhists like Nishida put it, self and other—'man' and world—are 'co-originating': the 'self-emptying' which is the arising of a world is also the enabling of 'mankind to be mankind'.[63] Those most basic practices, perspectives, and interests on which, for the existential humanist, the identity of things depends, are not there in place and at the ready to 'condition' the world and confer identity on things. Rather, they too belong with the presencing of a world, 'co-arise' with it. It is not that *we*, embroiled in our practices and perspectives, then 'disclose' a world to suit. Instead, there is—'es gibt', in Heidegger's German pun—a disclosure that at once 'gives' a world and 'gives' us. This is, to be sure, 'a human world' in which nothing 'lights up' except in relation to our practices and perspectives. But there is nothing human in what 'gives' a unity of world, practices and perspectives.

To appreciate this, writes Nishida, is to accept 'Amida's grace'. Amida Buddha is the central figure in Shin or Pure Land Buddhism, a school that emphasizes the absence of our 'self power' in relation to the 'other power' of 'suchness' as personified by Amida. Nishida's remark is made in the context of holding that any conception of the world—that of natural science, say—is, *au fond*, not *our* determination or expression, but the 'self-determination', 'self-expression' of 'the absolute'.[64] However much human

---

[62] See especially 'Letter on Humanism', in *Basic Writings: Martin Heidegger*, ed. D. F. Krell (London: Routledge, 1993). But see Chapter 10, n.28, for a qualification of these remarks.

[63] *Last Writings*, 100.   [64] Ibid. 107.

effort goes into forging that conception, ultimately the wherewithal for that effort 'just comes', in a manner popularly and pictorially represented as a gracious gift of Amida's.[65] 'Grace' indeed sounds a felicitious metaphor for the notion being advanced here. Nishida's sympathy for Zen references to our being 'absolutely nothing', to our 'becoming things' when we think and perceive, and to the identity of subjects and objects is also explained, I think, by his construing these as graphic expressions of the truth that what we are is inseparable from a world disclosure that, *au fond*, cannot be of our making, that 'just comes'.

So the problem that launched the discussion of grace—how to reconcile the rhetoric of emptiness, 'presencing', and 'advancing' with the thesis of 'the human world'—is resolved. That thesis remains: there is no discursable world—no world at all—except in relation to human language and perspective. More poetically put, 'man' is the 'clearing' or 'house of Being' in which alone beings can 'light up' or be 'gathered' and 'lodged'. But since the disclosure of the world embedded in language, and hence inseparable from the practices and perspectives that enable meaning, is not our 'handiwork', it and the world have 'just come'. World/disclosure is a present, a gift: it presences for us through grace. The thesis of 'the human world' remains, but with the appeal to something 'beyond the human', raw, uncompensated humanism does not.

The view of mystery emerging here requires elaboration by saying something more helpful than so far attempted about the notion to which those of transparency and grace point. This is the notion I label 'epiphany', and which is gestured at by talk of 'presencing', 'self-emptying', 'advancing', 'sending', 'repealing' and so on. For it is in those terms that both what we 'see through' to in 'compensating experience', and the operation of grace, have been characterized. One might say: to 'see through' the world to a presencing whose 'gift' it is, is to experience the world as an epiphany.

To speak of the world as an epiphany is not to provide some new information about it, to register some momentous feature of the world so far overlooked. Like other terms invoked, the role of 'epiphany' is to intimate a way of experiencing the word. It can be given this role by exploiting two features of the word in its familiar employment. By exploiting these, one

---

[65] For a modern, sympathetic, and massive 'reconstruction' of Shin philosophy, see Tanabe Hajime, *Philosophy as Metanoetics*, trans. T. Yoshinori (Berkeley: University of California Press, 1986).

may hope to attune both to the intimacy between what is mysterious (self-emptying, presencing, or whatever) and the world, and to the 'wondrousness' of the experience of mystery.

The word derives from a Greek one meaning 'show' or 'appear'. Epiphany, however, is not 'mere' appearance or show, a façade or mask that, itself out in the open, hides or distorts. Nor does an epiphany show in the manner of a sign or symptom: those tell-tale spots may show that the disease is present, but they are not an epiphany of it. Nor is something 'represented' by its epiphany. The reason why, for Berkeley, 'the mighty frame of the world' is, in effect, God's epiphany—why 'we need only open our eyes to see' him—is that our 'ideas' do not represent a material intermediary, but are directly shared by him with us.[66] Again, it is not through his representative or *avatar*, Krishna, that the god Vishnu truly appears to Arjuna in the *Bhagavad Gītā*: only in a late chapter—sometimes called 'the epiphany chapter'—when, dispensing with such an intermediary, does Vishnu show himself in his full tremendousness.

To regard the world as an epiphany, then, is not to treat it as the open-to-view veneer, product, symptom, or viceroy of something hidden, but as the showing up of something for what it is. But even this fails to capture the intended intimacy between the world and what it is an epiphany of, for the genitival form of the expression 'epiphany of . . .' encourages a continuing dichotomy between what shows and its showing, faithful and direct as the latter may be to the former. That is an encouragement, however, that we may resist by construing the expression as more akin to 'flash of lightning' than to 'flash of a knife'—as akin to expressions where it would obviously be mistaken to imagine a divide between what shows and its showing.

Resistance of that kind is certainly intended by both Buddhist and Heideggerian rhetoric. According to the latter, 'Being "is" nothing', not 'a cause that is added, not an encompassing that stands behind and above beings': rather, as a 'lighting' or 'presencing', it 'needs' a world in which things are 'lit', 'unconcealed', or 'present'.[67] Buddhist references to 'the emptiness of emptiness', to suchness as 'self-emptying', and to a Buddha-nature that is 'nothing special', have a similar point. That point, one might

---

[66] George Berkeley, *Philosophical Writings*, ed. T. Jessop (London: Nelson, 1952), 148.

[67] *Contributions to Philosophy (From Enowning)*, trans. P. Emad and K. Maly (Bloomington: Indiana University Press, 1999), 180–2.

say, is that, as with the lightning that 'needs' to flash, what is mysterious—
Being, presencing, self-emptying, or whatever—is not an entity of which the
world is an epiphany, rather it *is* an 'epiphanizing'. While it is that 'out of'
which a world 'comes to be'[68]—and only a world thus 'seen through' is
experienced as epiphany—it is, as it were, exhausted by that 'coming to be'.

Earlier, apropos of the 'double exposures', the question arose, '"See
through" the world to *what?*', to which the stop-gap answer 'Presencing' was
offered. Recent reflections suggests this is not a question to agonize over. It
would be so only in the expectation of identifying something at once substantial and hidden to which an informative name might be given. That
expectation is misplaced, and it matters little what name serves as the grammatical dative or genitive in such expressions as 'see through to . . .' or
'epiphany of . . .'. All that matters, perhaps, is that the name more or less
indicates that what it gestures at is intimate with the world, is nothing
'behind and above' what 'comes to be'. If so, then 'presencing' and 'self-
emptying' are not 'stop-gaps', but about as evocative and attuning as one
could hope for.

If 'epiphany' suggests an intimacy between the show and what is shown,
there is something further it intimates. A pale, watery gleam in an otherwise
leaden sky is not the epiphany of the sun that a flame-red dawn is. Only the
latter, for most of us, is something to wonder at, and aptness to inspire wonder is required, surely, for a phenomenon to invite the term 'epiphany'. This
is so even though different phenomena invite it for different reasons—
because they are resplendent or sublime, tremendous or awesome, and so
on. So to experience the world as a whole as an epiphany is to see it as wondrous, a term already encountered during this chapter from the pens of various authors. Nāgārjuna's phrase 'True emptiness, wondrous being', for
example, was cited when criticizing the downbeat equation of emptiness
with *saṃsāra*: where, on that equation, was there scope for regarding the
world as wondrous?

There is, however, an issue here. It is not only Buddhist downbeaters who
will challenge the idea that champions of mystery have a monopoly on talk
of a wondrous world—the idea, in effect, that wondrousness requires the
notion of epiphany. After all, aside from devotees of an 'ontological argu-

[68] Ibid. 182.

ment' for the logical necessity of the world, it is agreed on all sides that explanations for the existence of and the fundamental features of the world run out. Provided that the force of 'wondrous' is to register the final contingency, the 'brute facts', of there being anything at all and of its being the fundamental way it is, then the term is surely available to everyone. For opponents of mystery, more fully, exclamations of wonder register a recognition of brute fact and of a mood that may accompany this: astonishment, perhaps, rather than a shrugging of the shoulders, at there being a world that is as it is—a mood, perhaps, further encouraged by perceptions of the world's variety, symmetry, and immensity.[69]

This way of wresting sole entitlement to wonder away from champions of mystery could not, however, be acceptable as it stands to humanists. For, with its reference to a brute fact of the way the world is, in its most fundamental aspects, it incorporates 'the independence thesis', the absolutist's conviction that there is a discursable way reality anyway is. For the humanist, there is no such fact, brute or otherwise, to wonder at. Nevertheless, raw, uncompensated humanism spawns its own version of the brute fact diagnosis of wonder. What is wondrous, since entirely contingent and excluding further explanation, is the human world in its most basic aspects—a world whose description necessarily and irreducibly contains an account of those perspectives, forms of life, or whatever that constitute 'the human contribution' without which there is no discursable world. This is the position espoused by James C. Edwards when he unfavourably compares Heidegger's appeal to 'some hidden source' of meaning in the world with the 'pathos' and 'wonder' at the 'brute contingencies' of our form of life—of our 'agreements and disagreements'—inspired, he believes, by Wittgenstein's later writings.[70]

Champions of mystery need not deny that their absolutist and raw humanist opponents can find *a* place for talk of wonder: what they deny is that this place is a legitimate one. The wonder spoken of by the absolutist

[69] See e.g. Mary Midgley, *Science and Poetry* (London: Routledge, 2001), 182–3, who holds that, if 'Gaian thinking' is approximately right in its account of the role played by 'the system of life' in the evoultion of the earth, then 'the only possible response . . . is surely wonder, awe and gratitude'.

[70] James C. Edwards, *The Authority of Language: Heidegger, Wittgenstein and the Threat of Philosophical Nihilism* (Tampa: University of South Florida Press, 1990), 236, 239–40. I find Edwards's description of a certain wonder at the existence of the world persuasive. What is much less convincing is the equation of this wonder with a recognition of 'brute contingencies'.

requires acceptance of a thesis that, as humanists have shown, is hubristic and unbelievable. The raw humanist's own diagnosis of wonder as register-ing the brute fact of the human world, meanwhile, is simply a reaffirmation of the conviction, at once hubristic and unlivable, that there is no measure 'beyond the human'.

But champions of mystery have a further complaint. Not only do their opponents' diagnoses of wonder reflect the mistakes of their respective positions, their very conception of wonder is too thin. For, on a doctrine of mystery that meets the desiderata specified, to experience the world as won-drous is not simply or mainly to register that its having 'come to be present' is inexplicable, that the presencing or emptying 'out of' which it comes is ineffable. Rather, it is to experience things as at once belonging to a 'human world'—as dependent on 'the human contribution'—and yet 'just as they are', in a favourite Zen expression. It is to experience ourselves as at once 'constitutive' and 'faithful', as 'world-makers' and 'world-receivers'. The object of wonder, therefore, combines, seemingly paradoxically, the respective truths in humanism and absolutism.[71] The world is a human one, yet our disclosure of it is answerable, and may measure up, to what is 'beyond the human'. In Heidegger's metaphor, as 'shepherds of Being' we are answerable to . . . for what is dependent upon us. More fully, if more tortuously, to experience things as wondrous is to experience them 'trans-parently', as belonging in a world, to whose very existence as a world we ourselves are essential, that is a grace-given epiphany—a showing up of things 'just as they are'.

Of course, the envisaged combination of the respective truths of absolut-ism and humanism would be genuinely paradoxical if expressions like 'just as they are' or 'measure up to' are construed in an absolutist fashion—as meaning that there is an independent layout of the world to which our con-ception or disclosure may correspond, may offer a true description of. The idea must instead be that a disclosure may be 'faithful' or 'in the truth' through appropriately answering to what is mysterious, and that within such a disclosure things may be said to figure 'just as they are'. The question

---

[71] Some sort of combination of these respective truths, but without appeal to mystery, has of course been the ambition of the many philosophers—Hegel and McDowell among them—for whom reality must be more or less as we take it to be, even though no 'sideways on' comparison between reality and our take on it is possible. If my earlier arguments are well taken, that ambition has been unrealized.

of how a disclosure—how ways of perceiving, describing, and evaluating—may be identified as faithful is the question of how mystery can provide any measure. That it should provide measure was one of the desiderata of a doctrine of mystery and, in the context of my discussion, an especially central desideratum. For, in that context, it was the need for measure 'beyond the human' that inspired the quest for such a doctrine. It is to this issue that the final chapter is devoted.

CHAPTER 13

Mystery, Measure, and Humility

The Issue of Measure

It is appropriate, at the beginning of this final chapter, briefly to rehearse how the issue it addresses was reached. The early chapters traced the development, from late medieval times, of tendencies that culminated in the 'human world' thesis of existential humanism. Attention then turned to assessment of this thesis and a rival 'independence' thesis embraced by absolutists. It turned, in particular, to the charges of hubris or lack of humility exchanged by proponents of the respective theses. The two charges were significantly different: that levelled by humanists was one of a 'hubris of belief', while that levelled against them was one of a 'hubris of posture'. In subsequent chapters, I argued that both charges could be secured. Of no description that we can envisage is there warrant to suppose that it offers an absolute account of the world, and no sense can be made of the idea of descriptions that we cannot envisage. Humanism is not similarly unbelievable, but the 'dis-incumbenced' stance or posture it requires us to adopt is not one that we have the capacity to maintain.

Or so it was argued in Chapter 10, on the basis of a number of 'testimonies' that attested to the 'unendurable' character of a 'raw' humanism 'uncompensated' by some further doctrine that relieves us from the dis-incumbenced stance. I interpreted those testimonies as manifesting a need that we inveterately teleological creatures have for our practices and purposes, and the beliefs and conceptions that inform these, to be 'answerable to' something 'beyond the human'. With absolutism already rejected, this 'something' cannot be found in a discursable way that the world anyway, and independently, is.

The impasse reached when both absolutism and raw humanism are judged hubristic may only be escaped through a doctrine of mystery, according to which, while there is indeed a 'beyond the human', this is not discursable. The prospects for a doctrine of mystery were examined by criticizing a number of pre-emptive dismissals, as were the prospects for saying something 'about' what is mysterious in a way that does not, self-defeatingly, 'eff' the ineffable. In Chapter 12, I drew upon Buddhist sources and the later writings of Heidegger to sketch a doctrine of mystery, in terms of a notion of 'emptiness', that satisfied various desiderata. One of those was that a doctrine of mystery should cater to the need for answerability and measure. Whether or not the doctrine of emptiness does satisfy that desideratum is the present issue.

Before addressing it, however, I make two remarks of a historical character. First, it would be wrong to convey the impression that people have only been attracted to doctrines of mystery because of a strategic role these may have. The attraction may have various grounds, not least actual enjoyment of the kind of experience to which a rhetoric of mystery 'attunes'—an enjoyment whose background context may not be of the 'intellectual' kind it was in my discussion. Maybe it was prompted by reading the right poets or by appropriate encounters with nature. That said, attention was certainly paid by the thinkers discussed in the previous chapter to the measure-affording role of a doctrine of mystery. The Mahāyānist notion of emptiness was partly intended to guard against a 'nihilistic', 'antinomian' response which rejection of 'eternalist', 'transcendentalist' views is apt to trigger. Heidegger was plainly endorsing Hölderlin's 'wish' to find in a mysterious 'godhead' what cannot be found 'on earth'—'the measure of man'.[1]

The Buddhists and Heidegger are not alone in holding that, not only may the mysterious be 'measure-setting',[2] but that this is an important reason for cultivating an openness to it. 'Being', wrote Gabriel Marcel, which is 'strictly ineffable', 'cannot be separated from the exigence of being'—from, for example, the need experienced by an artist who, for all his 'liberty of movement', fears that his work is 'meaningless or worthless'. This is a main 'reason for the impossibility of severing being from value'—from the

---

[1] Martin Heidegger, *Poetry, Language, Thought*, trans. A. Hofstadter (New York: Harper & Row, 1975), 219–20.

[2] Heidegger, *Contributions to Philosophy (From Enowning)*, trans. P. Emad and K. Maly (Bloomington: Indiana University Press, 1999), 359.

provision of measure—and for describing our relation to being as an 'appeal'.[3] Perhaps, to turn the clock back, it is in the Taoist classics that the emphasis on the mysterious as the provider of measure is most pronounced. *The* Way, that cannot be 'spoken of', measures all *our* ways. 'Always to know the standard', says the *Tao Te Ching*, is that 'profound virtue' which 'follows alone from the Tao', 'hidden and nameless' as it is. Man must 'model himself . . . after Tao' and 'hold on to the Tao of old in order to master', to take the measure of, 'the things of the present'.[4]

The second historical remark concerns the connections that have long been made between mystery and a theme that has gone quiet over the last couple of chapters, humility. Not that the theme disappeared, for in my semi-technical senses of the term, humility is precisely what the doctrine of mystery is intended to honour. To concede that reality is mysterious is to eschew an absolutist 'hubris of belief', just as to 'appeal' to what is 'beyond the human' is to abandon a humanist 'hubris of posture'. Many thinkers, without understanding the term in quite my senses, have evoked the ancient virtue that it names in connection with the appreciation of mystery. The humble sage, aware of the Tao at work in all that he does, does not 'claim credit for it'.[5] Lao Tzu's words recall the discussion of 'grace' in Chapter 12, where the point—Heidegger's and Nishida's among others—was that, while the world is indeed a 'human world', it is not our Promethean achievement. This is because what we are, as much as what the world with which we 'co-arise' is, owes to a mysterious 'giving'. The association of this point with humility is made explicit by Marcel. We should speak of our own being with humility, since 'this being is something that can only be granted to us as a gift'. Humility is a 'mode of being . . . incompatible with . . . the claim that . . . we are, or have the power to make ourselves, dependent only on ourselves'.[6]

A hyperbolic way of expressing this is found in the references, over the centuries, to the person of humility as one who appreciates his own 'nothingness'. Humility, writes Marcel, is 'not a taste for self-humiliation',

[3] Gabriel Marcel, *The Mystery of Being*, 2 vols., trans. G. S. Fraser (South Bend, Ind.: St Augustine's Press, 2001), i. 43; ii. 37, 46, 61.

[4] In Wing-Tsit Chan (ed.), *A Source Book in Chinese Philosophy* (Princeton, N.J.: Princeton University Press, 1969), chs. 65, 21, 41, 25, 14.

[5] Ibid. ch. 77.

[6] *The Mystery of Being*, ii. 32, 87.

but 'the recognition of our nothingness'.[7] In the mouths of some—the Sūfi mystics, say, and Kierkegaard—the point of the hyperbole is to emphasize the individual person's insignificance in comparison with, as well as his dependence on, a creator God. As employed by Marcel, Meister Eckhart and, as we saw earlier (p. 326), some Buddhists, however, the message of this rhetoric is that the world, though 'our' world, is not of our making. We and the world are 'co-arisen' from a mysterious 'font and source'.

The theme of humility will not disappear from this chapter. Indeed, to the degree that a case for mystery as 'measure-setting' is also one against a hubristic posture that dispenses with appeals to 'something beyond the human', that theme is the chapter's central one. But the possibility will also be explored that the virtue of humility, in a more familiar sense of the term, is manifested in a life which 'measures up'.

What is it, turning to the issue itself, that appeals to mystery are supposed to measure? The short answer is: our lives. These are the lives, we saw in Chapter 10, of inveterately teleological creatures who are not only engaged in purposive projects, but who need to see themselves as such. Unless perm- anently 'tranquillized', we are also reflective creatures who sometimes appraise, take stock of, our activities and purposes. Since these do not arise in a cognitive vacuum, but are informed by beliefs and assumptions about the world and ourselves, we will sometimes want to appraise them as well. To measure our lives, then, is to measure—as I shall label them—both our comportments and our conceptions. Under the former bland term fall our purposive activities and projects, and the evaluations, commitments, norms, moods, and sensibilities these typically register. Under the equally bland latter term fall the concepts we use to think and speak about the world, our empirical beliefs and wider 'world views'.

Two remarks on comportments and conceptions are in place. First, atten- tion will focus on ones of a very general kind. The need for answerability to which a doctrine of mystery might respond is not for measuring this or that particular empirical hypothesis, but for measuring some much larger pic- ture of the world in which such a hypothesis has its place. Again, the need is not for appraising how I treated someone on some occasion, but for measur- ing a more general moral comportment I display towards my fellows. To restrict attention to such general conceptions or comportments is not to 'dodge the issue', for what inspired the search for measure 'beyond the human' was critical reflection on the wider conceptual and normative frameworks within which, typically, particular beliefs and commitments get justified.

Second, while it is useful to break our lives down into comportments and the conceptions they presuppose, this division should be taken as rough and unstable. It was a truth in humanism that our concepts are always embroiled with interests and purposes. So it would be wrong, as we have seen, to suppose that, say, the physicist's view of the world is uncontaminated by our purposes, our general comportment towards the world. Equally, as we also saw, it would be a parody of our purposive behaviour to suppose that, generally, we first take 'neutral' stock of the facts and then adopt or 'choose' a moral or other evaluative stance towards them. When 'in the stream of life', seeing how things stand and seeing what it is appropriate to do—getting out the first aid box, running for cover, or whatever—are seamlessly merged. So we should not regard comportments as bolt-on extras to conceptions.

With this rough reply to the question of what is to be measured, the central question now arises of *how* an appeal to mystery can provide measure. It would take many more pages than I have available to show in any detail how a given conception or comportment does or does not 'measure up'. However, the form of an answer, to which some 'content' will be added, is suggested through considering the pessimistic judgement that an appeal to mystery can provide no measure at all. The pessimist will remind us that the self-emptying or presencing spoken of as the mysterious 'font or source' of the world is not a God who has revealed instructions for our comportment, or into whose mind we might delve to discover 'divine ideas' to which our conceptions should be tailored. If the mysterious really is ineffable, there is no description of it on which to draw in order to adjudicate our ways of belief and behaviour. Or rather, the pessimist might continue, in so far as sense can be made of a notion of mysterious measure, won't it be either totally hospitable or totally inhospitable to our conceptions and comportments? Either way, it will not allow for discrimination. Looked at one way, any conception or comportment is just one more 'gift' of Being, self-emptying, or whatever, hence not something to be refused. Looked at in another way, since no discursive conception corresponds to the way the world independently is, then everything we think and do is founded on illusion or *māyā*, hence nothing to welcome. So, says the pessimist, either our lives always measure up or they never do. Either we are always in the truth and the right or we never are.

The suggestion that a doctrine of mystery is totally inhospitable reminds one of the 'nihilistic' response, discussed in Chapter 12, of some Buddhists and transcendental idealists to the notion of mystery. I shall say no more about it, having been at pains to defend the doctrine of emptiness from the charge of rendering the 'human world' an illusion. The pessimist's alternative suggestion—that, on a doctrine of mystery, no conceptions or comportments could be rejected—ignores a crucial possibility. This is that some of them fail to be consonant with the experience to which the rhetoric of emptiness aimed to attune us. There may be conceptions and comportments to which someone thus attuned cannot subscribe. If so, they fail to 'measure up'. There are several ways, in my judgement, that there can be disconsonance with the experience of mystery. I label the three ways I shall discuss those of *confrontation*, *degradation*, and *occlusion*.

Disconsonant Conceptions (1): Confrontation and Degradation

Shortly, some reminder and elaboration of the notion of the experience of mystery will be required. Even without that, however, it is possible to see how certain accounts of the world and of human life are disconsonant with that experience through, as I call them, confrontation and degradation. An account confronts that experience when, quite simply, it denies truth or sense to any doctrine of mystery that endorses such experience. If the impugnments of mystery by Putnam and Rorty discussed in Chapter 11 really flow from their philosophical positions, then those positions disconsonantly confront the experience of mystery. Unsurprisingly, absolutist and raw humanist accounts of the world will be disconsonant in this way, for according to these, reality is discursable. There is no room in it for mystery in my sense. The absolutist, certainly, may allow for mystery of a less radical kind. Like Nagel, he may think it probable that there are aspects of reality that we shall never fully understand. But that is not to allow for a doctrine of mystery of the kind with which I have been concerned. A humanist may allow for this: indeed, the champions of mystery discussed in the previous chapter *were* humanists—but not *raw* humanists, of course. In their case, a doctrine of mystery *compensated* for the raw thesis of 'the human world'.

Since absolutism and raw humanism had already been rejected by the time a doctrine of mystery was introduced—since, indeed, it was introduced in order to escape the impasse created by their simultaneous rejections—it can come as no news that, according to this doctrine, neither of those metaphysical conceptions 'measures up'. It then follows that any conceptions, convictions, and beliefs that presuppose one or other of those metaphysical positions also fail to 'measure up'.

More interesting, because less obvious, is the failure to 'measure up' of conceptions that are disconsonant through their *degradation* of the experience of mystery. A conception degrades an experience when, without any direct doctrinal confrontation, it entails that the experience cannot be taken at face value. For example, on Schopenhauer's unromantic conception of erotic life, my experience of loving a woman for her admirable qualities is degraded: as the blind expression of a cosmic will to procreate, my 'love' is not what it seems to me to be, not—what is anyway impossible—'true love'.

It is not difficult to think of conceptions of human behaviour and motivation that degrade the experience of mystery, ones familiar from the many attempts to 'explain away' and otherwise 'rubbish' religious experience. If Marx, Nietzsche, and Freud—those 'masters', as Paul Ricoeur calls them, of a 'hermeneutics of suspicion'—are right, then we need not take seriously people's alleged experiences of the divine or the mysterious, since these are merely symptoms of a failure, however understandable, to take the world as it is. If I recognize the *pudenda origo*, as Nietzsche called it, of my experience—perhaps my need, as a weakling, for a 'higher world' to compensate for the one that oppresses me—I can no longer invest it with the significance I once did.

Such conditional statements may be true: but in that case, so are the logically equivalent 'reverse' conditionals. If, despite reading my Nietzsche or Marx, I *do* continue to invest my experience of mystery with its face-value significance, then I must reject their conceptions of the human condition. Indeed, if, convinced of the unbelievability of absolutism and the unlivability of raw humanism, I cannot but take seriously the attractions of mystery, then I am compelled to reject those conceptions. In doing so, I do not question-beggingly assume the truth of a doctrine of mystery in order to denounce those conceptions. Rather, as someone impelled to enjoy—or at least hold himself open to enjoy—a certain way of experiencing the world, I cannot then view the experience with 'suspicion'. Hence I am compelled to judge that the conceptions which enforce suspicion—which degrade my experience—fail to 'measure up'.

It is not only conceptions with the intent of suspicion that degrade the experience of mystery. Consider the physicist's conception of the world. If that conception embraces human life—as for many contemporary scientists it does—then it, too, entails that the experience of mystery cannot be taken seriously. This is because it belongs to that conception to regard all events and states as explicable in terms of the categories and laws of physics. Now, to hold that the experience of mystery is thus explicable is to degrade it: for it excludes an interpretation of the experience that is integral to it from the point of view of the experiencer. For him, it is an experience that is directed towards, is a response to, and has its 'font and source' in, what is mysterious. That experience could not survive the degradation it would undergo were he to accept that it was the product, simply, of physical laws. The physicist qua physicist need not deny and directly confront every doctrine of mystery. Maybe he is a Plotinian who thinks that the physical world is an 'emanation' of the ineffable 'One'. But what he must do, if his physicalism extends to the human mind, is divest any experience of mystery of the import it has for the experiencer. (This point, parenthetically, shares the logic of one made by Husserl and some more recent philosophers—to the effect that physics degrades *itself*. The physicist's conception entails that his own arguments and statements cannot have the epistemic status he requires if they are to command rational assent. For, on that conception, they are, like everything else, simply sets of physical events caused through the operation of physical laws.)[8]

Disconsonant Conceptions (2): Occlusion

The final way in which conceptions may be disconsonant with the experience of mystery is through *occluding* it. Here it will be useful to elaborate

---

[8] See Edmund Husserl, *The Crisis of European Sciences and Transcendental Phenomenology*, trans. D. Carr (Evanston, Ill.: Northwestern University Press, 1970), and, for a good recent example of the argument in question, Frederick A. Olafson, *What Is a Human Being: A Heideggerian View* (Cambridge: Cambridge University Press, 1995), ch. 7.

earlier remarks on this experience. In Chapters 11 and 12, it was emphasized that it should not be assimilated to perceptual experience of some object. Mystery is not an entity accessed by some mystical analogue to visual perception. To experience mystery is to experience the world in certain ways—those gestured at by the rhetoric of emptiness. For analogues in everyday experience, we do better to think of, say, a soldier's experience of the war, or a student's experience of university life—of, one might say, 'existential' experience. When the student describes his or her experience of the university, it may well include reports of sense-experiences, but these will hardly exhaust it, and we would expect even these to be more than 'bare' ones—to relate, for example, how the first sight of the ivy-clad buildings *impressed* the student. An account of experience in this richer, 'existential' sense narrates how someone's world—the university, the war theatre—figures for him, what it is like for him.

We may not agree with William James that 'the essence of religious experience' resides in the 'uneasy'sense that 'there is something wrong about us as we naturally stand', accompanied by a further sense that we 'are saved from the wrongness by making the proper connection with the higher powers'.[9] But one should applaud his attempt to think about religious experience, not on the model of sense-experience, but through the way a person's world is 'tinged' for him. Indeed, one might follow Marcel and speak of experience, in this richer sense, as a 'mode of being'—the soldier's, the student's, or one we generally share in. But 'mode of being' does not bring out an element central to experience in its many forms—that of 'receptivity'. The soldier recounting his experience does not analyse or theorize about the war, but tells how things and events impressed him, presented themselves to him, 'struck' him. In the case of sense-experience, a rough distinction is legitimately drawn between reports of an experience and further claims inferred *from* the experience. It is one thing, similarly, for our lives to be uneasily 'tinged' for us and another thing to conclude, on the basis of theological argument, that they are a certain way. Only the former—how we 'receive' our lives—belongs, for James, to religious *experience*.

Experience of mystery, then, is a receptive mode of being in the world, a way the world presents itself. More precisely, it is a reception of the world as

---

[9] *The Varieties of Religious Experience* (New York: Longmans, Green & Co., 1923), 508.

the transparent, grace-given epiphany 'about' which the preceding chapter spoke. It is this experience which conceptions may occlude. Something occludes an experience when it obstructs the having of it or distorts it. That conceptions may do this will only sound odd to those fixated on sense-experience. For, in the case of the latter, it is not conceptions but drunken-ness, jaundice, and other conditions that impede 'veridical' perception which provide the stock examples of occlusion. It is not odd, however, to propose that conceptions may occlude 'existential' experience. Clearly, for example, a student's (pre)conceptions can stand in the way of or distort his or her experience of university life.

Conceptions may be appraised in terms of their conduciveness to experience. They may be too one-sided, partial, or bland to enable an environment or world to be appropriately experienced or received. Occluding conceptions should, however, be distinguished from ones that are simply mistaken. Not every false belief about the university renders someone less receptive: indeed, some may render him more so. Importantly, such conceptions must be rejected—if not *in toto*, then to a degree—by anyone who does succeed in enjoying the experience that he recognizes them as occluding. The soldier who comes to experience the war as, in Sebastian Faulks's words, 'an exploration of how far man can be degraded',[10] cannot subscribe to the rookie's image of war as a theatre for noble heroism. A person's 'existential' experience, therefore, serves as a measure of conceptions, for those which would occlude the possibility of that experience cannot command assent from him.

These considerations apply to the experience of mystery. Some conceptions occlude that experience and so cannot 'measure up' for anyone who is receptive to it. It would be the subject for another book to establish which conceptions in fact occlude the experience of mystery. Here I can only indicate the occluding role played by at least a certain range of conceptions. The point is not to show that certain conceptions are false *because* they occlude the experience of mystery. The argument for mystery came earlier: it offered the only escape from the impasse reached by the end of Chapter 10. The aim, rather, is to explore how someone attuned by the doctrine of emptiness is then in a position to measure conceptions of the world, and hence to fulfil the promise that gave the doctrine its initial attraction.

---

[10] *Birdsong* (London: Vintage, 1994), 150.

My proposal is that, for someone attuned to mystery, certain conceptions indeed fail to 'measure up'—those that occlude the very experience attuned to.

Many conceptions perhaps occlude the experience of mystery, but I shall consider only one general kind—'theoretical conceptions', as I label them. My focus is not randomly chosen, for it is a cluster of theoretical conceptions that now passes for educated common sense and imbues our kind of culture. By a theoretical conception of X—of nature, the mind, language, or even the world as a whole—I mean a conception that *privileges* a theoretical account of X. Hence it is not, say, the chemical theory in which water is described as H_2O that is a theoretical conception, but the idea that this description is a privileged one. Again, one should distinguish the theory that gives an account of thoughts and desires in neurophysiological terms from the conception that privileges such an account. Theoretical conceptions should also be distinguished from certain metaphysical views on the status of the theories. It may be that someone who privileges a certain theoretical description is an absolutist, a scientific realist for whom it uniquely captures how things anyway, independently are. But it is possible for anti-realists— pragmatists or humanists, say—to privilege the description as well. Indeed, plenty of them do urge theoretical conceptions of the world on us.[11]

I need to explain 'theory' and 'privilege'. Roughly, I identify 'theory' with 'scientific theory', though since some of the theories in question belong to such disciplines as linguistics and anthropology, 'science' should be taken broadly, in something like the sense of 'Wissenschaft'. Scientific theory is often viewed as based on and answerable to experience, but the crucial feature of theories that I have in mind is their *remoteness* from experience. The chemist and the neurophysiologist describe water and desire in terms remote from people's familiar experience of these items. The generative grammarian and the functionalist anthropologist do not describe conversations and rituals as conversationalists and tribesmen do, for theirs is not the task of recounting 'existential' experiences of conversing or sacrificing. That theory is thus remote from experience is compatible with viewing scientific theory as empirical. That the anthropologist's description is not one that records the tribesman's experience does not mean that he cannot make

---

[11] Neither Quine nor Rorty are absolutists, but both urge upon us the privileged status of physics' account of the world.

observations that inspire and perhaps confirm his theory of tribal behaviour. I leave the distinction between theoretical and experiential descriptions of X vague—which indeed it is, especially in an age when people 'brought up' on science readily reach for terms borrowed from bodies of theory to describe their experiences. The distinction is nevertheless crucial and often stark: no one's desires figure for them *as* firings of neurones; no one enjoys his beer *as* a collection of molecules.

I leave the expression 'privileging of theory' vague as well. Instead of defining it, I rehearse some attitudes, popular among both modern philosophers and a wider intellegentsia, that surely invite the expression. Because theory is more or less remote from experience, the question arises of the ranking of the respective descriptions they generate. From Democritus to Quine, many philosophers have awarded the laurels to theory. For Democritus, judgements that reflect experience have only a 'bastard' claim to knowledge, while for Quine 'whatever can be known can be known by means of science' alone.[12] At its most brutal, as with Democritus, privileging theory takes the form of simply rejecting the narratives of experience as erroneous. Our experience of objects as coloured, of actions as unjust, of landscapes as sublime is in error if, as widely accepted theories inform us, the world is devoid of such properties.[13] Slightly less brutally, privileging may assume the form of declaring that descriptions of experience themselves embody 'folk' or ur-theories that fare badly in comparison to those of modern science. One hears, for example, that the vocabulary of 'folk psychology'—'belief', 'desire', and so on—deployed in everyday descriptions of our ('existential') experience with people and animals, is that of a 'failed', 'hopelessly primitive and deeply confused' conception that should be scrapped in favour of neurophysiological theory.[14] Less brutally still, privileging may take the form of holding that, while experience informs us of the relatively accidental or superficial aspects of things, theory is required to identify their essential aspects—to tell us what the things fundamentally *are*.

---

[12] Democritus, Fragment DK 68 B11, in Jonathan Barnes, *The Presocratic Philosophers* (London: Routledge & Kegan Paul, 1982); W. V. Quine, 'Philosophical Progress in Language Theory', *Metaphilosophy*, 1 (1970), 1. See also the quote from Wilfrid Sellars on p. 175 above.

[13] I use the term 'error' as a nod towards J. L. Mackie, *Ethics: Inventing Right and Wrong* (Harmondsworth: Penguin, 1978), where a much discussed 'error theory' of moral experience is urged.

[14] Paul M. Churchland, *Matter and Consciousness: A Contemporary Introduction to the Philosophy of Mind* (Cambridge, Mass.: MIT Press, 1988), 45.

Experience shows that water is usually transparent and tasteless, but we need chemistry to spell out the essential *nature* of water, the one it has 'in every possible world'. The speaker's experience of his language enables him to gloss the sentences he utters, but it is the generative grammarian who identifies the deep structures where meanings really reside.

There are further ways in which theory gets privileged over experience, but those indicated suffice to convey the flavour of the privileging practices endemic in modern culture. Naturally, there have always been dissenting voices. Even Democritus hesitated: in a nice conceit, sense-experience admonishes intellect, 'you take your evidence from us and then overthrow us . . . [But] our overthrow is your downfall'.[15] In recent times, Heidegger and Wittgenstein have been tenacious critics of privilege. What is really 'messing up' modern thought, wrote the former, is 'the dominance and primacy of the *theoretical*', while, for the latter, 'it is by no means obvious' that the hegemony of science and technology is not 'the beginning of the end for humanity'.[16] As the strong language suggests, their concern is as much for the 'vital' dangers of 'the primacy of the theoretical' as with the philosophical confusions it reflects. In particular, the privileging of theory occludes experience. 'By looking at the world theoretically', said Heidegger, 'we have already dimmed it down to [a] uniformity', with the effect, as he later wrote, that 'ways of revealing' close to our experience of it get 'driven out'.[17] For Wittgenstein, similarly, the 'cold grey ash' of scientific theory extinguishes 'the glowing embers' of life.[18] There cannot be that 'celebration of . . . ordinary and everyday' experience, of which Nishida spoke (p. 314 above), in a climate where this is viewed as 'erroneous', 'primitive and confused', 'superficial', 'unserious'. And when such a view prevails, there will be occlusion: for who will cultivate and remain receptive to 'ways of revealing' thus impugned? If, in the case of some privilegers, there is no occlusion, this must be *despite* the privilege they accord to theory. Perhaps, like other figures encountered in this book, they are guilty of a 'fashionable put-on' in parroting the *idées fixes* of their age.

---

[15] Democritus, Fragment DK 68 B125, in Barnes, *The Presocratic Philosophers*.

[16] Martin Heidegger, *Gesamtausgabe*, vol. 56/57 (Frankfurt a. M.: Klostermann, 1987), 87; Ludwig Wittgenstein, *Culture and Value*, trans. P. Winch (Oxford: Blackwell, 1980), 6–7.

[17] *Being and Time*, trans. J. Macquarrie and E. Robinson (Oxford: Blackwell, 1962), 178; *The Question Concerning Technology and Other Essays*, trans. W. Lovitt (New York: Harper & Row, 1977), 27.

[18] *Culture and Value*, 56.

For Heidegger and Wittgenstein, certainly, experience both of art and the natural world is occluded by the 'the primacy of the theoretical'. There can, thinks Heidegger, no longer be experience of 'great art', which 'reveals' a world, since only science is these days held to 'reveal'. Artworks have a mere 'use-value' in a contemporary 'art business', as commodities for producing 'sensations' and other 'subjective' responses.[19] Wittgenstein, in similar vein, laments that 'people nowadays think that scientists exist to instruct them, poets, musicians etc. to give them pleasure'. They no longer imagine that artists, too, 'have something to teach' and 'reveal' about our world.[20] Nature cannot remain, argues Heidegger, one that 'stirs and strives', 'assails and enthralls us', once it is 'dimmed down' to a 'world-stuff' that, though still affording some pleasures and thrills, is the business, for all serious purposes, of science alone.[21] For Wittgenstein, 'the most important questions are concealed' when someone is dismissed as 'stupid' who does not understand that water simply '*consists* of the gases hydrogen and oxygen'.[22] For both philosophers, it is the abundance of ways in which natural things may figure for us that, to recall Feyerabend's phrase (pp. 150–1 above), gets 'conquered' through the privileging of theory. The conquest of abundance is the occlusion of experience.

Will occlusion of the experience of mystery simply be one instance of the much wider tendency just discussed? This suggestion may sound problematic, for what has been discussed is the occlusion of what should be familiar and available to all of us. Experience of mystery is surely too esoteric and *extra*-ordinary for its occlusion to belong to the tendency described. Nevertheless, it is an occlusion that Heidegger and Wittgenstein, once more, attribute to theoretical conceptions. If, for Heidegger, there is to occur that 'other beginning' to 'echo' the Greek experience of mystery, it will require loosening the grip that a scientific and technological 'way of revealing' has come to exert.[23] If, as Wittgenstein puts it, 'man has to awaken to wonder', then the hegemony of science, which is a 'way of sending him to sleep again', must be resisted.[24]

[19] Martin Heidegger, *On the Way to Language*, trans. P. Hertz (San Francisco, Calif.: Harper & Row, 1982), 42 ff.

[20] *Culture and Value*, 36.

[21] *Being and Time*, 100.

[22] *Culture and Value*, 71.

[23] *Contributions to Philosophy*, Pt. II.

[24] *Culture and Value*, 5.

For these philosophers, as for those in the Zen tradition, the contrast just mooted between the mysterious and the ordinary is a false one. To begin with, it should be re-emphasized that experience of mystery is not of something disjoint from or transcendent of the ordinary, familiar world. When Heidegger says that our modern 'way of revealing' heralds 'the oblivion of Being', he is not complaining, like some medieval ascetic, of distraction from the otherwordly. A main attraction of Wittgenstein's later philosophy, according to one perceptive commentator, is that it is 'focused on to ordinary aspects of life, without losing [a] sense of the mystery of things'.[25] And the thought that experience of mystery is a way of experiencing, of being with, the ordinary and familiar is encapsulated in the Buddhists' slogan that there is 'nothing special' about enlightenment. Indeed, says Dōgen, 'if you seek [enlightenment] outside of sense-experience, you will hinder the living meaning of Zen'.[26]

Champions of mystery, however, make a more radical complaint about the opposing of mystery to the ordinary. That the world presents itself as tinged with mystery is, so to speak, the *default* mode of experiencing it. Such experience seems esoteric and extra-ordinary only to people whom theoretical conceptions have educated out of that mode, people whose 'innocence' they have spoiled. It is no objection to this claim that 'people' here refers to nearly all of us, nor that some theories privileged by those conceptions long ago seeped into a widely received understanding of the world. If the Buddhists and Heidegger are right, these theories include, for example, the idea that things have 'own being', are 'substances' only externally, contingently related to one another. Modern scientific theories, on this view, only reinforce a relegation of experience that less 'professional' theories have for millennia been responsible for. Experience of mystery, far from having to be a virtuoso achievement, is the mode of experiencing the world that would be enjoyed by people innocent of theory and receptive to the world. This is Dōgen's message when he writes that we *are*, from the outset, Buddha-nature: enlightenment does not confer it, but removes obstacles to self-understanding. More generally, the Buddha-nature—the 'suchness' of everything, not just of ourselves—is 'manifest before us', or would be but

---

[25] David Pears, *The False Prison*, 2 vols. (Oxford: Oxford University Press, 1987–8), i. 17.

[26] In T. Cleary (ed.), *Rational Zen: The Mind of Dōgen Zenji* (Boston, Mass.: Shambhala, 1995), 59.

for occlusion. 'To look' with the 'innocent' eye 'at mountains and rivers is to look at the Buddha-nature'.[27]

The thought that people innocent of theoretical conceptions would experience a mysterious world is familiar among anthropologists. Typically, though, theirs is the thought that such people populate their world with dark, 'spooky' beings to explain the vicissitudes of life and nature. But this is to think of such people, not as 'pre-theoretical', but as up to their elbows in theory, albeit of a 'primitive' kind. This is the approach that Wittgenstein criticized Sir James Frazer for adopting, and a quite different one from that urged by champions of mystery. Their point is that, in the absence of theoretical conceptions, whether of a primitive or sophisticated type, the world would be experienced as a transparent, grace-given epiphany. If they are right, an experience of mystery available today will indeed be an 'echo' of innocence.

It remains to indicate how theoretical conceptions may occlude aspects of mystery, beginning with that of transparency. A target of several philosophers—Bradley and Bergson, for example—has been an 'atomistic' view of the world that, they argue, is the outcome of a theory-driven obsession with the 'analysis' of what is encountered in experience. It is theory-driven since the aim is to arrive at descriptions tailored to prediction and causal explanation. However sophisticated these descriptions are in modern science, and however 'micro' the elements described, the search for them is inspired by a focus on things as spatio-temporal particulars and on certain 'primary' features of them, like motion. And what lies behind that focus is the conviction that a conception of the world as so many contingently related particulars, whose causally efficacious features are their 'essential' ones, is the one most apt to enable explanatory ambitions. The critics' complaint is not that it is a 'mistake' to view objects, for certain purposes, as 'extended substances' or the like, analysable into 'micro' components and their relations. Rather it is to emphasize how constricted this view is, how 'abstracted' from the rich realm of experience that it threatens. This was surely Wittgenstein's point when complaining that the 'most important questions'—about the place of water in human life, say—are 'concealed' when water is understood simply as a stuff, H_2O.

---

[27] Dōgen, *Shobogenzo*, trans. G. Nishijima and C. Cross (London: Windbell, 1996), ii. 5–6.

This example invites expression in the language of transparency. To experience something as transparent, recall, is to experience it, in a 'double exposure', as empty, as 'dissolving' into, yet as a 'space' for the 'gathering' or 'con-centrating' of, a whole. ('I saw . . . what is meant by emptiness', relates a Tibetan monk, when 'the fruit . . . seemed at once so solid and so fragile that a breath could blow it away'[28]—so 'con-centrated' and 'dissolving', he might have said.) It is a way of experiencing remote from a focus on things as discrete particulars contingently or 'externally' related to one another. It is, for example, to appreciate the pool of water as what reflects the sky and children are baptized in, what animals struggle to reach and sustains the life of plants, and what men and women bathe in for pleasure or purification— as what, in these and innumerable other ways, 'points to' a world. It is to appreciate, as well, how a world, to be that world, 'gathers' into the pool, for things, practices, and creatures that do not so relate to water would not be the ones they are, not those that figure as they do in 'existential' experience.[29] Such experience of a pool, and hence of the world as a whole, can only be gestured at, only spoken 'about'. It belongs to the experience of mystery and is something that theoretical conceptions, with their predilection for the discrete and 'atomic', occlude.

The idea of grace was introduced (p. 324 above) when criticizing a Promethean humanism and a transcendental idealism that, while rightly proclaiming the thesis of 'the human world', treat this world as 'our handiwork', something 'constructed' or something conditioned by a priori structures of subjectivity. Both were guilty of ignoring that we ourselves, our subjectivity, 'co-originate' with the world, in Nishida's words, 'through mutual interexpression'. At a deep level, the world is not shaped or structured by us: rather we-and-the-world 'arise' or are 'given' together.

But why should the sense of we-and-the-world as grace-given be occluded by theoretical conceptions? After all, most theorists, one suspects, are neither Prometheans nor transcendental idealists. Nevertheless, there is reason to judge that the privileging of theory does occlude this sense. In Chapter 8, attention was drawn to the thoroughly active character of

---

[28] Quoted in Andrew Harvey, *A Journey in Ladakh* (London: Flamingo, 1983), 204.

[29] My elaboration of Wittgenstein's example consciously recalls Heidegger's notion of 'the thing' as 'the gathering of the fourfold'—gods, mortals, sky, and earth—in his *Poetry, Language, Thought*, 174.

theoretical enquiry—to theory construction, regimentation of data, experiment, and so on—and to scientific enquiry as a form of activity peculiar to a certain kind of culture. Attention was also drawn to the reliance of such enquiry upon 'ground-plans'—on criteria for what counts as real, on standards of reason and evidence, and the like—which settle in advance the type of results to be obtained. As Heidegger put it, 'science always encounters what *its* kind of representation has admitted beforehand as an object possible for it'.[30] In that chapter, such observations were deployed in a critique of scientific realism, in an attempt to secure the thesis of 'the human world'. In the present context, their purpose is different: to secure the contention that theoretical conceptions occlude the sense of grace.

The observations prompt two related thoughts vital to that contention. First, the products of theoretical enquiry—active, constructive, purposive as it is—are indeed 'our handiwork': that of people who, one might put it, are already 'defined', already there 'in place', their identities shaped and bequeathed by a certain kind of culture—people endowed with a relatively determinate 'second nature'. Hence to privilege theoretical enquiry is to regard the 'serious' revelation of the world as the achievement of creatures with identities and a 'nature' already 'defined' prior to that achievement. Correspondingly, it is to relegate ways of revealing or experiencing—ones belonging to forms of life that constitute the backdrop against which theoretical enquiry emerges—that cannot similarly be regarded as 'our handiwork'. They cannot be since, without these ways, there is no 'we'—no determinate subjectivity—whose handiwork the achievements of theory could be. We cannot be 'abstracted' from these 'primordial' ways of experiencing—and hence from the world as it figures in them—in the manner that the theoretician can be from his particular construals of the world. Dōgen wrote that 'the world realizes us [as much] as we realize the world'.[31] That stands to be forgotten when theory is privileged and when the focus is squarely on our achievement in 'realizing the world'.

The second thought begins by recalling that, theory being 'remote' from experience, the world it describes does not present itself to us *as* so described. Items and properties are attributed to the world not through 'innocent' reception, but in accordance with an actively determined

30 Ibid. 170.
31 Quoted in Cleary (ed.), *Rational Zen*, 133 n.

'ground-plan'. The theoretician's descriptions are not fitted to experience of the world, rather the world is fitted to the best theoretical descriptions of it—with what is 'best' already settled by 'ground-plans'. To privilege theory, therefore, is to promote a certain relation we can have to the world: not that of experiential engagement, but one we have as occupants of a standpoint from which we decide how the world is—the standpoint of 'world-makers', makers at any rate of those accounts that reality is required to satisfy. As occupants of that standpoint, we are, in a good sense, outside the world we 'make', and certainly not creatures who, in Nishida's sense, 'co-originate' with it. Representations of the world from that standpoint, when privileged, cannot have the status of anything represented by them—cannot, for example, be episodes either necessitated by nature or that 'just happened'.[32]

These two thoughts conspire towards the conclusion that theoretical conceptions occlude a sense of ourselves as 'given': a sense, better, of we-and-the-world as a single 'gift' that may only artificially be bisected into subjectivity and its objects. They occlude by fostering a more or less Promethean self-understanding, an exaggerated picture of what, as the Taoists put it, we can 'claim credit for'. For they inspire the conviction that 'serious' descriptions are the achievements of creatures who, far from being 'co-arisen' with and 'shaped' by the world in experiential engagement, act at a distance from the world whose nature they allegedly articulate.

How, finally, could theoretical conceptions occlude experience of epiphany? That experience, as gestured at in the previous chapter, was experience of the world as one to which we, as 'co-arisen' with it, are essential, yet—'wondrously'—as present to us 'just as it is'. For it is a world experienced as a 'gift' of—something come 'out of'—an ineffable, inexplicable 'presencing' or 'self-emptying' that is nothing 'hidden' behind what is present. Theoretical conceptions threaten occlusion of this for two reasons. First, a culture in which theoretical conceptions are entrenched is liable to be one where pretensions to total explicability impress the imagination. Nothing seems mysterious or inexplicable in principle: the explanation of everything may be just around the corner. Despite the frequency with which

---

[32] It is no rebuttal of this point to mention that human beings have themselves become objects of theoretical enquiry. This simply prompts the problem perceived by Foucault (p. 140 above): that of man as a 'strange empirico-transcendental doublet', at once within and without the domain of knowledge whose source is supposed to be his handiwork.

such pretensions are proclaimed, they are not, however, essential to theoretical ambition:[33] as we saw, there can be an admission of basic, brute contingency in the order of things. But that admission, while it allows for mystery in one sense, is, as we also saw, scarcely less inimical to the idea of the world as an epiphany of what is mysterious than are pretensions to total explicability. What is brutely contingent is not the 'gift' of anything, not a way that presencing issues in something present.

Occlusion is threatened in a second way. When recording the 'Asian experience' in Chapter 10, I expressed some sympathy with the feeling that, were there only 'the human world', it would be *māyā*, illusion, and, in Schopenhauer's words, 'pass us by like an empty dream'. Even if he, Śaṃkara, and others were wrong to suppose that raw humanism entails the illusoriness of the world, they were right to perceive that it is an unendurable position. I was less sympathetic to the Schopenhauerian and Advaitin alternative, that the world of ordinary experiece is not an *empty* dream, since it is a 'veil' between us and the noumenal—the 'veneer' of a cosmic will or *brahman*. The world as experienced is not, on that alternative, an epiphany of the real, but its façade.

These reflections are relevant since it is legitimate to regard Schopenhauer and the Advaitins as articulating theoretical conceptions. Both attribute to reality entities and properties that, while beyond the reach of familiar experience, serve to explain it. While the theoretical conceptions mentioned on pp. 342 f may be less dramatic, more 'modern' and 'scientific'—and while their champions may not impugn our pre-theoretical conceptions as 'illusory'[34]—they follow their metaphysical predecessors in treating what is encountered in experience as superficial. For 'serious' purposes, it is not this veneer that we should be describing, but the structures, processes, or whatever identified by theorists. This image of the world in which we are engaged through experience as a veneer is at odds with, and an occlusion of, the idea of it as epiphany. 'You will', to repeat Dōgen's warning, 'hinder the living meaning of Zen' by seeking enlightened

---

[33] Or so I suppose, but one should recall Kant's view that all scientific enquiries presuppose a regulative ideal of a total explanation to which they contribute.

[34] But remember the remarks of Churchland on 'folk psychology' (p. 343 above). It is worth recalling, too, that on one influential interpretation of Kant, his things in themselves are things considered in terms of the intrinsic physical properties that science has striven to identify. See Rae Langton, *Kantian Humility: Our Ignorance of Things in Themselves* (Oxford: Clarendon Press, 1998).

understanding 'outside' of experience. The ineffable which is, as he put it, 'something . . . coming like this', comes in full abundance—as the world we experience, receive, and describe in myriad ways. Descriptions of a 'dimmed-down' world of theory have their place, of course: but to privilege that place is to occlude the sense of our abundant world as epiphany.

This completes my indication of the modes—confrontation, degradation, occlusion—in which conceptions may be disconsonant with the experience of mystery. If these conceptions are thus disconsonant, they cannot be embraced by someone attuned to mystery. They fail, therefore, to 'measure up' by the measure that the sense of mystery itself provides.

Consonance and Comportment

In Chapter 10 and the present chapter, the issue of a measure for conceptions was presented as deriving from that of a measure for comportments—our purposive activities, projects, norms, and commitments. We need conceptions to answer to something 'beyond the human' because we need the comportments that presuppose them to be answerable. Once, as I put it, we become 'available' and reflection sets in, then, as inveterately teleological creatures, we seek measure for the direction of our lives. The present issue, then, is whether a doctrine of mystery—specifically one of emptiness—has the resources for providing any. How, if at all, may comportments be answerable to mystery? My treatment of the issue will be fairly brief, despite its emergence as a central one whose resolution is required if the doctrine of mystery is to provide more than a 'formal' escape from the impasse reached with the demise of raw humanism and absolutism. I shall be brief because I can partly follow the contours of the discussion of disconsonant conceptions, but also because treatment of so large an issue that went beyond promissory notes would require another book or the addition to this already lengthy one of several more chapters. What follows, then, is little more than a prologomenon.

Many writers have been sceptical of seeking guidance for the direction of our lives from doctrines of mystery. From the Confucian critics of Taoist appeals to an indescribable Way to critics of Heidegger's summons to hear 'the call of Being', the complaint has been that invocations of mystery are without implication for the conduct of life.[35] One thinks, for example, of the frequently voiced suspicion that Buddhism, with its emphasis on the achievement of enlightenment, is incapable of cogent provision of moral guidance.[36] Scepticism or suspicion has doubtless been encouraged by remarks on morality made by some champions of mystery. An 'artificial' concern with righteousness and virtue, according to the *Tao Te Ching* (ch. 38), only begins 'when Tao is lost'; for Wittgenstein, moral discourse, given that ethics is among the 'things that cannot be put into words', is 'just *gassing*';[37] Heidegger is invariably hostile to talk of 'values'. As for Zen, this can sound positively antinomial with respect to the moral life. 'If you are a real man, you may by all means . . . grab the food from a starving man', declared one master, while, according to a contemporary Zen philosopher, 'in Buddhism what is essential for salvation is to be emancipated from the . . . antinomy of good and evil'.[38]

No doubt these writers have their individual reasons for apparent hostility or indifference to moral discourse. I suspect, however, that they all share the sense, indicated by the remark from the *Tao Te Ching*, that, so to speak, ethics always comes too late: something has already gone wrong with our lives when preoccupation with good versus evil, with rights and values, sets in. The Way is already 'lost', the experience of mystery already 'forgotten'. Be that as it may, and despite their hostile remarks, it is clear that none of these writers is without a perception of how our lives should go. Moreover, there is surely an agreement among them that these should be lives led in awareness of the 'things that cannot be put into words'.

But what sort of lives or comportments are these? The issue returns: how may mystery provide measure? Perhaps the critic's scepticism or suspicion was due to a hope for, but failure to find, a certain sort of answer to that question: the identification of ultimate principles or moral facts to which our comportments are answerable. But, of course, that should never have

---

[35] For such criticism of Heidegger, see Herman Philipse, *Heidegger's Philosophy of Being* (Princeton: Princeton University Press, 1999), and Stanley Rosen, *The Question of Being* (New Haven, Conn.: Yale University Press, 1993).

[36] This suspicion has been voiced by, among others, Max Weber, Albert Schweitzer, and Hans Küng.

[37] Ludwig Wittgenstein, *Tractatus Logico-Philosophicus*, trans. D. Pears and B. McGuinness (London: Routledge, 1988), 6. 522, and Paul Engelmann (ed.), *Letters from Ludwig Wittgenstein with a Memoir*, trans. L. Furtmuller (Oxford: Blackwell, 1967), 143.

[38] Yuan-wu, quoted in Alan W. Watts, *The Way of Zen* (London: Arkana, 1990), 167; Masao Abe, in D. W. Mitchell (ed.), *Masao Abe: A Zen Life of Dialogue* (Boston, Mass.: Tuttle, 1998), 391.

been the hope. The mysterious is not a God whose moral word we may discern and communicate. That a doctrine of mystery cannot provide measure in that manner, however, does not entail that it cannot do so at all.

To begin with, certain comportments, like certain conceptions, may be disconsonant with the experience of mystery, in one or more of the modes discussed in the previous sections. Indeed, it seems obvious that certain 'lifestyles' and the normative attitudes they embody will *occlude* that experience. William James somewhere recalls his rueful realization that dedication to sensuality is incompatible with one to philosophic contemplation. While, as the Buddha learned, cultivation of a sense of mystery may not demand extreme austerity and self-denial, it surely does require the prolonged periods of calm concentration and detachment from more hedonistic pursuits that—despite tales of priapic or bibulous Taoist and Sūfi adepts— champions of mystery have consistently recommended. The 'Follow your fancy!' ethic of Nietzsche's 'last man' or of today's dedicated preachers of 'fun' is therefore disconsonant with the experience of mystery.

Less obviously, yet an implication of the preceding section, is that those comportments will occlude that inspire and are inspired by theoretical conceptions. Since those conceptions occlude, so do the norms and practices that help to entrench them. Consider, as a striking instance, the 'technological stance' or, as David Wiggins calls it when pitting it against the 'disposition of piety', the stance of 'rationalistic calculation'. This is, or entails, in Wiggins's words, a 'willingness to see the natural order and the palimpsest inscribed upon it by the efforts of all our human predecessors refashioned anywhere or everywhere in the image of our desires'.[39] Arguably that willingness alone, when translated into an unbooted 'refashioning' of our world, is itself disconsonant with a sense of mystery. But my present point is to connect that comportment with the privileging of theories of the kind discussed in the previous section. That connection was made by Heidegger in his discussion of technology. Theoretical 'ways of thinking' about the natural world are 'consequences of the hidden interpretation of beings in terms of machination'[40]—his term for the 'rationalistic calcula-

---

[39] David Wiggins, 'From Piety to a Cosmic Order', *Times Higher Education Supplement*, 4 Oct 1996, 22. In this article, Wiggins is generally endorsing points he locates in Roger Scruton, *Animal Rights and Wrongs* (London: Demos, 1996).

[40] *Contributions to Philosophy*, 88.

tion' elegantly characterized by Wiggins. Heidegger's thought is that it is 'by disenchanting beings'—by abstracting them, as theory necessarily does, from the 'abundance' of experience in which they figure—that 'machination' is made possible. 'Dimmed down' to clusters of atoms or cells, creatures and things become 'neutral', plastic objects, without any significance except for the value conferred upon them as 'equipment' to be 'refashioned' as we desire.

Heidegger could have added the point that it is not 'mechanistic and biological' theories per se that are 'consequences' of the technological stance. Rather it is the elevation of the descriptions they provide to the status of uniquely 'serious' and 'objective' ones—ones that, to recall Wittgenstein's H_2O example, we must be 'stupid' not to recognize as telling us how things fundamentally are. One might imagine a culture in which theoretical descriptions are accepted, but where they enjoy no special privilege. They are descriptions like any others—fine in their proper place and for their proper purpose. It is only when that place and purpose are privileged that other 'ways of revealing' are relegated to the 'non-serious'. In particular, it is when the imperatives of prediction, control and 'refashioning' dominate— when 'machination' gives its stamp to a culture—that theoretical descriptions assume paramount authority.

A salient example of occluding complicity between theoretical conceptions and comportments is provided by a development that Heidegger, with prescience and hyperbole, predicted when alluding to an 'attack upon the nature of man compared with which . . . the hydrogen bomb means little'.[41] This is the development of biotechnology and genetic engineering. It is impossible to miss the complicity between gung-ho enthusiasm for biotechnological intervention in life—resistance to which gets ascribed to 'ancient theological scruples'[42]—and the privileging of the descriptions of life provided by genetic theory. If, one enthusiast asks, there is 'no such thing as individuality anyway', only collections of genes, what possible objection can there be to engineering life to suit our purposes?[43] When Richard

---

[41] *Discourse on Thinking*, trans. J. Anderson and E. Freund (New York: Harper & Row, 1966), 52.

[42] The expression comes from an open letter, castigating objectors to genetic engineering, from an organization called, significantly, the International Academy of Humanists. Quoted in Gina Kolata, *Clone: The Road to Dolly and the Road Ahead* (Harmondsworth: Penguin, 1997), 97.

[43] Quoted ibid. 33.

Dawkins proclaims that we and other animals are 'merely vehicles for genes', like clouds for water droplets, it is no surprise to find another enthusiast wondering how anyone could doubt it 'legitimate to shunt genes around from one species to any other species'.[44] One understands why what has become extinct in the mentality and comportment registered by such pronouncements should be described as a 'disposition of piety'.

If biotechnological enthusiasms illustrate occlusion, then elements in the wider comportment it manifests also serve to *degrade* the experience of mystery. Many enthusiasts, after all, subscribe to E. O. Wilson's demand that ethics should be 'biologicized', that we should self-consciously heed what we are anyway compelled to obey, the 'biological imperative to maximize genetic fitness'.[45] It is time to admit that 'morality has no other . . . function' than as an arrangement whereby 'human genetic material has been kept intact'.[46] This is to insist, in effect, that any durable view of how our lives should go must honour this function. Precisely because it has endured, it must be performing that function, otherwise it would have suffered the fate of everything that fleetingly defies the 'biological imperative'. The sense that our lives should be in keeping with an experience of mystery cannot, therefore, have the standing that those who possess it imagine. Like any other comportment that has endured, it plays, unbeknownst to champions of mystery themselves, its evolutionary part. Cultures with a few mystics at large must have been more congenial to 'genetic fitness' than ones without. Since no champion of mystery can himself regard the experience of mystery merely as some genetically advantageous mutation, the 'biologicized' ethic urged by Wilson and his followers degrades that experience.

With the possibility of disconsonance with, and failure to 'measure up' to, the experience of mystery now illustrated, the question arises whether

---

[44] Dawkins, quoted in Alan Holland, 'Species Are Dead. Long Live Genes!', in A. Holland and A. Johnson (eds.), *Animal Biotechnology and Ethics* (London: Chapman & Hall, 1998), 236; for the 'cloud' analogy, see Dawkins, *The Selfish Gene* (Oxford: Oxford University Press, 1989), 34. The gene-shunting passage is quoted in Andrew Linzey, *Animal Theology* (London: SCM Press, 1994), 150–1. For fuller discussion of biotechnology and theoretical conceptions, see my 'Philosophy, Environment and Technology', in A. O'Hear (ed.), *Philosophy at the Millennium*, Royal Institute of Philosophy Lecture Series (Cambridge: Cambridge University Press, 2001), and 'The "Frankensteinian" Nature of Biotechnology', in A.-H. Maehle and J. Geyer-Kordesch (eds.), *From Paternalism to Autonomy: Historical and Philosophical Perspectives on Biomedical Ethics* (Aldershot: Ashgate, 2001).

[45] *Sociobiology* (Cambridge, Mass.: Harvard University Press, 1975), 562; *On Human Nature* (Harmondsworth: Penguin, 1995), 2.

[46] *On Human Nature*, 167.

something more 'positive' may be said. Are there comportments that are not only not disconsonant with, but that 'go with', are consonant or confederate with, that experience? A natural suggestion would be that a comportment is 'positively' consonant when it is a means to attunement to mystery. This, perhaps, is Alan Watts' suggestion when he writes that, for Zennists, certain 'improved human relations' have as their 'object' the experience of suchness or emptiness.[47] Certainly, if some 'life-styles'— bacchanalian ones, say—occlude the experience of mystery, it is a legitimate exercise in moral logistics to enquire whether others may instead prepare for it. But Watts's suggestion misses a central emphasis in the Mahāyāna texts. That emphasis is indicated by Nāgārjuna's reference to the 'practice of enlightenment, profound, awesome emptiness whose essence is compassion', and by the insistence, in a *prajñāpāramitā* text, that no one 'realizes emptiness' who does not have 'the great compassion'.[48]

Such remarks make it sound that compassion—the virtuous comportment *par excellence* for Buddhists—is partly constitutive or definitive of the experience of emptiness. If that is the idea, it serves as a useful antidote to the picture of the experience of mystery as some eureka-like 'mental event' rather than, as it was put earlier, a receptive mode of being. Of course, if compassionate comportment is a necessary ingredient *in* that experience, talk of its *consonance* with the latter will not be entirely felicitous. (Lower- and upper-C are consonant with one another, but not with the chord to which they belong.) But that is a fairly trivial worry. Nevertheless, those remarks are not best construed as defining the experience of emptiness in terms of compassion. Nor are Heidegger's references to certain comportments we should cultivate—a refusal, for example, to 'push on blindly with technology'[49]—to be construed as partial definitions of an openness to mystery. The building of certain comportments into the very 'essence' of the experience of mystery must rest, if it is not to be arbitrary stipulation, on the appreciation of an *intimacy* between those comportments and the reception

[47] *The Way of Zen*, 167.

[48] Quoted from the *Madhyamakaśāstra* in Robert Thurman, *The Central Philosophy of Tibet: A Study and Translation of Jey Tsong Khapa's* Essence of True Eloquence (Princeton, N.J.: Princeton University Press, 1984), 172; *The Large Sūtra on Perfect Wisdom*, trans. E. Conze (Delhi: Motilal Banarsidass, 1979), 426. As that Sūtra makes clear (p. 578), Mahāyāna compassion is not any old 'concern with the welfare of beings', but, specifically, with 'leading them to final Nirvāṇa'.

[49] *The Question Concerning Technology and Other Essays*, trans. W. Lovitt (New York: Harper & Row, 1977), 25–6.

of the world as a transparent, grace-given epiphany. Whether, at the end of the day, one talks of such comportments as partly constitutive of the experience does not, perhaps, matter overmuch. What does matter is to understand the intimacy that might inspire such talk.

A clue to that intimacy or consonance is provided by Heidegger's remark that appreciation of 'the mystery' is 'that which frees' from, inter alia, the 'stultified compulsion to push on blindly with technology', and by a commentator's reference to the enlightened Buddhist's *'spontaneous restraint* from wrong speech, action or livelihood' and hence, by implication, to a 'spontaneous' exercise of compassion.[50] Such remarks sound a theme salient in more than one tradition of mystery: that of the spontaneity, effortlessness, and naturalness of certain comportments on the part of those attuned to mystery. One thinks, for example, of the famous *wu-wei* ('notdoing') exhibited in the life of the Taoist sage, or of the Zennist's life that requires 'nothing special' since there has been a 'dropping off' of or a 'dying to' the desires and ambitions that inform the lives of most of us.[51] Buddhist compassion, so viewed, is not a muscular moral achievement, but something that 'just arises' once creatures and things are experienced in their transparency, as without 'own being' and as integral items in a world-as-a-whole.

When understood in keeping with this theme, consonant comportments are happily characterized not as means to, nor as definitional elements in, nor as contingent products of, the experience of emptiness. One doubts, indeed, that they can be much better characterized than by using metaphors like 'consonant' itself. Perhaps one may say this: consonant comportments are spontaneous ways of dealing, dwelling, and estimating that 'go with' with, are 'freed up' by, the experience of mystery. They are, to speak with Heidegger and the Taoists, the ways 'given' by The Way, the 'run-off' in the arena of human conduct of what *'makes way* for everything'.[52] Someone who must ask what these ways are and then strive to follow them is one in whom attunement to mystery is not, as the Buddhists say, 'deeply cultivated'. Compassion, for example, is not, for the Buddhist, something that

---

[50] Ibid.; Peter Harvey, *An Introduction to Buddhist Ethics* (Cambridge: Cambridge University Press, 2000), 38 (my italics).

[51] On 'dying to wordly desire', see Nishida, *An Inquiry into the Good*, trans. M. Abe and C. Ives (New Haven, Conn.: Yale University Press, 1990), 145.

[52] *On the Way to Language*, 92.

the enlightened Bodhisattva must struggle to express, for—to revert to Nāgārjuna's point—the experience of emptiness brings compassion with it. As *The Large Sūtra* explains, one who 'attends' to the emptiness of things—their 'lack of own being' and independence in a human world, their transparency—only fully 'dwells' in this experience when he also dwells in 'the attention of the great compassion'.[53]

With consonance understood in this manner, it is necessary to think of answerability and measure in ways different, perhaps, from those encouraged by my earlier discussion. I spoke of a need for our lives to answer to and find measure in something 'beyond the human'. Quite possibly, such talk conjures up a picture of that 'something' as providing a model or principles that comportments do or do not measure up to, properly answer to. Some such picture of measure as what justifies or gives reason for corresponds to a dominant ambition in western practical philosophy. Philosophers in that tradition are apt to assume that we can be content with comportments only when these have been justified, when reasons in support of them outweigh those against. This has not been the general assumption further east, and a different picture is evoked if we listen to other, older senses of 'answer to' than 'satisfy a demand', and other senses, too, of 'measure' than 'apply a standard'. Something may answer to when it simply 'goes with', is responsive to or 'echoes'. And to measure may be to 'moderate' and 'restrain'. When these senses of the terms are listened to, the picture is one of a comportment answering to an experience of mystery when it is among those 'spontaneous', 'freed up' ways that are consonant. The experience provides measure, not by acquainting us with a rule or standard, but by yielding 'spontaneous restraints', by leaving us—various desires and ambitions having 'dropped off' or been 'died to'—with comportments that no longer trigger the question 'Why?', comportments with which we are at peace. This is not the ostrich-like peace gained by the 'serene' or 'quietist' humanist encountered in earlier chapters who, maintaining that 'of course' we must 'work . . . from within our own framework', eschews all the 'old philosophical questions' about the credentials of that framework. It is the peace, rather, of someone for whom questions about the direction of life no longer press in, since it is one that just 'goes with' a sense of being in the truth, of receptivity to what is 'beyond the human'.

[53] *The Large Sūtra on Perfect Wisdom*, 201.

Humilities

My remarks have formed, to repeat, no more than a prologomenon to an account of consonant comportments, and I have made no serious attempt to identify just what these might be. I have hardly more than gestured towards the Buddhist view that universal compassion is such a comportment, and to Heidegger's notion of an appropriate 'coping' with technology. (A full discussion of the former, for example, would address the question of whether compassion spontaneously answers to—echoes—a sense of mystery only when this is yoked to certain doctrines, notably those of rebirth and *karma*.)

It would be nice to end, however, with a firmer indication of one kind of consonant comportment and, at the same time, with some final remarks on a term central to this book. I have generally used the term 'humility', following writers like Nagel, as something of a term of art: not as the name of a traditional virtue, but to label what contrasts with 'hubristic' attitudes—absolutist or rawly humanist—concerning our knowledge of an allegedly independent order of reality and the possibility of a dis-incumbenced stance towards our frameworks of belief and evaluation. Humility, so understood, turned out to require acceptance of a non-discursable mystery 'beyond the human'. As such, it sounds pretty different from the humility or modesty preached in various moral traditions. I suggest, however, that something close to this traditional virtue is indeed a comportment consonant with attunement to mystery. The virtue of humility 'goes with' humility in my quasi-technical sense.

The relation between the two humilities has been anticipated by Iris Murdoch. 'A genuine mysteriousness', she writes, 'attaches to the idea of goodness', and 'true morality is a sort of unesoteric mysticism'.[54] Within a morality properly informed by a sense of mysteriousness, she continues, the 'most central' of the virtues is that of humility, understood not as a 'habit of self-effacement', but as a 'selfless respect for reality'. As that phrase suggests, there are two discernible components of humility: respect for the integrity

---

[54] Iris Murdoch, *Existentialists and Mystics: Writings on Philosophy and Literature*, ed. P. Conradi (Harmondsworth: Penguin, 1997), 381, 375–6. Admittedly, her notion of mystery is not quite that entertained by the champions of mystery I have discussed. It's worth noting, however, Murdoch's increasing preoccupation and sympathy, in later years, with both Heidegger and Buddhism.

of things and what Murdoch calls 'unselfing'. By that term, she does not mean, simply, an individual's release from selfishness. More generally, it means abandonment of hubristic claims on behalf of human beings' capacities to, inter alia, know how things are, plan and control the future, and 'dominate the world'. In short, unselfing is the antidote to what she elsewhere calls the 'flimsy creed' of humanism.

The two aspects of humility—respect for integrity and unselfing— are closely related: 'the humble man, because he sees himself as nothing, can see other things as they are'.[55] They are surely aspects, moreover, of humility as familiarly and traditionally conceived. The humble person does not impose upon, does not mould and distort things to suit him, recognizes proper limits that it is not for him to transgress, and does not judge everything from within the orbit of his own particular aims. The Bodhisattva, we read, has 'respect . . . through being always humble' and is 'honest' towards all beings since he has 'slain pride'.[56] As for the talk of unselfing, that chimes with the rhetoric of 'dying to self' used by writers as various as Rūmi, Eckhart, Kierkegaard, and Nishida to lend hyperbolic expression to the notion of humility.

If the two aspects point, in one direction, towards the traditional virtue of humility, so they do, in another direction, towards themes central to the notion of mystery qua emptiness. Shorn of the absolutist image that a phrase like 'respect for reality' might encourage, the idea of an integrity of things that should be honoured evokes that of their transparency. To experience something as transparent is, to recall earlier metaphors, to see it as an open place or an intersection in a web of relations where the world as a whole 'gathers', is 'con-centrated'. It is what it is—has the integrity it does— precisely as such a place or intersection. The idea of unselfing, in turn, relates to that of the world as grace-given. Essential to that notion was the thought that this is not the givenness of the world to an 'us', a subjectivity, already there, up and running: rather, we too are 'given', our frameworks of beliefs and norms, our basic practices and our form of life no more our achievement than is the world which anyway cannot be prised apart from these.

To delineate comportments that manifest the humility of which

---

Murdoch speaks is, therefore, at once to articulate ingredients of the traditional virtue of humility and to specify complexes of attitude and behaviour consonant with an experience of mystery towards which my quasi-technical notion of humility drew us. In that delineation, the two humilities come together. What, briefly, might be the comportments delineated? To begin with, that stance towards creatures and other living beings, and indeed towards things generally, that Heidegger calls 'letting be' or, following Eckhart, 'releasement' (*Gelassenheit*). So to stand is to experience and treat things as what they are and not as they figure in some 'dimmed down', perhaps reductionist, vision that suits certain human purposes. It is, for example, to resist such practices as genetically engineering bulls so that, with the bovine equivalent of Down's syndrome (as one writer describes them), they become fat, placid lumps convenient for masturbation by machines. Such practices are blind to the integrity of bulls, to the 'place' they have in the world, to what they are. (I leave it to the reader to think of practices equally blind to the integrity of our fellow human beings.)

Second, the humble person will have respect for 'little things'—for, in Murdoch's words, 'the little accidental jumbled things like little stones, like bits of earth', and for inconspicuous, unglamorous activities, like eating a meal. 'Ways of life', she reminds us, 'imply times for breakfast'.[57] To be obsessed, as Heidegger thinks we have become, with the 'gigantic' and the striking—to be incapable of 'a celebration of the ordinary' and unassuming—is to have fallen victim to measuring the world by a yardstick that betrays an inflated reckoning of the scale of human achievement. The humble person, more receptive in his experience of the world, will recognize that, as a Zen poet put it, there is 'wondrous function' in 'carrying water and logging firewood'—that, as Dōgen saw, the Buddha-nature or 'the mystical power is realized' as much in the cypress tree, the bundle of flax or the reflection of the moon as in more dramatic and 'gigantic' vehicles.[58] A 'sense of the mystery of things', to recall the gloss on Wittgenstein's later philosophy, may be 'focused on to ordinary aspects of life'. Indeed, it is attention to— 'right mindfulness' of—something unassuming that might best attune to transparency, to the 'gathering' of a world in something. The reflection of

[57] *The Message to the Planet* (London: Vintage, 2000), 328, 149.
[58] Dōgen, *Shobogenzo*, 75.

the moon, writes Dōgen, is a 'place' where 'something ineffable exists'.[59] It is just such an experience of a pine tree's transparency—its 'con-centrating' of wind, sea, night, and moon—that the poet Saigyo records:

> Inviting the wind to carry
> Salt waves of the sea,
> The pine tree of Shiogoshi
> Trickles all night long
> Shiny drops of moonlight.[60]

Again, I leave it to the reader to consider the implications of a 'celebration of the ordinary' for the ways in which human beings might relate to one another—ways, for example, that, according to some, would call for rather 'simpler' and more 'local' forms of community than those seemingly required by current political and economic imperatives.

Finally, humility implies tolerance towards 'ways of revealing', schemes of thought and evaluation, different from those prevailing in the form of life in which one participates. This is not due to recognition of others' 'rights', nor to utilitarian calculation of the benefits of non-interference, nor to 'postmodernist' delight in 'difference' for its own sake. Rather it owes, in part, to a humanist recognition that, as Chuang Tzu puts it, a given way of revealing is 'rooted' in a given form of life, that people 'agree because they are the same', not because agreement is imposed upon them by the independent way that reality is.[61] It owes, too, to an appreciation, no longer a humanist one, that what is beyond the human, 'The Way', 'sends' or 'gives' many ways. The world on a given way of revealing is not, to repeat Dōgen's words, our 'possession', but a gift from 'something ineffable coming like this'. The person of humility will not be a triumphalist about, say, our modern democratic institutions or 'scientific culture': he or she will not want to see other ways of living together or thinking together automatically despised or obliterated. Humility is the virtue that exhorts us to accept that it is impossible, as Iris Murdoch warns, always to 'limit and foresee' what is 'required of us'.[62] It is a virtue distinctive, therefore, of those who do not

---

[59] Ibid. 17.

[60] Quoted in Matsuo Basho, *The Narrow Road to the Deep North*, trans. N. Yuasa (Harmondsworth: Penguin, 1966), 138.

[61] *The Book of Chuang Tzu*, trans. M. Palmer (Harmondsworth: Penguin, 1996), ch. 23.

[62] *Existentialists and Mystics*, 381.

prejudge which comportments, which 'spontaneous restraints', are intimated by attunement to mystery.

Mystery affords measure, then. Less gnomically, various conceptions and comportments may be judged consonant or disconsonant with the experience of, or attunement to, mystery as emptiness—an experience or attunement that reflective men and women persuaded of the hubris of both absolutism and raw humanism will be apt to cultivate.

Index